D0918322

Unless Recalled Earlier

DATE DUE

Euro-Pacific Investment and Trade

NEW HORIZONS IN INTERNATIONAL BUSINESS

General Editor: Peter J. Buckley
Centre for International Business,
University of Leeds (CIBUL), UK

This series is aimed at the frontiers of international business research. The study of international business is important not least because it gives researchers the opportunity to innovate in theory, technique, empirical investigation and interpretation. The area is fruitful for interdisciplinary and comparative research. This series is established as a central forum for the presentation of new ideas in international business.
Titles in the series include:

The Growth and Evolution of Multinational Enterprise
Patterns of Geographical and Industrial Diversification
R.D. Pearce

Multinational Enterprise and Public Policy
A Study of the Industrial Countries
A.E. Safarian

Transnational Corporations in Southeast Asia
An Institutional Approach to Industrial Organization
Hans Jansson

European Integration and Competitiveness
Acquisitions and Alliances in Industry
Edited by Frédérique Sachwald

The State and Transnational Corporations
A Network Approach to Industrial Policy in India
Hans Jansson, M. Saqib and D. Deo Sharma

Competitive and Cooperative Macromanagement
The Challenges of Structural Interdependence
Edited by Gavin Boyd

Foreign Direct Investment in Japan
Edited by Masaru Yoshitomi and Edward M. Graham

Structural Competitiveness in the Pacific
Corporate and State Rivalries
Edited by Gavin Boyd

Euro-Pacific Investment and Trade
Strategies and Structural Interdependencies
Edited by Gavin Boyd and Alan M. Rugman

Multinational Firms and International Relocation
Edited by Peter J. Buckley and Jean-Louis Mucchielli

Euro-Pacific Investment and Trade

Strategies and Structural Interdependencies

Edited by

Gavin Boyd

Honorary Professor, Political Science Department, Rutgers University, US and Research Associate, Centre for International Business Studies, University of Montreal, Canada

and

Alan M. Rugman

Professor of International Business, University of Toronto, Canada

NEW HORIZONS IN INTERNATIONAL BUSINESS

Edward Elgar
Cheltenham, UK • Brookfield, US

© Gavin Boyd and Alan Rugman 1997

Published by
Edward Elgar Publishing Limited
8 Lansdown Place
Cheltenham
Glos GL50 2HU
UK

Edward Elgar Publishing Company
Old Post Road
Brookfield
Vermont 05036
US

A catalogue record for this book is available from the British Library

Library of Congress Cataloguing-in-Publication Data
Euro-Pacific investment and trade : strategies and structural
    interdependencies / edited by Gavin Boyd and Alan M. Rugman.
        (New horizons and international business)
    "This book contains many of the papers that were presented at the
Halifax Euro-Pacific Investment and Trade Conference in May 1995" —
Frwd.
    Includes bibliographical references,
    1. Investments, Foreign—Congresses.   2. International trade—
Congresses.   3. International business enterprises—Management—
Congresses.   4. International economic integration—Congresses.
5. Europe—Commerce—Pacific Area—Congresses.   6. Pacific Area—
Commerce—Europe—Congresses.   I. Boyd. Gavin.   II. Rugman, Alan
M.   III. Halifax Euro-Pacific Investment and Trade Conference (1995)
IV. Series.
HG4538. E836   1997
332.6'73'099—dc20   96–23172
                                                             CIP

ISBN 1 85898 368 1

Typeset by Manton Typesetters, 5–7 Eastfield Road, Louth, Lincolnshire LN11 7AJ, UK
Printed and bound in Great Britain by Biddles Limited, Guildford and King's Lynn

Contents

Figures

Tables

Contributors

Michael Blaine is a Lecturer in the Max Fisher College of Business, Ohio State University, Columbus, Ohio, US. He authored *Cooperation in International Business* (1994) and has published in several business journals and books.

Gavin Boyd is an Honorary Professor in the Political Science Department at Rutgers University, Newark, New Jersey, USA, and a Research Associate at the Centre for International Business Studies, Ecole des Hautes Etudes Commerciales, University of Montreal. He edited *Structural Competitiveness in the Pacific* (1996) and *Competitive and Cooperative Macromanagement* (1995).

Drusilla K. Brown is Associate Professor of Economics at Tufts University, Medford, Massachusetts, US. She has published numerous papers on the theory and application of computable general equilibrium models to analysis of preferential trading arrangements.

Peter J. Buckley is Director, Centre for International Business, University of Leeds, UK and editor of the series New Horizons in International Business for Edward Elgar Publishing.

Mark Casson is Professor of Economics at the University of Reading, UK. His recent books include *Entrepreneurship and Business Culture* (1995), *The Organization of International Business* (1995), *Information and Organization: A New Perspective on the Theory of the Firm* (1996), and an edited volume on *The Theory of the Firm* (1996).

Patrick M. Crowley is Assistant Professor of Economics, Saint Mary's University, Halifax, Canada. His research concentrates on problems of monetary union in Europe.

Joseph R. D'Cruz is Professor of Management at the University of Toronto and one of Canada's leading authorities on international competitiveness. He was formerly an Adjunct Professor at IMD International, Switzerland.

Alan V. Deardorff is Professor of Economics and Public Policy at the University of Michigan, US. He has published numerous articles on aspects of international trade theory and policy. He co-authored, with Robert Stern, *The Michigan Model of World Production and Trade* (1996) and *Computational Analysis of Global Trading Arrangements* (1990).

J. Colin Dodds is Academic Vice-President, Saint Mary's University, Halifax, Canada and has been Vice-Chair of the Canadian Consortium of Management Schools and a Governor of the Canadian Institute of Bankers. He has published extensively on international financial topics and has served as a consultant to a number of international agencies and firms.

John H. Dunning is Professor of International Business, Rutgers University, New Jersey, US and Professor of Economics Emeritus, University of Reading, UK. He has published very extensively on the structures and strategies of international firms.

Heather A. Grant is Legal Counsel at the Canadian International Trade Tribunal in Ottawa, Canada. She has authored articles on NAFTA and dispute settlement procedures.

Ray Loveridge is Head of the Strategic Management Group, Aston Business School, Aston University, Birmingham, UK, Visiting Fellow, Science Policy Research Unit, University of Sussex and Visiting Professor, Ecole Superieure des Sciences Economiques et Commerciales, Paris. He has published extensively on technology policy issues.

Edward Mozley Roche is Assistant Professor of Management, Seton Hall University, South Orange, New Jersey, US. He has published extensively on information technology trends and policies.

Alan M. Rugman is a Professor in the Faculty of Management at the University of Toronto. He has held visiting appointments at the London Business School, Columbia University and the Massachusetts Institute of Technology, and was a member of Canada's International Trade Advisory Committee during the US-Canada free trade negotiations. He is the author or editor of 25 books, and his most recent publications include *Foreign Direct Investment and NAFTA* (1994) and a new text, *International Business: a Strategic Management Approach*. His collected works are being published by Edward Elgar.

Satwinder Singh is Senior Research Fellow, Economics Department, University of Reading, UK. His research focuses on multinational technology management and he co-authored, with Robert Pearce, *Globalizing R&D* (1992).

Robert M. Stern is Professor of Economics and Public Policy at the University of Michigan, US. He has published numerous articles and books on international trade and finance and collaborated with Alan V. Deardorff in developing the Michigan Model of World Production and Trade and in adapting it for computational analyses of preferential trading arrangements.

Gilbert R. Winham is Eric Dennis Memorial Professor of Government and Political Science, Dalhousie University, Halifax, Canada. He has served on Canada's International Trade Advisory Committee and on dispute settlement panels under NAFTA. He authored *International Trade and the Tokyo Round Negotiation* (1986) and the *Evolution of International Trade Agreements* (1992).

Foreword

This book contains many of the papers that were presented at the Halifax Euro-Pacific Investment and Trade Conference in May 1995. Sponsored by the Department of Foreign Affairs and International Trade, Ottawa, the Halifax Summit Office, Saint Mary's and Dalhousie Universities, the conference was a precursor to the G7 Summit. It had as a backcloth the recent enlargement of the EU, the potential expansion of NAFTA, the emergence of the free trade zone within APEC and the development of a multilateral agreement on investment (MAI) – an issue which the OECD hoped to conclude by 1997.

The bringing together of a distinguished group of international business experts provided a forum for a dynamic dialogue on cross-border capital and trade flows among participants, including business leaders, government officials and students. The papers have been revised to reflect these discussions. The result is a book which will provide a useful framework and source of reference for policy-makers in government, international agencies and the private sector to address the challenges and opportunities that arise from corporate, regional and financial integration of the world economy.

J. COLIN DODDS
Saint Mary's University, Halifax

Preface

This book reviews the activities of European and Pacific international firms, assesses their differing degrees of competitiveness and their effects on economic structures in the Triad pattern of industrialized democracies, and discusses options for corporate decision-makers and governments. The project developed out of an initiative by the Department of Foreign Affairs and International Trade, Ottawa, to encourage the convening of a conference on major economic issues in advance of the 1995 G7 meeting in Halifax. Papers from the conference, given by distinguished international political economists and business scholars, have been revised and arranged in what may be described as a macro briefing, serving the closely related needs of managements and policy communities, as well as the advancement of theory in the social sciences.

For managements, several chapters offer comprehensive surveys of major trends, problems and opportunities in the pattern of international operations by European, Japanese and North American firms. Transformations of markets and national economic systems associated with the activities of these corporations are posing many issues of adjustment and development, and are affecting decisions on long-term investments in industrial capacity. These decisions are becoming more knowledge intensive, because of technological advances, complex market uncertainties, and pressures on governments that cause unpredictable policy shifts. There are incentives for managements to lower risks and costs by forming international corporate alliances. Alliance capitalism is the principal trend examined in the first chapter, written by the prominent international business scholar John H. Dunning.

For policy communities dealing with trade, industrial, financial and competition issues the book offers contributions to the understanding of interconnected structural problems, and indications of ways of strengthening consultations with managements. Governmental quests for corporate cooperation are becoming more and more transnational, because increasing numbers of the major decisions shaping national economic structures are being made by global companies, and these are interacting simultaneously with numerous governments. Economic forecasts as guides for policy are becoming more difficult but are assuming greater importance for the management of policy mixes.

Social science scholars, it is hoped, will benefit from the interdisciplinary contributions to this book. Fundamentals affecting and affected by investment and trade flows have been studied with sensitivity to needs for the enrichment of theory and the formulation of sound economic advice to governments. The common tendency for policy learning to lag behind changes in corporate strategic innovations is examined in some of its principal dimensions. These have demanded attention because of the extensive structural consequences of largely independent corporate decisions regarding the location and development of industrial capacity.

Each contributor is grateful to numerous colleagues for insights shared over many years, and especially at the Halifax conference. All the exchanges of ideas, meanwhile, have assumed additional meaning with the publication by Mark Casson (co-author of Chapter 5) of his volumes on the Economics of Trust (*Entrepreneurship and Business Culture* and *The Organization of International Business*, Edward Elgar, 1995). Building trust is essential for balancing competition with cooperation, at the corporate and policy levels, as markets are internationalized.

GAVIN BOYD
ALAN M. RUGMAN

1. Reconfiguring the boundaries of international business activity

John H. Dunning

INTRODUCTION

Once upon a time, there was the firm, and the boundaries of its economic jurisdiction were clearly demarcated by its ownership. There were few intra-firm transactions, and all inter-firm transactions were conducted between independent parties at arm's-length prices. This is no longer the case. Once upon a time, there were identifiable and autonomous markets, the confines of which were unambiguously delineated by the particular assets, goods and services being traded, and by the parties to the exchange. This is no longer the case. Once upon a time, there were nation states, whose political domain largely corresponded with their economic domains, and whose governments produced largely independent macroeconomic and macro-organizational policies.[1] This is no longer the case.

The globalizing economy of the current decade is the outcome of a succession of radical technological and political changes, the lineage of which can be traced back to the industrial revolution of the late 18th century. At this former time, the boundaries of firms, markets and governments were easily recognizable and, for the most part, impermeable. Over the past two centuries, the extent and nature of economic activity has become increasingly specialized, complex and porous. At the same time, its spatial dimension has widened from the subnational to the national, and then to the regional, international and global.

Such changes have had widespread implications for both the macro- and micro-organization of resource allocation. The single-activity, autonomous firm is now the exception rather than the rule. Most contemporary firms are multi-activity, and are often part of a web of inter-firm cooperative alliances. Markets are increasingly interdependent, rather than independent, of each other; and the consequences of market-related transactions frequently affect institutions and individuals other than those who are the direct participants in the markets. As assets have become increasingly mobile, or 'quicksilver' across national boundaries, so the dichotomy between economic and political space has widened; and in the framing of their economic strategies, which affect the competitiveness and profitability of business activities within their jurisdiction, governments need to be increasingly aware of the strategies of the governments of other countries, which offer a comparable portfolio of location-specific assets.

This chapter has two main tasks. The first is to identify the extent and character of the changes which have taken place in the character and dimension of each of the three main organizational entities which govern the deployment of resources in a capitalist economy, and particularly those which arise from the globalization of business activity. The second is to look more specifically at the role of government as initiator, overseer and arbitrator of the economic system which determines the contribution and effectiveness of these entities.

THE DOMAIN OF THE FIRM

At one time, the formal or jurisdictional confines of the firm were assumed to be discrete and coincident with its ownership. Such confines related both to the scope of the value-added activities of the firm – be they process or product based – and to the geographical space in which it operated. Implicit in this assumption was that ownership conferred full sovereignty over decision-taking. Without such ownership[2] the firm was presumed to have no legitimacy or authority. All transactions within the firm, whatever their spatial dimensions, were presumed to be the responsibility of the owners of the company – although in practice, this responsibility was devolved to the Board of Directors and executive management. All transactions between firms were assumed to be off-the-shelf, and conducted at arm's-length prices. Little acknowledgement was given to cooperative agreements involving a continuing relationship between economic agents or an exchange (or sharing) of resources, experience, information or advice.

Over the years, the formal boundaries of the firm have steadily receded as a result of the internalization of intermediate product markets and the territorial extension of its activities. The contemporary multinational enterprise (MNE) is both the owner and orchestrator of a complex portfolio of interrelated assets, located in two or more countries. In some instances, these internal markets are closely integrated, and the parent company enjoys advantages of common governance and diversification of risk. In others, the MNE is better regarded as a multidomestic company in which the foreign subsidiaries operate more or less independently of each other (Porter, 1986). Over the last 30 years, and particularly as the range and extent of international production has increased, and as regional integration has facilitated the cross-border specialization of economic activity, an increasing number of MNEs have begun to embrace globally integrated strategies (UNCTAD, 1993).

At the same time the range and character of the *informal* boundaries of the firm have also been extended. Like that of intra-firm activities, the recent growth of inter-firm agreements has also been in response to the increasing costs of arm's-length transactions; but, unlike internalization, this response is better described as a *voice* rather than *exit* strategy.[3] We shall take this point up further in the next section of this chapter.

The net result of the growth of both inter- and intra-firm activities is that the boundaries of the firm have become more porous. Because of this, traditional analytical concepts are found wanting in a number of respects. First – and this is well known but deserves repeating here – the traditional, that is neo-classical theory of the firm, focused on its role as a *production* unit rather than a *transacting* and *coordinating* unit. However appropriate this emphasis may have been when firms engaged in one or a few activities, and served only limited markets, it is no longer the case today. As several economists (notably North, 1990) have shown, as society becomes more complex, the transaction and coordinating costs of economic activity become more important.[4] This is not only because of the increasing costs of acquiring information to measure the multiple dimensions of what is being exchanged, but also because of those associated with enforcing contracts and making credible commitments across time and space, necessary to realize the potential of technological and organizational advances.

About a half century ago, there was debate among economists as to the supply-side limits of the size of the firm producing in perfectly competitive conditions.[5] The consensus of opinion, at that time, was that the constraints to a firm's size were not its rising (marginal) production costs, but were the increasing difficulties faced by managers of coordinating resources, capabilities and markets, for example, rising transaction and coordinating costs. Although the debate was conducted mainly within the context of equilibrium analysis and firms were assumed to engage in only one activity, it is not difficult to argue that the more diverse the activities of a firm, the higher these latter costs are likely to be, and thus the profit-maximizing level of output will be less.

This analysis suggests that the de facto boundaries of the firm will be limited by its production and organizational competency, and by the size and geographical composition of the market. It follows, then, that any upgrading of the former, or extension of the latter, variables will enable the boundaries of the firm to be pushed out. And, indeed, history is replete with examples of the increased size of firms being brought about by changes in both exogenous variables, for example larger markets, falling transport costs and lower raw material costs, and endogenous variables, for example an improvement in labour or managerial productivity; while, from a dynamic perspective, the extent to which the boundaries are pushed out rests on the ability of firms to innovate new, or upgrade the quality of existing, products.

There is, however, another sense in which the boundaries of the firm are being reconfigured. This concerns the extent to which a firm is engaging in informal (that is, non-ownership) linkages with other firms which have an impact on their ability to sustain or enlarge their economic activities. Here we may introduce the concept of 'soft' boundaries as influencing both the organizational limits and the size and scope of production. Although the *de jure* boundaries of a firm may require little reconfiguration, as long as it has a 51 per cent equity interest in any joint venture, it may, nevertheless, be that the minority partner will have something to contribute to the efficiency of the majority partner. This may be no less so in minority-owned ventures, and, indeed, in non-equity alliances, for example subcontracting, research and development (R&D) agreements and management contracts. Of course, not all such agreements require a recasting of even the 'soft' boundaries of the firm. The key question is the extent to which such agreements – or, indeed, organizational arrangements associated with them[6] – may affect the production and organization activities of firms, for example by offering advice, providing additional inputs, or markets or by making possible economies in the common governance,[7] which in their absence would not have occurred.

There are, of course, a plurality of organizational modes by which the 'soft' boundaries of firms may be widened. These include vertical and horizontal alliances formed to accomplish very specific objectives, for example, access to new technology, management skills, learning and organizational capacity, markets, and so on; as well as more general alliances intended to share risks, accelerate the innovatory process and strengthen the overall competitiveness of the participating firms. These may variously affect a firm's performance. Thus a firm may lower its input prices or improve the quality of its end products by forming appropriate alliances with its suppliers. New markets may be tapped by franchising and other agreements with foreign distributors. A firm may best benefit from technological advances and their speedy application by jointly sharing R&D programmes with one or other of its competitors. It may gain the economies of intranational geographical clustering if it allies itself in space with related firms (Porter, 1990; Feldman, 1994).

Some scholars have argued that the world is entering into a new phase of capitalism – namely, *alliance capitalism*![8] The name implies that for firms to benefit most from innovation-led production, the upgrading of consumer demand and the imperatives of globalization, they need to engage in a network of cooperative agreements with other firms. This reflects the fact that economic activity is becoming more interdependent; and that to exploit their core assets effectively, firms have to combine these with the core assets of other firms – or of public authorities. However, rather than enlarge their hierarchical influence, they prefer to establish cooperative relationships with other firms, namely, extend their 'soft' boundaries. By so doing, they are able to improve and make better use of their own competencies, which, in turn, will help them sustain or push out further their market boundaries.

All these developments, then, point not only to the need for more flexible and readily changeable boundaries of firms; but to the fact that the very nature of these boundaries should be re-evaluated. So while a reduction in the scope of a firm's ownership may reduce its 'hard' boundaries, if such disinternalization is replaced by an increase in inter-firm cooperative agreements this may widen its 'soft' boundaries.

It is also quite clear that the nature and porosity of a firm's boundaries is both *industry* and *country* and sometimes *firm* – or even *activity* - specific. The porosity of the domain of firms would appear to be most marked in the information and technology intensity, manufacturing and service sectors (notably in the biotechnology, computer, telecommunications and financial services industries) and in countries, for example Japan and Korea, whose industrial culture seems to favour inter-firm cooperation as much as intra-firm hierarchies. Moreover, such boundaries tend to be even 'softer' when firms go abroad, particularly where, *inter alia*, because of ideological and political differences, there are substantial inter-country risks and uncertainties, and where the opportunities for synergistic economies are the most pronounced.

THE BOUNDARIES OF MARKETS

The neo-classical notion of a market is that it is an autonomous organizational entity in which the consequences of the transactions concluded are confined to the participants of the market, and are independent of those in other markets, that is there are no inter-market spillovers or externalities. It is also an implicit assumption of neo-classical economics that the costs of establishing and sustaining markets – be they factor or product markets – are minimal. Indeed, no real consideration is given at all to endemic or 'natural' market failure – it being presumed that any inability of markets to perform effectively is due to the distorting behaviour of one or other of the participants of the market, or to extra-market forces (for example, the intervention of the governments).

However, as North (1990) and others have demonstrated, as societies become more sophisticated, not only are markets likely to be less perfect (that is, in a Pareto optimality sense), but also any imperfection is reflected in the increasing transaction and coordination costs of using this organizational mechanism. Such endemic failures have been well addressed in the literature (see, for example, Wolf, 1988). In short, they reduce to the presence of uncertainties, economies of scale and externalities; and the increasing public good characteristics of intermediate and final products, which contain a high ingredient of *created* (as opposed to *natural*) assets.

In this chapter, we are interested primarily in the boundaries, rather than the character of markets, and we shall be most concerned with those properties which affect these boundaries. Essentially, these reduce to the externalities or spillover effects of market transactions, which lead to the interdependence between transactions and encourage the coordination of them. Such interdependence is of three kinds. First, some products need to be jointly demanded with others if they are to give the purchaser full satisfaction. In this case, the demand for one product is contingent upon the other being available at an acceptable price; in other words, the markets for the two goods are linked. Second, some products need to be jointly supplied if their combined worth (for example, productivity) is to be optimized. This is especially true of intangible assets, for example different kinds of information. Increasingly, as the demands of both industrial and final consumers become more sophisticated, several interrelated technologies may be needed to produce a given product. Again, the markets for these intermediate products are linked.

Third, there are the extra-market consequences of particular market transactions. The concept of external diseconomies, and the distinction between the private and social costs of producing a product – particularly where viewed in an environmental context – dates back to the time of A.C. Pigou and Alfred Marshall. The notion of the extra-market benefits of activities is perhaps more recent, and is currently best captured in those which arise from an increase in the created assets of firms – and especially of innovatory capacity and accumulation of human skills and experience. It is, for example, generally accepted that the social returns of R&D expenditure exceed the private returns;[9] which, *inter alia*, suggests that the private market for R&D cannot perform in a socially optimal fashion. The issue of apportioning the benefits of an investment no less applies to the upgrading of human capital, and to much transportation and communications infrastructure. The problem arises because the firm(s) investing in these activities do not necessarily capture all the benefits from them, or, if they do, the benefits are spread over an unacceptably long period of time.[10]

In some cases, of course, firms may (and do) respond to the kind of market failures just described by internalizing the extra-market benefits. This is most vividly demonstrated in the economies of common governance of interrelated activities. Indeed, much of the rationale for the diversified firm and for international business operations rests on the benefits perceived to arise from the economies of scale and scope. Such gains, it should be noted, arise as much from the reduction of transaction and coordination costs as from production economies. It surely follows that if such costs play a more important role in economic activity, then increasing attention should be given to organizational issues!

A later section of the chapter will deal with the implications of the reconfiguration of the domain of markets. Here we wish to emphasize that this reconfiguration may take a variety of forms depending on the nature of the markets. In some instances, the reconfiguration may be to strengthen the influence of arm's-length markets. In others, the nature of the market may be affected with arm's-length transactions being replaced by relational transactions between the parties to the exchange, or between these parties and others affected by it. Much will depend on the relative transaction costs of alternative market arrangements, and these will clearly vary over time and space. The fact that there are unique externalities of international business activities – associated *inter alia* with producing or transacting in countries with different language, ideologies, institutions and organizational structures – suggests that the international business scholar needs to consider the impact of globalization on the domain of markets very seriously indeed; for it is in those sectors which are most internationalized, where the boundaries of product and factor markets are becoming most porous. Examples include telecommunications, computers, biochemicals, robotics and financial services.

NATION STATES

In considering the spatial frontiers of MNE activity we shall distinguish between economic and political space.[11] Economic space comprises the geographical area in which production and transactions are undertaken by economic agents whose centre of governance, or residence, is within a particular country. Political space refers to the geographical area comprising the jurisdictional responsibility of a particular sovereign legislature. In the case of a national or federal government, this is usually coincident with a single country, although it may extend to its foreign possessions.

While over the past two or more centuries, economic space has continually widened, from the subnational to the national and, then, to the regional and international level, the main unit of political sovereignty has remained the nation state – even though, as we shall see, in their policies and strategies, national governments are increasingly having to take account of the widening of economic and other space. In a closed economy, political and economic territory are the same and easily identifiable. The boundaries of a nation state or a country represent the extent of the jurisdiction of authority and the legitimacy of its governing policy, for example, the national and federal government. Once, however, the economic agents of a country engage in international commerce, political and economic sovereignty may no longer be equated. For example, once a country's firms begin trading goods and services, although the political jurisdiction of its government remains the same, its economic sovereignty is reduced to the extent that it is dependent upon foreign buyers and sellers for part of its prosperity. As a country engages in deeper forms of integration, for example, foreign direct investment (FDI), then but not only are the boundaries of its firms and consumers widened, but so also are its geographical sources of wealth.[12]

Most scholars (for example, McGrew and Lewis, 1992) tend to think of the boundaries of nation states as being determined by the extent to which they are politically or economically independent or interdependent of each other. The opposite end of the spectrum of autonomous and self-sufficiency is one in which one country is merged with another. In between the two extremes are various stages and kinds of interdependence. The thesis we are suggesting is that the globalization of the world economy is leading to a watershed in, or a radical reshifting of, the *effective* boundary lines of a country, which we may define as the point at which, as a result of its association with other countries, there is no further effect on its *social* domestic production and transaction functions.

If the *extent* of interdependence influences the effective boundaries of nation states, the *form* of interdependence affects the degree and character of its porosity. Thus, for example, a regional free trade area impinges on the boundaries in a softer fashion than a customs union; and this, in its turn, less so than a monetary union. The deeper the integration between nations, the more widespread the implications for sovereignty of the participating nations.

The last twenty years have seen a number of trends, each of which is requiring scholars to reappraise the significance of national boundaries. The first is the increasing mobility of firm-specific assets between countries, one consequence of which is that (some) countries are becoming more like regions within a country.[13] This increased mobility has been especially revealed in the rapid growth of both intra- and inter-firm cross-border alliances, which, in turn, has been aided and abetted by (i) advances in transport and communications technology and (ii) the reduction of barriers to the movement of goods, assets and people brought about by regional integration.

The ability of firms to 'vote with their feet' is one thing. The extent to which they are willing to do so is another. Here a different but related aspect of the changing character of national boundaries is manifesting itself. That is that national governments, by their various actions (or non-actions), are increasingly influencing the competitiveness of location-bound resources and capabilities within their jurisdiction, in a way which determines the disposition of mobile resources and capabilities between countries. At one time, as we have seen, such government action was confined to influencing patterns of trade. Today, it extends to influencing the production and transaction costs of domestic resources, and the wealth-creating opportunities of its firms and people. No longer, then, are government (or country-specific) policies independent of each other. Governments, like firms, may, and do, act as oligopolists; and, in consequence, their spatial horizons are different than they used to be. They are broader in the sense that, by their organization and policies they may encourage or inhibit the flow of foreign assets to their borders; yet, they are narrower in the sense that other governments may affect the competitiveness of their own assets and sometimes cause domestic firms to relocate or restructure their activities outside their home countries.[14]

There is nothing new with the idea that governments may both cooperate and compete with each other, and that the balance of such interaction may be both country and time specific.[15] However, with the convergence of economic structure among at least the major industrial nations, and the widening of economic space, has come a burgeoning of both quasi-public institutions and intragovernmental agencies. In most cases, these have been activity or issue specific, but occasionally – especially in the area of macroeconomic policies – they have been more general. The geographical scope of the arrangements has also varied. In some cases it has been bilateral; in others it has been multilateral. Of the supranational arrangements, some, for example, as agreed in the United Nations (UN) or the United Nations Conference on Trade and Development (UNCTAD), have been informal and non-binding; others, for example, environmental and standards legislation in the European Union (EU), have been more binding. The point we wish to stress is that alliance capitalism is leading to more *inter*governmental intervention and, in an increasing number of cases, this intervention is taking the form of cooperation. But, at the end of the day, governments often compete with each other for the mobile created assets of firms and, as for example is demonstrated by the policies of member countries of the European Union and/or individual states in the United States, they have considerable leeway to do so.

By promoting the structural integration of nation states, the globalizing economy is restructuring the effective boundaries of both economic and political space. While some scholars have gone as far as to suggest that this may lead to the demise of nation states, the majority point to a change in its functions. Thus, while the EU is leading to a reduced role in some of the functions of the governments of the participating nations (compare those of the states in the USA with those of the Federal government), the macro-organizational actions of such national administrations – in influencing the production and transaction costs of economic activity in their midst – is becoming more important.

At the same time, such policies are being increasingly affected by those of other governments, who are seeking to upgrade the competitiveness of their own resources and capabilities. It is in this sense, and for this reason, that the spatial boundaries of nation states, and indeed the significance of the location-specific advantages of countries, need to be reconfigured.

THE RESPONSE OF INSTITUTIONS TO THE RECONFIGURATION OF BOUNDARIES

The previous sections have hypothesized that the boundaries of the main organizational forms used to allocate resources and capabilities in a capitalist economy are undergoing a radical shift as the global economy moves from a socio-institutional paradigm of *hierarchical* capitalism to one of *alliance* capitalism. Such a transformation, which is still in its early stages, is causing the relationships between firms, between markets and between nation states (or, more particularly, the governing bodies of nation states) to be changed in such a way that the boundaries are becoming blurred, and cooperation among firms is becoming as much a feature of capitalism as competition between them.

It is also worth mentioning that the boundaries between different organizational forms are also being reconfigured. Thus as nation states upgrade the issue of competitiveness on their national agenda, and firms (including MNEs) and governments evolve more cooperative and less adversarial relationships,[16] the interaction between governments and markets is also changing. While much government intervention has long been criticized by economists as market distorting – except where it is designed to inhibit or regulate anti-competitive behaviour by one or other of the participants in the market – it is being increasingly recognized that in an innovation-led globalizing economy, governments may play an important *market-facilitating* role. This they may do both by ensuring the supply of the public goods which private firms perceive to be too costly or risky to provide, and by assisting the readjustment of markets to technological change, wherever the social net benefits of such assistance are believed to be higher than the private net benefits.[17]

Finally, the interaction between firms and markets is changing. As its name implies, *hierarchical* capitalism emphasizes the importance of large vertically integrated and horizontally diversified firms in the organization of economic activity. But as we have already indicated, recent years have seen a growth of inter-firm cooperative agreements, which, in effect, represent a 'voice' reaction of the participants in the intermediate product markets to reduce the imperfections of those markets, rather than an 'exit' strategy of replacing the market by administrative fiat.

More generally, we have argued in this chapter that the globalizing economy is changing the costs and benefits of alternative modes of organizing economic activity, as well as affecting the systemic role of government as the organizational overlord of such activity. The responses to these changing costs and benefits by the various organizational forms are essentially fivefold. First, if the costs of supplying the product, asset or factor service in question are increased (or lowered) independently of the organizational mode, then the appropriate response may be to produce or transact less (more), that is, shift the organization supply curve to the left (right). Clearly this response will be highly sector specific; but as the transaction and coordination costs of economic activity rise, one may assume that a change in these will have a more pronounced effect on the level and structure of such activity than once it did.

The second response is to replace one organizational mechanism with another. Thus, the growth of hierarchies in the late 19th century represented a replacement of (that is, exit from) arm's-length markets; while the nationalization of private firms by the post-war socialist governments of the UK represented a replacement of the private by the public sector. The third response is to seek to reduce the deficiencies of an imperfect organizational mode rather than to replace it. So, rather than exiting from the costs of inefficient governments, by deregulating or privatizing markets, a 'voice' strategy would try to make the actions of governments more cost-effective. Rather than acquire subcontractors who fail to meet quality standards or adhere to delivery dates, the contracting firms might prefer to reduce such transaction costs by establishing closer and more productive working relations with such contractors. Similarly, governments, by reducing microeconomic uncertainties, removing market-inhibiting practices and lowering trade barriers, for example discriminatory purchasing procedures, might help lower the transaction and coordination costs of both hierarchies and arm's-length markets.

The fourth solution is for governments or some other extra-market institutions (for example, groups of firms) to counteract the intrinsic deficiencies of the market by offering producers and consumers inducements to behave as if a 'first-best' market existed. Examples include the provision of tax concessions and subsidies to increase the private benefits of R&D and training to the level of their social benefits; improving information about the export opportunities for small firms; setting up investment guarantee schemes to protect outbound MNEs against political risks; making certain that patent legislation and procedures properly reflect the needs of innovators; assisting the market in its provision of risk capital – especially for projects which are likely to generate social benefits and are long term in their gestation; and ensuring, directly or indirectly, that the hassle costs of doing business – for example, industrial disputes, inadequate transport and communication facilities, and time-consuming bureaucratic controls – are kept to the minimum.

It is not difficult to think of many other examples of endemic market shortcomings, but most reduce to the presence of X-inefficiency of one kind or another. But, there is another aspect of market failure which economists frequently neglect, mainly because they like to assume human beings behave in a consistent and rational manner and are interested only in the pursuance of wealth. Organizational theorists question this, and talk about the bounded rationality and opportunistic behaviour of producers and consumers; and about the *homo psychologicus* of cognitive psychology as compared with the *homo economicus* of economics.

Is it too unrealistic to extend this idea of psychological man to the mentality or culture of wealth-creating activities by countries and corporations? Even the most cursory glance at the ways in which the Arab countries and the Germans conduct their daily business; or the attitudes of the Japanese and Nigerians to inter-firm relationship and contractual obligations; or the ethos of work and leisure of the Taiwanese and Greeks; or the perceived responsibilities and duties of workers, business managers and governments of the Koreans, Chileans and Russians; or the cross-border operational and organizational strategies of Nissan and Toyota or Motorola and Texas Instruments, reveals wide differences in the culture or mentality of wealth-creating behaviour. The globalizing economy is affording a new importance to concepts such as trust, forbearance and reciprocity; and to informal, rather than formal, organizational forms in affecting national competitiveness, and, hence, the disposition of resources and capabilities.

The extent to which the culture of wealth-creating behaviour is an intrinsic characteristic of a country or corporation, or can be shaped by exposure to other cultures, by decree or economic pressure, or by a reorientation of personal or business values, is debatable. But, there can be little doubt that the forces of globalization are compelling firms and governments to review their respective roles in influencing mental attitudes towards wealth-creating activities. Whether we like it or not, the trade-offs between these and other activities, such as leisure pursuits, are changing; and, whether we like it or not, to a large extent, they are being set by countries which place the highest value on competitiveness. The grasshopper's attitude to life is fine as long as the grasshopper does not aspire to the living standards of the ant. The trouble is that most of us want to retain our lifestyles of work and leisure, but also enjoy all the material benefits of our economically more successful neighbours.

The fifth response, and one which is particularly germane to international business activity, is for supranational organization arrangements to either complement or replace national organizational arrangements. The argument here is that rather than a 'exit'[18] or 'voice' response to the costs of organizational failure by national institutions, the best solution would be for some agreement to be undertaken at an international level. The establishment of a range of early post-World War II supranational regimes, for example the General Agreement on Tariffs and Trade (GATT), the World Bank, the International Monetary Fund (IMF) and so on, was a recognition that national organizational forms were sometimes inadequate to optimize the international allocation of resources. With the spread of cross-border hierarchies and the globalization of an increasing number of markets, the areas for supranational intervention seem to be expanding.[19] In particular, the current debate over the widening of the terms of reference of the World Trade Organization (WTO) to embrace competition policy, labour standards and so on, and the growing pressure for a multilateral investment regime, is a recognition of the inability of national organizational modes to provide a first-best solution to minimizing the production and transaction costs of economic activity in a world in which national borders are porous to the movement of resources and capabilities. At the same time, there has so far been little systematic research on the costs and benefits of supranational governance, and we have no clear indication of the conditions under which the fifth response to organizational failure is the optimal one.[20]

THE SYSTEMIC ROLE OF GOVERNMENT

A review of the writings of past scholars on the appropriate role of governments in a market-based economy reveals that little attention has been given to the role of government as a creator and overseer of economic organization as opposed to a participator in the system (Dunning, 1995b). Apart from the institutional school of economists,[21] most scholars have either assumed that the setting up and management costs of a market-based system of resource allocation is zero minimal or they have ignored these costs altogether. At the time of Adam Smith, when most products were simple and natural resource based, the degree of division of labour was limited, and when most markets were subnational, this neglect was perhaps understandable – although it is perhaps worth observing that in the contemporary world economy, the costs of setting up even a rudimentary market system in a poor developing country are far from negligible. In today's structurally integrated world economy, and particularly in the Triad of advanced industrial economies, such an assumption is quite inappropriate, and it is becoming even less so as the components of the market system are becoming more complex and interdependent on each other.

Even accepting the almost intractable problems of both identifying the first-best system (which is likely to be both country and time specific) and the static and dynamic costs of supervising that system, it is none the less the case that, with the noticeable exceptions of Stiglitz (1989), Wade (1988) and Chang (1994), most mainstream economists, while implicitly acknowledging this role of government,[22] pay only lip-service to it. Yet as Amsden, Kochanowicz and Taylor (1994) vividly demonstrate, the failure of the East European economies to successfully and speedily embrace a market-based capitalism is at least partly due to the gross underestimation by Western economists of the institutionally related costs of setting up the system. Wade (1988) shows that there have been no such illusions among East Asian economists, who from the early post-war period have recognized the critical role of the state to fund most of the setting-up costs of the market system, and those associated with its efficient maintenance. The market system is *par excellence* a public good; and so it is reasonable that governments, on behalf of their constituents who benefit from it, should bear at least some of the costs of it. This, indeed, is the unique and special macro-organizational role of government, and it is the reconfiguration of this role, as much as its role as a participatory organizational entity, which the globalizing economy is currently demanding.

The precise character of the systemic and market-facilitating role of government is still a matter of debate; but gradually, with the increasing interaction between the particular macro-organizational strategies of national governments (for example, competition, innovation, environmental and educational policies), it is rising on the agenda of both these governments and supranational regimes. Except in East Asia, the idea that governments may beneficially coordinate (some of) their organizational arrangements in the same way they coordinate (some of) their macroeconomic policies has not yet gained credence, but this may well be forced on them in the emerging era of *alliance* capitalism.[23]

SOME CONCLUDING REMARKS

The aim of this chapter has been to argue that the boundaries of the main organizational entities in a capitalist economy are undergoing radical change as market-based capitalism is moving from being *hierarchical* to *alliance* in character; and as production and markets are becoming increasingly globalized. It has described the extent and form of these boundary changes in respect of firms, markets and governments (acting on behalf of the constituents for which they are responsible).

The chapter has four main conclusions. First, not only are the boundaries of each of the organizational forms becoming more porous and interdependent of each other, but there is a growing complementarity between them. Such interdependence is demanding a reappraisal of the cost-effectiveness of the alternative forms.

Second, the globalization of economic activity is requiring a reevalution of the optimal way in which the three main organizational entities, namely, firms, markets and governments, respond to changes in the costs of organizing resource allocation.

Third, not only is globalization causing the systemic role of national governments to become more important, but it is also compelling them to give more attention to how their policies might be integrated or harmonized with those of other governments, either formally through customs unions or other regional integration schemes, or by the participation in supranational regimes and arrangements.

The fourth conclusion is that scholars interested in the determinants and consequences of international business activity need to modify their paradigms and theories to encompass the implications of *alliance* capitalism for the boundaries of economic activity.[24] In particular the concept of the competitive or ownership advantages of firms needs to be widened to take account of the benefits to be derived from inter-firm alliances and networking; while that of the locational advantages of countries needs to give more attention to the consequences of the mobility of firm-specific assets and the role of governments in the ways in which such assets may be combined with those which are locationally immobile within their areas of jurisdiction. More generally, scholars need to give more careful attention to the alternative responses to organizational failure; and particularly those directed to trying to overcome, rather than exiting from, those failures.

The consequences of international business activity may also need re-examination as a result of the growing interdependence between firms, markets and nation states. The internal transfer of technology by an MNE to its subsidiary, which has few spillover effects and results of which only affect the recipient country, is one thing; such a transfer between two independent firms, the success of which depends on complementary technologies being available, and the output of which has social as well as private consequences, is quite another. By the same token, the competition for created assets by national governments, may, if it leads to the establishment or strengthening of supranational institutions which may constrain that behaviour, affect the cross-border alliance-related strategies of MNEs'; while a harmonization of national technical and environmental standards may have no less important consequences for the kinds of value-added activities (as well as their externalities) which MNEs and other firms undertake in particular countries.

It may be that this chapter has exaggerated the distinctive nature and consequences of alliance capitalism and the reconfiguration of the frontiers of international business activity. Only time will tell whether this is so or not.

NOTES

1. By macro-organization we mean the organization of a country's resources and capabilities, undertaken by governments on behalf of their constituents; and by micro-organization we mean the organization of a firm's or individual's resources and capabilities.
2. Or at least 51 per cent of the (voting) equity of shareholding.
3. The concept of 'voice' and 'exit' strategies was first put forward by Albert Hirschman (1970) to explain the responses of firms or nation states to threats to their sovereignty or economic prosperity. He postulated two such responses namely, 'exit' to a better alternative, and 'voice' which he defined as, 'any attempt at all to change rather than escape from an objectionable state of affairs (p. 30).
4. When the spatially specific transaction costs are added to the North model, then the significance of these costs further increases.
5. See, particularly, Knight (1921), Sraffa (1926), Kaldor (1934) and Robinson (1934).
6. As, for example, exerted by the banks on the German and Japanese systems of corporate governance (Prowse, 1995).
7. Albeit, perhaps, for a limited time period.
8. As described, for example, in Best (1990), Dunning (1994) and (1995a) and Gerlach (1992). To quote from Dunning (1995a), 'the expression *alliance capitalism* should be perceived partly as a socio-cultural phenomenon and partly as a techno-organizational one. The former suggests a change in the ethos and perspective towards the organization of capitalism, and, in particular, towards the relationships between the participating institutions and individuals. The latter embraces the formal structure of the organization of economic activity, including the management of resource allocation and growth. Alliance capitalism is an eclectic [sic] concept. It suggests both cooperation and competition *between* institutions (including public institutions) and between interested parties *within* institutions. *De facto*, it is also leading to a flattening out of the organizational structure of decision-taking of business enterprises, with a pyramidal chain of command being increasingly replaced by a more heterarchical inter-play between the main participants in decision-taking' (pp. 461–92).
9. One estimate is that the average social returns to R&D exceed those appropriated by the innovating firms by 50–100 per cent (Aaron and Schultze, 1992).
10. Implicit in these kinds of externalities is the 'free-rider' issue – which, of course, can work either to the advantage *or* disadvantage of firms, depending on whether they, or their competitors, are enjoying the 'free ride'.
11. There are, of course, other kinds of space, for example, cultural and ideological space; but, for the purposes of this chapter we shall consider these only as they affect economic and political space.
12. This may lead to a divergence between gross national product (GNP) and gross domestic product (GDP). Gross national product is the output produced by the residents of a country including the income earned on foreign assets. It is equal to gross domestic product plus income earned in foreign countries by its own residents (including subsidiaries of its firms) less income accrued to foreign residents on assets they own within their domestic territory. See Dunning, 1988, Chapter 4.
13. Compare countries in the EU with states in the United States.
14. For another, but complementary, view on the economic jurisdiction of national governments, see Helm (1989).
15. We appreciate that in classical and neo-classical economics, the concept of competing governments had no place. But in the late 20th-century globalizing economy, in which national competitiveness is innovation driven, where many assets are mobile across national boundaries, and where there is substantial unemployment, this particular tenet of neo-classical economics no longer holds true.
16. Although the form and extent of the cooperation varies markedly between countries. Compare, for example, the various forms of government/firm interaction in East Asian countries with those in the United States.

17. The subject of the optimal 'social' investment in dynamic public goods is one which has so far received only scant attention in the literature.
18. Paralleling an 'exit' response to rising costs, one could also consider an entry response to rising benefits of a particular organizational form.
19. No less are such institutions proliferating in a variety of non-economic fields, for example the environment, technical standards, defence, health and crime-related issues. See Eden and Hampson (1990).
20. It is hoped that some current research by David Vines (of Oxford University) and David Currie (of the London Business School) will help shed light on these issues. For a brief description of this research, see Currie and Vines (1992).
21. For succinct accounts of the evolution and contemporary views of this school, see North (1990) and Dunning (1995b).
22. See, for example, Friedman (1962) and Wolf (1988).
23. For an excellent analysis of recent changes in the macro-organizational policies adopted by East Asian and Latin American governments, especially towards innovation, trade, industrial development and competitiveness, see Bradford (1994a and 1994b).
24. An exploratory attempt to examine the implications of alliance capitalism for the eclectic paradigm of international production has been made by the present author (see Dunning, 1995a).

REFERENCES

Aaron, H.J. and C.L. Schultze (1992), *Setting Domestic Priorities: What can Government Do?* Washington: The Brookings Institution.

Amsden, A., J. Kochanowicz and L. Taylor (1994), *The Market Meets its Match: Restructuring the Economies of Eastern Europe*, Cambridge, MA and London: Harvard University Press.

Best, M. (1990), *The New Competition: Institutions of Restructuring*, Cambridge, MA: Harvard University Press.

Bradford, C.I. (1994a), *The New Paradigm of Systemic Competitiveness: Toward More Integrated Policies in Latin America*, Paris: OECD.

Bradford, C.I. (1994b), *From Trade-Driven Growth to Growth-Driven Trade: Reappraising the East Asian Development Experience*, Paris: OECD.

Chang, H.J. (1994), *The Political Economy of Industrial Policy*, New York: St. Martin's Press.

Currie, D. and D. Vines (1992), 'A global economic policy agenda for the 1990s: Is there a special British role?' *International Affairs*, **68** (4), 585–602.

Dunning, J.H. (1988), *Multinationals, Technology and Competitiveness*, London and Boston: Unwin Hyman.

Dunning, J.H. (1994), *Globalization, Economic Restructuring and Development*, Geneva: UNCTAD, The 6th Prebisch Lecture.

Dunning, J.H. (1995a), 'Reappraising the eclectic paradigm in the age of alliance capitalism', *Journal of International Business Studies*, **26** (3), 461–92.

Dunning, J.H. (1995b), 'Governments and the Macro-Organization of Economic Activity: An Historical and Spatial Perspective', Paper presented to Carnegie Bosch Conference on Governments, Globalization and Competitiveness, Washington, June.

Eden, L. and F.O. Hampson (1990), *Clubs are Trumps: Towards a Taxonomy of International Regimes*, Carleton University, C/TQS: Ottawa Center for International Trade and Investment Policies, pp. 90–102.

Feldman, M.P. (1994), *The Geography of Innovation*, Dortrecht: Kluwer Academic Publishers.

Friedman, M. (1962), *Capitalism and Freedom*, Chicago and London: University of Chicago Press.

Gerlach, M.L. (1992), *Alliance, Capitalism: The Social Organization of Japanese Business*, Oxford: Oxford University Press.

Helm, D. (ed.) (1989), *The Economic Borders of the State*, Oxford: Oxford University Press.

Hirschman, A. (1970), *Exit Voice and Loyalty*, Cambridge, MA: Harvard University Press.

Kaldor, N. (1934), 'The equilibrium of the firm', *Economic Journal*, **44**, 70–71.

Knight, F.H. (1921), *Risk, Uncertainty and Profit*, Boston and New York: Houghton Mifflin Co.

McGrew, A.G. and P.G. Lewis (eds) (1992), *Global Politics: Globalization and the Nation State*, Cambridge: Polity Press.

North, D. (1990), *Institutions, Institutional Change and Economic Performance*, Cambridge: Cambridge University Press.

Porter, M. (1986), *Competition in Global Industries*, Boston: Harvard University Press.

Porter, M.E. (1990), *The Competitive Advantage of Nations*, New York: The Free Press.

Prowse, S.D. (1995), *Financial Markets, Institutions and Instruments*, Oxford: Basil Blackwell.

Robinson, E.A.G. (1934), 'The problem of management and the size of firms', *Economic Journal*, **44**, 240–54.

Sraffa, P. (1926), 'The laws of return under competitive conditions', *Economic Journal*, **36**, 535–50.

Stiglitz, J. (1989), *The Economic Role of the State*, Oxford: Basil Blackwell.

UNCTAD (1993), *World Investment Report 1993, Transnational Corporations and Integrated International Production*, New York: UN, Sales No. E.93.II.A. 14.

Wade, R. (1988), 'The role of Government in overcoming market failure in Taiwan, Republic of Korea and Japan', in H. Hughes (ed.), *Achieving Industrialization in East Asia*, Cambridge: Cambridge University Press, pp. 129–63.

Wolf, M. (1988), *Markets or Governments*, Cambridge, MA: MIT Press.

2. Strategic foreign direct investment

Peter J. Buckley

INTRODUCTION

This chapter examines foreign direct investment by multinational firms in the modern world economy, which is characterized by increasing integration across national markets. This process – often termed 'globalization' – has radically altered firms' approaches to direct foreign investment. The following section introduces a simple model of the world economy which traces the effects of different degrees of integration across various types of markets and examines the consequences for direct foreign investment, paying particular attention to cross-investment in the 'Triad' of North America, Europe and Japan. The next section examines strategic foreign direct investment and its crucial relationships with trade and GDP. This section introduces some key data on the role of foreign direct investment in world economic activity in both the long run and short run. It demonstrates the crucial role of foreign direct investment in achieving the firm's strategic objectives, be they market access, control of key inputs or cost reduction. Then relationships among the Triad are examined in detail. International strategic alliances are introduced and analysed in a separate section and the conclusion brings various elements together.

A SIMPLE MODEL OF THE INTERNATIONAL ECONOMY

Figure 2.1 shows a highly simplified picture of the world economy. It attempts to show different degrees of integration across various types of market. The suggestion is that financial markets are substantially integrated so that the world financial market can, for many purposes, be regarded as a single market. The market for goods and services is differentiated on a regional basis with 'single markets' either existing or emerging (European Union (EU), North American Free Trade Area (NAFTA) and so on). Such markets are increasingly uniform in regulation, standards, codes of practice (for example, anti-trust) and business behaviour and so they offer the possibility of

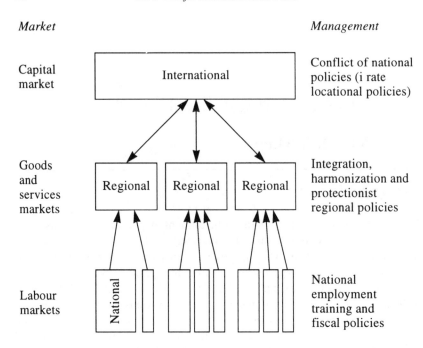

Figure 2.1   Internationalization of firms – conflict of markets

economies of scale across the market, but are substantially differentiated by these factors (and possibly by a common external tariff) from other regional markets. Labour markets, however, remain primarily national. Governments wish to regulate their own labour market and to differentiate it (protect it) from neighbouring labour markets. Many of the current difficulties in governmental regulatory policy arise from the difficulty of attempting to pursue independent labour market policies in the presence of regional goods and services markets and an international market for capital.

In contrast, multinational enterprises are perfectly placed to exploit the differences in international integration of markets. The presence of an international capital market enables capital costs to be driven to a minimum. The existence of regional goods and services markets enables firms to exploit economies of scale across several economies. Differential labour markets enable costs to be reduced by locating the labour-intensive stages of production in cheap labour economies. Horizontal integration is served by regional goods and services markets, vertical integration by differentiated labour markets and the spatial distribution of supplies of key raw materials. Strategic trade and foreign direct investment can be seen to take place within this overall framework.

STRATEGIC TRADE, STRATEGIC FOREIGN DIRECT INVESTMENT AND GDP

Does the notion of 'strategic' when appended to trade or foreign direct investment make a difference? It adds the dimension of competition – rivalry – to that of the firm simply responding to external market signals. As Graham (1992) has pointed out, many models of multinational firms assume the firm to be a monopolist. Formal modelling becomes more difficult when 'strategies' are included, because an interaction term with other firms is being added to the firm's decision set. It is not now simply aiming for the least-cost operation, it has goals defined in opposition to its rivals (market share for example, national or global). This suggests an analysis in which strategic goals are proximate goals, shorter-run goals or means towards an end which may be long-run survival or profit maximization. The competitive game is played under constraints. These constraints are the external environment, demand and technology conditions. Part of the modelling of strategy aims to make technology conditions endogenous by examining the creation of technology via R&D expenditure and combining this with assumptions on increasing returns to scale in the firm's various activities. These refinements can take place within the orthodox (non-strategic) environment. The twist is the market-share rivalristic game, such as the entry pre-emption case analysed by Horstmann and Markusen (1987). (See also Brander and Spencer, 1985; Krugman, 1990.)

From the point of view of the individual firm, trade can be strategic. Exports can be a weapon to gain access to a foreign market. When this is cast as a two-person game with national champions contending for a share of the prize (the international market) then subsidies can alter the payoffs and under certain restrictive assumptions can lead to gains in national welfare (payoffs to individual firms of national ownership) in the post-subsidy game.

As Casson (1990) points out, strategic trade policies suffer from the same difficulty as adversarial business strategies – they can be imitated and the results of the imitation can be disastrous. Classic strategic trade policy under which government subsidizes 'national champions' (Brander and Spencer, 1985; Krugman, 1987b) can result in foreign governments matching the subsidies. This can result in escalation of threat and counter-threat as each government guarantees the credibility of its national champion's threat to spoil the rival's market. Only when slow response or poor liquidity of the foreign rival causes it to exit the industry is a permanent gain likely to be achieved. The analogy with protectionism ('beggar-my-neighbour') policies is strong. While a subsidized or protected firm may sometimes gain, domestic consumers and taxpayers will normally lose. The first part of this sentence explains rent-seeking lobbying for government intervention to protect or subsidize putative 'national champions'.

This leaves aside the political feasibility of the 'tax generally and subsidize specifically' policy combination. In the USA this must (at the least) be constrained by the budget deficit and in the European Union it is constrained by the lack of a centralized body (Holmes, 1995). In addition, observation suggests that the ability of governments to pick winners (national champions) is severely limited. Institutional failure is greater than market failure.

From a macro view, trade, based on comparative advantage, is a non-zero-sum game. It is from this viewpoint that Krugman views the notion of national competitiveness as a meaningless concept (Krugman, 1994).

Krugman (1987a) reviews the arguments based on externalities and strategic trade consideration for interventionist policies, but he concludes that the optimal policy is so sensitive to the technological and behavioural parameters that the results of intervention are uncertain even in areas where externality and monopoly arguments abound (like semiconductors). Information available to the government will be biased – not least by lying on the part of rent-seekers: 'We have a sadder but wiser argument for free trade in a world whose politics are as imperfect as its markets'.

Strategic trade theorists have played a valuable role in introducing elements of imperfect competition, such as product differentiation, into trade models and focusing attention on to increasing returns to scale. There has, perhaps, been too little attention paid to *firm*-level economies of scale rather than *plant*-level economies. It is often firm-level economies of scale – gaining the maximum return from a specific sunk cost in R&D, which leads to internationalization rather than external transaction. The same logic, when combined with the firm's search for the most efficient operation by minimizing its overall costs of production by optimally locating its subunits, often dictates foreign direct investment.

Trade, however, is not redundant. The expansion of multinational firms by subdividing activities and locating them where overall costs are minimized creates a network of intra-firm trade. This intra-firm trade can take place at prices which diverge from market or 'arm's-length' prices in order to afford the corporation the ability to reduce its overall tax bill. Such transfer pricing policies add an additional, purely international (inter-tax jurisdiction) reason for firms to invest abroad.

This is not to say that foreign direct investment (FDI) will be always and everywhere the preferred means of doing business abroad. Figure 2.2 shows a simple model for the determination of the optimal form of doing business in a given foreign market (Buckley and Casson, 1981). It attributes fixed costs of entry and variable costs of exposure to each mode of doing business abroad: exporting, licensing and FDI. In the example given, the firm should switch from exporting to foreign direct investment only at point q, where the lower variable costs of foreign direct investment outweigh its higher fixed costs of

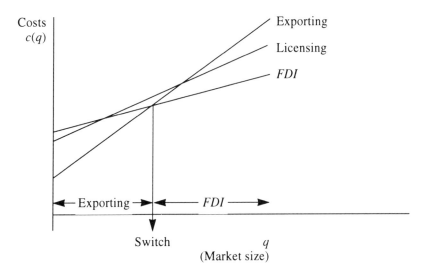

Note: In this example, licensing is never the preferred alternative.

Source: Reproduced from Buckley and Casson (1981), p. 80.

Figure 2.2   The timing of a foreign direct investment

entry. If q is large, then the point will never be reached where the firm should choose *FDI*. If *FDI* has unusually high set-up costs – large fixed capital requirements, for instance in a petrochemical complex – only in the largest markets will such a strategy be feasible.

Table 2.1 shows the role of foreign direct investment in selected years as a share of world output (stocks and flows), as a share of world capital formulation and an estimate of the world sales of foreign affiliates as a share of world exports. The importance of the sales of foreign affiliates as a percentage of world exports shows a rising long-term trend to the point at which the sales of foreign affiliates exceed the volume of world exports. This is particularly notable given the decline in tariffs (Table 2.2).

Intra-firm international trade is also a factor of growing importance variously estimated as between 30 and 40 per cent of world trade (Table 2.3). This arises in large part because of the increase in foreign sourcing of intermediate inputs as shown in Table 2.4.

Strategic foreign direct investment is a notion which arises from the competitive behaviour of firms. Foreign direct investment is carried out for a variety of motives, most notably:

Table 2.1   The role of foreign direct investment in world economic activity,
*   1913, 1960, 1975, 1980 and 1991 (percentage)*

Item	1913	1960	1975	1980	1985	1991
World FDI stock as a share of world output	9.0[a]	4.4	4.5	4.8	6.4	8.5
World FDI inflows as a share of world output	—	0.3	0.3	0.5	0.5	0.7
World FDI inflows as a share of world gross fixed capital formation	—	1.1	1.4	2.0	1.8	3.5
World sales of foreign affiliates as a share of world exports	—	84[b]	97[c]	99[d]	99[d]	122

Notes:
a.   Estimate.
b.   1967 based on United States.
c.   Based on United States and Japanese figures.
d.   1982 based on German, Japanese and United States data.

Source: UNCTAD. Division on Transnational Corporations and Investment, based on UNCTAD-DTCI, FDI data base, UN-DESIPA data base; Dunning, 1993 and Bairoch, 1994. *Taken from World Investment Report 1994, UNCTAD, Division on Transnational Corporations and Investment,* p. 130.

Table 2.2   Average tariff rates on manufactured products in selected
*   developed countries, 1913, 1950 and 1990 (weighted average;*
*   percentage of value)*

Country	1913	1950	1990
France	21	18	5.9
Germany	20	26	5.9
Italy	18	25	5.9
Japan	30	—	5.3
Netherlands	4	11	5.9
Sweden	20	9	4.4
United Kingdom	—	23	5.9
United States	44	14	4.8

Source: Bairoch, 1993, Table 3.3 *Taken from World Investment Report 1994,* p. 123.

1.   market access;
2.   resource control and foreign sourcing of key intermediate inputs;
3.   cost reduction (efficiency seeking).

Table 2.3 *United States and Japan: intra-firm trade, 1977, 1982 and 1989 (percentage of total exports or imports)*

Year	United States		Japan[a]	
	Exports	Imports	Exports	Imports
1977	36	40	24[b]	32
1982	33	37	31[c]	18
1989	34	41	33	29

Notes:
a. Refers to Japanese TNCs only.
b. Refers to 1980.
c. Refers to 1983.

Source: *World Investment Report* (1993), p. 143.

Table 2.4 *Ratio of imported to domestic sourcing of intermediate inputs, selected countries (percentage)*

Country	Early 1970s	Mid-and late 1970s	Mid-1980s
Canada	34	37	50
France	21	25	38
Germany	—	21	34
Japan	5	6	7
United Kingdom	16	32	37
United States	7	8	13

Source: *World Investment Report* (1993), p. 145.

Each of these motives contains the notion of 'stealing a march' on rivals either by securing (foreign) market share, excluding rivals from key inputs or raw materials and undercutting prices by least-cost location.

Foreign direct investment centrally incorporates the notion of control. This is the defining characteristic which distinguishes direct foreign investment from portfolio foreign investment. Control is easy to recongize but difficult to define. Control may be exercised not only through equity shares but also through control of technology, management and even information flows. The issue of foreign control raises a large number of questions related to conflicting national jurisdictions. It further complicates the targeting of policy. For whom should policy be designed? (All firms resident in the national economic space, including foreign-owned ones or all firms of 'our' nationality wherever they are located?)

Foreign direct investment represents a package of resources. Not only capital but also management skills, technology, labour services and access to markets are often elements of the package. These dimensions of the FDI give it a centrality in international economic relations which does not apply to trade flows. FDI represents a conduit through which flow information and resources.

The relationship between flows of trade and flows of foreign direct investment is a complex one. In some instances FDI will replace exporting by the parent corporation of a multinational firm. This so-called 'defensive investment' may be put in place to protect a market share initially established by exporting. 'Tariff-jumping' FDI would also be in this category. A local presence through FDI enables the firm to respond more rapidly to demand in a particular foreign market, but also serve as a 'listening post' in order to spot trends more quickly and to enable adjustment to the local business culture. Thus even when intended to be export replacing, FDI will often increase exporting capability and may serve to 'piggy-back' other products on to the original export line. FDI will be expected to enhance exports of semi-finished goods if it is aimed at a final foreign market (assembly, fabrication or finishing).

As pointed out above, it is not necessarily the case that the market will be a key motive for FDI. Securing access to resources and cost reduction are alternative motivations. The latter motive may result in a more differentiated pattern of trade as the firm moves towards globally integrated production. Casson et al. (1986) attempted to capture some of the complexities of this pattern by classifying the structure and content of world trade by six types of industry: new product industry, mature product industry, rationalized product industry, resource-based industry, trading services and non-tradable services.

Thus foreign direct investment is a strategic weapon which can serve a variety of motives. In high-technology multinationals, FDI represents the most important conduit for the international transfer of technology. In these instances FDI is intended to diffuse technology spatially, at the same time protecting its proprietary nature (ownership). In contrast to licensing, FDI represents the internal transfer of information and knowledge, risking diffusion less by reducing exposure to the market.

Foreign direct investment is the major method of penetrating markets in the non-tradables sector (largely services) which actually make up a majority of world economic activity!

TRIAD RELATIONS IN THE INTERNATIONAL ECONOMY

North America, Europe and Japan (the Triad) represent the centres of the world's emerging regional trade blocs – NAFTA, the EU and the putative Asia–Pacific Economic Cooperation (APEC) zone. Much of the analysis of flows of trade and FDI takes place on an implicit or explicit framework of this tripolar world. This must be held in mind as an abstraction or at best an approximation to trade and investment relations in the international economy. The decisions which are being aggregated are those of individual firms. The outcomes of these decisions are aggregated by national groups. Flows of

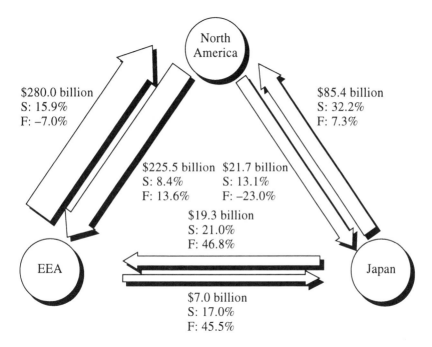

Note: Dollar figures show estimated values of stock of FDI based on data on inward and outward investment from North America and the European Economic Area (EEA), excluding Iceland and Liechtenstein. Intra-North American investment and intra-EEA investment have been netted out. Percentages show average annual growth rates for stocks (1980–90) and flows (1985–91). North America includes Canada and the United States. The European Economic Area includes the European Community (EC) and the European Free Trade Association, excluding Iceland and Liechtenstein.

Source: UNCTAD, Programme on Transnational Corporations, foreign-direct-investment database.

Figure 2.3   Intra-Triad foreign direct investment, 1990 (billions of dollars)

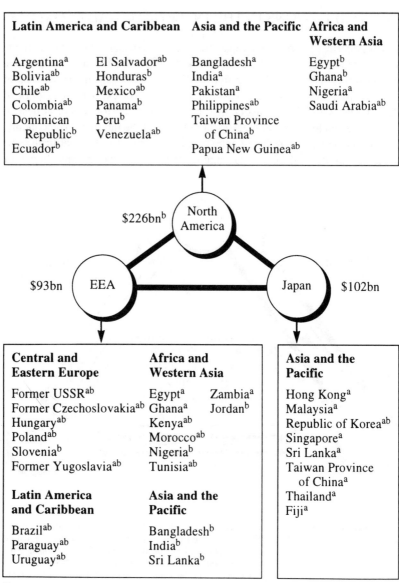

Latin America and Caribbean		Asia and the Pacific	Africa and Western Asia
Argentina[a]	El Salvador[ab]	Bangladesh[a]	Egypt[b]
Bolivia[ab]	Honduras[b]	India[a]	Ghana[b]
Chile[ab]	Mexico[ab]	Pakistan[a]	Nigeria[a]
Colombia[ab]	Panama[b]	Philippines[ab]	Saudi Arabia[ab]
Dominican Republic[b]	Peru[b]	Taiwan Province of China[b]	
Ecuador[b]	Venezuela[ab]	Papua New Guinea[ab]	

$226bn[b]   North America

$93bn   EEA   Japan $102bn

Central and Eastern Europe		Africa and Western Asia		Asia and the Pacific
Former USSR[ab]		Egypt[a]	Zambia[a]	Hong Kong[a]
Former Czechoslovakia[ab]		Ghana[a]	Jordan[b]	Malaysia[a]
Hungary[ab]		Kenya[ab]		Republic of Korea[ab]
Poland[ab]		Morocco[ab]		Singapore[a]
Slovenia[b]		Nigeria[b]		Sri Lanka[a]
Former Yugoslavia[ab]		Tunisia[ab]		Taiwan Province of China[a]
Latin America and Caribbean		**Asia and the Pacific**		Thailand[a]
				Fiji[a]
Brazil[ab]		Bangladesh[b]		
Paraguay[ab]		India[b]		
Uruguay[ab]		Sri Lanka[b]		

Notes:
a. In terms of average inward FDI flows, 1987–91.
b. In terms of inward FDI stock for 1991.

Source: UNCTAD, Division on Transnational Corporations and Investment.

Figure 2.4   The Triad of foreign direct investment and its clusters, 1991

trade are defined by spatial factors, flows of investment by ownership. There is a real sense that aggregating flows risk adding apples to pears. This is only useful when one wishes to know the weight of fruit. All such analyses should carry a health warning. Given these problems analyses of flows across the Triad can be very revealing.

Figure 2.3 shows the imbalance of foreign direct investment stocks across the Triad. The weakest link is the European FDI in Japan which represented only $7.0 billion. North American FDI in Japan too, accounted for only $21.7 billion as against $85.4 billion of Japanese direct investment in North America. Figure 2.4 shows clusters of countries attached to the main poles of the Triad. Developing countries have consistently declined as hosts to foreign direct investment, in terms of their share of world FDI (which is directed to a small number of less-developed countries (LDCs)). One Triad pole is the dominant investor in the countries listed. A pattern emerges of European dominance in Central and Eastern Europe and Africa, North American dominance in Latin America and Japanese dominance in non-Indian Subcontinent Asia (Figure 2.4).

In terms of firms' strategic positioning, it might be suggested that global firms need to maintain a (strategic) position in each of these three key markets in order not to let rivals have a 'free run' in any one market which would allow them to accumulate resources to enable the firm to mount a subsidized concerted attack on its rivals. This is a variant of the 'exchange of threat' model, usually expounded on a bilateral basis (Flowers, 1976; Graham, 1978, 1990).

TRADE AND INVESTMENT BETWEEN TRIAD POLES

Tables 2.5 shows the shares of different national ownerships of the world foreign direct investment stocks. In terms of Triad investment only, the figures in Table 2.6 show inward stocks.

The weak link is clearly inward investment to Japan. This issue brings us back to the idea of the 'centrality' of foreign direct investment (Buckley, 1994). FDI has a crucial role in cementing international economic relations. FDI is more than just a strategic weapon in a multinational firm's armoury or a choice among several possible foreign market-servicing strategies (Buckley and Casson, 1976; Buckley and Prescott, 1989; Buckley and Smith, 1994). It is a manifestation of a serious competitive commitment in the increasingly interdependent international economy. In many markets, it is not possible to gain a sizeable market share without an investment presence. Increasingly, arm's-length exports to major markets are futile. Selling through agents or distributors does not allow control of the operation or effective flow-back of

Table 2.5   *Share in world outward stock of foreign direct investment, by selected countries, 1914, 1960, 1978 and 1992 (percentage of world total)*

Country	1914	1960	1978	1992
France	12.2	6.1	3.8	8.3
Germany	10.5	1.2	7.3	9.2
Japan	0.1	0.7	6.8	13.0
United Kingdom	45.5	16.2	12.9	11.4
United States	18.5	49.2	41.4	25.3

Source: Dunning, 1993; Annex Table 4. Taken from *World Investment Report 1993*, p. 131.

Table 2.6   *Intra-Triad flows: inward stocks, 1990 (billions of dollars)*

North America	365.4
EEA	244.6
Japan	28.7

Source: Figure 3 – Intra Regional Flow (e.g. US–Canada) netted out.

information to the principal. (Buckley, Pass and Prescott, 1990). In markets such as Japan, the complexity of the distribution system demands a presence and the necessity for investment increases the cost of entering the market (Buckley, Mirza and Sparkes, 1987).

The institutional form of foreign direct investment is also important. Multinational firms have to make crucial choices on ownership strategy (wholly-owned subsidiary, majority- or minority-owned joint ventures) and in entry mode (takeover versus greenfield venture). The difficulties of takeover in certain countries such as Japan increase the costs and problems of market penetration by outsiders, particularly in a competitive game where the entrant firm is seeking rapid access to the market.

Ownership strategies, too, differ across the Triad. Joint ventures are the most common means of entry into the Japanese market and there is a lively dispute on the efficiency of using Japanese joint-venture partners (at home or abroad). In essence, new entrants are unlikely to gain a foothold in Japan without a local partner. However, such an arrangement is not fixed for all time and many US and European investors in Japan later increase their ownership share of an existing joint venture or add a parallel wholly-owned operation, utilizing the accumulated experience (American Chamber of Commerce in Japan, 1991; Buckley, Mirza and Sparkes, 1996). This double-entry form of accessing the Japanese markets is particularly marked among European high-technology firms (Buckley, Mirza and Sparkes, 1996).

In addition to securing market penetration, FDI is used by multinationals to reduce costs. There is considerable evidence that such indirect targeting of markets via production bases in Third World countries is increasing. The use of Mexico to penetrate the US market and of North Africa, Central and Eastern Europe or peripheral EU locations to penetrate Europe is increasing. This does not seem to work in the case of Japan – in Japan a presence is necessary. Japanese multinationals use neighbouring cheaper labour countries to reduce costs of production aimed at the Japanese market as well as Europe and America. Japanese multinationals, however, have an advantage in accessing the Japanese distribution system. It is not the case that a manufacturing presence is necessary in FDI. Indeed, an optimal global location strategy will often dictate the separation of production from distribution. Coordination costs then become important and the superior management of activities can confer competition benefits (Buckley, Pass and Prescott, 1990).

INTERNATIONAL ALLIANCES

International alliances can be defined as inter-firm collaborations over a given economic space and time for the achievement of corporate goals (this is a modified version of Buckley's definition (1992, p. 912)). The essence of an alliance is that it operates across the boundaries of the firm using resources from at least two firms. Alliances can be defined locally, regionally, nationally or internationally and can operate in some defined real time or until certain goals are reached. The goals may be defined in terms of physical output, market share, technological achievement or managerial objective. It is possible that the partners to an alliance will have different, even conflicting goals. These factors make it extremely difficult to assess the success (or otherwise) of an alliance. Alliances may be reconfigured or even dissolved but this does not necessarily mean that they have failed. Indeed, one of the primary virtues of alliances is their flexibility. They can be formalized by equity holdings – joint ventures are alliances cemented by equity exchange – but non-equity alliances enable great flexibility to be built into international corporate strategy.

There has been a dramatic growth in international (strategic) alliances in recent years. Glaister and Buckley (1994) show a rising trend in UK joint-venture formation in the decade of the 1980s. This is confirmed by Table 2.8, which shows figures on the growth of strategic alliances in the Triad for the same decade. Glaister and Buckley show that the motives for joint-venture/ strategic alliance formation are very similar to those for foreign direct invest-

Table 2.7 *Joint-venture formation by industry, 1980–1989*

Industry	Year										Total	
	1980	1981	1982	1983	1984	1985	1986	1987	1988	1989	No.	%
Food and drink	3	0	1	0	0	3	2	4	3	2	18	3.5
Metals and minerals	4	1	2	2	0	1	1	0	2	3	16	3.1
Energy	4	1	1	0	1	0	0	1	2	2	12	2.3
Construction	2	1	1	1	0	2	2	2	1	6	18	3.5
Chemicals	6	2	1	4	2	2	1	3	4	2	27	5.2
Pharmaceuticals	1	1	1	5	1	1	3	1	2	1	17	3.3
Computers	0	3	1	1	2	4	2	2	2	4	21	4.0
Telecommunications	2	4	7	5	3	4	10	7	7	10	59	11.3
Other electrical	1	3	4	3	5	0	1	4	1	6	28	5.4
Automobiles	2	3	3	2	3	6	5	5	6	3	38	7.3
Aerospace	6	4	4	2	4	7	7	3	7	12	56	10.8
Other manufacturing	2	8	2	5	5	7	9	6	10	13	67	12.9
Transport	1	2	0	0	0	1	1	2	2	2	11	2.1
Distribution	0	1	1	0	2	4	5	2	2	6	23	4.4
Financial services	7	7	8	4	13	5	3	6	6	12	71	13.7
Other services	6	3	4	1	1	4	1	0	7	11	38	7.3
Total	47	44	41	35	42	51	53	48	64	95	520	100.0

ment and that the strategic alliance phenomenon is best analysed as a form of direct investment.

Tables 2.7 and 2.8 show that international alliances form a key element of strategy in certain industries.[1] Financial services, other manufacturing tele-communications and aerospace stand out as key sectors. Automobiles, bio-technology and information technology have all shown rapid growth in alli-ance formation, particularly in US–Japanese firms (for example, Reich and Mankin, 1986) but the perceived benefits clearly outweigh the risks of oppor-tunism in many cases.

Strategic alliances extend the ability of multinational firms to achieve their goals and they complement direct foreign investment as a corporate weapon. Alliances make it easier to access difficult, regulated and protected markets and resources. They also provide an option on entry – where a firm is undecided whether to make a full direct investment commitment, joint ven-tures and alliances help it to 'keep its options open' for a later, full investment commitment. (Such an approach is currently prevalent in Central and Eastern

Table 2.8   Growth in strategic alliance formation, 1980–1989 (number and percentage)

Industry/region	1980–1984		1985–1989		Percentage change
	Number	*Per cent*	*Number*	*Per cent*	
Automobiles	26	100	79	100	203
United States–Europe	10	39	24	30	140
United States–Japan	10	39	39	49	290
Europe–Japan	6	23	16	20	167
Biotechnology	108	100	198	100	83
United States–Europe	58	54	124	63	114
United States–Japan	45	42	54	27	20
Europe–Japan	5	4	20	10	300
Information technology	348	100	445	100	28
United States–Europe	158	45	256	58	62
United States–Japan	133	38	132	30	–0.8
Europe–Japan	57	16	57	13	—
New materials	63	100	115	100	83
United States–Europe	32	51	52	45	63
United States–Japan	16	25	40	35	150
Europe–Japan	15	24	23	20	53
Chemicals	103	100	80	100	–22
United States–Europe	54	52	31	39	–43
United States–Japan	28	27	35	44	25
Europe–Japan	21	20	14	17	–33

Source: United States Congress, Office of Technology Assessment, 1993, Figure 5.3.

Europe.) Alliances may also be construed as signals – to competitors, customers, suppliers and other interested bodies. They may be a signal that the firm has a credible commitment to enter a particular market or segment.

Alliances, therefore, are a useful complement to an international strategy based on strategic direct investment.

CONCLUSION

Strategic trade, driven by government policy in order to back national champions, has severe defects. It can work only in a limited number of sectors where retaliation is limited by the lack of a rival's response. Even then, it is politically infeasible to subsidize rent seeking in a few firms from general tax revenue. The efficacy of 'backing winners' in the industrial policy of governments does not inspire confidence in the historical record – especially in advanced countries.

Trade is also a limited weapon in strategic games. There are swathes of industry where it is not possible to enter foreign markets by exporting, non-tradables make up for a far larger share of the world economy than do tradable goods. Even where tradable goods exist, foreign direct investment is often a more important weapon in gaining access to foreign markets than are exports (or licensing). There is very little enthusiasm for subsidizing outward foreign investment because the majority of value-added activity takes place outside the political remit of the (political) subsidizer.

In many situations, foreign direct investment is the most powerful means of penetrating foreign markets. FDI has been rising relative to world trade, output and capital formation. Intra-firm trade is also increasing rapidly as firms source intermediate goods on a worldwide basis and serve global markets. Despite the decline in tariff protection, FDI outpaces the growth of trade.

Policies on FDI worldwide are skewed. There is a great deal of effort expended on attracting inward FDI but most governments follow a policy of neutrality towards outward FDI. Tax neutrality is often an explicit objective of policy towards domestic and foreign locations.

NOTE

1. Some authors have made alliances the centre of an analysis of the firm, rather than a strategic alternative. This trend was exemplified by Gerlach (1992) in entitling his book on the Japanese *keiretsu Alliance Capitalism* – although his analysis is specific to Japan. This trend is continued by John Dunning who refers to 'the age of alliance capitalism' (see his chapter in this volume and Dunning, 1995). Dunning sees alliances as spreading rather like

a virus through the global political economy, posing new issues of governance, regulation and competition. While alliances are not new – witness the cartel movement of the Western economy in the interwar years – they are salient in key sectors of the world economy. However, it is currently claiming too much to see alliances as replacing the unitary firm as the dominant player in competition, innovation and production. Intercorporate ties are important and growing but remain one strategic choice among many in the mosaic of competition and cooperation facing multinational firms.

REFERENCES

American Chamber of Commerce in Japan (ACCJ) (1991), *Trade and Investment in Japan*, Tokyo: ACCJ.

Bairoch, Paul (1993), *Economics and World History*, Brighton: Wheatsheaf.

Bairoch, Paul (1994), 'Globalisation, Myths and Realities – One Century of External Trade and Foreign Investment', in R. Boyer and D. Drache (eds), *The Future of Nations and the Power of Markets*, Toronto: University of Toronto Press.

Brander, J.A. and B.J. Spencer (1985), 'Export Subsidies and International Market Share Rivalry', *Journal of International Economics*, **18**, 83–100.

Buckley, P.J. (1992), 'Alliances, Technology and Markets: A Cautionary Tale', in P.J. Buckley, *Studies in International Business*, London: Macmillan.

Buckley, P.J. (1994), 'Comment on Investment and Trade by American European and Japanese Multinationals Across the Triad', in M. Mason and D. Encarnation, *Does Ownership Matter – Japanese Multinationals in Europe*, Oxford: Clarendon Press.

Buckley, P.J. and M. Casson (1976), *The Future of the Multinational Enterprise*, London: Macmillan.

Buckley, P.J. and M. Casson (1981), 'The Optimal Timing of a Foreign Direct Investment', *Economic Journal*, **861**, 55–94. Reprinted in Buckley and Casson (1985), *The Economic Theory of the Multinational Enterprise*, London: Macmillan.

Buckley, P.J., H. Mirza and J.R. Sparkes (1987), 'Direct Foreign Investment in Japan as a Means of Market Entry: The Case of European Firms', *Journal of Marketing Management*, **2**, 241–58.

Buckley, P.J., H. Mirza and J.R. Sparkes (1993), 'The Development of European Direct Investment in Japan', A Report to the Japan Foundation, University of Bradford.

Buckley, P.J., H. Mirza and J.R. Sparkes (1996), 'Contrasting Perspectives on American and European Direct Investment in Japan', *Business Economics*, **XXXI** (1), January, 42–8.

Buckley, P.J., C.L. Pass and K. Prescott (1990), 'Foreign Market Servicing by Multinationals: An Integrated Approach', *International Marketing Review*, **7**, 25–40.

Buckley, P.J. and K. Prescott (1989), 'The Structure of British Industry Sales in Foreign Markets', *Managerial and Decision Economics*, **10**, 189–208.

Buckley, P.J. and G.E. Smith (1994), 'An International Comparison of the Structure of Foreign Market Servicing Strategies', *International Business Review*, **3**, 71–94.

Casson, M. et al. (1986), *Multinationals and World Trade*, London: George Allen & Unwin.

Casson, M. (1990), 'Entrepreneurial Culture as a Competitive Advantage', in *Research in Global Business Management*, **1**, 139–51.

Dunning, John H. (1993), *The Theory of Transnational Corporations*, London: Routledge.

Dunning, John H. (1995), 'Reappraising the Eclectic Paradigm in an Age of Alliance Capitalism', *Journal of International Business Studies*, **26**, 461–91.

Flowers, E.B. (1976), 'Oligopolostic Reactions in European and Canadian Direct Investments in the United States', *Journal of International Business Studies*, **7**, 43–55.

Gerlach, Michael, L. (1992), *Alliance Capitalism: The Social Organisation of Japanese Business*, Oxford: Oxford University Press.

Glaister, K. and P.J. Buckley (1994), 'UK International Joint Ventures: An Analysis of Patterns of Activity and Distribution', *British Journal of Management*, **5**, 33–51.

Graham, E.M. (1978), 'Transatlantic Investment by Multinational Firms: A Rivalristic Phenomenon?', *Journal of Post Keynesian Economics*, **1**, 82–99.

Graham, E.M. (1990), 'Exchange of Threat between Multinational Firms as an Infinitely Repeated Non-cooperative Game', *The International Trade Journal*, **4**, 259–77.

Graham, E.M. (1992), 'The Theory of the Firm', in P.J. Buckley (ed.), *New Directions in International Business*, Aldershot: Edward Elgar.

Holmes, P. (1995), 'European Industrial Policy and Subsidiarity after Maastricht', University of Rennes I, mimeo.

Horstmann, E.J. and J.R. Markusen (1987), 'Strategic Investment and the Development of Multinationals', *International Economic Review*, **28**, 109–21.

Krugman, P. (1987a), 'Is Free Trade Passé?', *Journal of Economic Perspectives*, **1** (2), Fall, 131–44.

Krugman, P. (1987a), 'Market Access and Competition in High Technology Industries: A Simulation Exercise', in H. Kierzkowski (ed.), *Protection and Competition in International Trade*, Oxford: Blackwell.

Krugman, P. (1990), *Rethinking International Trade*, Cambridge, MA: MIT Press.

Krugman, P. (1994), *Peddling Prosperity*, New York: W.W. Norton & Company.

Reich, R.B. and E.D. Mankin (1986), 'Joint ventures with Japan give away our future', *Harvard Business Review*, **64** (2), 78–86.

World Investment Report: Transnational Corporations and Integrated International Production (1993), New York: United Nations.

3. Strategies of multinational enterprises and governments: the theory of the flagship firm[1]

Alan M. Rugman and Joseph R. D'Cruz

INTRODUCTION

Today there is renewed interest in the strategies of multinational enterprises (MNEs) and governments. At the Halifax G7 summit, investment issues obtained the same status as trade issues. The critical role of foreign direct investment (FDI), undertaken by MNEs, is now at the centre of analysis of international economic activity. This viewpoint is consistent with the recent interest of policy-makers on market access issues in the context of 'deeper integration', as explored at a conference reported in OECD (1995). The new agenda for international policy arises less from traditional border measures (tariffs) impeding trade in goods, than from domestic policies and regulations that affect international investment and the activities of MNEs. The linkages between trade and investment policies and between strategies of MNEs and governments demand new analysis.

This chapter is organized in a manner which permits discussion of the issue of deep integration by a focus on MNEs. It is organized at three degrees of complexity. First, there is a brief review of recent discussion about the need for, and nature of, a potential multilateral agreement on investment (MAI) with MNEs at its heart. Next, there is a review of key literature on the strategies of MNEs, and their interaction with governments. This uses internalization theory and recent work on business networks. To proceed to a meaningful level of analysis the D'Cruz and Rugman (1992, 1993) five partners/'flagship' model of business networks is developed. Third, an application of the flagship model is made to the regionalization of MNE strategy in the Canadian chemicals industry.

MULTINATIONALS AND THE MAI

The conceptual framework for a multilateral agreement on investment (MAI) is to be found in the theory of the multinational enterprise. It is the MNE which is the vehicle for FDI, and the negotiation and implementation of a rules-based, market-access system for investment requires a clear understanding of the nature and role of MNE activity and strategy.

The rationale for an MAI can be traced to comparatively recent literature, with the main contributions being by Bergsten and Graham (1992), Sauvé (1994), Julius (1994), Brewer (1995), Lawrence (1995) and Graham (1995b). Previous thinking consistent with the complementarities of trade and investment (in the context of innovation and science policy) can be found in Ostry (1990), while Ostry and Nelson (1995) discuss the need for a type of MAI to deal especially with technology. The ways in which NAFTA's investment provisions are relevant for an MAI have been explored in Gestrin and Rugman (1994, 1995), Graham and Wilkie (1994), Sauvé (1994) and Brewer and Young (1995). The NAFTA investment regime is discussed in Rugman (1994b). The role of an investment accord for APEC is discussed by Guisinger (1993) and Graham (1995a).

Building on the investment-related aspects of the GATT Uruguay Round the agenda for the next round of negotiations, in the new World Trade Organization (WTO), will have to incorporate investment issues, especially the attempt by the Organization for Economic Cooperation and Development (OECD) to conclude a comprehensive multilateral agreement on investment, the so-called MAI, over the 1995–97 period. It is anticipated that the MAI will be an investment-enhancing and market-access-opening accord, rather than the protectionist and nationalist investment regimes of the past. Previous regulations on FDI and screening agencies, such as Canada's Foreign Investment Review Act (FIRA) from 1974–85, are to be replaced by a pro-MNE set of rules with guarantees for the free movement of FDI. The MAI will need to include key provisions, such as: the right of establishment; national treatment; dispute settlement in cases of expropriation and/or unilateral changes in the rules; transparency, notifications, binding obligations and dispute resolution procedures; and agreements on transfer pricing, taxation and competition policy. This agenda is so long that it involves writing out the relative roles of the MNE and the state in the multilateral trade and investment system. This will be a complex task and one confused by efficiency versus distributional issues. It is because of these underlying tensions between the MNE and the nation state that the conceptual framework for an MAI must be based on the modern theory of the MNE.

A Framework for the MAI

The idea of economic efficiency and globalization as made operational by the activities of MNEs can be shown on the vertical axis of Figure 3.1. A movement up the axis results in a greater degree of globalization, yielding a useful dichotomy between low and high globalization. With low globalization there is local small and medium-sized business. With high globalization there are MNEs.

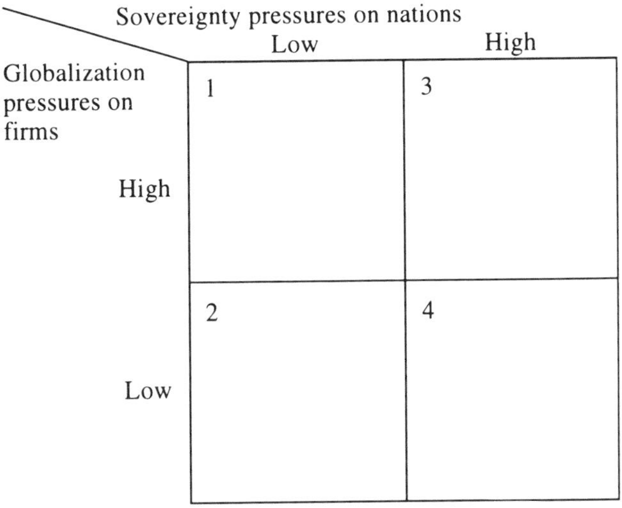

Figure 3.1   The globalization and sovereignty analysis of investment regimes

The concept of sovereignty and the independence of the nation state can be illustrated in the horizontal axis. Towards the right of the axis there is, conceptually, a high degree of sovereignty, where the regime passes its own laws and regulations, and has enforcement ability. To the left there is low sovereignty, meaning, in this context, that the regime has given up some of its power to others (either to firms or to other states in a multinational system). The matrix is a variant of Bartlett and Ghoshal (1989) and has been explored previously in Rugman (1993, 1994a).

The matrix yields four cases:-

Quadrant 1:   where Triad-based MNEs would prefer to operate today with no regulations whatsoever (an economic power-based quadrant of pure globalization).

Quadrant 2: where small and medium-sized enterprises (SMEs) operate – mainly domestic non-traded issues arise and there is no need for an MAI.

Quadrant 3: the ideal quadrant for the MAI – it allows MNEs to be efficient yet affords key aspects of sovereignty (by way of sectoral exemptions from the national treatment principle and other non-conforming measures); also where the NAFTA investment rules-based system operates. This requires a deeper understanding of the strategies of MNEs and how MNEs interact with governments. This is addressed in the next section.

Quadrant 4: a nationalist view of the MAI, in which regulation of MNEs is advocated on distributional grounds and performance requirements are enacted by screening agencies such as FIRA. For a critical analysis of such investment reviews and the economic costs of regulation of FDI, see Safarian (1993).

To make domestic markets internationally contestable (Lawrence, 1995), it is necessary for MNEs to have national treatment and right of establishment and also for them not to be subject to discriminatory domestic policy in a variety of fields, such as: competition policy; government procurement; technology policy; standards; tax policy; corporate governance rules and other government regulations. This is a quadrant 3 agenda. As both globalization and regionalization measures increase (such as NAFTA, and EC 1992 measures), nations became more similar as bases for internationally sourced production. Lawrence (1995) argues that, paradoxically, the differences in domestic policy also became more important since these differences act as market-access barriers to MNEs, especially when the barriers are in the Triad markets. The only weakness of Lawrence's proposition that domestic markets be made more internationally contestable is that it ignores the international negotiating process and the existence of domestic market imperfections.

In principle, the development of a broad MAI would be a 'public good' for MNEs and the world's consumers since there would be increased technical and allocative efficiencies. However, the political economy of the negotiating process for an MAI is not unambiguously welfare enhancing. For example, in the negotiations for the Canada–US Free Trade Agreement, and for NAFTA, influential sectors lobbied the US and Canadian governments for exemptions from the national treatment provisions (see Rugman, 1990, 1994a). In Canada, cultural industries, health, social services and education were exempted, whereas in the United States, the transport sector was exempted. In the NAFTA, the US auto sector lobbied for discriminatory rules of origin to protect its Mexican affiliates from new entry by European or Japanese competitors (see Gestrin and Rugman, in Rugman, 1994b). For a discussion of how the NAFTA investment rules could be used as a prototype for the MAI, see Rugman and Gestrin (1996).

The manner in which corporate (and other) groups can lobby and sometimes 'capture' the process by which trade-related and investment measures are negotiated and administered in international agreements has been analysed by Rugman and Verbeke (1990) in discussion of the theory of 'shelter'. The nature of shelter-based activities as applied to the NAFTA negotiating process is discussed by Rugman and Verbeke in Rugman (1994b). In terms of negotiating an MAI it is important to keep the market failure issue in mind, especially when asymmetries exist in the relative size of countries, a point also recognized by Graham (1995b). In other words, it will be difficult to arrive safely at a quadrant 3 solution; there will be pressures from some governments (and domestic business lobbies) for continued regulations in quadrant 4, as these can be 'captured' by domestic producers and used as a form of shelter, or entry barrier, against foreign competitors. Despite such practical difficulties in moving towards quadrant 3, an MAI remains a viable goal for the new WTO and associated international organizations.

MULTINATIONAL ENTERPRISE STRATEGY

Today the competitive strategies of MNEs are determined by a complex web of factors at regional, country, industry, firm, business unit and organizational task level. To cut through this dense jungle of potential cognitive and motivational factors affecting managerial decision-making in MNEs it will be useful to build upon a recent synthesis of work on the theory of the MNE and its interactions with key partners. This is the 'five partners' or 'flagship' model of business networks, as developed by D'Cruz and Rugman (1992, 1993). The five partners model has been applied to analysis of the Canadian telecommunications industry by D'Cruz and Rugman (1994b) and to the European telecommunications industry by D'Cruz and Rugman (1994a). It has been applied to the Canadian chemicals industry by D'Cruz, Gestrin and Rugman (1995). The five partners model emphasizes cooperative behaviour in network relationships and it can be contrasted with the five forces model of Porter (1980), which emphasizes rivalry and entry barriers as mechanisms to exercise market power and achieve competitive advantage.

The linkage of the D'Cruz and Rugman (1992, 1993) five partners model to earlier work on the theory of the MNE comes through the role of the MNE as a 'flagship firm' at the hub of the five partners model. The MNE is competing globally and it provides strategic leadership to partners such as key suppliers, key customers, and the non-business infrastructure. The rationale for the MNE is still explained by transaction-cost economics and internalization theory, as first developed by Buckley and Casson (1976). They demonstrated that economic activity takes place by MNEs when the benefits of internalization outweigh its costs and that this usually occurs under conditions when there are market imperfections in the pricing of intangible knowledge. This work was further refined by Casson (1979) and in essays collected in Buckley and Casson (1985). It was expanded into the 'eclectic paradigm' of international business by Dunning (1979, 1981). Internalization theory has been extended and applied in a North American context by Rugman (1980, 1981, 1986).

The relationship between the modern theory of the MNE and the five partners model, with its implication for some de-internalization (when successful network relationships are developed) has been discussed by Rugman, D'Cruz and Verbeke (1995). They argue that the internalization decision for an MNE takes into account concepts of business policy and competitive strategy and that proprietary firm-specific advantages yield potential economic profits when exploited on a worldwide basis. Yet the MNE finds these potential profits dissipated by internal governance costs of its organizational structure and the difficulty of timing and sustaining its FDI activities. This leads to de-internalization when the benefits of internalization are outweighed by its costs. De-internalization usually occurs within a business network when successful partnerships are found, as in the five partners model. The movement from internalization to business network requires analysis of parent–subsidiary relationships and the governance costs of running an MNE versus managing relationships in a business network.

Recently internalization theory has been linked to the resource-based theory of the firm by Kogut and Zander (1992, 1993), and others, who argue that issues of organizational learning complicate, and may even undermine, the argument for internalization. To help reconcile the basic thrust of internalization theory with the need for explicit consideration of organizational relationships, it is useful to consider the network relationships captured within the five partners model.

The Five Partners Flagship Model

Business networks are becoming increasingly common in industries where internationalization and globalization are advanced. In a business network a set of companies interact and cooperate with each other from the manufacture of basic raw materials to final consumption.

Conventional business relationships are characterized by arm's-length competition between firms as they buy and sell. Such relationships, which are the basis of Michael Porter's (1980) five forces model of competitive advantage, are based, to a large extent, on the development and exercise of market power. They tend to foster a short-term orientation among participants, with each participant being concerned primarily with its own profitability.

The D'Cruz and Rugman five partners flagship model is based on the development of collaborative relationships among major players in a business system. Its focus is on strategies that are mutually reinforcing. By their very nature, such relationships tend to foster and depend upon a collective long-term orientation among the parties concerned. Hence, they form an important facilitating mechanism for the development of long-term competitiveness.

There are two key features of such a system: one, the presence of a flagship firm that pulls the network together and provides leadership for the strategic management of the network as a whole; and two, the existence of firms that have established key relationships with that flagship. These relationships are illustrated in Figure 3.2 by black arrows that cross organizational boundaries, symbolizing the nature of inter-firm collaboration that characterizes them.

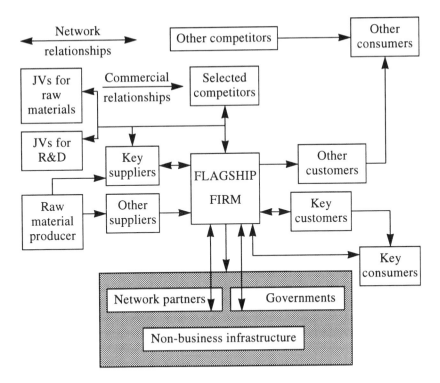

Figure 3.2   The flagship firm and its business network

Conventional arm's-length relationships are shown as grey arrows that stop at organizational boundaries.

The five partners business network consists of a group of firms and non-business institutions competing globally and linked together through close inter-firm organizational linkages (D'Cruz and Rugman, 1992). There are five partners in the business network: the flagship firm (which is an MNE), key suppliers, key customers, competitors and the non-business infrastructure. The latter partner includes the service-related sectors, educational and training institutions, the various levels of government, and other organizations such as trade associations, non-governmental organizations, and unions.

The five partners model is characterized by the flagship firm's asymmetric strategic leadership over the network partners in common areas of interest (D'Cruz and Rugman, 1993). The MNE sets the priorities of the partners in regard to their participation in this flagship firm's business system. Only the flagship firm has the global perspective and resources to lead a business network and to establish the global benchmarks necessary to lead the development of the network. The network's 'key' relationships are the organization's mechanisms for achieving the strategic purposes of the network. For example, in the automobile sector in North America, asymmetric relationships are made easier by the exclusivity of the Big Three's key suppliers and key customers. Like Ontario-based Magna, there are many auto parts suppliers whose sales are almost exclusively to the Big Three. Equally, because the vast majority of the automobile manufacturers' key customers are car dealers, who represent only one manufacturer, the dealers are an integral part of the strategy of the manufacturers and are dependent on that strategy. When telecommunications services are an integral aspect of a customer's operations, then the customer may be more willing to have its telecommunications strategy set by the telecommunications network's flagship firm (see D'Cruz and Rugman, 1994b). If a company such as McCains has a large component of international sales and depends upon telecommunications (such that they are a strategic 'asset') then McCains may be willing to use its telecommunications provider as a key supplier.

Another distinguishing feature of the five partners model is the deintegration of business system activities from the flagship firm – a de facto re-engineering of the value chain. This feature is a reflection of the complexity of competition in the global markets of today. Rather than internalizing ownership of core competencies and firm-specific advantages (Rugman, 1981), firms are deintegrating selectively those aspects of their value chains which they feel, for cost or strategic reasons, can better be performed elsewhere (Rugman, D'Cruz and Verbeke, 1995).

As a result of deintegration, key suppliers can expect to experience increased volumes through the flagship firm's outsourcing of activities. There is a reduction in the total number of suppliers serving the flagship, thereby creating value added to key suppliers outside the MNE; and a reduced business risk of more long-term contracts. The key supplier benefits through this partnership by having to benchmark its operations to the global standards of the flagship firm, for example, in adopting quality standards. The technologies, processes and systems of the supplier will reflect global standards of competitiveness.

Key customers in the five partners business network, by virtue of ceding strategic control to the flagship, fulfil a valuable role beyond being a market for the flagship. These customers are the testing grounds for product and service development. Specifically, by having thick and tight relationships with network members, the customer provides market feedback and, in return, receives products which respond to their needs. Often, the key customers will be intermediaries between the flagship firm and the end consumer, such as with car dealers.

For the non-business infrastructure (NBI), the flagship firm provides leadership and vision in terms of resource allocation, competency exploration, and mobilizing financial resources (as they apply to the NBI organization's participation in the flagship's business system). Such organizations contribute human resources, facilities, equipment and institutional arrangements as their role in business network activities.

Relationships with key competitors include joint ventures in new markets, market-sharing arrangements, technology transfers, supplier development, and so on. These are discussed in detail in D'Cruz and Rugman (1992). Unlike static contractual arrangements of the past, five partners–flagship model relations depend more on joint working teams and managerial interaction to elaborate and operationalize strategic purpose. This more fluid approach recognizes the adaptability required to change with the market but does not hinder the accrual of benefits through interaction. The strategic management aspects of this model have been further refined by D'Cruz (1995) and the flagship model is now applied in a Canadian context.

The Theory of the Flagship Firm

The flagship firm is an entity that provides strategic leadership and direction for a vertically integrated chain of businesses that operate as a coordinated system or network, frequently in competition with similar networks that address the same end markets. As the central coordinating authority in its network, the flagship firm establishes relationships with its key suppliers and key customers and ensures that they operate to implement a strategy for the network that is formulated by the flagship. We have called this relationship *strategic asymmetry* (D'Cruz and Rugman, 1994b). This is meant to imply that the flagship exercises control over the strategy of its network partners who have no reciprocal influence over the flagship's strategy. It determines and sets limits to the product/markets in which its network partners will be allowed to operate, it chooses the courses of action they will adopt to develop competencies in these fields of endeavour and it directs their capital investment programmes. In return, network partners are given membership in the flagship's network which usually carries with it the prospects of significant sales volumes, access to advanced technology and participation in the benefits of the brand image of the flagship.

In addition to such relationships with suppliers and customers in a vertical chain, modern flagships have also established similar alliances with organizations in the non-business infrastructure – universities, unions, research institutes and government bodies. The key feature of these links to the non-business infrastructure is that they are designed to enhance the access of the rest of the network to intellectual property and human capital. In that sense, these institutions are really suppliers of intangible inputs to the vertical chain. Consequently, it should be expected that the nature of these relationships will resemble those devoted to tangible inputs. Thus, the flagship will tend to exercise significant influence and control over the strategy of these non-business partners as it relates to their membership in the network. For example, the flagship will prescribe the areas for research inquiry of its university partners, set the terms of reference for human capital development projects with unions and provide leadership for business–government initiatives aimed at enhancing the competitiveness of the networks.

Finally, some flagship firms have established limited alliances with direct competitors. These include joint ventures for development of raw material projects or the manufacture of specialized inputs; in both cases, the minimum economic scale of the undertaking is usually larger than would be justified by the requirements of either partner on its own. Other forms of collaboration with competitors are joint efforts for research and development of a precompetitive nature, membership in consortia to bid for large projects and agreements on technical standards for the industry. While the flagship's relations with its competitors do not share the strategic asymmetry feature of its links with other network partners, it has another characteristic in common.

A fundamental feature of these relationships is their focus on collaborative rather than competitive behaviour. Thus, in transactions based on a network alliance relationship, the parties are motivated to work closely with each other to further the aims of the network which they regard as compatible with their own welfare. This can be contrasted with the competitive behaviour described in the five forces model by Porter (1980). The latter model encourages firms to behave in competition with their suppliers and customers for a share of the profits in transactions with each other. It focuses on the development and exercise of a market power in business systems, with managerial attention devoted to optimizing results on a transaction-by-transaction basis – a short-run orientation. On the other hand, the network mode of collaboration requires that both parties to a relationship apply the calculus of the benefits they hope to obtain and the costs they will incur across an indefinite stream of transactions rather than on one transaction at a time. It encourages the sharing of market intelligence and intellectual property without recourse to formal contracting to protect the self-interest of either party. In sum, these relationships are collaborative and long term in orientation.

The large car manufacturers are often cited as examples of firms that have adopted the flagship mode of operations. Thus Chrysler, for example, has developed close collaborative relationships with its key suppliers who are often encouraged to establish their own plants close to its assembly plants. These relationships are of a collaborative nature with both sides operating on the assumption that they will continue indefinitely. This facilitates the making of highly specialized capital investments by both parties to optimize their joint operations. Similarly, Chrysler develops close long-term relationships with its dealers who operate as an integral part of the overall system which is directed by the car manufacturer. The entire chain – suppliers, car manufacturer, dealers – is managed as a single system whose strategic direction comes almost exclusively from the car manufacturer, who functions as its flagship. The amount and nature of coordination necessary for effective functioning of this system can best be appreciated by considering what occurs when a new platform is created. Decisions about positioning and timing, for example are the exclusive preserve of the car manufacturer. The introduction of a new platform also involves adoption of new process technology. On the other hand, there are a myriad of operational issues that are the responsibility of the network partners, who are frequently required to make considerable investments in new equipment and training.

As a second example, let us examine the role of France Telecom as the flagship of that country's principal telecommunications system (D'Cruz and Rugman, 1994a). Its strategic role is to provide the vision and direction for the technological choices and associated commercial initiatives for the system. Thus, France Telecom determined to develop a system that was at the leading edge in such technologies as fibre optics and digitalization. It required its suppliers and distributors to devote resources to developing their own capabilities in these areas. Equally important, it provided strategic leadership to the network of government-funded research centres on telecommunications to coordinate the development of technology in these areas. It also directed the country's training institutions in telecommunications to make appropriate changes to their curricula to ensure availability of a workforce skilled in these technologies. What has emerged is an advanced telecommunications system with a highly centralized process for strategic decision-making coupled with decentralized operational capability. The key features of a flagship network – strategic asymmetry and collaborative relationships – are abundantly evident.

Some of the better-known flagship networks are those that have been created by the Japanese. Known as *vertical keiretsu*, these networks have succeeded in building formidable global competitive positions in such diverse fields as consumer electronics (Sony, Matsushita), automobiles (Toyota, Nissan) and computers (NEC, Toshiba). It should be mentioned that the strategies and structures of a *vertical keiretsu* are significantly different from the traditional Japanese *keiretsu* which is a family of broadly diversified companies with a bank/trading company at its centre. For dimensions of Japanese business networks see Fruin (1992), Gerlach (1992) and Westney (1995).

The structure of the flagship firm

Having described the flagship firm and provided some examples, let us now turn to the central questions of this chapter – the theoretical rationale for its existence. To do so, we need to establish certain assumptions about the management structure of the typical flagship firm. Treating it as a single, unitary actor is unsatisfactory. First, this assumption inhibits development of theory about the behaviour of the flagship firm towards its network partners because it requires a constellation of follow-on assumptions about: its objective function regarding profits maximization or shareholder value maximization; the unity of purpose at various levels of the firm; the dominance of economic/financial rationality in decision-making.

Second, it introduces a subtle bias in the nature of hypotheses that will be developed for empirical research about business systems led by flagship firms. Hypotheses about a unitary actor naturally tend to be based on expected regularities in its behaviour towards its network partners, given certain conditions. Take the probability of opportunistic behaviour in post-contract transactions. A unitary actor will be hypothesized either to have a non-zero probability or one that is not significantly different from zero, but not both. Researchers in the transaction-costs tradition are likely to be biased towards the former while those with a resource-based view may not, since they regard the firm's reputation as a key resource that managers value and protect. Chandler (1962) initiated a scholarly tradition of inquiry that firmly established the multiple-actor assumption, while Mintzberg (1979) legitimated the assumption that even a single actor may work with multiple conflicting objectives.

The structure we propose involves desegregating the flagship firm into three components. These components are based on the function that is being performed by the component, and will generally map closely to specific individuals and organizational positions.

1. *Strategy functions* These involve articulation of the goals and objectives of the network as a whole as well as the flagship firm itself, the formulation or ratification of the principal courses of action to be undertaken to achieve those goals and the allocation of resources for their implementation. Readers familiar with the strategy literature will quickly recognize the similarity of this definition with those used to define strategy itself (Chandler, 1962). However, it should be recognized that a flagship firm exercises domain over its entire network and not just over its own organization. This posits that it has a substantial or almost complete measure of control over the strategy of its network partners who, in turn, have given up their strategic autonomy in exchange for the putative benefits of belonging to the network.

2. *Management functions* These involve guiding and directing the work of others in the flagship firm and its network partners to achieve the objectives established by the strategy function. The commonly held view in the organizational behaviour and strategy literatures is that this includes activities such as planning and decision-making (Glueck, 1976), organizing, staffing, leading and controlling (Koontz and O'Donnell, 1972), but not the strategy functions described above. Here, too, it is useful to focus on the distinctive aspects of management in a flagship firm – the domain of its management function extends beyond the boundaries of its own organization and includes a substantial measure of control over the work of its network partners.

3. *Operational functions* These include all the other work performed by employees of the flagship firm, but they do not include any work that is done by employees of the network partners.

The preference for vertical integration
There is a substantial body of theoretical work devoted to vertical integration in chains of production processes where the output of one process becomes a significant input into the next process. In the discussion that follows, we will generalize the propositions of this work beyond the supply of raw materials and the distribution of final consumption goods to include also vertical relationships involving the production of service inputs (engineering services, transportation, systems integration, and so on) and ancillary products and services associated with final consumption (warehousing, after-sales service, and so on).

Three schools of thought have had a major influence in this area. The central concern of these theorists has been on the choice of mode between vertical integration, spot market transactions or long-term contracts. Under what conditions is one mode more likely to be preferred over the others? Which mode is more likely to remain stable as conditions change? And which is likely to induce firms to make investments which will contribute to the overall capacity and efficiency of the system as a whole and its various components? Each school provides a different perspective on the conditions and reasons why markets fail to operate satisfactorily and firms are driven to choose vertical integration.

1. *Traditional industrial organization theory* was primarily concerned with the behaviour of firms in oligopolistic and near-monopolistic markets – the so-called small numbers condition – and the related ability of incumbents to extract rents. Vertical integration (backward) is preferred when a firm anticipates that its suppliers have or can develop the potential to monopolize the market for an important input; similarly, forward vertical integration is a defence against foreclosure of markets for the firm's outputs or a pre-emptive attempt to gain the benefits of foreclosure for the firm itself.

2. *Transaction-cost/internalization theory*   The literature on transaction costs shifted the focus of attention to the nature of assets involved in vertical integration and on difficulties associated with long-term contracts. It argues that when investments are required in assets that are specific to the vertical relationship, the problem of *ex post* opportunistic behaviour by the partner is difficult to deal with and causes firms to prefer vertical integration to dealing on the spot market or through long-term contracts. The latter option has the additional problem of costs/difficulties related to writing, monitoring and enforcing contingent contracts. These contracting hazards discourage firms from dependence on long-term contracts when it is feared that adjustment of contract terms to changes in market conditions will be difficult to make or hard to enforce.

    Extending this concept to MNEs, *internalization theory* explains their preference for the FDI mode for international expansion as a function of their need to protect property rights, particularly those of a less tangible nature. Similarly, the theory suggests that MNEs will undertake vertical integration abroad whenever there is a need to protect firm-specific assets such as know-how or a brand name.

3. *Resource–based theory* encourages us to regard the firm as a bundle of hard-to-replicate *sticky* resources, with particular attention to managerial capability or similar less tangible resources. This theory suggests that a firm will prefer vertical integration when it has surplus managerial and other resources that it anticipates being able to deploy more effectively

in the vertical chain than would independent suppliers or customers. These arguments are particularly powerful when transactions in the vertical system involve a significant element of intangibles that are hard to price and monitor.

Failures of vertical integration

Given such powerful arguments favouring the vertical integration mode when conditions which frequently lead to market failure exist or are anticipated, why then have so many large firms chosen to move away from this solution and adopt the flagship form? There are two classes of explanations, which we will deal with separately below. First, are explanations based on the capture of rent in vertically integrated firms; this involves the appropriation by individuals and groups in the firm of some of the rents that accrue to the firm by virtue of its ownership of resources that are scarce or difficult to replicate. The second set of difficulties relate to failures of the management systems that have been developed within large firms.

Rent capture   A major motivation for avoiding vertical integration is to circumvent rent capture by employees in an upstream or downstream unit who are members of the union, particularly but not exclusively when the same union represents employees of the focal unit. Should this union attempt to negotiate wages and employment terms that capture a portion of the rents, management may respond by establishing network relationships with upstream or downstream firms that are not unionized or have less onerous union contracts. It is common for suppliers in the automotive industry to experience lower wage costs than their customers, partly because they are regarded as having fewer opportunities to earn rents. Sometimes this is achieved by establishing operations in low-wage locations. Similarly, firms engaged in the distribution of computer products pay lower wages than their flagship suppliers. In both cases, flagship firms are able to circumvent rent capture by employees in the upstream and downstream parts of their business system when they use network partners for these functions. The alternative of paying lower wages in vertically integrated divisions is usually not available because of a form of conscious parallelism practised by many unions whereby they resist such differentiation.

Note that inflexibilities in personnel practices in large firms can lead to similar outcomes in the absence of unions. For example, many large firms adopt highly structured systems for pay and grade levels and operate a form of seniority system where the employee's length of service is a determinant of wages. The tendency of these firms to apply such schemes uniformly across all vertically integrated divisions can impose a high-wage structure on upstream and downstream divisions.

Rent capture by employees in management positions can also raise costs in a vertically integrated firm. In addition to salaries and benefits, rent capture may take the form of management perquisites that are costly. For example, managers in upstream and downstream units may be entitled to similar office space and administrative staff support as their colleagues in the focal division, thus raising the costs of their units above those in firms in the upstream or downstream industry. A common response to these problems has been for large firms to spin off upstream and downstream activities into separate companies with whom they then establish a network relationship.

Management failure   It is our contention that the second major set of reasons have to do with managerial failures in the vertically integrated mode. To explain the causes of such failure of vertical integration, we need to establish the characteristics of the organizational structure and processes used by large, vertically integrated firms. The fundamental organizational form that underlies most structures for the management of vertically integrated firms is the multidivisional or M-form arrangement. The basic characteristics of this form of interest here are: multi-tier levels of management, the profit centre concept, and divisional autonomy.

Management roles and functions are specialized by level in this form. Corporate management has stewardship of the overall direction of the firm, including appointment of divisional managers and establishing the rules of engagement between divisions. Divisional general management is responsible for planning and implementing strategies for the division. Functional management in the division reports to the divisional manager and holds responsibility for running a particular function.

The profit centre concept is that each division is treated as a quasi firm within the firm; it is given responsibility for managing the affairs of the division to achieve profit performance targets that are negotiated with corporate management.

Divisional autonomy defines the scope of authority of divisional management and their responsibility for producing results. Despite prescriptions by organizational theorists about the need to make areas of responsibility co-extensive with the scope of divisional authority, in practice corporate management may choose to ignore this principle for pragmatic reasons.

Why do vertically integrated firms sometimes fail to perform as effectively as rivals who are less integrated?

1.   *Internal rivalry among general managers*   Corporate systems for the management of divisions in the M-form firm have a built-in bias towards enhancing rivalry among divisional general managers. Three systems in particular tend to create internal rivalry. First, financial performance measure-

ment systems based on the profit-centre principle of treating the division as a quasi firm place emphasis on overall results calculated by measures such as Return on Net Assets (RONA) and contribution to shareholder value. The message to the divisional general manager is: run your division as it if were an independent firm whose shareholder is the corporation. Since overall financial results of divisions are easily compared with each other, the incentives for competitive behaviour between upstream and downstream divisions are strong, and the incentives for cooperative behaviour almost non-existent. In effect, financial systems of this nature internalize the competitive aspects of the Porter five forces model described above.

Second, the reward and punishment system for divisional managers is similarly biased towards enhancing rivalry. Since they have overall responsibility for running their divisions, both the formal and informal reward systems are focused on outcomes measured by the financial performance measurement systems mentioned above. Good performance is rewarded through bonuses, management perquisites and formal recognition. Poor performance is punished ultimately by removal of the divisional general manager from that position. A close and frequently reinforced linkage between divisional financial performance and the self-interest of the general manager encourages rivalry between managers of divisions; many corporate managers believe that such rivalry is healthy because it provides incentives to divisional managers to strive to improve the financial performance. However, when applied to divisions in a vertical system, such rivalry also provides disincentives for cooperative behaviour.

Promotion is a special form of reward in large firms. Divisional general managers compete with each other for opportunities for promotion to positions in the corporate office. Since the number of positions available usually gets smaller towards the top of the hierarchy, there is a natural tendency for divisional managers to regard each other as rivals for promotion. Performance in their current job is frequently a major criteria for promotion; hence the incentive for competitive behaviour with a view to enhancing one's promotion prospects.

2. *Asymmetry of power among divisional managers* Corporate directives regarding terms and conditions for interdivisional transactions can have a significant impact on a division's ability to achieve its performance targets. For example, transfer-pricing policies, accounting conventions, and even such relatively trivial matters as the scheduling of maintenance shutdowns, can all be subject to corporate directives that impact on divisional performance. The formal and informal power of divisional managers to influence such directives can also vary considerably because of a number of factors.

Most important is the historical position of the division itself. Divisions that formed the main base from which the vertically integrated firm grew are

likely to wield considerable power. Senior corporate managers may have
worked their way up through the division, personal relations between division and corporate managers may be deep and of long duration, and the belief
may persist that the prosperity of the firm as a whole is intimately connected
to the prosperity of the division. This can be particularly true when the
acquisitions or internal development of the other components of the vertical
system were originally sponsored by the division with a view to enhancing its
own profitability.

The power of a divisional general manager can also be enhanced by the
capital intensity of the division, particularly when this is driven by economies
of scale in its technology. When the division's assets account for a large
proportion of the firm's total assets, its general manager tends to acquire
special status in the minds of corporate managers. The divisional imperative
of operating capital-intensive assets at high-capacity utilization rates can
easily be reinterpreted as corporate policy. Corporate directives may then be
issued to other divisions to support efforts to achieve these high-capacity
utilization rates, even when they may not be in the interest of these divisions.
For example, an upstream division may be discouraged from seeking new
customers when its outputs are needed by the downstream division.

Similarly, managers of a division that is seen as the custodian or repository
of the technology base of the firm can wield considerable influence with a
corporate office which regards the firm's technology as a core asset. Divisions which hold proprietary technology or which contain research facilities
used for generating new technology can come to have a preferential status in
corporate offices leading to influence that goes beyond matters strictly related
to technology.

3. *Failures of transfer pricing*   Policies about setting prices for transfers
between vertically integrated divisions are essential for the functioning of
performance measurement in a decentralized firm. The preferred theoretical
solution is to use some form of market price because that provides the most
accurate signals about the performance of both upstream and downstream
operations. However, market prices, even when they are readily available,
may fail to capture a number of additional considerations that must be addressed. First, market prices may need to be modified to take account of
location benefits, product modifications which improve operations in either
the upstream or downstream division, and investments in learning that are
specific to the relationship or capacity that has been dedicated to the vertical
relationship and would otherwise lie idle. Readers familiar with Williamson's
(1985) classification of asset specificity will recognize that these characteristics have been derived from his scheme. In the absence of market-price data
that closely reflect such conditions, corporate management may have to establish rules for transfer pricing that depart from strict reliance on data from

the market. Three classes of such departures need to be recognized. Each is prone to a particular type of failure.

First, corporate management may apply the best alternative rule – specifying that the selling division be allowed to charge the best price it could obtain outside the firm for similar transactions or that the buying division should only pay the same price as it can negotiate with an outside supplier or both. In any case, such policies are vulnerable to opportunistic behaviour from one side or the other. Either division may seek offers from third parties that comply with corporate rules but which are based on tacit understandings which are kept secret from others in the firm. For example, the upstream division may make tacit commitments to outside customers about the level of technical support that will be offered in the future or indicate a willingness to take back unused products at full price. Conversely, the downstream division may entice an outside supplier with forecasts of future requirements that are substantially in excess of its plans. In general, tacit aspects of supply contracts with third parties may be particularly difficult for the internal partner to detect. Should the corporate office be called upon to arbitrate, it is likely to experience even greater difficulty in making judgements about whether or not there are tacit aspects to the offer from the outside party, and may be forced to make its determination on the basis of the explicit features of the arrangement.

An alternative arrangement is some sort of cost-plus pricing formula which sets transfer prices at the costs of the upstream division plus some agreed-upon formula for profit. Apart from vitiating the firm's performance control system with respect to the upstream division, cost-plus formulae create incentives for several kinds of dysfunctional behaviour in both divisions. An upstream division that is treated as a cost centre by the corporate office may seek ways of keeping its costs below budget targets by underspending on maintenance or process development. Downstream divisions may underinvest in market opportunities that are made inaccessible by a high-cost upstream supplier to which it is tied by corporate edict.

The third class of solution is to use corporate staff to analyse the transfer-pricing issue and recommend a price or pricing formula which corporate management then imposes by edict. This approach suffers from disadvantages associated with inadequate expertise in corporate staff (for example, lack of deep knowledge about the industry, inadequate market contacts and scarcity of tacit knowledge). Assuming that these problems can be overcome by, for example, promoting an expert from one of the divisions to the corporate staff, there remains the problem of acceptance by divisional management of solutions which they have not played a part in developing. Variations of this approach which involve corporate officials or staff serving as facilitators for negotiations between divisions about transfer prices merely arrive at the same outcome through a different mechanism and do not deal with its fundamental weaknesses.

REGIONAL CORPORATE STRATEGIES OF MNES[2]

To demonstrate the interaction between the corporate strategies of MNEs and the strategies of governments, in the remainder of this chapter the focus will be upon Canadian MNEs operating within the regional framework of the North American Free Trade Area (NAFTA). As an example of the regionalization of corporate strategy, challenges to the Canadian chemicals industry will be explored in detail. With reference to the earlier discussion of the MAI, the NAFTA is an institutional device which is increasing the international contestability of the three nations' markets, but on a regional basis rather than the global basis desired by an MAI.

In all industries dominated by MNEs, the key insight required to understand the impact of regional trade agreements on competitiveness and the spatial organization of productive capacity is that they now operate as integrated North American networks. The critical questions to ask therefore relate to the transition of the Canadian manufacturing industries from the earlier branch plant and national economy-based organizational structure to the current North American network structure. For example, what function should Canadian-based managers perform as MNE network managers? What qualities in the Canadian economy will continue to attract a share of the economic activity of these North American networks?

The principal challenge faced by Canadian managers in industries dominated by MNEs, of which chemicals is a typical example, will be to make the transition from a multi-domestic organizational structure, in which Canadian operations are largely autonomous, to a network organizational structure in which the Canadian affiliates are actively integrated into global networks. The key strategic issue is how Canadian managers of these affiliates should try to adapt their operations to the new demands of international network operations.

In anticipation of the Canada–US Free Trade Agreement (FTA) and, subsequently, the NAFTA, multinationals in the Canadian chemicals industry began repositioning on a North American basis in the mid- to late-1980s. For bulk chemical producers this often meant a retrenchment of operations to the United States in order to capture the new potential for scale economies generated by free trade. For speciality chemical producers, where local responsiveness pressure is high (for example, automotive paint producers) regional trade liberalization also gave rise to the need for radical reorganization and a rethinking of the function of Canadian subsidiaries.

The analysis which follows uses the five partners model (applied to the Canadian chemicals industry by D'Cruz, Gestrin and Rugman, 1995.) Examples are drawn from different segments of this industry (paints, soaps and detergents, adhesives, agricultural chemicals and organic chemicals). It is found that international competitiveness is increasingly a function of the quality of the network relationships developed by firms in the chemicals industry. This analysis leads to different insights from others such as Quintella (1993), which examines the strategic management of technology in internationalizing chemicals industries. This is not the focus of this study of the network relationships in the Canadian chemicals industry. In the next section the five partners model is applied to the regional strategies of firms in the Canadian chemicals industry.

Regional Strategy in the Canadian Chemicals Industry

The Canadian chemicals industry can be divided between two types of firms: MNEs and small and medium-sized enterprises (SMEs). Both types are faced with the same challenge and overarching strategic objective: how to become useful participants in the increasingly internationalized structure of the global chemicals industry. However, for each type of firm, either MNE or SME, the appropriate strategy to adopt in order to successfully attain this objective is heavily influenced by the structure of network relationships.

In the following sections we examine the implications of regional integration for MNEs and SMEs in turn. The value of the five partners flagship model is that attention can be paid to MNEs (because of their dominant role in the Canadian chemicals industry) as well as SMEs, since the latter are increasingly serving as sources of innovation and employment and promise to play an important role in the future of the industry.

The relevance of the five partners model to competitiveness lies in the contribution of network relationships and the roles of key suppliers, key customers and flagships. An understanding of where an MNE subsidiary lies with respect to the particular network with which it is associated is critical for the formulation of a suitable business strategy.

Canadian managers of MNEs are confronted with a dual challenge. During the current phase of global restructuring by these firms, Canadian managers must find ways to sell the benefits and capabilities of the Canadian operation to the parent within the context of the latter's plans for a rationalized global network. Unless they succeed in this objective, they will not have sufficient resources at their disposal to fulfil the second objective, which is to refocus and concentrate the contribution of the Canadian operation to the MNE's global network. In other words, Canadian managers of MNE subsidiaries need to find a niche within the global operations of the company so that they become active participants in the global restructuring of the company rather than victims of the downsizing which usually accompanies restructuring. This niche will usually consist of establishing key supplier relationships, either directly with the parent (an intra-firm key supplier relationship) or with independent MNE flagships in the form of regional or global supplier arrangements (an inter-firm key supplier relationship).

The Canadian paint business

One of the clearest examples of inter-firm key supplier relations is in the paint industry. MNEs dominate this business system in both of its distinct segments: industrial and decorative. With respect to shipments, both segments are approximately equal in size. The paint industry made shipments worth $1,498.7 million in 1993, reflecting continued growth and recovery from the recession when industry shipments reached a low of $1,370.6 million in 1991. However, pre-1990 shipment levels ($1,659.6 million in 1989) have yet to be reattained. In 1992, there were 131 establishments in this sector, wages and salaries accounted for 28 per cent of variable inputs costs, and value added for the industry as a whole equalled $829.6 million, or 57 per cent of the value of shipments.

The industrial segment serves primarily the automotive industry in both OEM assembly plants and the refinish aftermarket. The firms in this segment are essentially all large multinationals whose relationships with the automotive original equipment manufacturers (OEMs) are organized to shadow the North American patterns of OEM operations. Output is concentrated in the hands of just a few large players and a few smaller niche players. The MNEs that account for most of this sector's output include BASF Coatings and Inks Canada Ltd., DuPont Canada Inc., PPG Canada Inc. and Akzo Coatings Ltd.

The key issues for paint manufacturers in the industrial segment revolve around the importance of the auto OEMs as flagships. Indeed, in some instances, paint manufacturers have developed a strategy of serving only the auto OEM market. For example, DuPont Canada Inc. produced paint for both the decorative and the broader industrial segments when it entered the business in 1956. However, its focus has progressively narrowed to the point where today it only produces for the automotive industry. PPG Canada Inc. is also highly focused in the area of automotive finishes, although the company does still manufacture some industrial coatings in Canada.

The suppliers to the automotive OEMs are responsible for researching colour trends, new product development and technical support. Each of the major paint manufacturers serving the automotive OEMs is capable of covering all of the stages in the paint process. Yet, the automotive OEMs generally allocate assembly lines among the various paint manufacturers and also distribute responsibility for the different layers in the automotive painting process (E-coat, topcoats, clearcoats, primers) to their key suppliers. Generally, each OEM facility has no more than two key suppliers. Only four Canadian automotive plants are sole-sourced. One reason for multiple sourcing by the automotive OEMs is that the paint manufacturer may have led in the development of certain products. For example, PPG established an early market position in E-coat. Another likely reason relates to the efforts by the OEM flagships to keep their suppliers competitive and avoid becoming too dependent in any one area upon a given supplier.

In addition to dealing directly with the OEMs, paint manufacturers are also key suppliers to the automotive parts suppliers – who in turn supply painted parts to the OEM. In this instance, however, the paint manufacturer interacts with the parts manufacturer that has won a contract with an auto OEM. In this case, the auto OEM is still clearly acting as the flagship, even though the paint manufacturer deals directly with the automotive parts manufacturer.

Most of the paint manufacturers that have specialized in the automotive OEM segment have also developed relations with the Japanese transplants. In order to enhance their relationship with the Japanese automotive manufacturers, DuPont has established a joint venture with a major Japanese paint supplier – Kansai. In this case, the flagship status of the auto manufacturer and the key supplier role played by the paint manufacturer is again evident. To become a supplier to the Japanese OEMs, the joint venture was required to adopt a different technology – the technology that the Japanese OEMs were familiar with in their domestic operations in Japan. Furthermore, the joint venture was required to source its basic inputs from the traditional suppliers to Kansai Paint Co. Ltd. Even though DuPont would like to source more inputs from its own supplier network, the strategic force in this relationship has clearly been the Japanese OEMs.

The paint manufacturers that serve the automotive OEMs are organized to conform to the spatial organization of the OEMs themselves. In the case of DuPont, sales contracts with the automotive OEMs (both American and Japanese) are negotiated in Detroit (indeed, DuPont has a reputation in the industry for having regionalized the structure of its operations most rapidly). Likewise, all of PPG's contracts with the North American-based automotive OEMs are negotiated on a regional basis by the OEM office in Detroit. However, business with the transplants (mainly Japanese firms) is negotiated by the Canadian subsidiary. In the OEM paint segment there are significant examples of horizontal integration. For example, in addition to being a major paint supplier to the automotive OEMs, PPG also supplies glass and DuPont supplies engineering plastics, fibres and windshield laminating adhesive film.

Canadian agrochemical sector

Whereas the paint industry provides a good example of inter-firm key supplier relations in the Canadian chemicals industry, an excellent example of intra-firm key supplier relationships occurs in the agrochemical sector. Uniroyal Chemical Ltd. maintains a sophisticated R&D facility in Guelph which is integrated into Uniroyal's global research and development programme. This facility supplies 100 per cent of the in-house compounds for biological screening to Uniroyal's main R&D facility in Connecticut, where environmental chemistry is conducted. In effect, the high technical capacity of the Canadian operation has made it an important part of Uniroyal Chemical's global R&D organization.

In addition, Uniroyal Chemical's technical capacity has given it a leadership position with respect to field testing and its relationship with customers. Its field testing programme is among the most sophisticated in Canada and the company works closely with customers to determine and then provide for their needs. In this respect, the Guelph facility contributes an important service function to the parent facility and to the international R&D network in general.

Canadian soap and detergent business

Unlike the two previous examples in which the flagship in the network is clearly identifiable (the automotive OEMs in the paint industry and the parent R&D facility in the agrochem sector), in the soap and detergent business system a transition of flagship status is currently under way. This industry comprises two broad groups of manufacturers: name brand producers and private label producers. Name brand production accounts for approximately 80 per cent of industry shipments (with 60 per cent going to the customer market and 20 per cent going to the commercial/institutional market), while private label production accounts for the remaining 20 per cent (most of which goes to the consumer market). The Canadian market, then, is 80 per cent consumer and 20 per cent commercial/institutional. In 1991, raw materials accounted for 49 per cent of the cost of inputs, containers 19 per cent, wages 26 per cent, miscellaneous services and inputs 4 per cent, and fuel and electricity 2 per cent. Total shipments in 1991 were worth $1.7 billion. Value added equalled $887 million, or roughly 52 per cent of shipments.

The industry is dominated by MNEs. Proctor and Gamble Inc. and Lever Brothers Limited are the predominant name brand producers for the consumer market, with approximately 75 per cent market share. The rest of the consumer market is divided between: (i) smaller, specialized producers (often regionally based) such as Lavo Ltd. (Montreal); (ii) MNEs that service a smaller share of the market through a distribution presence only (or minimal manufacturing) such as Colgate-Palmolive Canada Inc.; and (iii) private label manufacturers such as Witco Canada Inc. and CCL Industries Inc. The industrial segment is also dominated by MNEs, such as Diversey and Ecolab Ltd., that specialize in producing cleaning and sanitizing products for the hospitality, institutional and industrial markets.

Two MNEs have acted as flagships in the soap and detergent industry: Lever Brothers Limited and Procter and Gamble Inc. These companies are characterized by significant levels of both vertical and horizontal integration. Lever Brothers Limited, for example, has integrated backwards into higher value-added inputs such as isethionate and fatty acids and has sourced other critical inputs from third-party suppliers.

Key suppliers to these flagship firms are the large integrated chemical companies. For example, Rhone-Poulenc has been a key supplier of surfactants to many of the major soap and detergent manufacturers in Canada (Procter and Gamble Inc., Colgate-Palmolive Canada Inc., Lever Brothers Limited, Diversey Corporation, and CCL Industries Inc.). As a key supplier, Rhone–Poulenc interacts with its flagship customers on a North American basis reflecting the nature of flagship strategy in this industry.

In some cases, the soap and detergent flagships will closely coordinate the activities of several of their key suppliers. For example, the production of ethoxylate for a major soap and detergent manufacturer involved the coordination of three key suppliers: one supplied the ethylene oxide; alcohol was supplied by another; and the third supplier provided the reactors on a service fee basis. Therefore, in addition to negotiating all of the contracts for the inputs with its key suppliers, the soap and detergent manufacturer also directed its key suppliers to do the blending of a critical input for them.

Although Proctor and Gamble and Lever continue to act as flagships, their longstanding flagship positions have come under attack recently and the networks for which they have served as a hub for so long are on the verge of radical transformation. Competition for flagship status in this industry has emerged in the retail sector, both from traditional retailers, such as Loblaws, and from the new entrants in the Canadian retailing scene, mass merchandisers such as Price Club and Wal-Mart.

The new entrants in the Canadian retail sector have set new standards for efficient distribution networks and heightened price competition. While the soap and detergent industry has always been subject to price pressure from retailers (since soaps and detergents are among the 'basic products' that retailers frequently feature as specials), the traditional soap and detergent flagships will likely see their leverage with respect to retailers substantially eroded due both to the increased market power of the new large-scale retailers that have entered the market recently and to the rise of the private label segment. Furthermore, with advertising costs already accounting for approximately 25 per cent of selling price, it is unlikely that the soap and detergent manufacturers will be able to improve their leverage with respect to the retailers by means of increased promotion at the consumer level.

Therefore, the long-run outlook for the soap and detergent industry is for a transition from flagship to key supplier status. This does not necessarily imply that this sector cannot be competitive or profitable (as the automotive paint manufacturers can attest). However, the transition from flagship to key supplier is likely to be rocky, especially if the traditional soap and detergent flagships decide to engage the retailers head on in a battle to maintain flagship status.

Regional Strategies for Canadian-based MNEs

While most Canadian chemical companies play key supplier roles, a few examples can be found of flagship activity. One of the strongest instances of a flagship firm operating from a home base in Canada is a subsidiary of Sterling Chemicals, Inc. known as Sterling Pulp Chemicals, Ltd. This company has its Canadian head office in Toronto and operates a chlorine dioxide-based business in two sectors – bleaching systems for the pulp industry and disinfection systems for water treatment. The technology and commercial vision for this business have been developed in Canada by Sterling Pulp and its predecessor companies. In operationalizing this vision, it has made extensive use of network relationships with its partners in the business system.

Sterling's relationships with its key suppliers are instructive. Sterling has designed the technology for production of chlorine dioxide by its customers using generators which have also been designed by Sterling. However, the generators are produced by suppliers who have long-term relationships with Sterling. Similarly, Sterling works with a network of general contractors who have the expertise to install the generators at the customer's site.

Sterling's relationship with its customers in the pulp industry offers a number of useful lessons. Sterling is working with one of its key customers to find ways to develop closed-loop systems for using chlorine dioxide for bleaching pulp. These systems allow pulp mills to meet and exceed government emission regulations regarding free chlorine, a major environmental issue for the pulp industry. By addressing an important strategic issue facing its key customers, Sterling not only helps the Canadian pulp industry maintain its competitiveness but also consolidates it own position in the business system.

Sterling's experience with respect to the non-business infrastructure is also informative. Much of the fundamental technology for using chlorine dioxide in the pulp process was developed by collaboration between Sterling and the Pulp and Paper Center of the University of Toronto. This collaboration has been in existence for many years and was inspired by the work of Dr Howard

Rapson of the University of Toronto, an acknowledged leader in the field. Over the years, Sterling and the University team have developed improved processes to manufacture chlorine dioxide and are developing the technology for the closed-loop system for use in pulp mills. Without the latter, it might not be possible to meet current and future environmental standards. Both Sterling and the University have had essential roles in this collaboration. Sterling provided the strategic leadership for the commercial aspects of the project and made important financial contributions to the research. On the other hand, the University provided the research environment and talent for the projects.

Business Network Strategies for SMEs

For SMEs, healthy key customer relations with relevant MNE flagships in the business network are critical for survival in an economy increasingly driven by global benchmarks of competitiveness. SMEs are, in several key respects, better placed to benefit from globalization than subsidiary operations of MNEs. For example, SMEs can help MNEs to access small markets that require flexibility and quick response. This natural correspondence of interests means that SMEs have been and can continue to be a source of dynamism and growth in the Canadian chemicals industry.

With respect to SME decorative paint manufacturers that have positioned themselves in the upscale markets (for example, Para Paints Canada Inc.), the critical business relationship is the key customer relationship they can develop with the large integrated chemical manufacturers. Through these relationships, the paint manufacturers gain access to the output of research programmes that only the larger chemical companies can support. The larger companies are willing to share this information with the smaller paint manufacturers because these do not represent a strategic threat to the flagship and because these SMEs are small enough to be able to access markets in which the MNE would otherwise not be able to sell its products.

Another segment in which SMEs have established key customer relationships has been in the adhesives segment. Large industrial adhesives producers, like their industrial paint counterparts, usually perform a key supplier function (also mostly with automotive OEMs). SMEs in this segment, however, have developed niches in new, fast-growing product areas, such as pressure-sensitive labels. As such, they have become key customers of the MNE adhesive manufacturers. Their advantage lies in their ability to respond quickly to changes in markets and to new market opportunities. From the perspective of the MNE flagship, this relationship allows the MNE to reach markets it otherwise could not serve while the close network relationship ensures that cooperation with SMEs will not lead to a loss of proprietary control over new technological developments in the area of basic inputs and active ingredients.

CONCLUSIONS

Two broad themes have emerged from this analysis of the Canadian chemicals industry and its adjustment to regionalization under the NAFTA. First is the significance for competitiveness of key supplier relationships for subsidiaries of MNEs in the face of the rapid regional integration of the Canadian industry. Second is the significance for competitiveness of key customer relationships of SMEs with flagship suppliers.

Many of the larger MNEs in Canada are now doing very well as key suppliers. For example, in the paints industry key suppliers such as PPG and DuPont Canada have profitable businesses as key suppliers to the US and Japanese car manufacturers (OEMs) in Canada. The strategic direction for these businesses are partly determined in the United States but the production mandate to implement these contracts can result in a successful Canadian business, with many jobs, profits for the company, and a net positive contribution to Canada's social and economic well-being. Therefore, managers of MNEs need to continue to adopt a North American 'regional' strategic vision. Especially important within the context of MNEs will be the ability of Canadian managers to articulate in the appropriate strategic forums of the parent the Canadian subsidiary's potential contribution as a key supplier.

Within the institutional format of NAFTA, the Canadian MNEs are adopting new and relevant regional strategies and any new MAI-based rules for FDI should be NAFTA consistent to minimize further adjustment costs. The MAI will need not only to enshrine national treatment and right of establishment but to go well beyond these. To secure truly contestable conditions on a North American regional basis, or a global basis, additional domestic discriminatory practices must be ended and replaced by new trade, investment and competition rules.

Somewhat in contrast to the dramatic retrenchment affecting the larger MNEs, there is a more subtle change affecting SMEs. These are often 'niche' players driven by entrepreneurs who have a sense of the market. The SMEs are close to their customers; they can build and maintain long-term successful businesses through their marketing skills and flexibility. The SMEs act as intermediaries between the larger MNE suppliers and the wholesale or national distributors. Their flexibility and marketing know-how are vital firm-specific advantages. They can use their labs to customize products and/or respond very quickly to customer demands. They can manage these service functions better than larger MNE suppliers. As 'key customers' of the MNEs, they can actually expand the total market for the MNEs, while not acting as a threat to them. In this sense, the SMEs have to manage the key supplier role with skill and foresight. They can develop close working relationships with a variety of MNEs provided they preserve secrecy and develop a reputation for discretion and non-disclosure to rival MNEs.

SMEs therefore promise to be a source of considerable growth and dynamism in the Canadian chemicals industry as MNEs seek to rationalize the productive structure of their global (or regional) operations while at the same time accessing as many markets as they can. SMEs are, in effect, the keys to new markets in so far as (a) they are able to penetrate markets that are simply too small for MNEs to cater to given the scale of operations to which most MNEs are committed; and (b) they allow for more rapid roll-out of technological advances by making smaller, more specialized product development economically viable. Once again, the lesson from the Canadian chemicals industry is that even SMEs can adjust to new institutional frameworks, such as NAFTA.

From this case study of adjustment by the Canadian chemicals industry to the regionalization of strategic management signalled by NAFTA, three conclusions can be drawn. First, an MAI must be investment enhancing, with market-access provisions for business for smaller countries (like Canada) to Triad markets like the United States. Second, the key FDI principle is to have national treatment for investment and right of establishment. As discussed by Warner and Rugman (1994), the use of reciprocity provisions by Triad members will effectively discriminate against smaller countries and their firms, who require national treatment in order to operate in quadrant 3 of Figure 3.1. In addition, domestic markets must be made truly internationally contestable by the negotiation of non-discriminatory rules covering competition and tax policies, among other 'domestic' regulations. Third, policy-makers keen on negotiating an MAI should approach the task from the efficiency viewpoint of corporate strategy rather than the traditional distributional basis of tit-for-tat trade-related tariff-cutting 'concessions'. Such a regime has been proposed by Gestrin and Rugman (1994, 1995) and it is to be hoped that the valuable forward-looking investment rules of NAFTA can be used as a basis for the MAI.

NOTES

1. This is a revised version of two papers given at the Halifax Pre-G7 Conference on Euro-Pacific Investment and Trade, Halifax, 3–5 May 1995. Helpful comments have been received from Gavin Boyd, Peter Buckley, Steven Guisinger and Pierre Sauvé.
2. This, and succeeding sections, is a digest of a recent study of the Canadian chemicals

industry using the five partners framework and is reported in detail in D'Cruz, Gestrin and Rugman (1995).

REFERENCES

Bartlett, Christopher and Sumantra Ghoshal (1989), *Managing Across Borders: The Transnational Solution*, Boston: Harvard Business School Press.

Bergsten C. Fred and Edward M. Graham (1992), 'Needed: New International Rules for Foreign Direct Investment', *The International Trade Journal*, 7, Fall, 15–44.

Brewer, Thomas L. (1995), 'International Investment Dispute Settlement Procedures: The Evolving Regime for Foreign Direct Investment', *Law and Policy in International Business*, **26** (3), 633–73.

Brewer, Thomas L. and Stephen Young (1995), 'The Multilateral Agenda for Foreign Direct Investment: Problems, Principles and Priorities for Negotiation at the OECD and WTO', *Journal of World Trade*, **29** (1), 32–52.

Buckley, Peter J. and Mark Casson (1976), *The Future of the Multinational Enterprise*, Basingstoke and London: Macmillan.

Buckley, Peter J. and Mark Casson (1985), *The Economic Theory of the Multinational Enterprise*, London and Basingstoke: Macmillan.

Casson, Mark (1979), *Alternatives to the Multinational Enterprise*, London: Macmillan.

Chandler, Alfred D. Jr. (1962), *Strategy and Structure: Chapters in the History of American Industrial Enterprise*, Cambridge, MA: The MIT Press.

D'Cruz, Joseph R. (1995), 'The Theory of the Flagship Firm', paper for Halifax Pre G7 Conference, Halifax, May.

D'Cruz, Joseph R., Michael Gestrin and Alan M. Rugman (1995), 'Is the Canadian Manager an Endangered Species?', Toronto: Faculty of Management, University of Toronto, mimeo of study prepared for Ontario's Ministerial Advisory Committee on Chemicals.

D'Cruz, Joseph R. and Alan M. Rugman (1992), *New Compacts for Canadian Competitiveness*, Toronto: Kodak Canada Inc.

D'Cruz, Joseph R. and Alan M. Rugman (1993), 'Developing International Competitiveness: The Five Partners Model', *Business Quarterly* **58** (2), Winter, 101–7.

D'Cruz, Joseph R. and Alan M. Rugman (1994a), 'The Five Partners Model: France Telecom, Alcatel, and the Global Telecommunications Industry', *European Management Review*, **12** (1), 59–66.

D'Cruz, Joseph R. and Alan M. Rugman (1994b), 'Business Network Theory and the Canadian Telecommunications Industry', *International Business Review*, **3** (3), 275–88.

Dunning, John H. (1979), 'Explaining Changing Patterns of International Production: In Defence of the Eclectic Theory', *Oxford Bulletin of Economics and Statistics*, **41**, November 269–96.

Dunning, John H. (1981), *International Production and the Multinational Enterprise*, London: George Allen & Unwin.

Fruin, Mark (1992), *The Japanese Enterprise System: Competitive Strategies and Cooperative Structure*, Oxford: Clarendon, Oxford University Press.

Gerlach, Michael L. (1992), *Alliance Capitalism: The Social Organization of Japanese Business*, Berkeley: University of California Press.

Gestrin, Michael and Alan Rugman (1994), 'The North American Free Trade Agreement and Foreign Direct Investment', *Transnational Corporations*, **3**, February, 77–95.

Gestrin, Michael and Alan Rugman (1995), 'The NAFTA Investment Provisions: Proto-type Rules for International Investment', paper for OECD Conference, February, to be published by the C.D. Howe Institute.

Glueck, William (1976), *Business Policy, Strategy Formation and Management Action*, New York: McGraw-Hill.

Graham, Edward M. (1995a), 'Towards an Asia Pacific Investment Code', *Transnational Corporations*, **3** (3), August, pp. 1–28.

Graham, Edward M. (1995b), 'Investment and the New Multilateral Trade Context', paper for OECD Conference, February, to be published by the C.D. Howe Institute.

Graham, Edward M. and Christopher Wilkie (1994), 'Multinationals and the Investment Provisions of the NAFTA', *The International Trade Journal*, **8**, Spring, 9–38.

Guisinger, Stephen (1993), 'A Pacific Basin Investment Agreement', *ASEAN Economic Bulletin*, **10**, November, 176–83.

Julius, DeAnne (1994), 'International Direct Investment: Strengthening the Policy Regime', in Peter B. Kenen (ed.), *Managing the World Economy*, Washington, DC: Institute for International Economics, pp. 269–86.

Kogut, Bruce and Udo Zander (1992), 'Knowledge of the Firm, Combinative Capabilities, and the Replication of Technology', *Organization Science*, **3** (3), 383–97.

Kogut, Bruce and Udo Zander (1993), 'Knowledge of the Firm and the Evolutionary Theory of the Multinational Corporation', *Journal of International Business Studies*, **24** (4), 625–46.

Koontz, Harold and Cyril O'Donnell (1972), *Principles of Management*, New York: McGraw-Hill.

Lawrence, Robert Z. (1995), 'Towards Globally Contestable Markets', paper for OECD Conference, February, to be published by the C.D. Howe Institute.

Mintzberg, Harry (1979), *The Structuring of Organizations*, Englewood Cliffs, NJ: Prentice-Hall.

OECD (1995), *New Dimensions of Market Access in a Globalising World Economy*, Paris: Organization for Economic Cooperation and Development.

Ostry, Sylvia (1990), *Governments and Corporations in a Shrinking World*, New York: Council on Foreign Relations.

Ostry, Sylvia and Richard R. Nelson (1995), *Techno-Nationalism and Techno-Globalization*, Washington, DC: Brookings Institution.

Porter, Michael E. (1980), *Competitive Strategy: Techniques for Analyzing Industries and Competitors*, New York: Free Press, Macmillan.

Quintella, Rogerio H. (1993), *The Strategic Management of Technology in the Chemical and Petrochemical Industries*, London: Pinter and St. Martin's Press.

Rugman, Alan M. (1980), 'Internalization as a General Theory of Foreign Direct Investment: A Re-appraisal of the Literature', *Weltwirtschaftliches Archiv*, **116**, 365–79.

Rugman, Alan M. (1981), *Inside the Multinationals: The Economics of Internal Markets*, New York: Columbia University Press.

Rugman, Alan M. (1986), 'New Theories of the Multinational Enterprise: An Assessment of Internalization Theory', *Bulletin of Economic Research*, May, 101–18.

Rugman, Alan M. (1990), *Multinationals and Canada–United States Free Trade*, Columbia: University of South Carolina Press.

Rugman, Alan M. (1993), 'Drawing the Border for a Multinational Enterprise and a

Nation-State', in Lorraine Eden and Evan H. Potter (eds), *Multinationals in the Global Political Economy*, New York: St. Martin's Press, pp. 84–100.

Rugman, Alan M. (1994a), 'A Canadian Perspective on NAFTA', *The International Executive*, **36** (1), January–February, 33–54.

Rugman, Alan M. (ed.) (1994b), *Foreign Investment and NAFTA*, Columbia: University of South Carolina Press.

Rugman, Alan M., Joseph R. D'Cruz and Alain Verbeke (1995), 'Internalization and De-Internalization: Will Business Networks Replace Multinationals?', in Gavin Boyd (ed.), *Competitive and Cooperative Macromanagement: The Challenge of Structural Interdependence*, Aldershot: Edward Elgar, pp. 107–28.

Rugman, Alan M. and Michael Gestrin (1996), 'A Conceptual Framework for a Multilateral Agreement on Investment: Using NAFTA as a Prototype', in Daniel Schwanen and Pierre Sauvé (eds), *The Multilateral Agreement of Investment*, Toronto: C.D. Howe Institute, forthcoming.

Rugman, Alan M. and Alain Verbeke (1990), *Global Corporate Strategy and Trade Policy*, London: Routledge.

Safarian, A. Edward (1993), *Multinational Enterprise and Public Policy: A Study of the Industrial Countries*, Aldershot: Edward Elgar.

Sauvé, Pierre (1994), 'A First Look at Investment in the Final Act of the Uruguay Round', *Journal of World Trade*, **28** (5), 5–16.

United Nations Conference on Trade and Development (UNCTAD) and the World Bank (1994), *Liberalizing International Transactions in Services: A Handbook*, New York and Geneva: United Nations, United Nations publication, Sales No. E.94.II.A.11.

Warner, Mark A.A. and Alan M. Rugman (1994), 'Competitiveness: An Emerging Strategy of Discrimination in U.S. Antitrust and R&D Policy?', *Law and Policy in International Business*, **25** Spring, 945–82.

Westney, Eleanor (1995), 'The Japanese Keiretsu in Perspective', *Perspectives*, 3 (2), Toronto: Centre for International Business, University of Toronto.

Williamson, Oliver (1985), *The Economic Institution of Capitalism*, New York: Free Press/Macmillan.

4. Structural transformations: information systems and organizational networks[1]

Michael Blaine and Edward Mozley Roche

INTRODUCTION

In the 1986 article 'The Hollow Corporation', *Business Week* proclaimed the emergence of a new type of organization – 'the post-industrial' or 'network' corporation. They noted, 'these new corporations are "vertically disaggregated", relying on other companies for manufacturing and many crucial business functions. They are industrial companies without industrial production' (3 March 1986, p. 64). Among the early adopters of this 'new' form of economic organization were Nike, Esprit, Liz Claiborne, Emerson Radio, TIE, Schwinn, Sun Microsystems and Lewis Galoob. In 1985 these companies generated revenues of $50 million to $1 billion using workforces of less than 3,500 – and in some cases less than 150 – employees, and in almost all cases, the proportion of manufacturing employees to total employees was less than 20 per cent. A decade later, the 'network' or 'virtual' corporation had captured the imaginations of managers and academics alike, and was viewed by many as the appropriate response to competitive environments characterized by high levels of uncertainty and rapid rates of technological change.

Traditional economic analysis suggests that there are two means of organizing economic activities: the market and the firm (Coase, 1937; Richardson, 1972; Williamson, 1975). However, the sharp dichotomy between markets and hierarchies ignores a vast middle ground of 'intermediate' or 'hybrid' mechanisms which exhibit characteristics of both 'conscious planning' and 'arm's-length exchange'. These 'new forms of investment', as they have been called, are typically contractually based, and include such popular arrangements as licensing, management contracts, joint production or R&D, subcontracting, and minority joint ventures. Kester (1992) notes that these various forms of 'contractual' governance span a continuum ranging from explicit, detailed contracts enforceable in a court of law to implicit, 'relational' contracts based on trust and informal sanctions. The network firm lies at the latter end of this spectrum.

According to Powell (1990), 'In network modes of resource allocation, transactions occur neither through discrete exchanges nor by administrative fiat, but through networks of individuals engaged in reciprocal, preferential, mutually supportive actions' (p. 303). The informal, reciprocal nature of these arrangements has prompted Hakansson and Johanson (1993) to argue that the network is a unique form of governance that is difficult to explain using the traditional theory of the firm.

As used in this chapter, a 'network' or 'virtual' firm is a company that provides goods and services without directly owning the assets – and in some cases the knowledge – involved in the production and distribution of those goods and services. Instead, the network firm serves as the 'nexus' for a complex set of cooperative or contractual relationships with asset owners, and adds value by providing the 'vision' or design for a new product, service or technology, and by assembling and managing the relationships required to deliver that vision to customers. Like all organizational archetypes, networks exhibit a wide range of structural diversity in practice. Three factors can be used to discriminate between individual network firms: (1) the percentage of the firm's activities that are organized through contractual (versus equity) means, (2) the extent to which external partners are included in the firm's decision-making processes, and (3) the length of the firm's industry and product cycles. The arguments developed in this chapter are specifically aimed at firms which contractually control their value-adding chains, offer partners considerable input in group decision-making, and operate in highly dynamic, often emerging, industry settings. As a result, this analysis provides an interesting counterpoint to the flagship' model developed by Rugman and D'Cruz (see Chapter 3 of this volume).

In general, network firms are the result of two occurrences that have radically altered the relative costs and benefits of hierarchical governance. The first involves the growing complexity and uncertainty of many business activities. *Inter alia*, shortened product life cycles, increased international competition, converging national and product markets, and rapid advances in technology have introduced a new level of complexity into the competitive environment. As Halal (1994) notes, 'Hierarchy is too cumbersome under these conditions, so modern economies require organic systems composed of numerous small, self-guided enterprises that can adapt to their local environment more easily' (p. 69). By replacing the equity control of the firm's value-adding chain with more flexible contractual arrangements between independent companies, the network form of governance allows companies to reduce high production and overhead costs, increase rates of innovation and product introduction, and adapt to unstable demand or shifts in technology.

But the virtual corporation would not be possible without a second development – advances in telecommunication and information technologies. These new technologies have enabled firms to create complex 'inter-organizational systems' (IOSs) which can electronically link a company with its suppliers and customers, allowing it to manage the flow of information and products in 'real-time' along a value chain. These systems are important because they provide an alternative to the traditional, hierarchical coordination of economic activities. Further, as the exchange of products and information within the network grows, it becomes increasingly difficult to identify the boundaries between individual entities. Davidow and Malone (1992) underscore this point in their description of the virtual corporation, noting that, 'To the outside observer, [the virtual corporation] will appear almost edgeless, with permeable and continuously changing interfaces between company, supplier, and customers' (p. 5). Consequently, the network or virtual firm violates the most basic assumption of traditional economic theory – that transactions occur between discrete actors.

Although the theoretical rationale for the network is compelling, there are several reasons to question the adequacy of this form of governance. Contrary to most recent work, this chapter argues that the 'network' is fundamentally a costly and inefficient form of organization for a simple reason: as the number of components – or nodes – in the network increases, the cost of managing the complex contractual relationships which compose the network rises accordingly. While firms may be able to reduce administrative and production costs, increase flexibility, and access unique expertise by adopting the network form, at some point, the costs of protecting the interests of individual entities and the problem of dividing responsibilities and benefits between constituents will outweigh the potential economies gained from this form of organization. Equally important, as the size and complexity of the network expands, so does the practical problem of managing the technological infrastructure or 'information architecture' that supports the exchange and processing of information between constituents. Thus, at some point the network may collapse under its own weight.

But there is an even more important problem facing the network firm. Since network firms are often composed of relatively small, independent subunits, it may be difficult for these firms to forge the critical political alliances needed to influence the evolution of national and international legal and regulatory policies. This follows because networks are by definition flexible, and therefore, the components of a network are in constant flux. In addition, many of the components of one network are components of other networks which comprise their own unique sets of relationships. As a result, the ability of these diffused groupings to define a common set of interests and to effectively influence national and international institutions may be limited. Thus, network firms face a severe disadvantage relative to large, national or multinational firms that have cultivated long-term relationships with key national and international actors.

Finally, it is unclear whether network firms can remain innovative over successive generations of technology. Ideally, a network firm scans the environment for promising new technologies and assembles the production and marketing expertise – or 'complementary assets' to use Teece's (1988) term – required to commercialize them. As technologies change, the network simply assembles a new set of linkages with the owners of more appropriate assets. However, the owners of many sophisticated complementary assets – particularly on an international scale – are large, integrated firms; and as a result, these firms may be in a better position to commercialize promising new products and technologies than more diffused network firms. For example, in industries characterized by rapid rates of innovation, large firms routinely purchase small stakes in start-up companies in order to monitor their progress. As promising new technologies are developed, large firms have been eager to purchase their smaller partners in order to control the commercialization process or suppress competition. As a result, network firms may be at severe disadvantage in the battle to control emerging technologies and to access critical complementary assets.

Interestingly, most network firms are involved in the creation of new products and technologies, particularly information- and bio-technologies. Since these activities generate high rates of return when they are successful, it is possible that the monopoly rents associated with proprietary knowledge have masked the high costs and inefficiencies of network governance. Thus, despite its compelling theoretical rationale, the network or virtual corporation may not provide a useful general model for the organization of economic activity. The remainder of this chapter explores these ideas in greater detail.

THE EVOLUTION OF ORGANIZATIONAL STRUCTURES

Four major structural innovations have occurred over the past century and a half: the vertical hierarchy, the multidivisional (M) form, the matrix, and the network. These innovations were responses to specific environmental conditions and technological innovations which greatly increased the complexity, scale, and scope of the firm. Each innovation increased the firm's 'information-processing' capacity, enabling it to better adapt to a changing external environment.

According to Chandler, Bruchey and Galambos (1968), the basic hierarchical structure of the modern industrial corporation was a response to the creation of a national system of railroads and canals between 1830 and 1870. Since contemporary administrative practices could not handle the size and complexity of these mammoth organizations, the growth of the railroads fostered a number of structural innovations. These included the functional department, the geographic division, and the holding company. More importantly, however, the railroads precipitated the separation of long-range, strategic activities from the day-to-day operations of the firm, thus establishing management as a separate activity demanding the full attention of specialized personnel. Thus, by the latter half of the 19th century, small firms run by individual entrepreneurs were giving way to larger, hierarchical organizations run by professional managers.

Although the vertical hierarchy greatly enlarged the firm's span of control, technological advances and the drive towards vertical and horizontal integration in many industries pushed the firm's size and complexity beyond the capabilities of this relatively simple structure. The next major advance was the 'multidivisional' structure, which combined a number of distinct vertical hierarchies under central control. Chandler (1962, 1990) chronicles the rise of these large, integrated, industrial corporations in the early 20th century and examines the environmental conditions that led to their characteristic multidivisional form (M-form). By clearly separating the strategic and planning functions from the firm's day-to-day operations, the M-form allowed greater decentralization of decision-making and enabled the firm to coordinate and control a vastly expanded range of activities.

The M-form precipitated a revolution in the organization of business activities and was responsible for the geometric growth of the size of the firm. However, by the 1960s, many firms began to reach the organizational limits of this structure because of the increasing internationalization of their activities. As companies shifted from exporting to foreign production, an additional level of complexity was added to the management of the firm: controlling a growing system of foreign subsidiaries. Chandler (1986) notes that many of the forces responsible for the development and diffusion of the multidivisional structure also account for the rise of the multinational enterprise (MNE). Specifically, he cites the increasing scale of production resulting from new technologies and mass production which encouraged firms to expand vertically – to acquire resources and/or distribution channels – and horizontally – to increase their access to distant markets. As the search for resources and markets extended beyond national borders, the result is the multinational enterprise. (For more on the theory of the MNE, see Hymer, 1960; Kindleberger, 1968; Buckley and Casson, 1976; Dunning, 1977, 1979, 1980).

MNEs faced an even more complex operating environment than domestic firms of the same size since they had to coordinate diverse functional and product areas across national environments which exhibited widely divergent economic, socio-cultural and legal characteristics. The effect of these demands was to pull the firm in two directions: one reflecting the products or industries in which the firm operated, the other reflecting the geographical and cultural dispersion of these activities. Stopford and Wells (1972) were among the first to study the structural changes that accompanied the firm's entry into foreign markets. They found that most companies initially added an international division to their existing multidivisional structure; but, as their foreign activities increased, the international division often grew as large as the rest of the firm combined. At this point most firms undertook a major structural reorganization in an attempt to integrate the firm's domestic and international operations while still retaining the ability to respond to differences in local markets.

The structure designed to accomplish this task was the 'matrix' or 'grid'. According to Kingdon (1973), matrix management originated in the aerospace industry in the late 1950s and was an attempt to manage large-scale projects which required close collaboration between government and industry, and involved high levels of uncertainty and technological innovation. In order to cope with these highly complex, uncertain environments, the matrix combined a hierarchical structure with a loosely structured team design. Davis and Lawrence (1977) note that three forces encouraged the adoption of the matrix: (1) two distinct and equally important focuses in a single organization, (2) the need for high information-processing capacity, and (3) the need to fully employ scarce resources in order to achieve high levels of performance and quality. In most cases, however, the matrix failed to deliver its desired results because the structure proved too difficult to manage in practice. As a result, over time, many firms abandoned the matrix and returned to a simpler, multidivisional structure with operations organized along either product or geographical lines. Unfortunately, the need to simultaneously achieve the benefits of 'global integration' and 'local responsiveness' remained.

During the 1970s and 1980s a number of factors radically altered the international competitive environment, creating both new opportunities and some serious challenges for the firm. The growing similarities between national and product markets, the emergence of large and fluid international capital markets, falling trade barriers, advances in technology, the increased dissemination of technology and information, and the rise of new global competitors eroded many of the traditional advantages of large, vertically-integrated firms. At the same time, the declining importance of natural resources in the production process diminished the need for vertical integration. In both cases, the traditional model of the firm (MNE) based on the internalization of markets, vertical and/or horizontal integration, and the central control of an international system of subsidiaries was brought into question. Instead, a new model emerged which stressed the 'externalization' of certain activities, cooperation with host governments and other firms, and the coordination of activities through contractual agreements rather than equity ownership. This led to a growing interest in various types of inter-firm cooperation called 'new forms of investment' (NFIs).

According to Hennart (1989), '"New Forms" include arrangements that fall short of majority ownership, such as various forms of contracts (licensing, franchising, management contracts, turnkey and product-in-hand contracts, production sharing-contracts, and international subcontracting) as well as joint ventures' (p. 212). The growing body of literature on joint ventures, strategic alliances, and other contractual arrangements (Killing, 1983; Mariti and Smiley, 1983; Harrigan, 1985; Anderson and Gatignon, 1986; Morris and Hergert, 1987; Contractor and Lorange, 1988; Kogut, 1988; Hennart, 1989), suggests that the opportunities presented by the 'new' international environment do not readily lend themselves to the traditional structures of the past. Through the use of computers and telecommunications, organizations can overcome the increased complexity and bounded rationality that limited earlier designs. This, in turn, has encouraged smaller, flatter organizations controlled by specialists rather the middle managers. Carried to an extreme, this vision yields a large, complex 'network' of independent organizations loosely linked through R&D, production, and distribution agreements.

As noted above, the network or virtual firm represents a new organizational form that is more amorphous than the equity-based structures of the past. By coordinating the firm's (international) activities through contractual agreements with host governments, other MNEs, and local firms, the network firm becomes the nexus for the exchange of capital and information within this larger grouping of independent organizations. By externalizing the firm's value-adding chain, the network firm may be in a better position to respond to the rapidly changing threats and opportunities which characterize the international competitive environment. But more importantly, by replacing routines and hierarchical referral with flexible lateral relations between independent entities, the network form greatly increases the firm's capacity to process information (Galbraith, 1973; Egelhoff, 1991).

THE EVOLUTION OF INFORMATION SYSTEMS

To a large extent, the evolution of organizational structures discussed above reflects the firm's increasing need to manage and process information. As the scale and scope of the firm's activities expanded, the firm needed to manage and process larger amounts of information. This, in turn, encouraged structural and technological innovations designed to increase the firm's information processing capacity. One of the most important technological advances in this regard has been the introduction of telecommunications equipment and computers which enabled the firm to complement its organizational structure with an 'information infrastructure'. This development has been particularly useful for coordinating and controlling the firm's international activities due to the great distances involved.

The relationship between telecommunications and international business goes back more than a century to the first use of the telegraph in conducting international commerce (Roche, 1992). In the multinational enterprise, for example, headquarters locations have been tied together with overseas subsidiaries in order to coordinate manufacturing, financial reporting, management control and other activities. The data-processing and telecommunications infrastructures which have evolved make it possible for companies to build large, extended enterprises, spanning the globe and operating in many countries on a 24-hour basis (Vignault, 1987; Harasim, 1993).

The existence of information 'networks' linking headquarters with their subsidiaries has been known for some time, but these systems have been difficult to study because of their complexity and scale. In the days before computers, methods of coordinating the flow of information within and between firms included the telegraph, the telex and the telephone. Surprisingly, these 'primitive' technologies were the primary means of coordinating the activities of firms until the end of the 1960s. In the 1970s, the first remote terminal linkages were established when Texas Instruments built the world's first private satellite network to link its Texas headquarters with its semiconductor manufacturing operations in the Far East. Evolving technology made it possible to place terminals and cluster controllers at distant locations, but this approach was relatively expensive since it relied on analog networks supplied through public telephone companies. But these early innovations, however primitive they appear today, allowed remote locations to share information with headquarters or regional centres. The velocity of information was accelerated and decision-making was improved by the faster transfer of information and feedback cycles. Theoretically, this translated into better decisions (Rapoport, 1985), although it has been difficult to measure and verify this in practice (Egelhoff, 1991).

Next, the proliferation of leased and dedicated lines allowed companies to build increasingly large and complex information systems, but these were primarily within individual nations – generally the United States. Although this technology made it possible to link together sites in other countries, national legislation and standards coupled with high costs and many practical problems inhibited the growth of these linkages (Rada and Pipe, 1984; Junne, 1988; Jussawalla, 1987; Ives and Jarvenpaa, 1991).

During the latter half of the 1980s, however, the growth of intra-firm information systems accelerated on an international scale as user groups such as INTUG (International Telecommunications User Group) worked to ease restrictions at the international level. Many of the problems associated with international computer networking have supposedly been alleviated in the recent round of trade negotiations, but the wide divergence of national goals virtually guarantees a continuing struggle between the firm and the nation state, making it more expensive and complex to create, enhance, or expand these international information networks (see Wallenstein, 1990). At the current rate of change, it is unreasonable to expect transborder data flow problems to be completely resolved before the end of the first or second decade of the next century, particularly since the explosion of the Internet is creating a host of new regulatory problems. Nation-state-imposed controls on computer networking may yet set a practical limit to the international expansion of the virtual corporation.

As the size and complexity of these intra-organizational systems increased in the 1980s, technological advances made it possible to establish *external* linkages between companies. For the first time this created a schism in the management of the firm's information infrastructure. Before, there had been only internal systems, now many firms had to manage external systems as well. At the time, very few writers recognized that the development of these external information networks had the potential to change the structure of the firm and even entire industries (Piore and Sabel, 1984; McGee, 1991; Konsynski, 1993).

These external information networks – or inter-organizational systems (IOSs) as they have been called – were initially termed 'strategic systems' in the Multinational Information Systems (MIS) literature (Wiseman, 1988). Figure

Early (1980s) forms of electronic strategic networking

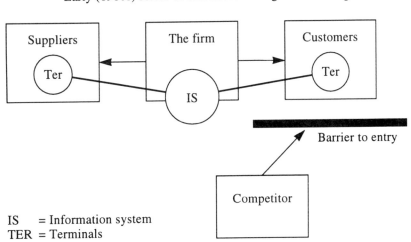

IS = Information system
TER = Terminals

Figure 4.1 Electronic strategic information networks, circa early 1980s

4.1 provides a graphic depiction of a typical IOS. Many believed that these systems could provide strategic advantages to the firm, since once they were installed, it became difficult and costly for the customer to switch to another vendor (McFarlan, 1984). These computer linkages resulted in 'information bonding' (Venkatraman and Loh, 1994) which further tied the customer to the firm and created an entry barrier which blocked firms from establishing competing linkages. For example, the strategic advantage Citibank gained from its introduction of the automatic teller machine has rightly been hailed as one of the most important strategic innovations in information technology (IT), and there are many similar examples of the use of IT to establish forward and backward linkages along the firm's value chain (see White, 1979; Blackwell, 1983; Mulqueen, 1987).

Other writers, however, claimed that the strategic advantages associated with IOSs were largely accidental (Clemons and Row, 1988) and that firms were building these networks out of 'strategic necessity' (Clemons, 1986, 1988, 1991; Clemons and Kimbrough, 1986). This view contradicted the popular notion that a firm's information system was an important source of innovation and competitive advantage. The optimistic view of IT-based competitive advantage was further dampened by a number of studies which suggested that the growing investments in information technology provided little or no increase in productivity. For example, Roach (1987, 1988) found that by the end of the 1980s almost half of the capital investment in the US economy was in information technology, but this investment yielded no discernible improvement in productivity. Regardless of whether these inter-firm information linkages were a source of competitive advantage or an unproductive investment, one thing is clear, during the 1980s firms faced considerable national and international obstacles to building them (Roche et al., 1992).

These problems did not, however, prevent some firms from experimenting with novel ways of linking companies together electronically. In fact, these experiments ultimately gave rise to the network or virtual firm. Breakthroughs in understanding the social impact of network governance came from scholars such as Castels (1989), Scott (1993) and Saxenian (1994) who compared the economic efficiency and competitive power of the network firm with that of the traditional hierarchical company. Saxenian's analysis is perhaps the most dramatic. She compares the more traditional computer and high-technology companies around Route 128 in Boston with the emerging network firms of Silicon Valley. In explaining the demise of Digital Equipment and Wang versus the success of Hewlett Packard, Sun Microsystems and Silicon Graphics, she concluded that these differences were related to the way these companies organized their external relationships. By using a high proportion of outsourcing and co-engineering, the latter 'network' firms were better able to adapt to rapid shifts in technology and consumer tastes than the former firms.

At the hear of this analysis was the belief that the hierarchical, centralized, vertically-integrated firm was a weak and vulnerable form of organization. With shorter product life cycles, firms were forced to bring products to market faster, resulting in time-sensitive competition (Stalk and Hout, 1990; Anderson and Tushman, 1991). The Silicon Valley firms were successful because they retained their 'core competencies' (Kesler et al., 1993; Prahalad, 1993; Bakker et al., 1994; Kozin and Young, 1994; Simpson, 1994), and subcontracted out everything else. In short, they replaced the equity control of their value-adding chains by using contractual arrangements with independent suppliers. Sun Microsystems is the quintessential example of the resulting network firm where most activities are performed by others. Adopting this form of organization meant that the smaller virtual firm could often successfully out-manoeuvre its larger rivals.

As realization of the advantages of network governance spread, large, vertically-integrated firms also began to reevaluate their operations. Re-engineering, down-sizing, and outsourcing were the common results of this process. Firms 'dis-integrated' business functions which were not central to their core mission or competencies and either spun these activities off into separate companies or subcontracted them to others (Morton, 1991). In many cases, this led to the creation of the 'flagship' firms studied by Rugman and D'Cruz. But it is important to note that this new approach to industrial organization may have severe repercussions for the firm's 'stakeholders', particularly its workforce. Since many virtual firms transfer production to suppliers overseas or in low-wage, non-union domestic sites, the widespread adoption of the network model may weaken and impoverish domestic workers. Consequently, industrial reorganization has often had the effect of depressing wages and reducing employment through the elimination of middle managers and production workers. In American, the job security of the 1950s to 1970s now appears to be an artifact of a bygone age (Newman, 1993; Bridges, 1994; Handy, 1994).

The efforts to build strategic, inter-organizational systems and the breaking apart (disintegration) of large, industrial organizations has been made possible by rapid advances in computer and telecommunications systems. It is only with the rapid and efficient transfer and manipulation of information between firms and their customers, subcontractors, service providers and other partners that the virtual company can exist (Gilroy, 1993).

Perhaps the greatest irony of these inter-organizational information systems is that many multinational enterprises appear to be moving in the opposite direction. Much of the strategic management literature in the 1980s focused on 'globalization' – the process of consolidating available functional areas of the firm in order to obtain economies of scale and scope. Globalization is the antithesis of 'dis-integration' through information and telecommu-

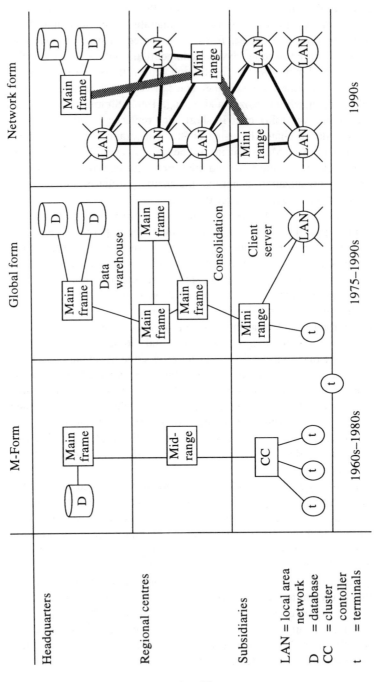

Figure 4.2 *Structural transformation and the firm's information system*

M-Form   Global form   Network form

Headquarters

Regional centres

Subsidiaries

LAN = local area
        network
D   = database
CC   = cluster
        contoller
t   = terminals

1960s–1980s   1975–1990s   1990s

Data
warehouse

Consolidation

Client
server

Main
frame

Mid-
range

CC

Main
frame

Main
frame

Main
frame

Main
frame

Mini
range

Mini
range

Main
frame

nications technologies. The information infrastructure of the MNE – defined as the set of rules governing the hardware and software infrastructure supporting the creation, processing, storage and distribution of information and data, including voice, video and multimedia signals – suffers from a paradox of complexity related to the overall distribution of data-processing sites, and the type of information architecture the firm already has in place (see Deans and Karwan, 1994; Palvia et al., 1992).

Figure 4.2 provides a graphic depiction of the advances in the firm's (MNE's) information systems over the past three decades and associates these changes with corresponding changes in organizational structure. As the preceding discussion suggests, the information systems associated with the network firm are extremely complex and may impose a practical limit on the growth of these firms in the near-term, particularly when firms are being linked across countries.

ASSESSING THE COSTS OF NETWORK GOVERNANCE

As noted above, the 'network' or 'virtual' corporation can be seen as a structural response to changing conditions in the (international) competitive environment, particularly the growing uncertainty associated with many business activities due to rapid advances in technology. By increasing the flexibility and information-processing capacity of the firm, network governance enables the firm to adapt to these highly complex and uncertain external conditions more quickly and at far lower cost than large, integrated firms. As a result, network firms should exhibit superior performance, and over time challenge the archetypical hierarchical firm for organizational dominance. But as compelling as this proposition is – and as profitable as some network companies have become – there are many important factors this simple 'contingency' argument ignores. The two most important are: (1) the costs of maintaining the contractual and cooperative relationships that comprise the network firm, and (2) the relative ability of the network firm to effectively 'lobby' national and international actors. Therefore, in order to accurately assess the costs and benefits of network governance, it is necessary to examine each of these factors in greater detail.

There are costs associated with all forms of governance. Although these costs are difficult to measure, transaction-cost analysis (Williamson, 1975, 1985) provides a useful theoretical tool for comparing the relative costs and benefits of alternative methods of organizing economic activities. Traditionally, only two forms of economic organization were recognized – the market and the firm. Coase (1937) was perhaps the first to recognize that the firm was the product of costs associated with market-mediated exchange. Specifically, Coase cited the cost of discovering relevant prices, the cost of writing and enforcing contracts, and the cost of uncertainty, and noted that in some cases these costs could be high enough to justify the 'supersession of the price mechanism' and the coordination of economic activities through the firm.

Although hierarchical governance (the firm) may generate certain economies, such as economies of scale and scope (Chandler, 1990) and the reduction of contracting and enforcement costs, the firm also incurs unique costs. The most important of these is the cost of creating and maintaining the administrative apparatus that coordinates the firm's activities. As the size of the firm increases, so does the cost and complexity of managing it. Thus, at some point, the firm may grow so large that it begins to experience 'transactional diseconomies' as Williamson (1975) calls them. These include internal procurement bias, internal expansion bias, programme persistence bias, communication and information distortions, and employment disincentives. Taken together, these 'diseconomies' can raise the cost of hierarchical governance above that of market-mediated exchange so that the firm no longer provides an efficient alternative to the market.

It is difficult to explain why cooperative mechanisms – including the network firm – should have an advantage over either market or hierarchical governance. Williamson (1979, 1985) has developed a scheme that explains the advantages of alternative forms of governance based on the nature of the transactions involved. Simply stated, market exchange is appropriate for any transaction that is nonspecific in nature, such as buying and selling basic commodities. As transactions become more idiosyncratic or require more specialized investments, alternative forms of governance are preferred. If highly idiosyncratic transactions occur frequently or generate large economies, the costs of hierarchical governance can be defrayed and the firm becomes the preferred option.

On the other hand, if transactions are moderately idiosyncratic and occur frequently, various types of 'relational contracting' – or 'bilateral' governance as Williamson calls it – are favoured. Relational contracting arises because the moderate idiosyncrasy of the transaction gives parties an incentive to continue their relationship, but no incentive to shift the exchange to the market or to 'internalize' it within the firm. Instead, longer-term, contractual arrangements are established between parties, as in the network firm. But these alternative forms of governance are subject to high contracting and enforcement costs. Thus, network governance replaces one set of costs – managing the administrative apparatus and assets of the firm – with another – managing the complex contractual relationships which compose the network. As a result, for network governance to offer an advantage over traditional hierarchical governance, these latter costs must be less than the former.

It is not at all clear why the cost of managing a complex set of contractual relations should be less than the cost of managing an integrated firm of comparable size, or why a network firm should be able to manage these relationships better than a traditional firm. On the contrary, a large integrated firm may be able to forge more advantageous relationships than a network firm because of its ability to engage in more comprehensive search activities and its bargaining power relative to potential partners. Further, by virtue of its size, an integrated firm may be able to attract higher quality managerial and legal expertise, allowing it to write more complete contracts. Finally, a network firm faces many of the same problems coordinating and integrating its activities as an integrated firm, but lacks the ability to use hierarchical mechanisms to resolve disputes among partners.

There are, however, at least four conditions under which network governance may be preferred: (1) when the value of a particular product does not justify the costs of owning the physical assets required to produce it, (2) when large firms experience high 'transactional diseconomies' due to the nature of their activities, (3) when the returns associated with a particular activity are so high that the form of governance is irrelevant, and (4) when the cost of negotiating and enforcing contracts are lower for a network than an integrated firm.

While the first of these conditions may initially appear trivial, it is particularly relevant in 'sunset' industries or industries which have experienced a radical change in product or process technologies or consumer tastes. As a result of these occurrences, the value of a firm's product – or its current cost of production – no longer justifies the firm's investment in existing plant and equipment. However, the firm still possesses valuable knowledge, relationships and goodwill which may be profitably employed in another way. For example, by replacing the cost of internal production with contractual agreements between more efficient, low-cost suppliers, the firm may be able to substantially reduce its cost of production and to continue to operate *sans* a large portion of its assets and workforce. Interestingly, this process of 'disaggregation' – or 'dis-integration' as we have called it – is a common way network or virtual firms are created. It also describes the way many 'flagship' firms have evolved.

The second condition – when large firms experience high 'transactional diseconomies' – may also produce network firms through the process of 'dis-integration'. In this case, the cost of production *per se* is not the problem, but inefficiencies associated with the firm's management. Organizational theory has identified a large number of 'organizational pathologies', most of which involve the social dimension of organizations and the unique characteristics of their members. But whatever the cause, in many cases large firms become unable to accurately assess their environment and ignore critical threats to their activities. As a result, performance declines and the firm may be forced to 'down-size', 'right-size', or 're-engineer' its operations in order to survive. In each case, the result is a smaller, more focused (often network) organization. In other cases, the pathologies of large firms may provide an opportunity for smaller, less cumbersome network firms to compete. In either case, however, the network emerges because of the *mis*-management of the integrated firm, not the advantages of network governance.

The third condition – when returns are extremely high – also represents a contrary view of network governance. In this case, the network firm emerges not because it offers advantages over hierarchical governance, but because the products or knowledge created by the firm generate such high returns that *any* form of governance would suffice. This would explain why the bulk of network companies are in industries that generate high monopoly profits from unique technologies or knowledge such as biotechnology, computers and information technologies, entertainment, and even fashion. In many cases, these firms adopt the network structure as start-ups since the network requires relatively little capital investment because of its limited asset base. As these companies enter periods of rapid growth, familiarity – *not* efficiency – encourages them to retain this form of organization. Thus, the high returns associated with proprietary products or knowledge – not the advantages of network governance – may explain the apparent success of network firms in many instances.

The most interesting of the four conditions is when network firms find a less expensive way to negotiate and enforce contracts and manage relations between partners. In fact, many of the explanations of cooperative forms in general, and the network in particular, have focused on the use of low-cost, semi-formal means of coordinating activities and guaranteeing compliance. Three explanations for these low-cost safeguards have been offered.

The first is characterized by Hill's (1990) argument that traditional economic theory has grossly exaggerated the need for safeguards against opportunism, and thus overestimates the cost of writing and enforcing contracts. If this argument is correct, then the cost of managing the relationships which comprise a network could be far less than traditional theory would suggest. A second explanation is that there are economies associated with long-term reciprocal trading which traditional economic analysis does not recognize (Elg and Johansson, 1993; Blaine, 1995). Over time, partners may develop more efficient methods of trading or the administrative apparatus used to coordinate one exchange may lower the cost of a second related exchange. In either case, the cost of a 'stream' or 'system' of transactions becomes less than the sum of the costs of the individual transactions. The final explanation is that network firms (and other cooperative arrangements) employ 'trust' or similar informal mechanisms to reduce the cost of 'writing and enforcing contracts under conditions of uncertainty' (Ouchi, 1980; Johanson and Mattsson, 1987; Powell, 1990; Grabher, 1993). To the extent that trust between parties is well-founded and maintained, the need for costly contracting is clearly abrogated. Further, to the extent that contracts may be implicit rather than explicit, the firm's flexibility is enhanced. Thus, by providing an inexpensive alternative to explicit contracting, trust – when it is well-founded – may lower the cost of network governance relative to traditional hierarchical governance.

The kinds of informal, social bonds which tie the partners of a network together may be easier to establish and more effective in some cultural settings or institutional structures than others (Blaine, 1995). For example, in a legalist society like the United States, replacing formal contracts with informal, trust-based agreements seems naive at best. On the other hand, in a tight-knit society like Japan, where social sanctions and reputations effects are strong, informal agreements may be adequate. Interestingly, Japanese and Swedish scholars have produced a large and sympathetic body of literature on 'networks' and other cooperative arrangements (for a review, see Blaine, 1995). Additionally, these writers have often vehemently rejected transaction-cost principles. This may suggest that the cultural or institutional characteristics of these nations significantly reduces the need for formal, contractual safeguards, thus eliminating one of the major obstacles to network governance.

However, even with informal, trust-based agreements, the network firm still incurs the costs of managing relationships, coordinating the production process, and dividing responsibilities and profits among partners. These are clearly difficult and complex tasks even when the fears of free-riding, non-compliance and opportunism are substantially reduced. Further, unlike hierarchical governance – where position and authority can be used to resolve conflicts between members and subunits – the network firm must negotiate and enforce solutions to internal disputes within the group itself. This can be a costly process, particularly when parties differ in their activities or expertise, contributions or expectations, or cultural or legal backgrounds. As a result, we would expect network governance to be more costly when: (1) partners differ substantially in their functional or cultural backgrounds, (2) external institutions require formal, legal or contractual safeguards to assure compliance, or (3) institutions do not recognize or support agreements based on informal, social safeguards, or (4) a larger number of parties are involved. Consequently, international networks involving parties from different cultural backgrounds and operating under different legal institutions may be extremely costly and are unlikely to encompass a large number of parties.

THREE WAYS TO MANAGE A NETWORK

In a study of the headquarters–subsidiary relationships of MNEs, Ghoshal and Nohria (1993) identify three structural mechanisms that can be used to integrate the activities of diverse subunits. They are: centralization, formalization and normative integration (socialization). Centralization is well known and involves the use of authority to manage the firm's internal relationships. Formalization involves the use of rules and procedures to maintain cohesion and resolve internal disputes. Finally, normative integration uses a strong set of behavioural norms (corporate culture) to manage internal relationships. These three mechanisms may also be used to manage relationships and resolve disputes between members of a network firm.

For example, when the firm at the centre of the network has greater bargaining power than its partners, decision-making and dispute resolution can be centralized as in the 'flagship' model. This situation could arise when the centre controls key knowledge or technologies, or is the only partner capable of assembling and coordinating the network's components. The problem with this approach, however, is that over time the use of authority may create tension and animosity within the group, increasing the need for formal contractual safeguards, and raising the cost of governance. Formalization, on the other hand, would require the members of the network to develop a formal set of rules or procedures that would be used to manage internal relationships, resolve disputes between partners, and divide responsibilities and profits. Although this would initially require lengthy negotiations, once a set of rules has been established, managing internal relations should proceed smoothly. The major drawback of this approach is that rules make it difficult for the network to remain flexible and adapt to changing external conditions. They also make it difficult for the network to expand or incorporate new members. Thus, a network firm founded on centralization or formalization is an oxymoron – hierarchical governance without the hierarchy.

This leaves normative integration (socialization) as a basis for managing relations within the network. In this case network partners develop a strong set of norms, myths or behaviours which give the group a unique identity. If this identity is strong enough, partners will place the interests of the group above their own individual interests, and 'trust' may evolve. As noted above, trust among network members may significantly lower the cost of governance and provide a key advantage over traditional hierarchical mechanisms. This approach may be more appropriate in cultures that are strongly group-oriented, tightly-knit, or employ strong social sanctions such as reputation effects. In addition, certain institutional configurations may encourage the kind of social or group behaviour which supports network governance. As a result, networks may be more prevalent in some countries or cultures than others.

But whatever the external conditions, a critical factor in the success of the network form of governance lies in its ability to manage internal relationships and disputes, and coordinate activities among partners in a way that is less costly than either market exchange or hierarchical control. Based on the discussion thus far, achieving this objective should not be taken for granted.

A RESOURCE-DEPENDENCY PERSPECTIVE

Before the full potential of network governance can be assessed, it is necessary to examine a second factor, namely, the relative ability of the network firm to 'lobby' national and international institutions in order to influence the evolution of the international commercial regime. The question is this: by replacing the equity control of a (globally) dispersed set of assets with the cooperative or contractual control of a diverse set of relationships, does the network firm's ability to influence the global institutional structure increase or decrease, particularly relative to large, integrated (multinational) firms? This question is important because to the extent that any organization can enhance its influence, it may use that influence to shape the rules regulating competition and trade to its advantage. According to Pfeffer and Salancik (1978), 'There are two broadly defined contingent adaptive responses – the organization can adapt and change to fit the environment, or the organization can attempt to alter the environment so that it fits the organization's capabilities' (p. 106). Although the bulk of organizational and strategic management theory deals with the process of adaptation, modifying national and international legislation and regulation is clearly an option – albeit a difficult one. Thus, if integrated firms have some inherent advantage in lobbying national and international actors, network firms may fail to prosper even if they possess certain inherent efficiency or cost advantages – which is far from certain.

Pfeffer and Salancik (1978) have developed an approach to the study of organizations that focuses on the relationship between the firm and the environment in general, and the firm's need to access critical external resources in particular. They argue that in order to survive, an organization (firm) must assemble a coalition of parties that contribute requisite resources, and that these parties in turn define the organization and its activities. Once this grouping has been assembled, however, the organization becomes a 'market for influence and control', and within that market, parties which control more valuable resources are awarded more influence. Clearly, this 'resource-dependent' view of the firm can be used to explain the relationships and behaviours of parties within the firm, as well as the relations between two or more firms, and between the firm and other social and economic actors. This view is also useful in examining the firm's ability to effect national and international legislation and regulation.

There are several reasons to believe that network firms will be less effective in lobbying rule-making institutions than their larger, integrated rivals. First, because of their diverse and diffused structure, network firms are likely to have an extremely difficult time identifying critical issues, formulating effective policy responses, gaining a consensus among network partners, and coordinating the lobbying activities of these partners in different countries and in different international fora. Second, since network firms typically own few assets and often subcontract manufacturing activities to partners in low-wage foreign locations, they may have little to offer powerful institutional actors in return for support in shaping legislation and regulation. Although some network firms do have large shareholder bases, since they generally lack large domestic workforces, network firms (which are not intimately associated with national defence or in critical industries) have few strong constituents to support their lobbying efforts on a national level and, as a result, have no strong advocate for their preferences on the international level. Thus, network firms appear to be at a severe disadvantage to larger (multinational) firms in influencing policies and regulations at the national and international level.

On the other hand, a profitable network firm can purchase the services of the same professional lobbyists, lawyers, and 'agents of influence' as a large, integrated firm, and can also make substantial (legal and illegal) political contributions. Further, if the network contains international partners, and if those partners can agree on issues and responses, these parties can attempt to lobby local institutions, and the network can (theoretically) achieve the same lobbying effectiveness as a coordinated multinational – provided that at least one party focuses its lobbying activities on key international institutions and agencies and trade and industry organizations.

Thus, in order for the network firm to engage in effectively lobbying at the (inter) national level, it must: (1) have a number of (foreign) partners, (2) be able to identify key national and international policy issues, (3) gain consensus among its partners regarding appropriate responses, (4) encourage its foreign partners to lobby local governments and institutions, (5) provide partners with the resources necessary to lobby effectively, and (6) coordinate these activities on a global basis, while simultaneously lobbying key international organizations. Given the diverse interests of network partners, their often small size, and their geographical and cultural dispersion, successfully accomplishing these tasks seems unlikely in most cases. As a result, most network firms will operate in institutional and regulatory environments that are created by others.

If large firms have an inherent advantage in effectively lobbying national and international institutions – as we would argue – what does this suggest about the future of the network form of organization? Will large (multinational) firms use their influence to shape the international commercial regime to their own advantage, ultimately leading to the 'extinction' of their more flexible rivals? While we would agree that this outcome is possible – particularly since many network firms are involved in the creation of new technologies which severely disrupt the operations of large, integrated firms, two alternatives seem more likely.

The first is that the network becomes a transitional organizational structure appropriate for the early stages of industry competition. During this phase of an industry's life cycle, activities and technologies are poorly defined and common standards and production techniques have not emerged. As a result, the institutional environment is weak or nonexistent. Under these conditions, the flexibility inherent in the network form enables firms to adapt to changing technologies, standards, and regulations, and to substantially reduce the cost of assembling the 'complementary assets' needed to commercialize new products and technologies. These advantages far outweigh the costs of managing the complex relationships among partners. Further, since only a few firms survive the early stages of industry competition – generally those whose products or technologies become widely accepted, the costs of network governance are more than offset by the gains of those fortunate few, and are irrelevant to the casualties. Interestingly, network firms appear to populate the early stages of rapidly evolving, often high-technology industries.

Once standards become widely accepted, however, competition shifts from innovation to production, and cost becomes an increasingly important competitive factor. In addition, as institutional structures begin to take shape, the ability to influence legislation and regulation or gain special subsidies or tax breaks becomes critical. In both cases, the advantages of hierarchical control begin to outweigh the advantages of flexibility and innovation and, over time, successful network firms may metamorphose into traditional integrated firms. A variant on this scenario is that as the survivors of the early stages of industry competition become apparent, large firms may absorb smaller network firms through mergers or acquisitions. Examples of both of these outcomes are widespread.

The second possibility is that large integrated firms and network firms will continue to coexist in largely unrelated worlds, performing vastly different activities and functions. For example, network firms appear well suited for highly complex, rapidly shifting environments, yet face difficulties effectively lobbying national and international institutions. Conversely, large integrated firms may be effective in shaping institutional structures, yet find it difficult to adapt to changing environmental conditions. Consequently, network firms may continue to perform highly complex tasks in small niche markets, while integrated firms continue to perform more clearly defined tasks in large, increasingly global markets. Thus, peaceful coexistence is also possible. In fact, Piore and Sabel (1984) suggest that these two types of organizations have coexisted and in some cases supported each other for some time. Specifically, they note that traditional 'craft' or 'small batch' production – which in some ways resembles the production processes used by network firms – has continued to occur alongside mass production –which is typical of large integrated firms – in many industries since each way of organizing production is appropriate for very different activities. Thus, it is not unreasonable to envision a bifurcated organizational environment in which large, integrated (multinational) firms and smaller, flexible network firms coexist more or less peacefully in a largely unrelated world.

CONCLUSIONS

At this point it is useful to ask what we have learned about network governance and the network firm. Before offering these remarks, it is important to note that the types of organization we have considered here consist of small centres controlling larger peripheral activities through a complex system of non-equity agreements. They are *not* large centres holding hands with other large centres through strategic alliances and joint ventures, nor are they large centres controlling 'networks' of small suppliers through equity and non-equity arrangements as in Rugman and D'Cruz's 'flagship' model. What makes network governance unique – and contradicts traditional organizational theories – is that it coordinates complex activities *without* the use of hierarchical or equity control. Thus, explaining the ability of a network to organize economic activities more efficiently than either the market or the firm becomes a primary objective.

Our analysis suggests that, even under the best of circumstances, network governance will be costly and perhaps inefficient since it involves the management of highly complex relationships that are not easily amenable to contracting. In fact, to the degree that the network firm becomes more contractual or more hierarchical, it may become more efficient, but it also begins to look increasingly like the traditional market or firm, respectively. What makes network governance interesting, is that it employs a 'negotiated' approach to relationship management and dispute resolution. But since these negotiations are costly – and may reduce the flexibility of the firm – some factor must be found which explains why networks can manage these processes effectively and at little cost.

We have followed others in suggesting that 'trust' may be that factor, and have added cultural and institutional characteristics as other possibilities. However, we also recognize the distinct possibility that there is little long-term advantage to network governance, particularly given the widespread acceptance of Anglo-American institutions and cultural assumptions. As a result, the network may ultimately serve as a transitional mechanism or emerge in activities that generate returns high enough to compensate for its inherent costs. Although we do not attempt to resolve this question, we find it curious that at the same time some firms are moving towards the 'dis-integration' of their structures through outsourcing and other cooperative and contractual arrangements, others are continuing to concentrate and consolidate the hierarchical control of their operations around the globe. Interestingly, in both cases advances in technology are driving these trends.

NOTE

1. The authors would like to thank Peter Buckley, Mark Casson, Joseph D'Cruz, J. Colin Dodds, Hamid Etemad, Edward Graham, Bernard Wolf, and the participants of the Halifax Conference on Euro-Pacific Investment and Trade for their constructive comments on an earlier draft of this chapter. We also benefited from discussions with Annalee Saxenian regarding network firms in Silicon Valley. Finally, we wish to thank Alan Rugman and Gavin Boyd for their valuable editorial suggestions, although we must take full responsibility for any errors or omissions.

REFERENCES

Anderson, Erin and Hubert Gatignon (1986), 'Modes of Entry: A Transaction Cost Analysis and Propositions', *Journal of International Business Studies*, **17** (3), Fall, 1–26.
Anderson, Philip and Michael Tushman (1991), 'Managing Through Cycles of Technological Change', *Research Technology Management*, **34** (2), 26–31.
Bakis, Henry (1988), *Enterprise, Espace, Telecommunications: Nouvelles Technologies de l'information et Organisation d'Economique*, Caen, Calvados, France: Paradigme.
Bakker, Hans, Wynford Jones and Michele Nichols (1994), 'Using Core Competencies to Develop New Business', *Long Range Planning*, **27** (6), 13–27.
Bar, François Marie (1990), 'Configuring the Telecommunications Infrastructure for the Computer Age: The Economics of Network Control', Ann Arbor: UMI (Doctoral Thesis).
Blackwell, Richard (1983), 'DP Rises to the Challenge of Electronic Banking', *Canadian Datasystems*, **15** (4), 34–9.
Blaine, Michael (1995), 'Comparative Contractual Governance', in Gavin Boyd (ed.), *Competitive and Cooperative Macromanagement: The Challenge of Structural Interdependence*, Aldershot: Edward Elgar, pp. 67–106.
Bridges, William (1994), *Job Shift: How to Prosper in a Workplace Without Jobs*, Reading, MA: Addison-Wesley Publishing Company.
Buckley, Peter and Mark Casson (1976), *The Future of the Multinational Enterprise*, London: Macmillan.

Business Week (1986), 'The Hollow Corporation', 3 March 57–85.

Castells, Manuel (1989), *The Informational City*, Oxford: Blackwell.

Chandler, Alfred (1962), *Strategy and Structure: Chapters in the History of the Industrial Enterprise*, Cambridge, MA: MIT Press.

Chandler, Alfred (1986), 'The Evolution of Modern Global Competition', in Michael Porter (ed.), *Competition in Global Industries*, Boston: Harvard Business School Press, pp. 405–48.

Chandler, Alfred (1990), *Scale and Scope: The Dynamics of Industrial Capitalism*, Cambridge, MA: Belknap Press of Harvard University Press.

Chandler, Alfred, Stuart Bruchey and Louis Galambos (1968), *The Changing Economic Order: Readings in American Business and Economic History*, New York: Harcourt, Brace & World Inc.

Clemons, Eric K. (1986), 'Information Systems for Sustainable Competitive Advantage', *Information and Management*, **11** (3), 131–6.

Clemons, Eric K. (1988), 'Strategic Necessities', *Computerworld*, **22** (8), 79–80.

Clemons, Eric K. (1991), 'Corporate Strategies for Information Technology: A Resource-Based Approach', *IEEE Computer*, **24** (1), 23–32.

Clemons, Eric K. and Steven Kimbrough (1986), 'Information Systems, Telecommunications and Their Effects on Industrial Organization', *Proceedings: 7th International Conference on Information Systems*, San Diego, pp. 99–108.

Clemons, Eric K. and Michael Row (1988), 'A Strategic Information System: McKesson Drug Company's Economist', *Planning Review*, **16** (5), 14–19.

Coase, R.H. (1937), 'The Nature of the Firm', *Economica*, 386–405.

Contractor, Farok (1990), 'Contractual and Cooperative Forms of International Business', *Management International Review*, **30** (1), 13–54.

Contractor, Farok and Peter Lorange (eds) (1988), *Cooperative Strategies in International Business*, Lexington, MA: Lexington Books.

Davidow, William and Michael Malone (1992), *The Virtual Corporation: Structuring and Revitalizing the Corporation for the 21st Century*, New York: Edward Burlingame Books/Harper Business.

Davis, Stanley and Paul Lawrence (1977), *Matrix*, Reading, MA: Addison-Wesley.

Deans, P.C. and K.R. Karwan (eds) (1994), *Global Information Systems and Technology: Focus on the Organization and Its Functional Areas*, Harrisburg: Idea Group Publishing.

Dunning, John (1977), 'Trade Location of Economic Activity and the MNE: A Search for an Eclectic Approach', in B. Ohlin, P. Hesselborn and P. Wijkman (eds), *The International Allocation of Economic Activity*, London: Macmillan.

Dunning, John (1979), 'Explaining Changing Patterns of International Production: In Defense of the Eclectic Theory', *Oxford Bulletin of Economics and Statistics*, **14** (4), November, 269–95.

Dunning, John (1980), 'Towards an Eclectic Theory of International Production', *Journal of International Business Studies*, **XI** (1), Spring/Summer, 9–31.

Egelhoff, William G. (1991), 'Information-processing Theory and the Multinational Enterprise', *Journal of International Business Studies*, **22** (3), 341–68.

Elg, Ulf and Ulf Johansson (1993), 'The Institutions of Industrial Governance', *International Studies of Management and Organization*, **23** (1), 29–46.

Galbraith, Jay (1973), *Designing Complex Organizations*, Reading, MA: Addison-Wesley.

Ghoshal, Sumantra and Seok Kim (1986), 'Building Effective Intelligence Systems for Competitive Advantage', *Sloan Management Review*, **28** (1), 49–58.

Ghoshal, Sumantra and Nitin Nohria (1993), 'Horses for Courses: Organizational Forms for Multinational Corporations', *Sloan Management Review*, **34** (2), 23–35.

Gilroy, Michael Berhard (1993), *Networking in Multinational Enterprises: The Importance of Strategic Alliances*, Columbia, SC: University of South Carolina Press.

Grabher, Gernot (ed.) (1993), *The Embedded Firm: On the Socioeconomics of Industrial Networks*, London: Routledge.

Hagström, Peter (1991), *The 'Wired' MNC: The Role of Information Systems for Structural Change in Complex Organizations*, Stockholm: Stockholm School of Economics.

Hakansson, Hakan and Jan Johanson (1993), 'The Network as a Governance Structure: Interfirm Cooperation Beyond Markets and Hierarchies', in Gernot Grabher (ed.), *The Embedded Firm: On the Socioeconomics of Industrial Networks*, London: Routledge, pp. 35–51.

Halal, William E. (1994), 'From Hierarchy to Enterprise: Internal Markets are the New Foundation of Management', *Academy of Management Executive*, **VIII** (4), 69–83.

Handy, Charles B. (1994), *The Age of Paradox*, Boston: Harvard Business School Press.

Harasim, Linda M. (ed.), (1993) *Global Networks: Computers and International Communication*, Cambridge, MA: MIT Press.

Harrigan, Kathryn Rudie (1985), *Strategies for Joint Ventures*, Lexington, MA: Lexington Books.

Hennart, Jean-François (1989), 'Can the "New Forms" of Investment Substitute for the "Old Forms"? A Transaction Cost Perspective', *Journal of International Business Studies*, **19** (2), 211–33.

Hill, Charles (1990), 'Cooperation, Opportunism, and the Invisible Hand: Implications for Transaction Cost Theory', *Academy of Management Review*, **15** (3), 500–513.

Hymer, Stephen (1976, original 1960), *The International Operations of National Firms*, Cambridge, MA: MIT Press.

Ives, Blake and Sirkka Jarvenpaa (1991), 'Applications of Global Information Technology: Key Issues for Management, *MIS Quarterly*, **15** (1), 33–49.

Johansson, Jan and Lars-Gunnar Mattsson (1987), 'Interorganizational Relations in Industrial Systems: A Network Approach Compared with the Transaction-Cost Approach', *International Studies in Management and Organization*, **XVII** (1), 34–48.

Junne, Gerd (1988), 'The Emerging Global Grid: The Political Dimension', in George Muskens and Jacob Gruppelaar (eds), *Global Telecommunication Networks: Strategic Considerations*, Dordrecht, Netherlands: Kluwer Academic Publishers, pp. 125–36.

Jussawalla, Meheroo (1987), *The Calculus of International Communications: A Study in the Political Economy of Transborder Data Flows*, Littleton, CO: Libraries Unlimited.

Kesler, Mark, Diana Kolstad and W.E. Clarke (1993), 'Third Generation R&D: The Key to Leveraging Core Competencies', *Columbia Journal of World Business*, **28** (3), 34–44.

Kester, W. Carl (1992), 'Industrial Groups as Systems of Contractual Governance', *Oxford Review of Economic Policy*, **8** (3), 24–44.

Killing, Peter (1983), *Strategies for Joint Venture Success*, New York: Praeger.

Kindleberger, Charles (1968), *International Economics*, Homewood, IL: Richard Irwin, Inc.

Kingdon, D.R. (1973), *Matrix Organization*, London: Tavistock Publications Limited.

Kogut, Bruce (1988), 'Joint Ventures: Theoretical and Empirical Perspectives', *Strategic Management Journal*, **9**, 319–32.

Konsynski, Benn R. (1993), 'Strategic Control in the Extended Enterprise', *IBM Systems Journal*, **32** (1), 111–43.

Kozin, Marc D. and Kevin C. Young (1994), 'Using Acquisitions to Buy and Hone Core Competencies', *Mergers and Acquisitions*, **29** (2), 21–6.

Mariti, P. and R.H. Smiley (1983), 'Co-operative Agreements and the Organization of Industry', *Journal of Industrial Organization*, **XXXI** (4), 437–51.

McFarlan, F. Warren (1984), 'Information Technology Changes the Way You Compete', *Harvard Business Review*, **62** (3), 98–103.

McGee, James Jr. (1991), 'Implementing Systems Across Boundaries: Dynamics of Information Technology and Integration', Ann Arbor: UMI (Doctoral Thesis).

Morris, Deigan and Michael Hergert (1987), 'Trends in International Collaborative Agreements', *Columbia Journal of World Business*, **XXII** (2), 15–21.

Morton, S. Scott (ed.) (1991), *The Corporations of the 1990s: Information Technology and Organizational Transformation*, New York: Oxford University Press.

Mulqueen, John T. (1987), 'Networking Dollars and Sense: ATMs Uniting Nationwide', *Data Communications*, **16** (11), 85–92.

Newman, Katherine (1993), *Declining Fortunes: The Withering of the American Dream*, New York: Basic Books.

Ouchi, William (1980), 'Markets, Bureaucracies, and Clans', *Administrative Science Quarterly*, **25**, 129–41.

Palvia, Shailendra, Prashant Palvia and Ronald Zigli (1992), *The Global Issues of Information Technology Management*, Harrisburg: Idea Group Publishing.

Pfeffer, Jeffrey and Gerald Salancik (1978), *The External Control of Organizations: A Resource Dependency Perspective*, New York: Harper & Row.

Piore, Michael J. and Charles F. Sabel (1984), *The Second Industrial Divide: Possibilities for Prosperity*, New York: Basic Books.

Powell, Walter (1990), 'Neither Market nor Hierarchy: Network Forms of Organization', in Barry Straw and L.L. Cummings (eds), *Research in Organizational Behavior*, Vol. 12, Greenwich, CT: JAI Press Inc., pp. 295–336.

Prahalad, C.K. (1993), 'The Role of Core Competencies in the Corporation', *Research Technology Management*, **36** (6), 40–47.

Rada, J.F. and G.R. Pipe (1984), *Communication Regulation and International Business*, Amsterdam: North-Holland.

Rapoport, Anatol (1985), *General Systems Theory*, Tunbridge Wells, Kent: Abacus Press.

Richardson, G.B. (1972), 'The Organisation of Industry', *Economic Journal*, **82** (327), September, 883–96.

Roach, Stephen (1987), 'America's Productivity Dilemma: A Profile of the Information Economy', Special Economic Study, Morgan Stanley, 22 April.

Roach, Stephen (1988), 'White-Collar Productivity: A Glimmer of Hope', Special Economic Study, Morgan Stanley, 16 September.

Roche, Edward M. (1992), *Managing Information Technology in Multinational Corporations*, New York: Macmillan.

Roche, E.M. (1994), 'International Business Enterprises and Telecommunications: A User Perspective', in E. Bohlin and O. Granstrand (eds), *The Race to European*

Eminence: Who Are the Coming Tele-service Multinationals?, Amsterdam: North-Holland.

Roche, E.M., S.E. Goodman and H.S. Chen (1992), 'The Landscape of International Computing', *Advances in Computers*, **35**, 325–71.

Saxenian, Annalee (1994), *Regional Advantage: Culture and Competition in Silicon Valley and Route 128*, Cambridge, MA: Harvard University Press.

Scott, Allen J. (1993), *Technopolis: High-technology Industry and Regional Development in Southern California*, Berkeley: University of California Press.

Simpson, Dan (1994), 'How to Identify and Enhance Core Competencies', *Planning Review*, **22** (6), 24–6.

Stalk, George Jr. and Thomas M. Hout (1990), 'Competing Against Time: How Time-Based Strategies Give Technological Innovators the Competitive Edge', *Research Technology Management*, **33** (2), 19–25.

Stopford, John and Louis Wells (1972), *Managing the Multinational Enterprise: Organization of the Firm and Ownership of the Subsidiaries*, New York: Basic Books.

Tassey, Gregory (1992), *Technology Infrastructure and Competitive Position*, Norwell: Kluwer Academic Publishers.

Teece, David (1988), 'Capturing Value from Technological Innovation: Integration, Strategic Partnering, and Licensing Decisions', *Interfaces*, **18** (3), 46–61.

Venkatraman, N. and Lawrence Loh (1994), 'The Shifting Logic of the IS Organization: From Technical Portfolio to Relationship Portfolio', *Information Strategy: The Executive's Journal*, **10** (2), 5–11.

Vignault, Walter (1987), *Worldwide Telecommunications Guide for the Business Manager*, New York: John Wiley & Sons.

Wallenstein, Gerd (1990), *Setting Global Telecommunication Standards: The Stakes, the Players and The Process*, Norwood: Artech House, Inc.

White, George Jr. (1979), 'Electronic Banking and Its Impact on the Future', *Magazine of Bank Administration*, **55** (12), 39–42.

Williamson, Oliver (1975), *Markets and Hierarchies: Analysis and Antitrust Implications*, New York: The Free Press.

Williamson, Oliver (1979), 'Transaction-Cost Economics: The Governance of Contractual Relations', *Journal of Law and Economics*, **22**, 223–61.

Williamson, Oliver (1985), *The Economic Institutions of Capitalism*, New York: The Free Press.

Wiseman, Charles (1988), *Strategic Information Systems*, Homewood, IL: Irwin.

5. Corporate culture in Europe, Asia and North America

Mark Casson, Ray Loveridge and Satwinder Singh[1]

INTRODUCTION

The growth of Asia–Pacific trade to rival North Atlantic trade and European trade has encouraged the view – particularly in the United States – that the world economy has evolved into a Triad, comprising three great trading blocs, centred in North America, Europe and South-East Asia (Ohmae, 1985). Each of these trading blocs has one or more leading industrial economies. A distinctive feature of these economies, according to Whitley (1992), is the 'national business system'. Evolutionary and institutional economists such as Nelson (1993) and Lundvall (1992) represent these systems as having greater or lesser adaptive capability and therefore entitle them 'national innovation systems'. Porter (1990) regards the 'national competitive advantages' of these systems as stemming from relatively tangible factors such as the competitiveness of local markets for new products. By contrast those writers who stress advantages derived from inter-firm cooperation rather than competition often see softer and less tangible factors, such as business culture, as crucial. Dore (1973), Chandler (1990) and Lodge and Vogel (1987) argue that industrializing elites within the newly industrializing countries (NICs), like the elite of the archetypal 'late developer', Germany, deliberately retained traditional aspects of their social structure to reinforce 'cooperative capitalism' or 'communitarianism'. They contrast this legacy with the socially fragmenting individualism that they associate with the Anglo-Saxon ideology of capitalism.

It might be conjectured that the business cultures of the leading countries in each of the Triad blocs will be reflected in the organizational structures and business strategies of their leading firms. An important rationale for outward direct investment from these countries appears to be the transfer of superior corporate culture overseas (Casson, 1995, p. 271). The competitive advantage of leading firms may derive more from their culture than from their technology – particularly in the 1990s, which Dunning (1995) has dubbed the era of 'alliance capitalism'. Human resource management (HRM) is an obvious area of business strategy in which cultural factors might prove especially influential (Brewster and Tyson, 1992).

The object of this chapter is to report the results of a recent empirical investigation into the HRM practices of leading firms from a number of major economies, and to consider how far domestic business culture is reflected in the firm's overseas operations. The methodology also makes it possible to consider the contribution of host-country culture to the HRM practices of affiliates.

Discussion of global trends in foreign direct investment in terms of Triad interactions naturally raises the question of how far there is homogeneity within each Triad group so far as HRM practices are concerned. Any suggestion of such homogeneity is firmly rejected by the evidence reported here. Even in North America, there are distinctive differences between US and Canadian firms. Within Europe, UK firms are in many respects more similar to their US counterparts than they are to French and German firms. Japanese firms are strikingly similar to US firms in some respects, although many of the obvious differences remain. Within Asia itself, Japanese, Taiwanese and Indian firms all operate in different ways. If there is a sound generalization to be made, it involves the distinction between the mature industrial countries (MICs) on the one hand and the newly industrializing countries (NICs) on the other. The NICs are far more traditional in their cultural values. Their corporate values resemble those which prevailed in Europe and North America in the 1950s and 1960s. Job security, career progression and a congruence between corporate and national goals are more typical of the NICs than of the MICs. The differences are particularly striking *vis-à-vis* the Anglo-Saxon world (the UK and the USA, and to some extent, Canada and Sweden too) where there appears to have been significant cultural change over the last twenty years.

The results suggest that the survival of traditional values is indeed a major source of strength. They suggest, furthermore, that some large Anglo-Saxon firms are entering into a period of organizational crisis as a result of the mismanagement of corporate culture over the last decade. The problem has not been that Anglo-Saxon firms in general have lacked an entrepreneurial culture. While many of them did indeed become bureaucratic in the 1960s and 1970s, and needed to strengthen their entrepreneurial culture, it would in many cases have been possible to build upon the core of entrepreneurial culture that was already present. Instead many firms swept away what they already had and misguidedly adopted a highly competitive and individualistic concept of culture recommended by management gurus. Many firms have fallen prey to the intellectually vacuous prescriptions of the strategic HRM movement (see, for example, some of the contributions to Blyton and Turnbull, 1992). In 'delayering' their firms and 'empowering' their employees, they have demotivated many of their employees by reneging on implicit contracts regarding promotion and job security. Indeed, some firms appear to have been delayered to the point where they are no longer organizationally viable – there are simply too few people left to process all the information that is required for correct decision-making (Casson, 1994).

These conclusions need to be interpreted with caution, of course. They are not intended to be taken uncritically as an alternative set of generalizations with which to sweep away earlier views. Rather, they are intended as an antidote to the excesses of the strategic HRM literature itself, and as a sidelight on some of the organizational changes that have accompanied the liberalization of trade. There is, indeed, a close connection between the emergence of competitive global markets on the one hand and recent changes in corporate cultures on the other, as this chapter makes clear. The liberalization of trade has created a more turbulent competitive environment for most multinationals. Multinationals based in MICs have faced particular problems because of high wages and relatively low productivity growth in their home countries. By changing their culture to achieve greater flexibility, however, they may have sacrificed long-run growth prospects for short-run survival. The long-term perspective, which underpins the traditional values noted earlier, is increasingly the prerogative of the more dynamic NICs, although some non-Anglo-Saxon MICs have managed to retain it too. The study reported in this chapter is simply a snapshot of a process of rapid change, and it is inevitably a matter of conjecture as to where this process will ultimately lead. For the Anglo-Saxon world, however, the omens are not good.

THE SURVEY AND ITS METHODOLOGY

The survey has been described in detail elsewhere (Casson, Loveridge and Singh, 1996) and only a brief account of it will be given here. The study, based on a sample of Fortune 500 firms, involved both questionnaires and interviews, and covered both parent firms and their overseas affiliates. The original intention was to focus on ten countries, chosen to generate a reasonable geographical and cultural mix. Because of the wave of mergers and acquisitions which occurred in the late 1980s and early 1990s, however, many of the affiliates that we contacted had recently changed ownership, either through individual divestment and acquisition, or as part of a comprehensive takeover of their parent firm. At the finish, 13 parent countries (in which firms were headquartered) were represented in the study, together with 12 host countries in which they operated. Some countries, such as France, are represented only as parents, while other countries, such as Brazil, are represented only as host countries because they have not yet developed many major multinationals of their own.

Some 200 affiliates and 56 parents responded to our postal questionnaire, and a total of 47 firms were subsequently interviewed including, for control purposes, some of the non-respondents. The non-respondents were mainly the smaller firms, and the chief reason for their non-response was that they felt intimidated by some of the questions and were suspicious as to how our random sampling technique had singled them out. This in turn reflects the fact that we addressed the questionnaire to Personnel Directors rather than to Chief Executives and that, contrary to what is said in the strategic HRM literature, it is only in the very largest firm that the Personnel Officer has any sort of strategic role. The overall response rate of 17 per cent is indicative of the additional problems created by the process of delayering that many firms were going through at the time of the study. Many Personnel Directors were affected by the demoralizing experiences of their employees, and were under additional stress because delayering was being applied to the Personnel Office too.

A separate questionnaire was supplied to parents and to affiliates, though there was considerable commonality between the two to allow the responses of parents and their affiliates to be compared.

The most interesting results are those obtained from the affiliates, because it is at the affiliate level that the interaction between the parent-firm culture and the host-country culture occurs, and so it is the affiliate responses that are emphasized here.

Both questionnaires were in five parts. The first part inquired about the objectives of the company and its principal strategies. Responses to this part were used to interpret the responses to the other parts, in a manner described below. The second part asked about how the HRM function was organized and what the principal responsibilities of the Personnel Director were. The third part concerned policies for the recruitment, training and retention of staff. The last two parts addressed the issues which form the focus of this chapter: the system of incentives and rewards and the role of corporate culture.

The modern economic theory of the firm (Milgrom and Roberts, 1992) has quite a lot to say about the design of incentive systems, including the way that non-pecuniary incentives can be reinforced using corporate culture (Casson, 1991a). The functionalist perspective adopted by this literature suggests that incentive systems and corporate culture will adapt themselves to the requirements of the industry in which the firm operates. For example, industries that depend heavily on major innovations with long-term paybacks, such as the aircraft industry, are unlikely to favour incentive pay schemes which reward only short-run performance. Conversely, industries that depend on driving down costs through sustained hard work, such as the metals industries, are much more likely to favour such schemes, and to invest much less in the professional reputation mechanisms appropriate to industries with very long-term horizons.

The objectives and strategies of the firm are also likely to influence its use of pecuniary incentives and corporate culture. In order to capture the influence of nationality on the behaviour of the firm, therefore, it is necessary to take account of not only industry-specific factors, but also firm-specific factors such as objectives and strategies. The basic statistical methodology is therefore to analyse the responses to questions on incentive systems and corporate culture by regressing these responses on the industry in which the affiliate is involved, and on its objectives and strategy, as well as on the parent country, and the host country in which it is based.

The roles of industries and countries are captured using dummy variables. In constructing these dummy variables the paper industry is used as the control industry, while the USA is used as the control for both the parent country and the host country. The paper industry was chosen because it is a relatively homogeneous industry with a medium level of technological sophistication and one for which a reasonable number of responses is available. Some writers prefer to use 'other manufacturing' as the control industry, but the drawback to this is that because the industry is so heterogeneous it is difficult to know exactly what is being compared with what when the regression coefficients for industry dummy variables are being interpreted.

Finally it is evident from the responses to the questions about organization of HRM that the size of the affiliate is an important factor, and to allow for this factor the size of the affiliate has been incorporated as an explanatory variable in all the regressions. The results are not reported here, however, because they are the subject of a separate paper. All the regressions were estimated by ordinary least squares and, where appropriate, by tobit and logit regressions. As previous experience has shown, however, the different methods make hardly any difference to the results and so, on the grounds of their simplicity and robustness, only the OLS results are reported here.

To illustrate how this methodology works in practice, a typical set of results is reported in Table 5.1. The five main categories of variable – industry, parent country, host country, firm-specific objectives and firm-specific strategies – are listed down the left-hand side. As already indicated, the results on the sixth category – size of firm – have been suppressed. Two separate ·regressions are shown for purposes of comparison. The first analyses the responses to a question about job security while the second analyses views on career prospects. This idea of presenting results on related issues together in the same table is extremely useful. It demonstrates the congruence between the answers to related questions and thereby provides reassurance that the responses are meaningful ones. At the same time it highlights anomalies that require explanation.

For each regression two columns of figures are shown. The left-hand column shows the estimated coefficient. The important thing here is whether the sign is positive or negative – to interpret the magnitude it is important to refer to the scale on which the dependent variable is measured, as described in the footnote to the table. In the case of Table 4.1, both dependent variables are measured on a five-point Likert scale. Looking at the magnitude of the coefficients in this light, it can be seen that many of them are quite sizeable. Magnitude does not guarantee statistical significance, however, as the right-hand columns made clear. These columns report the significance level associated with the coefficients, indicating by an asterisk those cases where significance is greater than 10 per cent. The overall significance of the various groups of dummy variables is indicated at the bottom of the table by the F-statistics, but the statistic is reported only in those cases where the significance is 10 per cent or more. The overall significance of the entire regression is also shown, together with the number of responses to the particular question involved. Because not all respondents answered all questions, this number is normally less than the two hundred who replied altogether.

The results in Table 5.1 give the first intimations of the scenario set out in the introduction. Japanese-owned affiliates regard job security as far more significant for their managerial employees than do US-owned affiliates. Japanese foreign investors, it seems, export to their affiliates the emphasis on job security that is indigenous to Japan. In Japan itself, foreign-owned affiliates also report that job security is important to their employees, reinforcing the view that this is still an important component of the employment relation in Japan. But Japan is not the only host country where job security is emphasized. The NICs – Brazil, India and Taiwan – all rate it as important, as does Italy.

It might be thought that the responses to the second question – on career prospects – would be similar to the first, in the sense that companies that rate job security highly would also emphasize career progression. This is not the case. For a start, the expectation itself is culturally specific, reflecting an individualistic view that no manager would wish to stay with a company unless he or she expected to be promoted. This view may not prevail in more 'organic' societies (Casson, 1993). Despite the emphasis on job security in Japan, for example, the results show that Japanese-owned firms accord career prospects less weight that their US counterparts (though not significantly so). Thus the job security of the 'window watcher' may be valued in a Japanese-owned firm, even though job security of this kind could be considered humiliating in a US-owned firm.

Table 5.1 Responses to the questions 'How important are the social and psychological benefits of job security to a manager working for your company?' and 'How important are better career prospects than other firms in the same industry in retaining key staff?'

	Job security		Career prospects	
Explanatory variable	**Coefficient**	**Significance**	**Coefficient**	**Significance**
Industry				
Aircraft and electrical engineering	+0.12	0.79	−0.46	0.31
Chemicals	+0.78	0.09*	−0.36	0.44
Coal and petroleum	+0.24	0.65	−0.25	0.64
Food, drink and tobacco	+0.56	0.25	−0.48	0.33
Mechanical engineering	+0.46	0.36	−0.23	0.66
Non-metals	+0.46	0.40	−0.36	0.53
Office equipment	+0.28	0.62	−0.05	0.94
Pharmaceuticals	+0.67	0.17	+0.01	0.99
Other manufacturing	+0.69	0.19	+0.10	0.85
Metals	+0.65	0.19	−0.10	0.84
Motor vehicles	+0.81	0.12	−0.06	0.91
Parent country				
Japan	+0.65	0.05*	−0.03	0.92
Canada	−0.67	0.25	+1.00	0.09*
UK	−0.24	0.40	−0.61	0.04*
Germany	+0.28	0.36	+0.02	0.95
Sweden	+0.06	0.89	+0.66	0.16
Finland	−0.60	0.32	+1.02	0.10*
France	+0.75	0.20	+1.13	0.06*
Switzerland	−0.30	0.54	+0.43	0.39
Netherlands	−0.09	0.85	+0.85	0.08*
Other Europe	+0.06	0.90	−0.54	0.26
Host country				
Brazil	+1.44	0.00*	+0.60	0.09*
India	+1.00	0.04*	+0.71	0.14
Japan	+1.18	0.01*	+0.16	0.72
Taiwan	+1.39	0.01*	+0.59	0.27
Canada	+0.28	0.42	+0.24	0.51
UK	+0.29	0.36	+0.49	0.13
Germany	+0.57	0.15	+0.36	0.38
Switzerland	−0.23	0.67	+1.13	0.04*

Table 5.1   continued

Explanatory variable	Job security		Career prospects	
	Coefficient	Significance	Coefficient	Significance
Italy	+0.79	0.04*	+0.70	0.07*
Other Europe	+0.57	0.56	−0.96	0.34
Objectives				
Growth of total sales	−0.08	0.51	−0.03	0.83
Growth of market share	−0.00	0.99	+0.04	0.74
Profitability	+0.11	0.37	+0.09	0.45
Maximize share price	+0.04	0.62	+0.03	0.73
Company reputation	−0.29	0.02*	+0.15	0.24
Communal well-being	−0.01	0.91	+0.31	0.00*
Strategies				
Product innovation	−0.02	−0.86	+0.01	0.92
Investment in traditional products	+0.25	0.02*	−0.01	0.96
Basic research	+0.10	0.20	+0.03	0.67
Relations with customers and suppliers	+0.57	0.00*	+0.19	0.28
Sophisticated advertising	+0.01	0.87	−0.04	0.64
Competitive prices	+0.00	0.96	−0.08	0.38
Aggressive acquisitions	−0.12	0.19	+0.02	0.84
Joint ventures and cooperation	+0.06	0.50	+0.08	0.41
Size of firm	−0.35	0.01*	+0.08	0.57
Intercept	+0.61	0.58	+0.35	0.76
Mean	+3.44		+3.90	
R^2	0.47		0.48	
F industry	0.71	0.73	0.47	0.92
F parent	1.14	0.34	2.44	0.01*
F host	3.08	0.10	1.20	0.30
F overall	1.98	0.00*	1.97	0.00*
Number of responses	148		146	

Notes: Size of firm is measured by the logarithm of employment in the affiliate. The control industry is paper. The control country is the United States. Responses to both questions are on a scale from 1 (not important) to 5 (very important).
*   Significance greater than 10 per cent.

In general, the attitude to career progression seems to reflect not only indigenous attitudes but also the degree of long-termism in the parent firm, as reflected in its confidence in the future and in its sense of commitment to communal well-being. It is interesting to note that UK-owned firms consider career prospects even less important than US-owned firms, while Canadian firms consider them much more important. Career prospects are also important in French and Dutch firms. One interpretation of this is that UK- and US-owned firms have pursued delayering and 'empowerment' much further than others and can therefore no longer offer career progression of the traditional kind. If this interpretation is correct then it suggests that Canadian, French and Dutch firms have stuck more to the traditional hierarchical view of the firm. This could reflect greater confidence in the firm's long-term growth – greater confidence means that delayering is considered unnecessary, or at any rate is not pursued as far, and so career prospects remain intact.

Job security, but not career progression, is emphasized by firms which invest in traditional products and make special efforts to maintain good relations with customers and suppliers. These strategies are typical of firms producing industrial products, often as subcontractors to other large firms. The emphasis on managerial job security almost certainly reflects the importance to the firm of the manager building long-term personal relationships with his 'opposite numbers' in other firms. By keeping the same employee in the same job for a considerable time, job security is emphasized at the expense of career progression.

BUSINESS OBJECTIVES AND BUSINESS STRATEGY: ARE THEY COUNTRY SPECIFIC?

Business Objectives

It is widely held that Japanese firms are less concerned with short-term measures of financial performance than their US counterparts. It is also alleged that German firms are fairly traditional in their outlook, emphasizing straightforward measures of profitability and growth computed from routine accounting information. Both of these stereotypes are supported by the evidence in Table 5.2. Both Japanese-owned affiliates and foreign firms operating in Japan attach less weight to current profitability than do their US counterparts. German-owned firms are less likely to emphasize objectives that are difficult to measure, such as reputation or contribution to communal well-being. Like the Japanese, the Swedes and the Finns, German-owned firms also report less concern with the share price than their US counterparts. A simple explanation of this is that all these countries have a strong tradition

Table 5.2 Responses to the question 'What are the main business objectives of the company?' (scale 1–5)

Objective	Mean	Standard deviation	Industry	Country Parent	Country Host	R^2	N
Profitability (post-tax) rate of return on assets	4.52	0.78		− Japan (0.00) − Finland (0.05)	− Japan (0.00) − Italy (0.01)	0.29	172
Growth of total sales	4.35	0.75		+ Canada (0.08) + Finland (0.03)		0.19	172
Growth of market share	4.19	0.87	− Coal and petroleum (0.07) − Non-metals (0.07)	− Switzerland (0.06)		0.25	171
Maintain or improve reputation within the industry	4.03	0.99		− Germany (0.02) − Sweden (0.05)	+ Germany (0.01) + Italy (0.05)	0.30	168
Contribute to communal well-being	3.33	1.14		− Germany (0.05) − Sweden (0.02)	+ Brazil (0.07)	0.26	167
Maximize the share price	3.06	1.39		− Japan (0.05) − Germany (0.00) − Sweden (0.05) − Finland (0.01)	+ Brazil (0.04) + Canada (0.02) + Germany (0.06) + Other Europe (0.04)	0.35	161

Note: The regressions control for the affiliate's size, as measured by the number of employees (in logarithms). Control industry is other manufacturing. Control country is the United States.

of industrial banking and, until recently, had relatively underdeveloped equity markets.

There is another stereotype that does not fare so well at the hands of the data, though. Swedish-owned firms do not appear to be as concerned with reputation and communal well-being as might be expected; they seem, like their German counterparts, to be more concerned with the measurable aspects of their business. Part of this may be explained by the relative importance in the sample of one particular Swedish multinational (which cannot be named for reasons of confidentiality) which places considerable emphasis on the installation of sophisticated financial control systems in its newly-acquired affiliates. Another part of the explanation, however, is that unquantifiable criteria such as communal well-being mean different things in different cultures, as will be shown later (Brewster, Holden and Lundmark, 1993).

The influence of the host country on business objectives is even less clear cut. This is hardly surprising, since the parent's influence would be expected to dominate on an issue of this kind. Foreign investors in Italy appear to rate reputation more highly, and profitability less highly, than foreign investors in the USA. This could represent a foreign investor's view of how the business system works in Italy, but this is only a speculation. More intriguing still is that foreign investors in Germany and Brazil rate both long-term unquantifiable criteria – reputation and contribution to well-being – and short-term financial criteria – maximizing the share price – relatively high. One explanation could be that Germany and Brazil are, for different reasons, very tough environments in which to operate, but very profitable for really strong firms. They therefore attract a distinctive type of foreign investor which is able to reconcile short-term and long-term objectives in a way that ordinary firms cannot.

Business Strategy

Industry factors have a negligible influence on business objectives but, as might be expected, they are more important in the choice of business strategy. Their impact is fairly predictable, however. Table 5.3 shows that mature industries like food, mechanical engineering and metals emphasize investment in traditional products. Joint ventures and acquisitions are important in high-technology industries with large and expensive R&D projects – aircraft, chemicals and pharmaceuticals, for example. The parent country has much less influence on strategy. German firms place less emphasis on joint ventures and collaboration than others. Swedish firms (and one in particular) emphasize aggressive acquisitions. But the most interesting results are to be found by comparing the role of a country as a parent and as a host.

It is often alleged that the UK is good at invention but poor at innovation, and the results provide strong support for this view. UK-owned parents are less

Table 5.3 Responses to the question 'What are the major business strategies employed by your company?' (scale 1–5)

Strategy	Mean	Standard deviation	Industry	Country Parent	Country Host	R^2	N
Good long-term relations with major customers and suppliers	4.52	0.67		− France (0.02)	+ Japan (0.02) + Italy (0.01)	0.27	172
Continuous innovation of new and improved products	4.30	0.86		− UK (0.10) − Other Europe (0.05)	+ Taiwan (0.07)	0.20	173
Continued investment in traditional products	3.44	0.99	+ Food (0.01) + Mechanical engineering (0.07) + Metals (0.03) − Office equipment (0.08)		− Germany (0.09)	0.26	171
Strategic commitment to basic research	3.26	1.23			+ UK (0.09)	0.17	169
Selling standardized products at highly competitive prices	3.22	1.21				0.18	169
Sophisticated advertising and promotion	2.99	1.16	− Mechanical engineering (0.04)		− UK (0.02) − Sweden (0.03)	0.26	172
Strategic use of joint ventures and cooperative arrangements	2.86	1.21	+ Aircraft and electrical engineering (0.02) + Chemicals (0.07) + Coal and petroleum (0.02) $F=0.05$	− Germany (0.09)	− Italy (0.06)	0.27	170
Aggressive acquisitions policy	2.34	1.21	+ Chemicals (0.02) + Mechanical engineering (0.04) + Pharmaceuticals (0.09)	+ Sweden (0.01)	+ Germany (0.07) + Sweden (0.09)	0.27	168

Note: The regressions control for the affiliate's size, as measured by the number of employees (in logarithms). Control industry is paper. Control country is the United States.

likely than other parents to be committed to the continuous innovation of new and improved products. On the other hand, foreign investors in the UK reveal a strong commitment to basic research. This corroborates the results of a previous study (Casson, 1991a) which found that foreign firms were attracted to the UK by the strength of its university science base – particularly in biochemistry – but that UK firms lacked the skills to manage the product development process properly. Firms with larger, more competitive and more sophisticated home markets – in the USA. Germany and Japan – tended to have these skills instead, and to use their UK affiliates to channel basic science to them.

So far as Sweden is concerned, considerable rationalization of ownership is going on, with Swedish firms making acquisitions and being acquired as well. A relatively high proportion of acquisitions involve German firms, and firms in the mechanical engineering industry. The overall impression is one of Swedish and German engineering firms restructuring though acquisition to maintain their competitive strengths within the widening borders of the European Union.

Turning finally to business strategies in host countries, it is worth noting that foreign firms operating in Italy and Japan emphasize the importance of good long-term relations with customers and suppliers. This appears to be a fairly straightforward case of adaptation to culture-specific norms in those countries. More striking is the importance of continuous innovation to foreign investors in Taiwan. Taiwan's flexible and sophisticated subcontracting system, backed by its highly skilled workforce, is clearly attracting a distinctive and potentially very desirable type of foreign investor.

Further Light on Business Objectives

A more detailed analysis of business objectives is provided in Tables 5.4 and 5.5. Rather than asking respondents simply to rate the importance of different objectives, the respondents are here presented with a dilemma, and asked to rate the priority given to different interest groups in the resolution of a conflict. The results are broadly similar to those obtained earlier, but they reveal two important nuances which have been overlooked so far.

Table 5.4 shows the importance attached to the interests of customers and suppliers (mean value 4.08). This corroborates the dominance of good relations with customers and suppliers indicated in Table 5.3 (mean value 4.52). The direct connection between the two is confirmed by the regressions results reported in Table 5.5. Giving priority to customers and suppliers connects with mainstream objectives such as profitability and growth of sales. It is important in achieving price competitiveness as a subcontractor, and in maintaining joint ventures and collaborative arrangements on which long-term sales prospects will depend.

Table 5.4   *Means and standard deviations of responses to the question 'When top management faces an issue where the interests of different groups may conflict, what priority is given to the interests of the following groups?' (scale 1–5)*

Group	Mean	Standard deviation
Firm's major customers and suppliers	4.08	0.92
Equity shareholders	3.71	1.28
Employees	3.64	0.91
Local community in which the firm is based	2.97	1.10
National interests of the country in which the firm is based	2.62	1.15

Note: Number of responses 182.

Equity shareholders come second in the list of priorities (mean value 3.71). The regression results show that this priority is very closely tied to the objective of maximizing the share price – a result which provides some reassurance about the consistency with which questionnaires were filled in.

It is interesting, though, to note that the interests of shareholders represented here receive far more priority than does the maximization of the share price, as reported earlier, suggesting that our respondents did not share the neo-classical economist's narrow view of where the interests of shareholders lie. It is possible that the respondents were thinking of the interests of loyal shareholders, committed to the firm on a long-term basis, rather than those shareholders interested simply in short-term capital gains.

Firms engaged in joint ventures also give priority to equity shareholders – presumably because they provide the risk capital to fund the firm's equity stakes. The share-price objective and the joint-venture strategy are also correlated with the mergers and acquisitions strategy, but in this particular regression mergers and acquisitions does not emerge as significant in its own right because of multicollinearity.

Employees are the last of the three main groups which receive a significant degree of priority (mean value 3.64). Not surprisingly, companies which value their reputation accord high priority to employee interests. In the light of the coefficient on company reputation in Table 5.1, however, it would be a mistake to identify employee interests with job security. It is more appropriate to relate it to long-term career prospects associated with a steady growth of sales. Firms involved in joint ventures take their employees seriously. This

Table 5.5 Regression analysis of responses to the question 'When top management faces an issue where the interests of different groups may conflict, what priority is given to the interests of the following groups?'

Group	Objectives and strategy	Industry	Country		R^2
			Parent	Host	
Firm's major customers and suppliers	+ Growth of total sales (0.00) + Profitability (0.01) – Communal well-being (0.03) – Investment in traditional products (0.04) – Relations with customers and suppliers (0.00) – Sophisticated advertising and promotion (0.01) + Competitive prices (0.09) + Joint ventures and cooperation (0.07)	– Aircraft and electrical engineering (0.05) – Coal and petroleum products (0.09) – Non-metals (0.09) – Office equipment (0.04)	– Sweden (0.07)		0.50
Equity shareholders	+ Maximize share price (0.01) + Joint ventures and cooperation (0.07)	– Aircraft and electrical engineering (0.02) – Chemicals (0.02) – Coal and petroleum (0.05) – Non-metals (0.05) – Pharmaceuticals (0.03)	– Sweden (0.08)	Japan (0.01) Canada (0.03) Italy (0.05)	0.48

Employees	+ Growth of total sales (0.06) + Company reputation (0.05) – Investment in traditional products (0.01) + Joint ventures and cooperation (0.01)	– Non-metals (0.09) – Office equipment (0.04)		0.43
Local community	+ Communal well-being (0.01) + Relations with customers and suppliers (0.05)	– Metals (0.03) – Office equipment (0.08)	+ Sweden (0.07)	0.47
National interests	+ Communal well-being (0.00)	– Aircraft and electrical engineering (0.09) – Chemicals (0.01) – Coal and petroleum (0.01) – Office equipment (0.03)	– Germany (0.01)	+ Brazil (0.00) + India (0.02) + Japan (0.03) + Taiwan (0.00) + Canada (0.02)	0.34

Note: The regressions control for the affiliate's size, as measured by the number of employees (in logarithms). The control country is the United States. Respondents were also asked priority given to the interests of the management team, but the results were very similar to those for employees as a whole. In the interests of space, only the latter are reported here. Number of usable responses 146.

agrees with the point made earlier, that joint-venture success depends on employees cultivating relationships as individuals which are valuable to the firm as a whole.

The low priority accorded to the local community and to national interests accords with the relatively low mean values for the business objective of communal well-being reported in Table 5.2. The correlation between these priorities and the relevant business objective is very high. What is interesting, though, is the way that Swedish parents, which before appeared to weight financial objectives very highly, now appear to favour the local community instead. What this shows is that while Swedish-owned firms attach little weight to rather vague objectives like communal well-being, they attach considerable weight to more tangible and focused objectives such as the interests of the local community. The Swedes, in other words, appear to have a very specific idea of what communal well-being means, which is different from that of any other country in our study.

It was noted earlier that the Germans, like the Swedes, favour quantifiable performance measures so far as business objectives are concerned. The Germans differ from the Swedes, however, in that when they take social factors into account, they tend to think in national rather than local terms. More specifically, German-owned foreign affiliates are more likely to align their affiliates' interests with those of the host-country government than with those of the local community in which they are based because for them communal well-being has a national rather than a local connotation.

Perhaps the most notable feature of Table 5.5, though, is the relative prominence accorded to host-country national interests in NICs such as Brazil, India and Taiwan. The natural interpretation of this is that Personnel Directors working for foreign firms in these countries see the firms that they work for as being important instruments of national economic development. This is a perspective which, it appears, would be seen as most natural by headquarters in German-owned firms.

It is interesting to note that Japan and Canada also have nationalistic affiliates. This is not unexpected in the case of Japan, but quite remarkable in the case of Canada. The explanation may lie in the predominance of US investment in Canada and the 'branch plant syndrome' of being vulnerable to an economically powerful neighbour; the nationalist factor may represent the ambition of the Canadian affiliate to maintain its cultural identity in spite of this.

THE ORGANIZATION OF THE FIRM

This leads on naturally to a discussion of headquarters–subsidiary relations. This is an area where national culture is seen, quite rightly, as an important factor. Table 5.6 shows that for most firms there is a simple strategic–tactical division of labour between headquarters and subsidiaries. This traditional hierarchical view of the multinational firm is particularly favoured in Brazilian affiliates. Subsequent results will reinforce the view that Brazil is a country in which a rather old-fashioned system of corporate values seems to persist – a set of values forged from US corporate attitudes of the 1960s and 1970s, combined with indigenous nationalism. As indicated at the outset, however, there is no reason to believe that this is a source of weakness in the economy – indeed, quite the opposite.

Anglo-Saxon culture has a reputation for individualistic attitudes, and in the corporate sector these seem to be the most apparent in UK-based firms. Compared to their US counterparts, managers of UK affiliates do not regard receiving instructions from headquarters as an important part of their job. Respect for central authority seems to be rather weak in UK-based firms.

The Dutch favour a consultative style of management in the firms they run. This style is also favoured in the food industry, in which Dutch multinationals are strongly represented. The Dutch are also happy to give their affiliates a high degree of autonomy – they much prefer their affiliates to develop strategies of their own than to lay down the strategies at headquarters. The fact that German multinationals also allow their affiliates considerable autonomy comes as something of a surprise, however, but with an important *caveat* suggested by the interviews reported later – that if the affiliate keeps to budget then the German headquarters keeps away, but that if there is a problem then a comprehensive audit will be initiated without delay.

Given the importance of culture in headquarters–subsidiary relations, it comes as quite a surprise to find that culture is not particularly important in the HRM function itself. More precisely, the ownership of the firm has little impact on how the HRM role is performed. The host country certainly does have an influence, but this is mediated by the legislative framework. Local culture impacts upon industrial relations and on labour law, and this in turn impacts upon the firm.

The parent country has little influence on the HRM function, it would seem, for two main reasons. The first is that there is a fairly standard professional view of what HRM involves among the leading firms. Much of this is reflected in Table 5.7, where six main factors achieve substantial weighting in terms of strategic significance – advising in organizational design, monitoring and assessing employee performance, planning careers paths for management development, organizing training programmes, job evaluation and en-

Table 5.6 Responses to the question 'What best describes headquarters–subsidiary relations?' (scale 0/1)

	Mean	Industry	Country		R^2	N
			Parent	Host		
Headquarters determines long-term strategy and subsidiaries determine short-term tactics within this framework	0.51		− Netherlands (0.03)	+ Brazil (0.06)	0.16	173
Headquarters gives instructions to subsidiaries and subsidiaries report regularly to headquarters	0.21			− UK (0.07)	0.21	173
Headquarters coordinates a network of subsidiaries as a 'first among equals'	0.17	+ Food (0.07)	+ Netherlands (0.06)		0.17	173
Subsidiaries decide for themselves how much support they need from headquarters	0.11		+ Germany (0.04) + Netherlands (0.03)			

Note: The regressions control for the affiliate's size, as measured by the number of employees (in logarithms). Control industry is paper. Control country is the United States.

Table 5.7   Means and standard deviations of the responses to 'What activities of the Personnel Director are of greatest significance to the company?' (scale 1–5)

Activity	Mean	Standard deviation
Advising on organizational design	3.77	1.12
Monitoring and assessing employee performance	3.66	1.05
Planning career paths for management development	3.57	1.17
Organizing training programmes	3.43	1.00
Job evaluation	3.37	1.13
Ensuring compliance with equal opportunities legislation	3.34	1.16
Industrial relations and wage bargaining	3.12	1.41
Counselling employees under stress	2.82	1.12
Head-hunting	2.30	1.26
Psychometric testing	1.76	1.01

Note: Number of responses 192. The statistics reported here are slightly different from those reported in Casson, Loveridge and Singh (1996) because of the inclusion of additional data from late respondents.

suring compliance with equal opportunities legislation. The second reason is that, despite the impression of strategic significance given in the recent academic literature, much of the HRM function that we observed through interviews was of a very mundane and mechanistic kind. Many Personnel Directors did not appear to have either the influence within the organization, or the personal capability, to contribute much to strategic thinking. It is, therefore, a mistake to think that differences in the HRM function hold the key to differences in corporate strategy. Whatever strategy a firm follows, there are certain basic HRM functions that need to be performed. Other functions may be performed as well, according to the strategy being followed, but these are not a consequence of strategic HRM thinking itself.

Table 5.8 shows that the overall weight given to the six main factors depends mainly on whether contribution to communal well-being is regarded as an important objective of the firm. Many respondents appear to regard good personnel practice as an aspect of corporate social responsibility. This concern is largely unrelated to other strategic concerns, confirming the view

Table 5.8 Regression analysis of responses to the question 'What activities of the Personnel Director are of greatest significance to the company?'

Activity	Objectives and strategy	Industry	Country		R^2
			Parent	Host	
Advising on organizational design					0.41
Monitoring and assessing employee performance	+ Communal well-being (0.06) + Growth of total sales (0.06)	+ Aircraft and electrical engineering (0.04) + Food (0.04) + Metals (0.02) + Mechanical engineering (0.07) + Motor vehicles (0.03) + Non-metals (0.05) + Pharmaceuticals (0.03) + Other manufacturing (0.03)			0.36
Planning career paths	+ Communal well-being (0.02) + Joint ventures and cooperation (0.07)				0.49
Organizing training programmes	+ Communal well-being (0.01) + Company reputation (0.00)		− UK (0.02)		0.48
Job evaluation	+ Communal well-being (0.05) + Aggressive acquisitions (0.05)			+ UK (0.03) + Brazil (0.08) + India (0.07)	0.37

Practice	Strategy/attitude	Industry		Value
Ensuring compliance with equal opportunities legislation	+ Communal well-being (0.04) + Aggressive acquisitions (0.04) − Investment in traditional products (0.07)	+ Aircraft and electrical engineering (0.04) + Chemicals (0.08) + Food (0.09) + Metals (0.00) + Mechanical engineering (0.01) + Non-metals (0.01) + Pharmaceuticals (0.07) + Other manufacturing (0.07)	− India (0.04) − Italy (0.03) − Germany (0.09)	0.44
Industrial relations and wage bargaining	− Maximize the share price (0.05) − Sophisticated advertising and promotion (0.05)	+ Chemicals (0.01) + Mechanical engineering (0.00) + Metals (0.00) + Motor vehicles (0.03) + Non-metals (0.01) + Pharmaceuticals (0.01) + Other manufacturing (0.00)	+ Brazil (0.01) + India (0.01) + Japan (0.01) + Canada (0.01) + UK (0.08) + Sweden (0.00) + Italy (0.02) + Other Europe (0.00)	0.51
Counselling employees under stress		+ Food (0.07) + Mechanical engineering (0.02) + Non-metals (0.06) + Pharmaceuticals (0.09) + Other manufacturing (0.09)	− Netherlands (0.05)	0.31
Head-hunting	+ Aggressive acquisitions (0.03) − Relations with customers and suppliers (0.05)	− Mechanical engineering (0.08)	− Sweden (0.03) − France (0.07) + India (0.02)	0.37
Psychometric testing	− Profitability (0.01)	+ Coal and petroleum (0.07)	− Other Europe (0.06) + Other Europe (0.09)	0.34

Note: The regressions control for the affiliate's size, as measured by the number of employees (in logarithms). The control industry is paper. The control country is the United States.

that the basic functions of HRM are largely independent of the strategies of the firm.

The most distinctive HRM functions are those that achieve the lowest ratings overall. A minority of Personnel Directors are heavily involved with industrial relations problems. This is particularly true of affiliates in the NICs, Canada, the UK, Sweden and Italy – all countries where trade unions remain a significant force in the market for skilled manual labour. Head-hunting is important to firms committed to an aggressive acquisitions policy. It seems to be characteristic of 'tough-minded' firms who are looking for outsiders to 'turn around' a new acquisition. People who are head hunted for jobs like this may move on fairly quickly because they can make themselves very unpopular with the workforce in the process. Consequently there is a regular turnover of head-hunted personnel in work of this kind. Of the other minority functions – counselling and psychometric testing – there is little to be said.

METHODS OF MOTIVATION

From an economic perspective the most important aspect of corporate culture is its role in motivation. In order to be motivated, employees need to know the performance criteria, and how these criteria are applied to them. Table 5.9 shows that overall professionalism and quality of output are the most widely used criteria. But what exactly does overall professionalism mean? A cynic might suggest that professionalism and quality are just a pair of buzz words

Table 5.9   Means and standard deviations of the responses to 'What are the main dimensions of individual or group performance used in assessing cases for promotion?' (scale 1–5)

Dimension	Mean	Standard deviation
Overall professionalism	4.23	0.76
Quality of output	4.21	0.74
Value of output (independent of profit margin)	3.83	0.88
Effort (independent of final result)	3.55	1.07
Contribution to profit	3.48	1.06
Keeping within budget	3.44	0.83

Note: Number of responses 188.

Table 5.10 *Regression analysis of responses to the question 'What are the main dimensions of individual or group performance used in assessing cases for promotion?'*

Dimension	Objectives and strategy	Industry	Country Parent	Country Host	R^2
Overall professionalism	+ Maximize share price (0.06) + Product innovation (0.06) + Joint ventures and cooperation (0.07) - Basic research (0.07)				0.31
Quality of output	+ Company reputation (0.02)	- Office equipment (0.07)	- Sweden (0.09)		0.37
Value of output	+ Maximize share price (0.09) - Communal well-being (0.01) + Relations with customers and suppliers (0.01) - Basic research (0.04)			+ Brazil (0.03)	0.40
Effort	+ Product innovation (0.05)				0.32
Contribution to profit	+ Profitability (0.00) + Aggressive acquisitions (0.02)	- Coal and petroleum (0.09)	+ Japan (0.06) + Switzerland (0.07)	+ Brazil (0.01) + Japan (0.02) - Other Europe (0.02)	0.42
Keeping within budget	+ Aggressive acquisitions (0.03)		- Canada (0.07)	+ Brazil (0.09) - Japan (0.09)	0.42

Note: The regressions control for the affiliate's size, as measured by the number of employees (in logarithms). The control industry is paper. The control country is the United States. Number of usable responses 149.

which any well-educated HRM professional will endorse. Professionalism does, however, appear to have a special meaning, and Table 5.10 suggests how it can be decoded. Professionalism, it would seem, is an attribute which is strongly desired in companies striving for greater flexibility. A typical company of this kind is committed to expansion through joint ventures in innovation-intensive industries where product life cycles are short and continuous investment is required to keep up with the competition. Top management is aware that fixating employees on any single performance criterion is likely to distort incentives. Much of their work may involve short-term assignments to project teams dedicated to meeting the special requirements of major customers. The firm's need for flexibility is incompatible with offering jobs for life, and the normal career progression associated with it. This suggests a link with the Anglo-American firms identified by the analysis of career prospects in Table 5.1

Another link with the Anglo-American axis is the importance of the share-price motive, which is characteristic of US and UK firms as opposed to continental European firms from Germany, Sweden and elsewhere. This supports the idea that professionalism is rated so highly because for a distinctive type of firm – predominantly, but not exclusively, from the USA or the UK – it describes the flexible alternative to the pyramid-climbing manager of the traditional hierarchical firm. Professionalism, it may be suggested, connotes an individual who is building his or her career by moving between firms, or from project to project within the firm, rather than following a narrowly defined path of promotion in which he or she hopes always to be successor to his or her current boss.

The idea that quality of output can be paired with professionalism as just a buzz word can be dismissed, at least partially, on the grounds that it is a rather different type of firm that embraces this criterion. The kind of firm that embraces quality is particularly concerned with its reputation in the industry, and is the same kind of firm that takes job evaluation and training seriously, according to Table 5.8. This emphasis does not seem to be particularly strong in any one country – it is certainly no longer a prerogative of the Japanese, who actually seem to emphasize profit as the performance criterion instead.

It was suggested at the outset that short-term incentives such as bonuses are inappropriate for firms pursuing long-term goals, and that only firms committed to short-term goals would tend to use them. The evidence on this issue in Table 5.11 is decidedly mixed however. Support for the basic principle comes from the positive and significant coefficient on profitability in the first regression, indicating that bonuses are regarded as particularly important in retaining key staff when a short-term objective predominates. The actual variation in bonuses, which measures the impact on management pay, is not significantly affected by the profit objective, though, as indicated in the

Table 5.11 Analysis of responses to the questions 'How important is the opportunity to earn large bonuses through greater efforts in retaining key staff?', and 'By what percentage do total bonus payments in a successful year of business exceed total bonus payments in a not-so-successful year of business?'

Explanatory variable	Opportunity for bonuses		Excess bonus	
	Coefficient	Significance	Coefficient	Significance
Industry				
Aircraft and electrical engineering	−0.53	0.39	−10.06	0.69
Chemicals	−0.70	0.28	−4.58	0.87
Coal and petroleum	−0.73	0.34	+45.59	0.18
Food, drink and tobacco	−1.65	0.02*	−42.14	0.20
Mechanical engineering	−0.71	0.31	−26.89	0.34
Non-metals	−0.99	0.19	−16.05	0.63
Office equipment	−1.05	0.19	−9.85	0.76
Pharmaceuticals	−0.00	0.99	−44.97	0.11
Other manufacturing	−0.01	0.99	−11.30	0.72
Metals	−0.57	0.40	−83.83	0.04*
Motor vehicles	+0.13	0.86	−51.76	0.14
Parent country				
Japan	+0.16	0.70	+4.99	0.14
Canada	+1.01	0.19	−0.24	0.99
UK	+1.04	0.01*	+31.99	0.04*
Germany	+0.09	0.83	+20.57	0.26
Sweden	−1.25	0.04*	+100.16	0.03*
Finland	+0.16	0.86	+18.73	0.56
France	+0.91	0.24	−80.15	0.02*
Switzerland	+1.68	0.01*	+25.11	0.35
Netherlands	−0.21	0.74	+42.47	0.26
Other Europe	+0.10	0.87	+45.47	0.23
Host country				
Brazil	+0.68	0.14	−12.86	0.58
India	−1.05	0.09*	−47.32	0.21
Japan	+0.83	0.16	−41.76	0.16
Taiwan	+0.34	0.66	+3.64	0.92
Canada	+0.70	0.14	−24.65	0.26
UK	0.18	0.67	−37.84	0.08*
Germany	−0.17	0.74	−21.04	0.44

Table 5.11   continued

Explanatory variable	Opportunity for bonuses		Excess bonus	
	Coefficient	Significance	Coefficient	Significance
Switzerland	+1.71	0.03*	−22.08	0.51
Italy	+0.47	0.34	−6.12	0.79
Other Europe	−2.19	0.13	—	—
Objectives				
Growth of total sales	-0.01	0.98	−15.38	0.06*
Growth of market share	+0.26	0.13	+1.79	0.81
Profitability	+0.32	0.04*	+1.76	0.79
Maximize share price	+0.10	0.37	+1.41	0.77
Company reputation	+0.14	0.39	+6.36	0.44
Communal well-being	−0.11	0.40	+3.89	0.53
Strategies				
Product innovation	+0.33	0.04*	+7.65	0.31
Investment in traditional products	+0.04	0.75	-5.31	0.43
Basic research	+0.02	0.83	−3.04	0.50
Relations with customers and suppliers	−0.20	0.36	−16.05	0.15
Sophisticated advertising	−0.30	0.02*	+5.44	0.39
Competitive prices	+0.18	0.11	+10.17	0.08*
Aggressive acquisitions	+0.11	0.40	+1.84	0.77
Joint ventures and cooperation	+0.01	0.96	−2.02	0.72
Size of firm	−0.11	0.57	+8.59	0.30
Intercept	−0.21	0.89	+80.72	0.30
Mean	3.12		+43.41	
R^2	0.45		0.52	
F industry	1.57	0.11	1.40	0.21
F parent	1.97	0.04*	1.78	0.09*
F host	2.22	0.02*	0.61	0.78
F overall	1.71	0.01*	1.09	0.39
Number of responses	143		91	

Notes: Size of firm is measured by the logarithm of employment in the affiliate. The control industry is paper. The control country is the United States. Responses to the first question are expressed on a scale from 1 (not important) to 5 (very important).
*   Significance greater than 10 per cent.

second regression. However, the growth of total sales – which is a long-term objective – carries a significant negative coefficient in the second regression, providing more support for the theory. Competitive pricing – another short-term objective – also carries the expected positive sign in this regression. The coefficients on the product innovation and advertising strategies carry the wrong sign in the first regressions, however, and the negative coefficient in food, drink and tobacco is counter-intuitive too.

The natural explanation of these results is that reliance on bonuses is not a calculated response to objective circumstances in the market or the industry, but rather a reflection of the culture of the firm. It is the culture of the firm, rather than the realities of the industry, that determine whether bonuses are heavily used or not. In this context, it is interesting to note the heavy reliance on bonuses in UK-owned firms, despite the fact that foreign firms in the UK make little use of them. It is tempting to conclude that most UK parent firms believe heavily in short-term incentives, and apply them to their foreign affiliates, while most foreign investors in the UK take a quite different view of what motivates workers in the UK. The UK is not the only country to emphasize bonuses – Switzerland does it as well, and is the only country to do so as both a parent country and a host country. This suggests a picture of Swiss culture as a highly materialistic one.

THE RISE AND DECLINE OF THE ANGLO-SAXON FIRM

The regression results clearly show that the influence of national culture on business strategies is much more complex than a simple Triad perspective suggests. If a simple scheme is desired, then the picture given in Figure 5.1 is recommended instead. This identifies four main groups of countries rather than three, and opens up each group to recognize the individual country differences to be found inside them.

The Anglo-Saxon group appears at the top of the figure. It includes the USA, the UK and Canada, although it has two close relatives in the European group – the Netherlands and Sweden. Germany may be taken as the country most symbolic of the European style of management, just as the USA is symbolic of the Anglo-American style. Laurent (1983) distinguishes a Mediterranean business culture within Europe, centred on Italy and France; the present study provides some indirect support for his view, in so far as it identifies some distinctive features of Italy as a host country which may be due to the influence of informal local business groups. There is, however, insufficient evidence to go any further than this. There is no evidence that the French-owned firms behave in a manner significantly different from their German counterparts, although there are too few observations on them to be

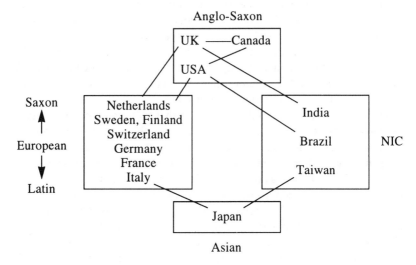

Note: The lines indicate possible channels of mutual influence. Only a few lines are shown in order to avoid complicating the figure.

Figure 5.1   Schematic representation of national cultures according to their impact on business strategies

really sure about this, and there is qualitative evidence from other studies which appears to contradict this finding.

The Anglo-Saxon group has relatives among the NICs as well – India is related to the UK, for example, and Brazil to the USA, although the statistical evidence for an India–UK connection is really quite weak. These relationships are almost certainly based on the legacy of Western business practices introduced into these countries during the 20th century. Taiwan appears as a relative of Japan, on account of its shared emphasis on national interests and job security, although it would of course be more meaningful to introduce the Chinese connection into the picture. Unfortunately, though, China is not a part of this study.

There are other countries which do not fit too neatly into the scheme: Finland, for example, reflects Russian as well as Swedish, German and Anglo-Saxon influence, but for obvious reasons Russia is not included in the study. Switzerland is positioned between Germany and Sweden, although this clearly understates the French (and to some extent the Italian) influence on its culture. Finally Japan is shown at the opposite pole to the USA, despite evidence which reveals many commonalities between large multinationals headquartered in the two countries.

Japan and the USA continue to differ in the business objectives of their companies, though, with the Japanese tending to emphasize a plurality of objectives and their US counterparts being focused on financial perform-ance – profitability and the share price in particular. Japanese firms are not all alike in this respect, however, any more that US firms are, as Ouchi (1981) noted some time ago. This is important, because firm-specific busi-ness objectives seem to be an important source of differences in business strategies.

So far as Japan as a host country is concerned, the statistical evidence suggests an interesting affinity with Italy. The explanation could be that both Japan and Italy are high-technology MICs in which traditional attitudes to-wards the local community remain a significant economic force. Integration into the local business community is a major challenge for foreign investors in both countries.

To appreciate the full significance of business objectives for the behaviour of the firm, it is useful to reinterpret the statistical results reported above in the light of the interview evidence. This evidence confirmed the impression gained from the statistics that firms which maximize the share price as a major objective are very different from those that do not. Many of these firms have recently been involved in mergers and acquisitions, and often have extensive networks of joint ventures and cooperative agreements too. They are mainly from the Anglo-Saxon countries, and as part of their post-merger rationalizations have relied heavily on consultants to engineer internal corpo-rate change. They have been described elsewhere as Post-modern firms (Casson, Loveridge and Singh, 1996).

These firms seem to differ from the more traditional firms, now typically based in Germany and other continental European countries, which empha-size conventional measurable objectives such as profitability and growth. These firms do not take HRM as seriously as the Post-modern firms because they are not so concerned with using it as an instrument of cultural change. Their HRM is more concerned just with the legal mechanics of hiring, firing and paying employees on time.

In some respects these traditional firms resemble what firms of the Anglo-Saxon type were like some ten or twenty years ago. In particular, they still have a discernible hierarchical structure, even though they may be structured divisionally or in a matrix form. They rely on the type of organization which first satisfactorily addressed the problems of multinational organization in high-technology industries. This is not to say that these firms are behind the times – their technology is often ultra-modern and their consumer advertising very slick. Indeed, it seems likely that one reason why they have not needed to restructure is that they are highly competent in their core business. Another reason may be that their home economies have performed fairly strongly, so they have not felt the same need to internationalize production as have their UK and US counterparts.

The Anglo-Saxon type of firm appears to have rejected this model because it proved too inflexible. The difficulty many US and UK firms experienced in meeting Japanese import competition – not only in the home market but in third-country markets where their affiliates were based – convinced them that they needed greater internal flexibility. This theme was taken up by management consultants, who persuaded them to 'down-size' by 'delayering' and to 'network' their newly empowered employees.

It is interesting to speculate whether this change arose because the individualistic personal values of their Anglo-Saxon managers made the bureaucratic structures they adopted in the 1950s and 1960s difficult to operate successfully. In Germany, and in continental Europe generally, fewer problems seem to have been encountered in making bureaucracy work efficiently, and this may be because of the more organic and collectivist outlook of the employees (Stewart, Barsoux, Kieser, Ganter and Wallenbach, 1994). In any case, a loss of confidence in bureaucratic methods in the Anglo-Saxon world led to greater emphasis on flexible working.

The price of this flexibility has, however, been the demise of job security and career progression for employees. To combat this, the delayered firms have adopted the concept of 'professionalism' to maintain a sense of identity and self-respect among managers whose security and prospects have disappeared.

Firms promoting flexibility aspire to share in the success of the Japanese by encouraging general rather than specific management skills. Concern over flexibility is a sequel to another Anglo-Saxon fad for imitating the Japanese, based on total quality management. But Japanese methods have become distorted in the process of transmission because they have to be fitted into the Anglo-Saxon framework of individualistic values. Beneath the veneer, the firms promoting Japanese values seem to be more concerned about the share price than they are about the mix of social and economic objectives found in the Japanese firm. They strive to achieve flexibility without job security rather than with it. Indeed in some cases, it seems, they use the threat of job loss to intimidate people into being 'flexible' by doing someone else's job as well as their own for the same wage as before.

There are, of course, some firms in the Anglo-Saxon countries which have not pursued the Post-modern approach. By and large, these are firms that have already achieved long-run success, and have little to learn from the Japanese approach. They have a consistent record in recruiting high-achieving professionals (in the true sense of that word) and in giving them whatever on-the-job training they require. They had achieved quality before the 'total quality' movement came along. These firms still remain much as they were twenty years ago so far as organizational structures and HRM policies are concerned. They are not remarkably different from the most successful German and Japanese firms. They have evolved over many years a culture which curbs the more selfish aspects of individualism among their employees, while giving full rein to those aspects of individualism conducive to innovation. These 'enterprising traditionalists' have a corporate culture which really works because it gains credibility from the past successes of the firm. It is regrettable that the Post-modern firms have not been able to learn from these successful examples close to home, and have preferred to adopt a Westernized version of exotic oriental practices instead.

While Anglo-Saxon firms have been in the throes of the transition to the Post-modern form, firms in the NICs have been busily exploiting their domestic advantage of relatively cheap and increasingly well-educated labour. This study has no direct evidence on the subject, but it is reasonable to infer that NIC parent firms can benefit from the same indigenous strengths that are reflected in the responses of foreign affiliates in these countries. They have achieved flexibility through local subcontracting arrangements embedded in networks of trust within the business community. Nationalism has provided a useful focus for extending these networks, and for legitimating government efforts to promote them. It could turn out to be a significant aspect of the Asian miracle that parent firms in the NICs have so far felt no need to experiment with the Post-modern form. The indigenous culture is not so individualistic that it creates insuperable problems for bureaucratic management. They have been more informed, and more critical than Western firms, in following Japanese methods. As 'second movers' they do not have the same imperative to invest in new technology as do the Anglo-Saxon firms, and hence the lack of individualism is not a handicap at their particular stage of development. While the Anglo-Saxon firms struggle with their self-inflicted problems, and the continental Europeans carry on in their traditional ways, the NICs look set to continue their multinational growth for the foreseeable future.

For many NICs, Japan is a natural model in the sense that Japan, like them, was a latecomer to international markets dominated by established multinational firms. It cannot escape notice that Japan itself – so recently the object of uncritical emulation in the West – has problems of its own. Just as the Post-modern firms have striven to assimilate Japanese methods into an individualistic environment, so in the post-war period leading Japanese firms have been assimilating US business methods into a much more organic environment. This too has created problems which, like those of the Post-modern firm, are not yet fully resolved.

This study cannot illuminate the problems of the Japanese firms in the way that it illuminates the problems of the Post-modern firms because there are far fewer Japanese firms in the sample. The evidence of five interviews suggests one important difference, however, which operates in favour of the Japanese firm. Unlike the Post-modern firm, which has tended to sweep away corporate traditions, and make a fresh start through a personality cult surrounding its top management, the Japanese prefer to emphasize the historical continuity of the corporation and to adopt a self-effacing management style. Thus, although Japanese firms face a serious problem in renegotiating the implicit contract of lifetime employment, their consultative processes may achieve more success in this rather than have the precipitate actions of the stock-market-driven Anglo-Saxon firms.

On balance, therefore, it seems that the competitive threat to the Anglo-Saxon firms from the Japanese will remain, though it may not be as severe as in the 1980s. The NICs, such as Brazil, India and Taiwan, will pose an increasingly formidable threat, however. Unless the Anglo-Saxon world can build on the strengths of its enterprising traditionalists, and curb the excesses of the Post-modern firm, it may perform even worse in global competition in the future than it has done in the recent past.

NOTE

1. The authors are grateful to the UK Economic and Social Research Council for funding supplied under research contract R 000233914. Valuable comments were received from Gavin Boyd, Matthias Kipping and Ken Starkey.

REFERENCES

Blyton, P. and P. Turnbull (eds) (1992), *Reassessing Human Resource Management*, London: Sage.
Brewster, C., L. Holden and A. Lundmark (1993), *A Different Tack: An Analysis of British and Swedish Management Styles*, Stockholm: Studentlitteratur.
Brewster, C. and S. Tyson (eds) (1992), *International Comparisons in Human Resource Management*, London: Pitman.
Casson, M.C. (1991a), *Economics of Business Culture: Game Theory, Transaction Costs and Economic Performance*, Oxford: Clarendon Press.
Casson, M.C. (ed.) (1991b), *Global Research Strategy and International Competitiveness*, Oxford: Blackwell.
Casson, M.C. (1993), 'Cultural Determinants of Economic Performance', *Journal of Comparative Economics*, **17**, 418–42.
Casson, M.C. (1994), 'Why are Firms Hierarchical', *International Journal of the Economics of Business*, **1**, 47–76.
Casson, M.C. (1995), *Entrepreneurship and Business Culture*, Aldershot: Edward Elgar.
Casson, M.C., R. Loveridge and S. Singh (1996), 'The Ethical Significance of Corpo-

rate Culture in Large Multinational Enterprises', in F.N. Brady (ed.), *Ethical Universals in International Business*, Berlin: Springer Verlag.

Chandler, A.D. (1990), *Scale and Scope: The Dynamics of Industrial Capitalism*, Cambridge, MA: Belknap Press.

Dore, R. (1973), *British Factory: Japanese Factory*, London: Allen & Unwin.

Dunning, J.H. (1995), 'Reappraising the Eclectic Paradigm in an Age of Alliance Capitalism', *Journal of International Business Studies*, **26** (3), 461–91.

Laurent, A. (1983), 'The Cultural Diversity of Western Conceptions of Management', *International Studies of Management and Organisation*, **13** (1–2), 75–96.

Lodge, G.C. and E.F. Vogel (1987), *Ideology and National Competiveness*, Boston, MA: Harvard Business School Press.

Lundvall, B. (1992), *National Systems of Innovation*, London: Pinter.

Milgrom, P.R. and J. Roberts (1992), *Economics, Organisation and Management*, Englewood Cliffs, NJ: Prentice Hall.

Nelson, R.R. (1993), *National Innovation Systems: A Comparative Analysis*, Oxford: Oxford University Press.

Ohmae, K. (1985), *Triad Power*, New York: Free Press.

Ouchi, W.G. (1981), *Theory Z: How American Business Can Meet the Japanese Challenge*, Reading, MA: Addison-Wesley.

Porter, M. (1990), *The Competitive Advantage of Nations*, New York: Free Press.

Stewart, R., J.-L. Barsoux, A. Kieser, H.-D. Ganter and P. Wallenbach (1994), *Managing in Britain and Germany*, London: Anglo-German Foundation.

Whitley, R. (ed.) (1992), *European Business Systems*, Chs 1 and 12, London: SAGE.

6. Regional economic cooperation: EU, NAFTA and APEC

Gavin Boyd

The transformations of markets and structures described in previous chapters are occurring within and across regional patterns of economic activity – the European Union, the North American Free Trade Area, and the Asia–Pacific Economic Cooperation forum. The European Union is a system of collective management capable of influencing and guiding market and structural changes in its area that result from the production and trading activities of its own and outside firms. Levels of structural competitiveness in the member states, however, lag behind that of the USA, the dominant state in the North American Free Trade Area, in which there is no system of collective management. Canada and Mexico are being linked more and more closely with the US economy, mainly through the operations of US firms, which are implementing their strategies very independently.

The USA, Canada and Mexico participate in the Asia–Pacific Economic Cooperation forum, in which they relate to market-economy East Asian states and China. The forum is committed in principle to regional trade liberalization, but understandings of potentials for free commerce are influenced by general awareness of substantial informal trade barriers in Japan and in the high-growth industrializing East Asian states. Sharp cultural differences and long distances, moreover, are recognized to be serious hindrances to productive negotiations between the North American and East Asian members of the forum.

The institutionalized cooperation in Europe has understandably attracted more theoretical and policy-related interest than the establishment of the North American Free Trade Area (NAFTA) and the discussions in the Asia–Pacific Economic Cooperation forum (APEC). The European Union has established a single market for goods and services, implemented a common commercial policy and a common competition policy, as well as a common agricultural policy, has made progress towards monetary union, and has promoted technological cooperation between member states, while subsidizing regional development in backward areas of the region. Collective decision-making institutions have prepared the way for the evolution of a federal structure. The advances to a higher level of integration, however, have been slow and difficult, because of problems of consensus building, and have not been sufficient to support macromanagement endeavours that would substantially raise structural competitiveness in the Union.

EXPANDING INTERACTIVE REGIONALISM

Understanding the different patterns of regional economic cooperation necessitates references to formative influences on national policies and on the activities of firms contending for international market shares. Cultural and political affinities between countries facilitate communications between governments and between firms, especially where geographic proximities are conducive to exchange and encourage the use of common resources. Major cultural and political contrasts, as in the Asia–Pacific context, hinder productive interactions, but may not prevent dynamic political economies from vigorously expanding their commerce. Very active exporting by Japan, South Korea and Taiwan over the past few decades has resulted in considerable penetration of the US market, arousing strong American interest in possibilities for the reduction of trade barriers through negotiations in APEC.

The European Union began as an integration endeavour assisted by cultural and political affinities. Shallow regional integration in a common market was followed by deepening integration through transnational production. Outside firms, based mainly in the USA, however, became very actively involved, with large resources that facilitated competition against European enterprises. Meanwhile new members were attracted by the region's growth prospects. An established pattern of confederal decision-making thus became more complicated, but the integrative motivations of participating governments were qualified by tacit opposition to the development of a strong role by the European Commission, although it had been given authority to aggregate regional interests and propose measures for more advanced integration. The Commission's functions did expand, mainly through regulatory measures, while member governments retained control of their finances, but increasing market integration tended to force acceptance of the logic of completing that process and establishing a monetary union.[1]

European corporate interests, influencing the policies of member governments, contributed, with advocacy by the European Commission, to a drive to eliminate non-tariff barriers and thus form a single market during 1992. With this process competition within the integrating market intensified: weaker enterprises were driven into declines by stronger European and outside enterprises. The spread of gains from intrazonal commerce was uneven, especially because of the presence of major US firms, and German competitive advantages, deriving from an integrated national intercorporate system. The single market was relatively protected against Japanese commercial penetration that was assuming strategic dimensions in the USA, and the German political economy adjusted more effectively than other European states to the destabilizing effects of US policies during the 1980s. During the first half of the 1980s, high US interest rates increased the costs of capital in Europe.[2]

The effort to form a single market evidenced slow policy learning, in the context of a shift in policy orientations towards increased reliance on market forces. The shift was most notable in France, following a large expansion of the French public sector at the beginning of the 1980s.[3] A Franco-German partnership in leadership of the European Community had been functioning since the 1970s, and French policy had been influenced, after the early 1980s, by economic difficulties resulting from expansionary fiscal measures associated with the growth of the public sector. French policy had also been influenced by German achievements in building structural competitiveness with much reliance on market forces – these achievements being possible because of the high degree of integration in the German intercorporate system.

Slow policy learning and insufficiently integrative commitments in the member states prevented the development of effective collective endeavours to overcome disparities in the spread of gains within the single market and raise levels of structural competitiveness, in response to US and Japanese challenges. The growth potential of the single market, however, attracted new members, and as the Community expanded it acquired greater bargaining strength in the world economy. Considerable assertiveness was displayed during the final years of the Uruguay Round of international trade negotiations, when US negotiators were seeking concessions for greater access to the single market.[4] US trade policy activism also presented an indirect challenge by working for regional trade liberalization, in North America, with indications of interest in Latin America, and in the APEC forum. The USA's trade policy activism reflected problems of governance related to losses of structural competitiveness which it had experienced, but problems of governance in several European states were also serious, and problems of collective management in what was now the European Union were in effect increasing the costs of its lags in structural competitiveness and of the disparities in gains from commerce in its single market.

The European integration experience has indicated how advances towards the formation of a single regional market open the way for largely independent corporate strategies that transform economic structures while causing asymmetries in intrazonal interdependencies and weakening national policy instruments. These effects challenge member governments to evolve a system for comprehensive collective management, but that becomes difficult because the intrazonal inequalities in gains tend to make policy orientations adversarial, while increasing problems of advanced political development in the disadvantaged member states. The future of the entire integration endeavour can thus depend very much on whether the initial commitments of the member governments were strong enough to ensure the establishment of a common institution for regional interest aggregation, and policy advocacy on that basis.

NAFTA, lacking a common institution like the European Commission, has had a shorter and less complex history than the European Union, reflecting primarily the market-opening interests of its dominant member, the USA, and the greater scope provided for market and structural transformation by US firms. Deepening integration, mainly through the activities of these firms, had long been under way before the NAFTA agreement, and its principal result was to facilitate regional rationalization of US corporate strategies. The configuration of the area thus tended to become more hierarchical as US enterprises strengthened their market positions in Canada and Mexico, while economic links between those two states remained small.

The establishment of a system for collaborative decision-making to manage the rising interdependencies in North America was not considered. Discussion of such a possibility had been excluded from debate about NAFTA in the USA, because of a strong tradition of unilateralism and of government aloofness from industry and commerce. The prominence of employment issues and questions about industrial relocations to Mexico, moreover, gave a strong domestic orientation to public discussions of NAFTA in the USA. The unilateral tradition had been strengthened by compulsive trade policy activism, aiming at NAFTA's extension to include Latin American states, primarily through bilateral interactions with the USA.

A major contrast with the European Union has concerned the systemic significance of the USA as the central state in NAFTA. In the European Union, Germany's macromanagement achievements have had positive demonstration effects, but the United States has been experiencing serious problems of governance, and these generate pressures to impose costs of adjustment on other states. This has become less and less feasible in dealings with European governments, because of the enlargement of the European Union, and market-opening diplomacy has thus tended to focus more on Canada, Mexico and Latin American states. The main US problem of governance – the difficulty of achieving fiscal discipline – has contributed substantially to large trade deficits which have motivated efforts to increase access to foreign markets. Canada and Mexico have become heavily dependent on the US market, and their options for trade diversification are more restricted than those of many states in the European Union, which are better placed to strengthen ties with each other and with outside countries.

THEORY

As an elementary form of regional economic cooperation, a free trade area allows firms wide scope to contend for market shares, and as they expand their operations the structural effects involve losses of economic sovereignty for governments, except where enterprises function as members of integrated intercorporate systems closely associated with their home-country governments. Depending on the attributes of the states in a free trade area, then, the structural changes resulting from corporate activity may diverge greatly or to a lesser extent from the policy preferences of member governments. This, of course, will happen in a context set by the terms of intrazonal trade liberalization, as determined by the bargaining that establishes the free trade area, and the significance of those terms will change with subsequent bargaining and with shifts in the gains from liberalized commerce as corporate competition intensifies. As firms become more active in shaping economic structures within the free trade area, governments have incentives to work for increased structural competitiveness in their economies but also to cooperate for the advancement of their structural objectives. Achieving such cooperation tends to be difficult, and, indeed, more difficult over time, because of the effects of the disparities in gains on national policy processes, shifts in relative bargaining strengths, changing political business cycles, the complexities of the issues, and uncertainties about the outcomes of collaborative endeavours.

In a hierarchical free trade area the dominant state (or states) tends to gain superior benefits because the firms most active in shaping structural change are based in its economy, and because its bargaining strengths ensure that the terms of intrazonal trade liberalization are favourable. If burdened with problems of governance it will tend to use considerable leverage to extract trade concessions from smaller partners in the free trade area. If advantaged by a high degree of integration in its political economy and by superior structural competitiveness, it will also become more dominant. Meanwhile the free trade area will attract new members seeking to avoid exclusion, thus providing opportunities for further enhancement of the dominant state's position. The free trade area may thus become a zone of influence. The dominant state, however, if not highly integrated, will tend to lose elements of economic sovereignty as the home-country ties of its international firms weaken. It may also experience increasing problems of governance, partly because of adjustment and welfare difficulties caused by outward sourcing and foreign production by its firms.

The formation of a free trade area will of course open the way for increased commerce, possibly with diversions of exports and imports. A rising proportion of the increased internal commerce will be intra-firm trade, and this will also be true of any increased external commerce. Higher growth following market integration in the free trade area will tend to contribute to higher-volume external commerce, and this trend will continue as outside states are attracted into the free trade area. There may be a strong protectionist consensus in the area, but international firms based in the area as well as those operating out of other states will increase transnational production links between it and the rest of the world, reducing the significance of its protectionist barriers. Interests in lowering those barriers through political action to effect policy changes will probably be evident in the strategies of the transnational enterprises based within and outside the area.

The formation of a free trade area can lead to widening recognition of benefits that would be gained by member states through advances towards collective management of the interdependencies rising in the area. Over time, however, that will be less likely if differences of size make the area very hierarchical and if the gains from liberalized commerce are spread unevenly. Leverage exerted by a large state or states will tend to shape the terms of trade liberalization, while smaller states remain within the area because exit would reduce access to its market. Continued membership, of course, will entail vulnerability to externalities associated with the policies of the dominant state or states. In NAFTA, Canada and Mexico are vulnerable to the effects of the USA's problems of governance on its economic policies.[5]

The wider scope for economies of scale and specialization in a free trade area leads to greater cross-border market efficiencies and failures. Firms acquiring increased market strength provide improved service for consumers but gain oligopoly power, used to reduce market contestability and extract higher profits. Externalities associated with the strategies of those firms have negative as well as positive effects on industrial sectors and communities. The most desirable international public good – balanced interdependent growth – will not be provided because of the shifts of gains to a smaller number of major competing firms and to the states with higher structural competitiveness and/or superior leverage on trade issues. In NAFTA the pattern of commerce is dominated by the major features of US trade policy.[6]

In a free trade area and in a more advanced system of regional economic cooperation the evolution of *firms* as production and marketing systems tends to be continuous, driven by managerial quests for commercial achievements, and generally weakens the economic policy instruments of individual governments. The evolution of national political economies, however, is generally affected by problems of governance, notably because functional imperatives are subordinated to vote-maximizing concerns that cause losses of allocative discipline and weaken institutions. Vicious circles can develop as fiscal laxity adversely affects growth and stability, activating distributional demands that hinder efforts to achieve fiscal restraint. Corporate responses to the effects of problems of governance on location advantages tend to result in shifts of industrial capacity to sites under more effective macromanagement, or to those where administrations offer appealing inducements. Incentives to cooperate with the industrial policy objectives of administrations burdened with problems of governance are understandably weak, and there are compulsions to adopt strategies that will maximize the exploitation of relative location advantages across all areas.

Corporate expansion, while linking national economic structures within a free trade area or economic union, also builds interdependencies between those structures and outside states. While national political economies are becoming more closely interconnected in the European Union, they are also being drawn into a transregional pattern of economic relations through commercial ties with the USA, and Japanese firms are increasingly involved in this Atlantic process.[7] It must be stressed, however, that the market and structural transformations, and the associated gains, reflect contrasts between the collective advantages of integrated intercorporate systems, in Germany and Japan, and the firm-specific advantages of major transnational enterprises, notably in the USA, operating within fragmented intercorporate systems. The entire pattern also reflects the effects of differing policy environments on corporate activities – the greater freedom for autonomous corporate operations in the USA, and the closer but not always functional relations between governments and firms in most of the European Union members.

Where a regional system of collective management is evolving, member governments mix competitive and cooperative behaviour in relations with their partners, mainly to increase shares in the benefits of intrazonal commerce. The interactions evidence differences in bargaining strengths and strategies, in macromanagement achievements and failures, and in degrees of trust and goodwill, as well as relative retentions and losses of economic sovereignty. The degrees of cooperative behaviour largely determine the scope for policy learning conducive to further development of the collective management system. Higher levels of competitive behaviour tend to force concentration on assertions of perceived national interests. In such contexts firms based in member states and outside enterprises tend to have wider scope for independent implementation of their strategies, while exploiting the rivalries between member governments. Resulting macromanagement difficulties for several of those governments can then cause their policies to become more competitive and less cooperative, thus hindering the development of a stronger system of collective management. Domestic contests for power, involving groups advantaged or disadvantaged by market and structural changes, have outcomes that subsequently drive stronger and less cooperative assertions of interests that make the collective decision-making more conflicted.[8]

The capacities of regional structures for transnational interest aggregation and the consensus-building capabilities of regional elite networks can thus have crucial importance for the development of a system of collective management. Where a regional integration endeavour begins with a common political will to establish an institution for the representation of common intrazonal interests and for integrative advocacy on behalf of those interests, the developmental prospects of the regional system will be greater. These prospects, however, will be negatively affected if member governments become reluctant to support the advocacy role of the institution representing common interests. This has been illustrated in the history of governmental attitudes to the European Commission, which have slowed the development of a system of comprehensive collective management.[9]

Regional elite networks can play constructive roles in a free trade area, but these will be less feasible if the configuration of the area is hierarchical, and if the development of such networks is hindered by cultural factors. In NAFTA the fragmentation of the US and Canadian intercorporate systems tends to hinder the evolution of regional elite networks, and this is also hindered by the distinctly national character of US and Canadian political parties, and by the more marked contrasts between the Mexican political economy and its two northern partners. The USA's political processes are not significantly receptive to cross-border interest representation from Canada or Mexico, and the scope for Canadian and Mexican lobbying in Washington is small compared with that for large American business groups. An expansion of NAFTA to include Latin American states, primarily through negotiations with the USA, would not alter the basically hierarchical configuration of the free trade area.[10]

In a relatively egalitarian free trade area the scope for regional elite networks will of course be greater if affinities are conducive to their formation, but the prospective gains from intrazonal commerce may not be sufficient to retain the members. A larger regional market may have a stronger attraction, even if it requires participation in a collective decision-making process. This has been illustrated by the drift of European Free Trade Area members into the European Union, after their administrations recognized that the growth prospects of their economies would be substantially improved through involvement in its single market.[11]

CHANGE AND CONTINUITY

Corporate expansion and development exhibits a high degree of continuity, with increasing concentrations that augment oligopolistic trends, within and across regional patterns of economic cooperation. International alliances between firms, driven by technological, financial and market-sharing interests, constitute patterns of alliance capitalism.[12] These are not as cohesive as the relationally bonded industry groups in Japan and Germany, which generate superior efficiencies through information sharing and concerted entrepreneurship. Japanese firms affiliated with their home-country industry groups are active in networks with enterprises operating out of fragmented intercorporate systems, and tend to be advantaged by the collective benefits of their industry groups, and by consultative links between those groups and their governments.

In the evolution of national political economies, which is less functional, overall, than the processes of corporate development, pressures for political change frequently aggravate problems of governance. In the European Union such pressures are active in several member states as high unemployment and slack growth increase demands for improved macromanagement but make policy processes more conflicted, necessitating fiscal compromises with weak allocative discipline. Diversions of investment into government debt, together with rises in the costs of government, hinder economic recoveries, contributing to further imbalances in gains from regional market integration.[13] The principal exception, it must be stressed, is the integrated German national political economy, where broad policy consensus is sustained by rather successful macromanagement. In the Union context Germany is a force for improved economic policies, that is through demonstration effects and as the main source of performance criteria in the drive for monetary union. The contrast with North America is highly significant, regionally and globally, because the USA's problems of governance have potentially destabilizing dimensions. These problems persist while US firms retain large shares of world markets, especially through foreign production that greatly exceeds Germany's but that in effect substitutes for exports.[14]

In the transregional Atlantic context, change at the corporate level results mainly from the operations of US enterprises, active in the European Union and North America. In Europe the American presence contributing to structural change is very large, and is active in competition against many weaker Union firms adversely affected by low levels of growth in much of the region.[15] In North America, US corporations have greater scope to cause structural change, and strengths gained in this context can support allocations of resources to further expansion in Europe. Direct investment by European firms in the USA, because of increases over the past decade, approximates the US direct investment position in Europe, on a historical cost basis, but structurally is less significant. It comprises several national investment positions, and Britain's, which is the largest, is based on holdings in numerous relatively weak enterprises acquired from US owners.

Change at the political level in the Atlantic setting results from the European Union's slow progress towards the development of a federal structure, while absorbing new members, and shifts of power during the political business cycle in the USA. The evolution of a multilevel integration consensus in the European Union, which had been given impetus by the drive to form its single market, was slowed by the recession caused by the costs of German unification, and by the modest size and unevenness of the gains from the single market. Other factors were the tendencies of several member governments to seek additional domestic support through patriotic posturing as issues of political integration were confronted in an adverse economic context. Because of an emphasis on unanimity in Union decision-making, the reluctance of some states to support political integration affected views of its feasibility in other members. The slackening of the political integration endeavour, however, in conjunction with slow growth in the single market, gave greater urgency to questions about structural competitiveness and the openness of the Union market. European firms clearly needed greater security for the exploitation of that market's opportunities.

The American interest in access to the European market has become more active because of its expansion and because rivalries between European Union governments can be exploited to secure increased access. Export expansion to reduce trade deficits is a constant imperative in US policy, and the lowering of trade barriers in East Asia tends to become more difficult as Japanese influence increases in that area. The US political business cycle, alternating in part because of problems of governance that inject differing pressures into decision-making, can be favourably influenced, from the administration's point of view, by agreements that promise increases in the openness of the European Union, and protection of the interests of US firms in Europe. Major issues that have to be confronted relate to the Europeanization of service industries, for improved efficiencies in the single market: this is a perceived requirement that influences European governments and the Union's decision processes.

EUROPEAN SYSTEMIC EVOLUTION

In the European Union the demonstration effect of German macromanagement has been a major factor in the development of the regional system of collective management, adding to the influence of market discipline on the economic policies of other member states, and inducing acceptance of the need for fiscal restraint in the context of a European monetary union. Effective macromanagement has been possible because of a broad consensus for building a competitive social market economy, sustained by an integrated intercorporate system and cooperative interactions between the two major political parties, the Christian Democratic Union and the Social Democratic Party. Solidarity in the intercorporate system has facilitated concerted entrepreneurship, but on a less exclusive basis than that in Japan, as there has been considerable openness to entries by other European firms.

The consensus sustaining continuity in Germany was strained by the recession caused by the high costs of national unification during the early 1990s. The ruling Christian Democrats, with support from the small Free Democratic Party, retained power with reduced legislative support after the 1994 elections. Unemployment, entailing high welfare costs, has remained well above levels before unification, due to a considerable extent to weak demand in the less dynamic states of the Union. High labour costs, together with tax increases associated with the welfare costs, were causing manufacturing firms to shift production to lower-cost foreign sites. This trend was changing what had been well-established corporate preferences for locating production activities in the home economy, so as to serve the regional and world markets primarily by exports. Outward direct investment is still significantly restrained by the integrating influences maintaining solidarity in the national political economy.[16]

Overall continuity in Germany has contributed substantially to the evolution of collective management in the European Union. A consistently constructive role has been maintained, for the building of a regional economic union with standards of collective management higher than those in many of the Union members, in line with German achievements in fiscal restraint and monetary stability. This role has accorded with German dominance of the Union economy, due to size and structural competitiveness, and has depended very much on French political cooperation. This has been forthcoming because of elite recognition of an extensive complementarity of interests, especially following the French policy shift during the early 1980s, towards greater reliance on market forces, with contraction of the public sector.[17]

French cooperation with Germany has become extremely important for progress towards European monetary union, but the fiscal standards set for such union require difficult allocative discipline in France. This has to be striven for while coping with high welfare costs and while endeavouring to raise structural competitiveness through reductions in the costs of government and the implementation of more effective industrial policy measures.[18] Fundamental problems which tend to defy effective engagement are a somewhat adversarial tradition of government–business relations, and a fragmented intercorporate system. Administrative authoritarianism and corporate distrust, together with a strongly individualistic managerial culture, tend to prevent synergies like those generated in the German system. Social unrest followed government efforts to reduce welfare costs in late 1995, but the administration lacked structures for the mobilization of public support, due to the organizational weaknesses of the conservative parties represented in the government. President Jacques Chirac and members of his administration became very dependent on their personal capacities for communication of their policy goals to all levels of French society.[19]

Most Union governments are responsive to Franco-German leadership for more advanced regional economic integration. There are vital interests in continued access to the markets of those two highly industrialized states, and there has been no coalition building to challenge the capacity of the dual leadership to draw majority support in Union decision-making. There are imperatives to raise levels of structural competitiveness, so as to share more in gains from intrazonal commerce, but for each administration in these less advantaged states, especially Italy, improvements in macromanagement are very difficult. Basic requirements for fiscal discipline will have to be met for membership in the projected European monetary union, and there is evidently some elite understanding that allocative restraint would be unattainable without pressure from regional institutions.

Institutionalized policy learning, in which the German role has been substantial, has aided advances towards regional monetary union, for effective operation of the single market, and to reduce the accumulating effects of failures in fiscal responsibility.[20] Challenges to the drive for more comprehensive collective management have come mainly from Britain, despite weak regional support for endeavours to hinder more advanced regional integration. Britain's structural links with Union members have become strong, but fragmentation in its intercorporate system has hindered aggregations of business interests for representation in policy-making. This fragmentation has also limited collaboration between enterprises in the interests of more dynamic growth, thus tending to perpetuate a lag in structural competitiveness which has disadvantaged Britain in the European Union.[21]

Union-level processes of continuity and change are activated mainly by bargaining between member governments responding to domestic pressures, European Commission initiatives, and shifts in alignments during interactions over collective management issues. Relative leadership capacities to guide the influence of domestic pressures are highest in Germany's political economy; most other administrations in member states tend to be more reactive to domestic pressures, and are thus inclined to incremental and experimental involvement in Union-level decision-making. In this decision-making, small member countries are overrepresented, and the decision rules allow considerable obstruction of majority preferences by governments endeavouring to extract concessions in return for their cooperation. With the accession of new members (Austria, Finland and Sweden in 1995) the number of small and medium-sized countries has become larger, increasing the scope for concession bargaining, thus tending to slow and complicate the system of collective management. European Commission initiatives to push forward the integration process have to contend with the bargaining dynamics associated with enlargement of the Union, and evidently tend to be cautious on issues over which France and Germany may be divided.[22]

While the Commission's role has expanded largely through regulatory functions, including especially a common competition policy,[23] its scope to make legislative proposals to the EU Council depends very much on governmental preferences in the more industrialized Northern member countries, whose voting strengths have been increased with the entries of Austria, Finland and Sweden. The Commission's scope for initiative will no doubt be reduced if prospective Central and East European members join the Union, because of the effects on intrazonal coalition potentials, and because Franco-German capacities for leadership will tend to be weakened. Increased multinational staffing, meanwhile, may also affect the Commission's aggregating and advocacy functions. All member governments secure representation in the staffing, through bargaining that can relativize functional considerations. There is an elaborate overlapping division of these functions within numerous Directorates in the Commission. The range and complexity of the functions increase with advances towards a higher level of regional economic integration and with the inclusion of new members. Rival specializations in the Directorates tend to make overall coordination difficult, that is, as these respond in differing ways to conflicting representations of interests by member governments.[24]

Institutional development in the Commission depends very much on its leadership and on Franco-German support for that leadership. The former President of the Commission, Jacques Delors, provided strong direction for organizational performance that mobilized multilevel cooperation for the drive to fully integrate the internal market.[25] A successor favoured by a majority of the Union governments was opposed by the Conservative administration in Britain, and a compromise resulted in the appointment of a lower-profile official, Jacques Santer, as Commission President in 1994. Franco-German cooperation in support of the integrating functions of the Commission then became all the more necessary for the development of comprehensive collective management in the Union.

The dominance of the Council (formerly the Council of Ministers) and the evolving role of the European Commission have evoked complaints about a 'democratic deficit', as the Council and the Commission have been seen to be acting with little accountability to national representative institutions.[26] Ratification of the Maastricht Treaty on European Union was somewhat unenthusiastic in several member countries because of feelings of remoteness from Union-level decision-making and concerns about losses of economic sovereignty. The Treaty was signed in 1992 and attitudes to its ratification were affected in the third quarter of that year by severe disruptions of the Exchange Rate Mechanism of the European Monetary System, resulting in the exit of the British and Italian currencies. Disagreements within and between member governments about the treaty commitment to establish a regional monetary union raised questions not only about the democratic deficit but also about the performance of the Union system of governance.

A basic developmental problem the for Union structure is its lack of a capacity for promoting growth through a common industrial policy supported by sound coordinated fiscal policies. This incapacity is a serious problem because the legitimacy of the structure is adversely affected by under-exploitation of the economic potential of the single market, for which macromanagement deficiencies in member states are primarily responsible. Governments in these states lack the political will to enhance and concert their industrial policies, and most of their intercorporate systems, which are fragmented, do not have strong cross-border links that would support collaborative industrial measures.

The European Commission could extend initiatives which it has taken in the technology area into a common industrial policy, for the implementation of a broad structural design, but this would require intensive well-directed consultative activity, and very active Franco-German support. The building of consensus would be difficult, because of uncertainties about the spread of initial and longer-term benefits, visualized in the context of existing disparities in levels of industrialization and in the sharing of gains from the single market. The vital requirement for Franco-German agreement on industrial policy fundamentals would be hard to meet because the German policy orientation places greater reliance on the autonomy of an integrated intercorporate system, while French policy, having to relate to a less-integrated intercorporate system, has interventionist tendencies. Problems in Union technology policy could be expected to become more serious if there were substantial ventures into a common industrial policy.[27]

NAFTA

In the North American Free Trade Area a less complex pattern of continuity and change is shaped by corporate development more advanced than that in Europe, with scope for more independent expansion, and by a greater concentration of political power, that is in the USA, the virtual hegemon, although the exercise of this power is affected by problems of governance. These cause macromanagement deficiencies which prevent the projection of a demonstration effect like that of the efficient macromanagement process in Germany. US corporations, as agents of structural change, extend their operations in Mexico and Canada more actively than German firms expanding in the European Union, raising imbalanced structural interdependencies that allow fewer options than those for the more numerous states relating to Germany in the European Union. The North American structural changes pose growth and adjustment issues, but these are not leading to collective engagement with the problems of interdependence. Only the USA has extensive scope for initiative, but the unilateral orientation in its political tradition remains strong, and this tradition also remains very liberal, allowing much corporate freedom for international operations.

Intense pluralism in the US system of divided government, which has to function with weak aggregating structures in a highly individualistic society, with low levels of trust, generates conflicting pressures that perpetuate problems of advanced political development. Consistent macromanagement that could promise extensive stable cooperation with partners in regional integration is not achieved. Allocative discipline is made very difficult by aggressive representation of unaggregated interests, and this necessitates extensive distributional compromises, causing large fiscal deficits to persist. As in other debt-laden states, large-scale government borrowing diverts considerable investment away from productive use, contributing to the availability of internationally traded government debt, and to volatility in global currency markets that reflects uncertainties about stability and growth in the US economy.[28] These uncertainties tend to increase a strong emphasis, in US corporate strategies, on foreign production for the service of external markets. Compared with other industrialized democracies the volume of foreign production is very high in relation to arm's-length and intra-firm exports from the USA.[29] Hence the effects on the balance of payments on and the growth of industrial capacity in the home economy are exceptional, although the vast size of the national economy provides much scope for domestically based corporate expansion.

Unemployment around the 5 per cent level, with very low wages for the unskilled, tends to persist because of the combined effects of outward movements of industrial capacity and a restrictive trend in monetary policy. This reflects the interests of a very influential financial community and a need to counter the inflationary consequences of the large fiscal deficits. Welfare spending, although providing benefits much smaller than those in major European states, is a major factor responsible for the high costs of government, and is a target for corporate pressures to reduce the fiscal deficits. The representation of lower-class interests, however, is much weaker in the American political economy than it is in most European states, because of the fragmenting effects of intensely individualistic political competition, and the degrees to which that competition is shaped by financial resources, especially for public relations activities.[30] Because of the organizational weaknesses of the major political parties, politicians have to build personal support mobilization networks, and these have to be financed mainly by corporate contributions, which are provided in anticipation of administrative favours.

The system of divided government has to operate with cooperation between the President and Congress, and this necessitates bargaining on multiple issues. Because of the weaknesses of the main political parties, contenders for the presidency emerge from rather unpatterned elite socialization processes, with distinctive idiosyncrasies, and gain office through competitive projections of personality traits, supported by large-scale publicity activities. Such projections continue when a contender gains office, through constant endeavours to secure broad popular approval for displays of decisive engagement with all major issues, with the Vice-President and Cabinet colleagues remaining in the background. The emphasis on repeated support mobilization through sequences of issues tends to result in executive overload, leading to disjointed and experimental decision-making, with little policy learning. The principal trend over the past two decades has been the evolution of a highly personalized presidency, influencing and responding to shifts in public opinion, partly in competition with the media. With this trend, urgent growth and employment problems have been increasing as the accumulating effects of unsustainable fiscal deficits have become larger, and as substantial trade deficits have been persisting. These problems have been important factors in a general rise of public dissatisfaction with the system of government over the past decade, and that has obligated more active presidential public relations activity. Engagement with the substantive tasks of macromanagement has thus been somewhat neglected: there have been tendencies to retreat from managerial responsibility in order to concentrate on image projection for maximum effect.[31]

The necessary executive bargaining with Congress, which presidential public relations activity is intended to assist, is extremely demanding, because the elected representatives seek to maximize benefits for their constituencies from the fiscal process in return for administrative favours. These multiply, with great complexity, and there is little institutional legislative restraint on the proliferation of requests that have to be met for the passage of legislation. In recent decades Democratic majorities have operated as large distributional coalitions in Congress, but since 1994 a Republican majority in each house, attuned more to business interests, has been exerting pressure for drastically reduced spending. In the dynamics of divided government the pressure has been directed against Bill Clinton, as a Democratic President, while signalling awareness that the heavy fiscal deficits, accumulating for a decade and a half, have become unsustainable.[32]

Macromanagement tasks have become more difficult for the system of divided government, with its liberal tradition, because of losses of structural competitiveness. The principal domestic cause has been the prolonged lack of fiscal discipline. While the adverse effects of that have been accumulating the advantages of the large internal market as a base for US firms have diminished somewhat: other major markets, including especially the European single market, have grown in size, the American domestic economy has been significantly penetrated by Japanese firms, and the intensification of global competitive pressures has made it all the more necessary for US firms to develop large operations in major foreign markets. With all these changes imperatives to achieve greater structural competitiveness, while applying fiscal restraint, have challenged the liberal political tradition.

The main structural imperative is increased government–corporate cooperation in the public interest. Complex patterns of corporate interdependence are evolving as markets are internationalized, and these interdependencies are giving rise to US forms of alliance capitalism. Technocratic inputs into the concerting of corporate strategies on a long-term basis can assist the development of these forms of alliance capitalism. States with capacities to provide such inputs become structurally advantaged. This can be stated without implicit neomercantilist advocacy because the USA has to earn substantial volumes of foreign exchange in order to pay large external debts that have resulted from balance of payments deficits and international borrowing.

Failures to reduce the balance of payments deficits provide opportunities for the growth of protectionist pressures and demands for trade policy activism. Competing imports can be limited through administrative discretion in the implementation of retaliatory measures against dumping and other forms of unfair trading. Such measures can be used without technical violation of the rules under which the World Trade Organization is intended to operate, and in recent years there has been considerable informal US protection of this kind.[33] Market-opening activism has been a related trend, but leverage for this purpose, which has been directed mainly against Japan, has been weakening because of dependence on Japanese investor confidence and, in the Atlantic context, because of the enlargement of the European Union. Increases in the openness of major foreign economies have been small, and have not significantly affected the emphasis of US manufacturing firms on foreign production for the service of external markets.[34]

Canada has been experiencing change primarily because of expansion and restructuring by US firms in the integrating NAFTA market. The constraints of a small domestic economy have prevented the development of balanced complementarity with the USA, and the scope for Canadian measures to promote improved structural competitiveness has tended to become more restricted. The national intercorporate system is fragmented, and is becoming more closely linked with that in the USA. Heavy deficit spending, reflecting common problems of governance in less-integrated industrialized democracies, has hindered growth by imposing high administrative costs and reducing productive investment. Tax and other inducements are offered to attract foreign direct investment, but the high level of government debt poses uncertainties about the future of the economy.[35] Canada's location advantages have to be frequently reassessed because of the effects of rising debt, and also because of the strength of a separatist movement in the province of Quebec.

At the federal level a strong parliamentary majority enables the present Liberal Party government to implement policy with much less domestic bargaining than is required in the USA. The policy orientation of this administration has some affinities with that of the more loosely organized Democratic Party in the United States, but could well be expressed in interventionist measures to reduce inequalities in the benefits of the close economic relationship with the USA.[36] Because of those inequalities there is a potential for strain in the relationship, and this potential may well become more significant if pressures for trade policy activism become stronger in the United States.

Mexico is the most seriously mismanaged political economy in NAFTA, and its rather dependent role in the North American regional pattern has been assumed after a long history of resistance to American territorial and corporate expansion, and a recent history of very disruptive economic reverses, including massive capital flight, major currency depreciations, and failures to meet rising debt obligations. These reverses, the most serious of which began in late 1994, have been due primarily to gross mismanagement by the ruling Partido Revolucionario Institucional, which maintains a form of soft authoritarianism. Gradual democratization has been tolerated, in part because of the penetration of concepts of representative government in the course of expanding economic links with the USA.[37]

Membership of NAFTA was accepted after a shift away from a tightly controlled and poorly managed strategy of import-substituting industrialization which had been implemented for several decades after World War II. The most drastic phase of the policy shift began in the mid-1980s, after the end of a period of strong fiscal expansion and heavy international borrowing that had seemed feasible because of large oil revenues. When these revenues declined, several balance of payments crises forced increased dependence on international lending agencies and on US economic cooperation, and the demonstration effect of the high-growth East Asian states was having a positive influence on the slow policy learning of the ruling elite. Serious capital flight, however, had begun in the early 1980s, mainly because of large rises in US interest rates, and limited prospects for growth under the new outward-oriented growth strategy. Large increases in the flight of capital exposed the currency to severe speculative attacks which precipitated the troubles in 1994. Foreign exchange reserves were depleted, and efforts to stabilize the economy became heavily dependent on US financial support. Mexican firms encountered severe difficulties because of high interest rates, high inflation and contractions of demand.[38]

Some stabilization was achieved by 1995, but implementation of the out-ward-oriented growth strategy remained difficult, because of the disruption that had been experienced, and because the technocratic capacities of the administration continued to be weak. Private sector confidence in the pros-pects for the economy had been discouraged by more than a decade of crises due to administrative failures; the style of macromanagement was still au-thoritarian, necessitating managerial subservience for favours; and industrial sectors had become more open to US corporate entries. In the NAFTA con-text the deterioration of Mexico's status, in circumstances dramatizing high-level incompetence, entailed losses of bargaining strength that would limit possibilities for attaining a less imbalanced relationship with the USA at some future stage.[39]

REGIONS AND FINANCIAL MARKETS

While the European Union has been enlarging and advancing towards eco-nomic union, and while trade liberalization has been increasing in the North American Free Trade Area, vast speculative flows in international financial markets have been increasing, far in excess of transactions in the real economy, and with some adverse implications for growth in Europe and North America. The establishment of a monetary union in Europe, in which Germany will have a strong role, will reduce opportunities for the predators manipulating world financial markets, and may prepare the way for effective collective regulation of those markets if the discipline of the monetary union leads to the formation of a well-controlled European regional financial system. Euro-pean leadership, with Japanese support, might then elicit US cooperation for the development of a Euro-Pacific system of financial regulation. With the formation of the European Monetary Union, German and other leaders of that Union will have to devise methods of coping with the danger of a financial crisis in the United States.[40]

The financial governance potential of an advanced system of regional collective management has been largely ignored in the international politi-cal economy literature, but it is quite clear that German-sponsored disci-pline in an emerging European monetary union will drastically reduce opportunities for speculative runs against weak currencies, and may well facilitate German initiatives for regulatory improvements in Union financial sectors. It is also clear that increasing international use of a strong Euro-pean currency will make the world monetary system less vulnerable to volatility associated with pressures on the US dollar, and may well encour-age sufficient political will in the USA to attain fiscal discipline. Some trade diversion related to the management of the European single market could well be justified if it assists building solidarity in support of an effective European monetary union.

Collective recoveries of elements of monetary sovereignty through regional cooperation in Europe could increase the concerns of Union financial authorities with the volatility in world financial markets. These concerns could motivate efforts to collaborate with the Japanese administration, especially because of the increasing use of the yen by industrializing East Asian states, and the relatively high level of asymmetric financial interdependence that has evolved between Japan and the USA, through the activities of Japanese investors. Germany and Japan share grievances about under-representation in the weighed voting system of the International Monetary Fund, and a European monetary authority, operating to a considerable extent under German leadership, would have an entitlement to strong voting power in a reformed IMF decision system.[41]

The drift of investment away from productive use, into the high-volume speculation in world financial markets, which must be regarded as a problem of international market failure, could be overcome through progressive increases in regional regulatory cooperation, beginning in Europe. Collaboration for this purpose, moreover, could lead to engagement with problems in the funding of industry from international capital markets. As these markets become more actively linked, virtually preferential funding for large transnational enterprises achieving high short-term profits is increased.[42] Oligopolistic trends in product markets thus tend to become stronger, and there is reduced funding for long-term ventures of potentially greater significance for growth and employment. Integrated national political economies such as Japan and Germany are better protected against the latter trend, and their financial enterprises benefit from extensive links with their national intercorporate systems, which in turn tend to be advantaged in the oligopolistic rivalry for domination of world product markets. The evolution of an integrated European system of corporate governance, guided by German experience, could reduce short-termism and instability in Union intercorporate systems as they become more closely linked. Increased regional growth and employment would then be possible.

More productive use of investment is imperative in the European Union, for economic recovery and stronger involvement in the world trading and transnational production systems, as well as for participation in organizations for transregional and global economic cooperation. Slow economic recovery may cause substantial flows of investment to firms in Japan, industrializing East Asian states, and the USA. It may also enable American and Japanese enterprises to strengthen their positions in the Union market, and limit opportunities for European firms to increase investments in advanced technology and to develop advantageous alliances with multinational corporations based in Japan and the USA. For more productive use of investment that will benefit all or most European Union member countries, however, it must be stressed, the region will need an integrated financial system that will guide capital into the funding of European industries.[43]

In North America a US-centred regional financial system is evolving as major banks and securities firms in the USA expand into Canada and Mexico, with the advantages of large resources derived from positions in their home market. There are dangers of instability because of weaknesses in the US banking system, inadequate regulation of the US securities firms, and the involvement of both types of institutions in the high-volume speculative activity that is growing rapidly within world financial markets, with volatility that imposes downward pressures on the dollar.[44] NAFTA, functioning simply as a liberalized trade area, has no mechanism for regional financial cooperation. US monetary and financial authorities seek primarily Japanese and German cooperation for the moderation of adverse trends in international capital markets. If NAFTA extends southwards, through the inclusion of more Latin American countries on the basis of bilateral ties with the USA, expansion of the US financial sector will follow, but the formation of a regional structure for collective financial regulation, although desirable, will depend on moderation of the unilateral emphasis in US monetary and financial policies.

THE WORLD TRADING SYSTEM

Discussions of regionalism in the policy literature have given much attention to the effects of economic integration arrangements on degrees of openness in the world trading system, and on the trading opportunities of countries that choose not to enter liberalized trade areas. Regional market integration can shift trade away from excluded countries, while enabling member countries to increase structural competitiveness as their firms exploit greater intrazonal economies of scale and scope. Higher regional growth may contribute to higher global growth, but possibly more through activating competitive dynamism in other regional systems than through productive exchanges with countries outside such systems. The efficiency and welfare effects, however, have to be considered with reference to direct investment flows that increase transnational production.

In Europe the gains of Union firms from involvement in the single market have to be achieved in competition against US enterprises with generally larger resources that are producing at high volumes within that market. Japanese firms, moreover, operating in industry groups, are penetrating that market through production in member countries. Formal and informal trade barriers are thus offering less and less protection for Union firms in their own market. For their futures industrial, competition and foreign direct investment policies adopted by or within the Union tend to become more significant, in so far as these can restrict penetration by outside enterprises while facilitating market gains.[45]

The formation of NAFTA was in part an expression of US dissatisfactions with progress towards openness in the world trading system during the Uruguay Round negotiations. It was argued that regional trade liberalization would give impetus to freer global trade, although US tendencies to resort to market-opening leverage were open to interpretations that could justify defensive reactions. Latin American countries were given incentives to form regional economic integration systems in their own area while responding to US initiatives for the expansion of NAFTA. As members of Latin American regional integration systems, any states negotiating entries into NAFTA could be advantaged by solidarity in those systems that might facilitate collective bargaining with the USA. The resulting openness could thus be more balanced than the aggregate effects of trade liberalization arrangements established through US bilateral dealings with Latin American states. There has been a long history of failures in Latin American regional cooperation schemes, however, which would explain ambivalence shown by states interested in the potentials of such schemes but drawn towards opportunities for preferential access to the US market, although on unequally negotiated terms.[46]

Regional trade liberalization, depending on its terms, provides scope for corporate restructuring to rationalize the use of intrazonal location advantages in manufacturing and marketing strategies, and these advantages are typically exploited in intensifying rivalries which drive weaker firms into declines. Firms acquiring market dominance are then able to deploy their growing resources for ventures into other areas, including regions in which markets are being integrated. Thus US firms strengthened through restructuring and expansion in NAFTA can compete more actively for shares in the European Union market, where restructuring and expansion is also facilitated by its process of market integration.

The extent to which oligopolistic trends can be strengthened in regional trade liberalization contexts, while of course continuing because of corporate rivalries outside those contexts, complicates questions about regionalism and openness in the global trading system. The openness considered in much policy literature is an international public good mixed with elements of market failure – principally because of the growth of oligopoly power, in the absence of a system of comprehensive collective management. A regional economic cooperation system may cope with this and with other elements of internationalized market failure, but of course may have weaknesses that allow oligopolistic trends and negative externalities to persist. Failures in collective action at the regional level may occur, for example, through the foreign direct investment bidding of member governments that lack the political will to develop a common industrial policy, as has been evident in the European Union.

Competition policy issues await resolution in multilateral trade negotiations, and linkages between these problems and trade policy issues can be expected to become prominent as non-tariff barriers to trade become more significant with the implementation of Uruguay Round tariff cuts. National competition policies generally do not deal with the anti-competitive practices of home-country firms in their foreign operations: cooperation between governments for this purpose is necessary, and often does not occur. Information problems cause difficulties, the firms engaging in anti-competitive practices can influence their home governments, and the issues tend to be seen mainly in the context of rivalries to achieve greater structural competitiveness.[47] In OECD discussions of competition policy cooperation focus has shifted, over the past decade, from the promotion of collaborative restraints on anti-competitive practices to the promotion of competitive activities, in line with an emphasis on the efficiency effects of market forces.[48] This change in orientation has reflected, in part, a relaxation of anti-trust enforcement in the USA, in the interests of efficiency, and appears to have been influenced by the concerns of major industrialized states to allow wide scope for international competitive activities by their firms.

The World Trade Organization is not well constituted to assume a leading role in the regulation of competitive practices, because of the diversity of its large membership, unresolved problems regarding the steering of its activities, and the proliferation of issues which tend to overload its dispute settlement mechanism.[49] At the regional level competition policy cooperation, and even a common competition policy, can be feasible, if a sufficiently advanced system of collective management has been developed. The European Union has a common, if not comprehensive, competition policy, but has yet to evolve a complementary common industrial policy. In NAFTA the dominant role of the USA gives its competition policy regional significance, without any prospect of evolution into a collective function, however, and implementation of this policy varies with changes in guidelines under each administration.[50] While US firms shape strategies for what is becoming a single regional market, their operations in Canada and Mexico are largely outside the scope of competition policy enforcement in their home economy.

SYSTEMIC DEVELOPMENT

The numerous complex structural interdependencies in the world economy which are being increased by expanding corporate activities can be distinguished according to the degrees to which their evolution is guided through national policies and systems of regional cooperation. With the expansion of these interdependencies the efficiencies and failures of linked markets have to be assessed in terms of diverse cross-border benefits and negative effects, and, accordingly, of imperatives for collective management. In the European Union there is extremely complicated interaction between national policies, of varied effectiveness, and the system of regional collective management, influencing corporate activities that strengthen mainly German domination of the single market. In NAFTA the USA's policies have a very extensive reach, facilitating but not significantly guiding the activities of its firms operating in Canada and Mexico. The changing European structural pattern sets imperatives for more comprehensive and more broadly representative collective management which have to be met through basically confederal decision-making. The North American pattern manifests a public good requirement for establishing the beginnings of a collective management system, but this does not accord with the present orientation of US policy.

National policies in the European Union evidence differing levels of advanced political development, at which holistically functional objectives in decision-making tend to order or be subordinated to concerns with maximizing group or popular support. Professional economic advice to the Union governments generally encourages allocative discipline, to moderate tendencies towards vote-seeking fiscal expansion, in line with standards that have to be met for membership in the European Monetary Union, and with needs to raise levels of structural competitiveness. Responsiveness to this advice, in most member governments, reflects strong vote-seeking compulsions and difficulties in reconciling welfare concerns with obligations to facilitate growth by lowering the costs of government. A strong stable holistically functional consensus shapes policy only in Germany, because of the relatively high degree of integration in its political economy. This, however, is a source of ambivalence towards imperatives for more comprehensive and more broadly representative European collective management, as the public interest consensus has developed in an ethos of economic nationalism.[51]

A regional policy consensus for comprehensive collaboration to increase Union structural competitiveness is not evolving because of rivalries to increase gains from the operation of the single market; the weaknesses of regionalized political parties and interest groups; the vote-seeking concerns of ruling political organizations and diverging views about the role of the state in the management of structural interdependencies. Associated with the contrasts in structural competitiveness at the national level are differences in industrial development, technocratic capacities, and technological capabilities, which cause awareness that a common industrial policy would be a vast and extremely difficult undertaking. This, of course, would require equally difficult efforts to build more integrated intercorporate systems in most member states and link them in organically at the regional level.

In the absence of an effective structural consensus, significant vulnerabilities are increasing as the imbalanced linkages in the European pattern become larger. Reactions in the states lacking structural competitiveness tend to reduce prospects for the evolution of a consensus for more comprehensive collective management. Instead of the necessary shared policy learning and community building, governments focus on measures to increase relative gains in the single market, within limitations set by its present degree of integration and its configuration of corporate strengths. The common competition policy, which is rather permissive, and is influenced by concerns to facilitate increases in international competitiveness by allowing concentrations of economic power, is not being implemented in ways that would motivate regional support for a common industrial policy. A dominant theme in European Commission studies has been the Union's need to become more competitive in world markets through the emergence of very large enterprises with secure bases in their home regional economy.[52] This is to happen as intensifying rivalries eliminate weaker firms, and as more efficient corporations operate with greater economies of scale and scope: less competitive states can thus be disadvantaged.

The European Commission's potential to promote policy learning and the building of trust has much significance for the development of a more advanced system of collective management. For the present, however, the operative region-building doctrine strongly emphasizes the efficiency effects and the positive structural changes expected from the operation of free market forces. This reflects the mixed consequences of tacit German preferences for the general avoidance of Union industrial policy initiatives, and the influence of uncertainties about the benefits of such initiatives on the calculations of decision-makers in most other member countries. Meanwhile the freedom for market forces, it must be stressed, allows wide scope for the consolidation of strong positions in the regional economy by US firms, and for penetration by Japanese firms, as member governments compete to attract foreign direct investment. Over time, then, the development of a structural consensus in the Union is tending to become more difficult, although losses of structural competitiveness experienced by individual states continue to affect Union involvement in world markets.

In North America the increasing US corporate activity shaping economic structures in Canada and Mexico, while drawing Canadian and Mexican firms into closer association with US enterprises, is limiting policy options for these two states. Their scope for independent efforts to increase structural competitiveness is being reduced, and it is less and less feasible for them to propose forming a regional system of collective management. This, however, may change if several Latin American states join NAFTA and strengthen their mutual economic ties, as well as those with Mexico. In such a context Canada would be left with quite restricted choices unless very intensive efforts were made to establish political bonds with the Latin American NAFTA members, on the basis of interests in negotiating the formation of an organization for regional economic cooperation.

The initial Canadian interest in free trade with the USA as an arrangement that would ensure less vulnerability to American protectionism has given way to concerns that on balance the vulnerability has increased, and that US corporate entry barriers have become more significant, while Canadian enterprises have been exposed to more severe US competition in their home market. The unfavourable change in relative bargaining strength, together with Mexico's severe loss of bargaining strength since 1994, has given NAFTA a more hierarchical configuration, with shifts of power to US firms as agents of structural change, pre-empting opportunities for European and Japanese enterprises. The contrasts with the European system of collective management, despite its problems of systemic development, are thus becoming stronger.

For discussions of regional cooperation in the Pacific the most instructive lessons are that states with weak structural competitiveness and weak bargaining strengths must build solidarity and press for the establishment of well-institutionalized systems of comprehensive collective management, instead of drifting individually into free trade arrangements with powerful national political economies. Such individual choices in effect allow international firms based in the larger states to operate more extensively in quests for market shares that cause structural transformation. Systemic development at the regional level, however, requires collective guidance of the entrepreneurial dynamism of the major intrazonal patterns of alliance capitalism.

Regionally and globally the reduction of governmental barriers to trade opens up possibilities for increasing gains from commerce, through economies of scale and scope, as firms extend operations across borders, but the actual benefits depend on market-entry barriers that change with increasing concentrations of oligopoly power, and on structural transformations effected in varying degrees by those concentrations. A general trend is that higher-performing enterprises, aided in some cases by higher-performing governments, eliminate weaker rivals. Associated with this trend is the transregional expansion of forms of alliance capitalism, influenced by changes in regional trade policies. The complex market efficiencies and failures indicate public goods requirements that demand wide-ranging governmental cooperation, and extensive corporate cooperation.

In systemic perspectives based on extended government responsibilities for international public goods, in contexts of deepening integration within and between regional systems of cooperation, the growth potentials of concerted entrepreneurship demand full recognition in designs for constructive statecraft. It is becoming more and more important to serve the international public interest through collaborative efforts by governments to facilitate the harmonious evolution of corporate strategies through continuing consultations with firms and industrial associations. This is necessary in regional contexts, and in the transregional settings of Atlantic relations and Euro-Pacific commerce. If government and corporate leaders rise to this challenge, rivalries for structural competitiveness will be balanced by goodwill for structural complementarity.

NOTES

1. See *West European Politics*, **18**, (3), July 1995, Special Issue on *The Crisis of Representation in Europe*, and Neill Nugent (ed.), *The European Union 1993: Annual Review of Activities*, supplement to *Journal of Common Market Studies*, **32**.

2. For surveys of regional growth problems see Andrew Scott, 'Developments in the Economies of the European Union', *Annual Review*, cited, pp. 87–104, and Andrew Gamble, 'Economic Recession and Disenchantment with Europe', *West European Politics*, **18** (3), July 1995, 158–74.

3. On French policy see Olivier Jean Blanchard and Pierre Alain Muet, 'Competitiveness through Disinflation: An Assessment of the French Macroeconomic Strategy', *Economic Policy*, **16**, April 1993, 11–56.

4. See Anne O. Krueger, 'US Trade Policy and the GATT Review', *The World Economy*, Special Issue on Global Trade Policy 1995, 65–78.

5. See Martin Feldstein (ed.), *American Economic Policy in the 1980s*, (Chicago: University of Chicago Press, 1994).

6. See Krueger, cited.

7. See John Cantwell (ed.), *Multinational Investment in Modern Europe* (Aldershot: Edward Elgar, 1992); B. Burgenmeier and J.L. Mucchielli (eds), *Multinationals and Europe 1992* (London: Routledge, 1991); and Stephen Young and Neil Hood, 'Inward Investment Policy in the European Community in the 1990s', *Transnational Corporations*, **2** (2), August 1993, 35–62.

8. See *The Crisis of Representation in Europe*, cited.

9. See review of the evolution of the Commission in George Ross, *Jacques Delors and European Integration* (New York: Oxford University Press, 1995).

10. See references to NAFTA in *Trade Liberalization in the Western Hemisphere* (Washington DC: Inter-American Development Bank and Economic Commission for Latin America, 1995).

11. See Brian Hindley and Patrick Messerlin, 'Guarantees of Market Access and Regionalism', in Kym Anderson and Richard Blackhurst (eds), *Regional Integration and the Global Trading System* (New York: St Martin's Press, 1993), pp. 358–84.

12. See John H. Dunning, 'Reappraising the Eclectic Paradigm in an Age of Alliance Capitalism', *Journal of International Business Studies*, **26** (3), Third Quarter 1995, 461–92.

13. See Gamble, cited, and Scott, cited.

14. See Gavin Boyd, *Corporate Planning and Policy Planning in the Pacific* (London: Pinter, 1993), Chapter 5.

15. See Gamble, cited, and Scott, cited. See also sectoral reviews in Frederique Sachwald (ed.), *European Integration and Competitiveness* (Aldershot: Edward Elgar, 1994) and in Kirsty S. Hughes (ed.), *European Competitiveness* (Cambridge: Cambridge University Press, 1993).

16. See Carl F. Lankowski (ed.), *Germany and the European Community* (New York: St Martin's Press, 1993), Chapters 1 and 3, and *Multinationals and Europe 1992*, cited.

17. See Blanchard and Muet, cited.

18. See Paul R. Masson (ed.), *France: Financial and Real Sector Issues* (Washington: International Monetary Fund, 1995).

19. See Andrew Appleton, 'Parties under Pressure: Challenges to "Established" French Parties', *West European Politics*, **18** (1), January 1995, 52–77.

20. See Emile Noel, 'Future Prospects for Europe', *Government and Opposition*, **30** (4), Autumn 1995, 452–68, and Andrew M. McLaughlin and Justin Greenwood, 'The Management of Interest Representation in the European Union', *Journal of Common Market Studies*, **33** (1), March 1995, 143–55.

21. See references to Britain in William D. Coleman, 'State Traditions and Comprehensive Business Associations: A Comparative Structural Analysis', *Political Studies*, **XXXVIII** (2), June 1990, 231–52, and in Michael Hodges and Stephen Woolcock, 'Atlantic Capitalism versus Rhine Capitalism in the European Community', *West European Politics*, **16** (3), July 1993, 329–44.

22. See Nugent, cited, and Ross, cited.

23. On the competition policy see Lee McGowan and Stephen Wilks, 'The First Supranational Policy in the European Union: Competition Policy', *European Journal of Political Research*, **28** (2), September 1995, 141–69, and Jeanne-Mey Sun and Jacques Pelkmans, 'Regulatory Competition in the Single Market', *Journal of Common Market Studies*, **33** (1), March 1995, 67–90.

24. See Ross, cited.

25. Ibid.

26. See Noel, cited, and Madeleine O. Holsti, 'The Balance between Small and Large: Effects of a Double Majority System on Voting Power in the European Union', *International Studies Quarterly*, **39** (3), September 1995, 351–70.

27. Problems in the evolution of a Union technology policy are discussed in Margaret Sharp and Keith Pavitt, 'Technology Policy in the 1990s: Old Trends and New Realities', *Journal of Common Market Studies*, **31** (2), June 1993, 129–50.

28. See symposium on capital markets, *Policy Sciences*, **27** (4), 1994, and Frederick S. Mishkin, 'Preventing Financial Crises: An International Perspective', *Manchester School Papers on Money, Macroeconomics, and Finance*, Supplement, **LXII**, 1993, 1–40.

29. The profitability of US majority-owned foreign affiliates is higher than that for domestic operations – 27 per cent compared with 16 per cent in 1989 – and for most host countries the share of GNP accounted for by US majority-owned affiliates is higher than the share of US GNP accounted for by that country's affiliates in the USA. US majority-owned affiliates in Britain accounted for 7 per cent of British GNP in 1991, but US affiliates of British companies accounted for only 1 per cent of US GNP, although Britain has the largest foreign direct investment position in the USA. See Raymond J. Mataloni and Lee Goldberg, 'Gross Product of US Multinational Companies, 1977–91', *Survey of Current Business*, **74** (2), February 1994, 42–63. Total sales to foreign countries by US majority-owned foreign affiliates in 1991 were $1,114,953 million, see Raymond J. Mataloni, 'US Multinational Companies: Operations in 1991', *Survey of Current Business*, **73** (7), July 1993, 40–58.

30. See Graham K. Wilson, 'Corporate Political Strategies', *British Journal of Political Science*, **20** (2), April 1990, 281–8, and *Journal of Law, Economics and Organization*, **6**, 1990, Special Issue on US Politics. See also Coleman, cited, and Robert F. Durant, 'The Democratic Deficit in America', *Political Science Quarterly*, **110** (1), Spring 1995, 25–48.

31. See Ronald C. Moe, 'Traditional Organizational Principles and the Managerial Presi-

dency: From Phoenix to Ashes', *Public Administration*, **50** (2), March–April 1990, 129–40, and M. Stephen Weatherford, 'The Puzzle of Presidential Leadership: Persuasion, Bargaining, and Policy Consistency', *Governance*, **7** (2), April 1994, 135–64.

32. On the history of the deficits, see Feldstein, cited, Chapters 1 and 4.

33. See Krueger, cited.

34. See references to foreign direct investment plans of US firms in Mahnaz Fahim-Nader, 'Capital Expenditures by Majority-Owned Foreign Affiliates of US Companies', *Survey of Current Business*, **74** (9), September 1994, 58–63.

35. See *Government Securities and Debt Management in the 1990s* (Paris: OECD, 1993), p. 190.

36. On Canada's situation in NAFTA see references in Khosrow Fatemi (ed.), *North American Free Trade Agreement* (New York: St Martin's Press, 1993), and Murray Smith, 'The North American Free Trade Agreement: Global Impacts', in *Regional Integration and the Global Trading System*, cited, pp. 83–103.

37. See M. Delal Baer and Sidney Weintraub (eds), *The NAFTA Debate: Grappling with Unconventional Trade Issues* (Boulder: Lynne Rienner, 1994), Chapter 7.

38. See Michael Adler, 'Mexico's Devaluation: The Beginning, not the End of its Problems', *Columbia Journal of World Business*, **XXX** (1), Spring 1995, 112–20.

39. See Gary L. Springer and Jorge L. Molina, 'The Mexican Financial Crisis: Genesis, Impact, and Implications', *Journal of InterAmerican and World Affairs*, **37** (2), Summer 1995, 57–82.

40. On this danger see Mishkin, cited.

41. See expressions of German concerns in comments by Horst Schulmann, in Peter B. Kenen (ed.), *Managing the World Economy* (Washington: Institute for International Economics, 1994), pp. 386–94.

42. See *Policy Sciences* symposium, cited.

43. For the present, Germany is advantaged with respect to industrial funding. See Kirsten S. Wever and Christopher S. Allen, 'The Financial System and Corporate Governance in Germany: Institutions and the Diffusion of Innovations', *Journal of Public Policy*, **13** (2), April 1993, 183–202.

44. See Mishkin, cited.

45. See Peter Lloyd and Gary Sampson, 'Competition and Trade Policy: Identifying the Issues after the Uruguay Round', *The World Economy*, **18** (5), September 1995, 681–706; Alexis Jacquemin, 'Towards an Internationalisation of Competition Policy', *The World Economy*, **18** (6), November 1995, 781–90; Robert D. Anderson and S. Dev Khosla, *Competition Policy as a Dimension of Economic Policy: A Comparative Perspective* (Ottawa: Industry Canada, Occasional Paper 7, 1995), pp. 62–6; and Hindley and Messerlin, cited.

46. See *Trade Liberalization in the Western Hemisphere*, cited.

47. See Lloyd and Sampson, cited.

48. Ibid.

49. See John H. Jackson, 'The World Trade Organization: Watershed Innovation or Cautious Small Step Forward?', *The World Economy*, symposium on Global Trade Policy, cited, 11–32.

50. See Lawrence J. White, 'Competition Policy in the United States: An Overview', *Oxford Review of Economic Policy*, **9** (2), Summer 1993, 133–50.

51. See Wever and Allen, cited, and Jeffrey A. Hart, *Rival Capitalists: International Competitiveness in the United States, Japan, and Western Europe* (Ithaca: Cornell University Press, 1992), Chapter 5.

52. See McGowan and Wilks, cited.

7.   Regional integration in Europe

Patrick M. Crowley

The extent to which a change in attitude, such as a more intensive competitive attitude, may further raise production remains completely uncertain. Suggestions, to the effect that doubling of production might be hoped for, are based on the assumption that most of the difference between American and European prosperity can be attributed to such a difference in attitude and that the establishment of the European Economic Community would bring about in Europe, an American level of competitive activity. This seems very doubtful.   (Jan Tinbergen, 1965)

INTRODUCTION

Regional integration is not new. It occurred in previous centuries, as consociationalist political structures such as Switzerland and Belgium as well as federalist structures such as Australia, Canada and the United States, attest. Historically, regional integration occurred for political and military rather than for economic reasons, so states, provinces, or cantons could better defend themselves against common threats and simultaneously take advantage of the economies of scale in government (for areas of common interest such as foreign policy and defence). As trade and investment have gained more importance in government policies, with the internationalization of markets, so the focus for regional integration has shifted to the economic and monetary sphere. Indeed, there are virtually no examples of contemporary regional integration that are motivated by political concerns (German reunification being the one notable exception). In Europe, plans for political union have been downplayed and do not gain unanimous support among member states, so that here, as elsewhere, future integration plans emphasize economic and monetary integration.

The recent growth of interest in regional integration no doubt reflects the failure to multilaterally agree on a blueprint for world economic integration during the past 15 years. During the last decade, the rush not to get left behind in the emerging tripolar world economy has led to new agreements in various areas outside of the main large regional blocs (notably South America, Eastern Europe and Central America). Statistical data now indicate considerable regionalization of trade flows, with the volume of trade in Europe, North America and Japan and the dynamic Asian economies increasing by about twice as much compared with income growth, as it did outside of these regions during the last 25 years.

Regional economic integration presently incorporates not only increased trade ties, but also liberalizing the flow of factors of production across borders, which can involve the dismantling of border posts (with liberalized labour flows), full currency convertibility and the elimination of capital controls (with liberalized capital flows). This result has now been achieved in several countries in Europe, after the single market '1992' legislation was passed by all member states, and it moves the whole notion of regional economic integration on to a different plane.

The economic pressures on governments to pursue regional integration are now intense, with economic benefits and increased government credibility the primary objectives in nearly all cases. Recent examples illustrate, ranging from the competition between certain East European countries to be first to be admitted into the European Union (EU) to the recent overtures made to Chile to join the North American Free Trade Area (NAFTA) which may then evolve into a pan-Americas free trade zone. Indeed, almost every continent in the world now possesses at least one regional economic grouping, so it is timely to look at the economic implications of such trends.

The emphasis in this chapter is on Europe as an example of advanced regional integration. The signing of the Treaty of Rome (1958) was one of three regional integration schemes that were initiated in the late 1950s in Europe (the others were the European Free Trade Association (EFTA) in Western Europe and the Council for Mutual Economic Assistance (CMEA) in Eastern Europe) and together they marked the formal inception of the regional trade bloc concept in the post-World War II era (moves that were originally motivated by political concerns, as noted by Ungerer (1993)). The main motivation behind this chapter is to see if there are any lessons to be drawn from the European experience.

The chapter comprises seven sections. In the next section, the hierarchies of regional integration are defined and applied to integration agreements. Regional economic, monetary and political integration are discussed in the following three sections respectively. Then fiscal policy concerns are addressed. In the final section, future political concerns are addressed and conclusions are drawn.

HIERARCHIES OF REGIONAL INTEGRATION

An exploration of the economic impacts of regional integration requires an analytical framework. Table 7.1 augments and refines Emerson (1991) to create a taxonomy of the different trade, monetary and political regime choices that form part of the hierarchy of options that countries have at their disposal when choosing to integrate.

Table 7.1   Hierarchies of trade, monetary and political regime choices

Category	Description
Trade	
T1	Multilaterally determined trade policy
T2	Free trade
T3	Customs union
T4	Single market
Exchange rate	
E1	Float
E2	Managed float
E3	Adjustable peg
E4	Fixed
E5	Monetary union
Convertibility	
C1	Current a/c convertibility for residents
C2	C1 plus convertibility for non-residents
C3	C2 plus capital a/c convertibility for residents
C4	C3 plus convertibility for non-residents
Politics	
P1	Sovereign/independent states (single member veto)
P2	Multilevel decision-making (majority voting)
P3	Consociation (power sharing among components)
P4	Federation (supranational powers supreme)

A newly independent inward-looking state would probably opt for T1+E1+C1+P1 and a small Swiss canton or European country such as Luxembourg, would operate under T4+E5+C4+P3 or P4. The combinations of options are clearly great, with increased levels of integration tending to move countries down the list.

In most cases the perception is that increased trade liberalization usually precedes increased exchange rate and monetary integration, but this is not always the case. Argentina is a case in point (see Cavallo, 1992). It has decided to 'irrevocably' peg to the US dollar (through a currency board) for macroeconomic stabilization reasons, even though it does a relatively small amount of trade with the USA. Scandinavian countries (Sweden and Finland) decided to peg their currencies to the European currency unit (ECU) long before they were accepted as members of the EU. Canada here is a particularly interesting case. Although it possesses a federal structure and therefore a single currency, it does not have a single market in all products – interprovincial trade barriers remain, even though trade barriers between provinces and states (in the USA) have now mostly been eliminated. Nevertheless, as McCallum (1993) shows, the Canada–US border matters, as there is substantially more trade between provinces (in spite of trade barriers) than would be predicted by a gravity model in a borderless and barrierless world. This result might also suggest that monetary union encourages economic integration, rather than vice versa, a theme that will re-occur later in the chapter.

At this juncture it is probably appropriate to attempt a description of the three regional 'poles' in terms of the above hierarchy. The EU moved to a single market (in capital and labour) in January 1993 (and therefore would classify as T4 in Table 7.1). The single market eliminates the relevance of national identity or residency in all economic relations, as differences in regulations for economic agents resident in London or in Madrid have been minimized to the extent that anyone can operate just as effectively out of London or Madrid. The single market was established under the principles of mutual recognition and minimum harmonization, an innovative way of removing barriers within the then European Community (EC). According to the principle of mutual recognition laws and regulations enforced in one member state must be recognised by all others. Thus if national authorities do not wish to put domestic firms at a competitive disadvantage, they relax regulations that impose additional constraints on these firms, leading to a greater degree of harmonization between national authority regulations. Therefore the principles work hand in hand, the former by legislation (enacted in the Single European Act of 1986) and the latter by market forces. It should also be noted that labour is completely mobile between all member states of the EU, and in addition a core of member-state governments (under the Schengen Agreement) have now dispensed with all border controls and customs between them. The EU has an adjustable peg exchange rate system, namely the Exchange Rate Mechanism (ERM) of the European Monetary System (EMS), which currently operates with +/- 15 per cent fluctuation bands for the most part (this would therefore be characterized as E3 in Table 7.1). With the elimination of capital controls as part of the single market legislation (208 directives in all), the EU, in large part (there are exceptions for Greece, Portugal and the new Scandinavian member states) operates with perfect capital mobility (and would therefore be classified under convertibility in Table 7.1 as C4). In political terms, policy decisions are made at summits using a rather complex formula, so that blocking votes can be mustered even when a majority vote is cast (so in terms of Table 7.1 the EU would lie somewhere between P1 and P2, but with some elements of P4).

To avoid repetition, Table 7.2 presents a rough categorisation for the three regional 'poles', using Table 7.1.

Table 7.2   Classification of the tripolar regional blocs by hierarchy

Category	EU1	EU2	NAFTA	ASEAN
Trade	T4	T4	(T2)	T2
Labour mobility	Yes	Yes	(No)	No
Exchange Rate	E3	E5	E2	E1
Convertibility	(C4)	C4	C4	C2
Politics	P1/P2	P2	P1	P1

Notes:
1. EU1 refers to the current situation, EU2 refers to if and when the Maastricht Treaty provisions are fully implemented.
2. Labour mobility refers to the free movement of labour between constituent countries.
3. A bracket refers to the existence of exceptions.

The three models of regional integration are quite different in range and scope. NAFTA is a free trade zone, but some exceptions (accounting for approximately 35 per cent of intra-NAFTA trade) remain. North American exchange rates operate under a managed float regime with perfect capital mobility and decisions are made on a unanimous vote basis. The Asian model is much less well defined, and has largely been based on unilateral trade liberalization and offshore investment from Japanese multinationals. The Association of South East Asian Nations (ASEAN), which consists of Singapore, Malaysia, Thailand, Indonesia, the Philippines and Brunei, have set out to reduce tariffs on manufactured goods, so as to achieve a free trade zone within the next 15 years. Japan, although absent from the ASEAN roster, maintains strong trade and investment links with ASEAN members.

REGIONAL ECONOMIC INTEGRATION

The economics of free trade zones has been adequately developed elsewhere (see Krugman, 1991) so is not repeated here. Rather, this section focuses on both the microeconomic and macroeconomic aspects surrounding the success or failure of regional integration arrangements, and also the nature of the impact of successful integration on countries external to the agreement.

Microeconomic Aspects

On a microeconomic level, Dunning and Robson (1988) note that the goals of regional integration projects usually can be described as 'the more efficient deployment of resources between member countries and sectors, and within countries and sectors, and an increased international technological and managerial capability'. From an economics perspective, this roughly corresponds to what is predicted under a trade theoretic model of imperfect competition, as firms and industries exploit economies of scale across national borders, leading to increases in intra-industry trade and intra-firm trade across borders (see Helpman and Krugman, 1985). On a macro-level, this trend leads to the formation of regional blocs and is broadly consistent with predictions based on the model of imperfect competition in international trade theory. In reality, this new configuration of trading patterns can also lead to unemployment in relatively uncompetitive regions, because of, for example, 'problems of economic structure or of geographical peripherality' (see Begg, Gudgin and Morris, 1995). Further, increased intra-firm trade may encourage a growth bias in favour of multinationals, leading to less competition overall where economies of scale are being exploited by a small number of firms in an industry. The former is addressed through an EU regional policy, under the rubric of structural fund spending, which incorporates the European Regional Development Fund (ERDF), the Economic and Social Fund (ESF) and the Cohesion Funds (see Commission of the European Communities, 1994 and Dignan, 1995). These funds allocate resources from the EU budget, mostly for infrastructure improvements in eligible states, and as an addition to member-state funding. The latter (less competition) has to a certain degree been addressed by the EU through its competition policy (although not always explicitly on economic grounds). The research in this area (see Greenaway, 1988), however, suggests that integration has been associated with a growth of intra-industry trade and intra-firm trade.

Jacquemin and Sapir (1991) classified regional economic integration as one of two different types: 'natural integration' and 'strategic integration'. Natural integration involves geographically close trading partners, which adopt a liberal trade policy towards countries outside the regional trading bloc, and strategic integration involves regional integration that is detrimental to nations outside the bloc. The former is likely to lead to trade creation while the latter will probably induce net trade diversion, and therefore both will have economic welfare implications. Most authors agree that EC integration was a catalyst for a lowering of Europe's external barriers, but there is not unanimous agreement on this point (see Commission of the European Communities, 1993) when non-tariff barriers are considered.

The case of the EC during the 1980s is a particularly interesting example of increased regional integration against the backdrop of dollar misalignment and nominal exchange rate volatility. Table 7.3 gives figures for the regional structure of EC trade.

Table 7.3   The regional structure of EC trade

Year	EC[1]	Western Europe[2]	Contiguous countries[3]	ROW:[4] Industrial	ROW:[4] Developing	Total
Exports						
1970	53.4	11.7	11.8	16.0	7.1	100.0
1975	52.4	10.6	15.2	12.2	9.6	100.0
1980	56.1	11.2	12.9	10.6	9.2	100.0
1985	55.2	10.0	10.3	15.8	8.7	100.0
1990	61.2	10.4	8.1	13.0	7.3	100.0
Imports						
1970	50.3	8.7	12.3	18.4	10.3	100.0
1975	49.5	7.9	11.1	15.2	16.3	100.0
1980	49.3	8.6	11.7	14.8	15.6	100.0
1985	53.4	9.4	12.5	14.9	9.8	100.0
1990	59.0	9.6	8.3	14.9	8.2	100.0

Notes:
1. EC = The 12 member states of the EC.
2. Western Europe = European Free Trade Organization (EFTA).
3. Contiguous countries = Eastern Europe, Mediterranean countries and ACP countries (those that are part of the Lomé Convention).
4. ROW = Rest of the World.

Source: Eurostat

Table 7.3 hints at the disruption to the integration process by the oil price shocks of the mid-1970s and the misalignment of the US dollar in the mid-1980s. The rapid fall of the US dollar against European currencies between 1985 and 1986 gave the USA a cumulative 12.2 per cent increase in export price competitiveness over these two years, but the EC suffered a cumulative 26.2 per cent loss in export price competitiveness over the same period. These price effects showed up in the trade data in the 1986–89 period, and undoubtedly fostered greater dependence on intra-EC trade, which is shown by the rapid fall in trade with contiguous countries. Nevertheless, taking the

1980s as a whole, there appears to have been a rapid increase in the proportion of intra-EC trade, irrespective of other factors.

It has been widely noted that the EC opted to foster intra-EC trade at the expense of integration with the rest of the world (see Padoa-Schioppa (1993) for commentary on the emergence of a tripolar economy). Winters (1993), while arguing that the EC, on balance, fostered trade creation, focuses on the Common Agricultural Policy (CAP) as a distortionary and protectionist policy, and notes a fivefold erection of non-tariff barriers for extra-EC trade. Indeed the growth of intra-EC trade was certainly aided by the large subsidies given to the agricultural sectors and the rather pernicious agricultural exchange rate system operated by the EC, which together gave economic agents an incentive not only to dramatically step up production but also to export their produce to specific countries. Winters comments that 'while every nation has its protectionists, I suspect that an organisation designed to promote mutual market penetration, and whose yard-stick is "integration", is particularly prone to such perceptions' (as an increasingly closed trading zone).

To summarize, while much of the push for increased European integration focused on integration of a 'natural' kind, several important sectors clearly pursued 'strategic' integration. Perhaps this is reflected, to a degree, in the macroeconomic performance of the EC during the 1980s. Certainly, with the unprecedented growth in European unemployment in the 1980s, it is difficult to argue that greater regional integration in Europe induced a superior macroeconomic performance.

Macroeconomic Aspects

Genberg and Nadal De Simone (1993) compare three regional integration agreements, the EU, the Central American Common Market (CACM) and the Latin American Integration Association (LAIA) to identify the roles of macroeconomic factors in their respective development. The most important findings were that real exchange rate variability matters, macroeconomic policy convergence also matters (in that persistent macroeconomic imbalances can cause real exchange rate overvaluation which makes trade liberalization more difficult), and inadequate policy coordination reduces gains from market integration. Their conclusion was that large shocks to real exchange rates are detrimental to regional economic integration.

The process of regional integration will automatically lead to a restructuring of production and employment, which with price and wage rigidities and imperfect mobility of factors of production will invariably lead to a transitional upsurge in unemployment in certain industries and/or regions. This will, in turn, prompt changes in macroeconomic policies, which may affect real exchange rates. If nominal exchange rates are fixed or kept relatively stable, convergence in monetary policies is essential to maintain such an exchange rate policy. Without convergence, eventually the monetary authorities will have recourse to various forms of capital and/or trade controls to maintain real exchange rates.

But even if policy coordination is adequate and there are negligible real exchange rate shocks, what is the impact of successful integration on macroeconomic policies? The answer obviously depends to some extent on the degree of integration and the exchange rate policies adopted by the respective governments and monetary authorities while the dynamic effects are in progress. If the imperfect competition model of trade creation is used, the expansion of trade will require new investment in the expanding sectors of each member country, and may even increase capital mobility, reflecting multinationals' plant relocation in other member countries (see Cantwell, 1988 and Dunning and Robson, 1988). Also, increased capital mobility would probably aid trade financing between countries. Thus trade liberalization would normally induce a greater degree of financial integration and therefore economic interdependence. Clearly, the implications for the exchange rate regime of such an increase in capital flows will undoubtedly highlight any asymmetries in the degree of financial integration, and so the nature of the exchange rate regime becomes critical.

Advocates of flexible exchange rates have argued that the existence of forward markets should obviate the currency risk under a flexible exchange rate regime. Frankel and Wei (1993) used a cross-section of countries to statistically test whether exchange rate volatility affected trade flows and found that the effect was in fact small in magnitude. This result is hardly surprising, though, as most companies make long-term commitments to either export and/or import into specific markets. A more telling measure of the effects of exchange rate volatility would be seen in terms of the profits of the companies involved in the trade flows. Recent anecdotal evidence reported by Mercedes-Benz of Germany in the financial press appears to suggest that the effects of exchange rate volatility are significant.

Also, even if one accepts the forward market argument, as Eichengreen (1993) notes, the lifespan of most types of plant and equipment exceeds the term to maturity of available forward contracts, so this should affect cross-border investment more than trade flows. Morsink and Molle (1991) report that direct foreign investment among EU member states was indeed depressed when currency risk was apparent. Table 7.4 shows the evolution of foreign direct investment flows for EU member states in recent years.

Table 7.4 illustrates not only the effects of the single market, but also the globalization strategies of multinational companies and more liberal policies towards foreign direct investment. In fact, since the mid-1980s the United Kingdom has been the largest direct investor in the EU in terms of flows, and

Table 7.4   Foreign direct investment (as a percentage of GDP)

Country	Inward		Outward	
	1980–86	1987–92	1980–86	1987–92
Belgium	1.15	3.85	0.36	3.30
Denmark	0.16	0.73	0.35	1.23
France	0.39	0.86	0.53	1.60
Germany	0.12	0.25	0.64	1.16
Greece	1.35	1.52	0.00	0.00
Ireland	0.85	0.24	0.00	0.00
Italy	0.20	0.45	0.38	0.51
Netherlands	0.79	2.04	2.02	3.82
Portugal	0.84	2.92	0.05	0.35
Spain	1.07	2.00	0.17	0.41
United Kingdom	1.14	2.51	2.13	3.03
EU Member States	0.53	1.16	0.85	1.55
OECD Countries	0.46	0.82	0.56	1.11

Source: OECD.

has also been the largest recipient of extra-EU investment, mostly sourced from Japan, causing some consternation among EU partners that were members of the Exchange Rate Mechanism (the UK only joined the mechanism briefly). Mergers and acquisitions also increased rapidly post-1987. A review of these trends can be found in Hoeller and Louppe (1994).

In macroeconomic terms, with a fixed exchange rate regime such as the ERM, increased financial integration suggests that macroeconomic policy interdependence will be significant, so that policy convergence would prove helpful, so as to minimize real exchange rate variability. The ERM, though, is an adjustable peg exchange rate regime, where realignments are permitted, so exchange rate volatility may not have fallen compared with the pre-ERM period. Artis and Taylor (1994) and Crowley (1995), though, show that the ERM did significantly reduce volatility for all member currencies, particularly during the post-1983 period when realignments were relatively infrequent. There is, therefore, a probable relationship between exchange rate volatility and direct foreign investment flows in the EU context, although it is difficult to isolate such an effect in the data, due to the other concurrent trends mentioned.

If exchange rates are fully flexible, there will still be substantial macroeconomic interdependencies which can manifest themselves through monetary and fiscal policy interactions and feedback, as well as through unphased business cycles (see Mussa, 1979 and Artus, Avouyi-Dovi, Bleuze and Lecointe, 1991). Also, to date, flexible exchange rate regimes have experienced misalignments in nominal exchange rates and a high degree of nominal exchange rate volatility. Long-term misalignments are often the root cause of protectionist pressures, so the EU has sought to proceed with establishing a single market while at the same time pursuing nominal exchange rate stability between member states.

There are other well-recognized macroeconomic effects of increased intra-regional trade which should also be considered. As intra-regional trade grows in importance, aggregate demand linkages are strengthened, due to larger marginal propensities to import and the effects of changes in the terms of trade. Also aggregate supply linkages increase as intermediate goods become specialized within the regional trade bloc (see Jacquemin, 1992). From a monetary policy perspective as well, inflation or exchange rate pass-through can have significant effects on domestic inflation and wage settlements.

Bini-Smaghi and Vona (1989) attempt to capture the effects of dynamic economic activity (aggregate demand) and price competitiveness on the volume of intra-EC trading flows. Their findings were critical of the lack of monetary and fiscal policy coordination in the EC during the 1980s. In particular, they deplored the lack of cooperation from those countries which experienced an improvement in price competitiveness and therefore current account balances, but refused to stimulate growth through more active domestic demand policies. The fact that countries that obtained a stimulating effect from their improved competitive position maintained restrictive demand policies (and vice versa for those that experienced a loss in competitiveness), led to growing trade imbalances, which, no doubt through expectations effects, caused a tightening in monetary policy in the deficit countries. More recently, Allsopp, Davies and Vines (1995) have also suggested that countries should take into account international coordination issues in a cooperative way when setting macroeconomic policy, but ensuring that short-term fiscal activism is not allowed to detract from medium-term fiscal control.

In other research, Vona (1990) opposes the use of nominal exchange rate adjustment, due to the inflation differential consequences, but favours monetary union as the only feasible method for eliminating intra-ERM trade imbalances, given that fiscal policy convergence would be desirable. This prescription naturally leads on to a discussion of monetary integration.

REGIONAL MONETARY INTEGRATION

There are few instances of monetary union that have attracted as much attention and academic study as the plans of the EU. Perhaps this is because single currencies have evolved over time (as in the USA and Canada), or they have been legislatively introduced (as in the post-World War II USSR satellites, post-communist East Germany and Hawaii's accession as a US state) as part of both aggressive and non-aggressive territorial acquisition. European plans for monetary union are unique, though, not only because the European Commission sees monetary integration as a logical step to both widen and deepen economic integration, but also because there is a significant proportion of Europeans that do not favour a loss of monetary sovereignty. As no other regional trading bloc has taken the step towards monetary union, the focus in later parts of this section will be solely on Europe.

The Theory of Optimum Currency Areas

The theory of optimum currency areas originates from a celebrated article by Mundell (1961). Its main gist is a weighing up of the benefits and costs of adopting a single currency.

The benefits are the elimination of the costs of changing one national money into another, the possible positive boost to economic integration (in trade and welfare terms) that such an elimination may foster, and the elimination of exchange rate uncertainty, which would also be expected to boost trade. In addition, there is alleged to be an added advantage over fixed exchange rates, in that when governments and monetary authorities possess imperfect policy credibility, the adoption of a single currency (as long as it is properly managed) will enhance policy credibility in other areas.

As well as the loss of seigniorage income, the costs of monetary integration would include the loss of the exchange rate as a policy instrument, and therefore increased vulnerability to asymmetric disturbances between participating countries. If shocks are asymmetric and permanent then the costs of adopting a single currency are likely to be significant, whereas if shocks are symmetric then the costs will be minimal (dependent on size differential). Also, Mundell pointed out the desirability of labour and capital mobility within the single currency area if costs are to be minimized.

The benefits of monetary union in the European context are difficult to quantify, but the Commission of the European Communities (1990) has estimated that monetary union would eliminate transaction costs, amounting to at most 0.4 per cent of EU GDP. As for the benefits from increased economic integration, the Commission (1990) estimated these as accumulating to up to 5 per cent of EU GDP. For other benefits, such as the boost to trade from the elimination of exchange rate volatility, there is little econometric evidence (see Frankel and Wei, 1993). Other benefits are almost impossible to quantify.

The calculation of the costs of monetary union in a European context is an extremely complex proposition, so only the seigniorage losses have been calculated by the Commission (1990), and they turn out to be less than 0.5 per cent of EU GDP. Much of the weighing up of costs over benefits therefore turns on a systematic evaluation of the incidence of shocks across member states. A recent study by Bayoumi and Eichengreen (1993) evaluates demand and supply shocks in the European context by using a vector autoregression technique using price and income data. Shocks with a permanent impact on output are interpreted as supply disturbances (as these are more likely to be technology shocks) and shocks with only a temporary impact on output are read as demand disturbances (being more reflective of national economic policies). The correlation of supply disturbances and demand disturbances for the major EU member states in this study are shown in Tables 7.5 and 7.6.

Table 7.5 suggests that only Germany, France and Italy experience supply shocks that are significantly symmetric, and Table 7.6 suggests that only France and Italy have significant symmetry in their demand shocks. It is noteworthy that the UK and France and Italy together appear to have demand shocks that are negatively correlated. Taken in isolation, this suggests that the UK is a less suitable candidate for a single currency zone. The results indicate that a small core of industrial countries (Germany, France, Belgium, the Netherlands and Denmark) are suitable candidates for a single currency zone.[1]

Other more recent literature on optimal currency areas has set out a formal model with microeconomic foundations, so as to combine some of Mundell's

Table 7.5   Correlation of supply shocks across EU member states

	Germany	France	Netherlands	UK	Italy
Germany	1.00				
France	0.54	1.00			
Netherlands	0.59	0.42	1.00		
UK	0.05	0.10	0.08	1.00	
Italy	0.23	0.33	0.33	0.38	1.00

Note: The significance levels are 0.43 and 0.51 for 5 per cent and 1 per cent levels of significance respectively.

Source: Bayoumi and Eichengreen (1993), Table 13.

Table 7.6   Correlation of demand shocks across EU member states

	Germany	France	Netherlands	UK	Italy
Germany	1.00				
France	0.35	1.00			
Netherlands	0.17	0.35	1.00		
UK	0.16	−0.22	0.38	1.00	
Italy	0.17	0.57	0.19	−0.27	1.00

Note: The significance levels are 0.43 and 0.51 for 5 per cent and 1 per cent levels of significance respectively.

Source: Bayoumi and Eichengreen (1993), Table 14.

insights with a more rigorous analysis of the costs and benefits of moving to a single currency. Bayoumi (1994) finds that a monetary union can increase welfare for participating countries, but in his model it lowers welfare for regions outside the union. This is because for regions outside the union whose consumption is most closely associated with the union, if prices are downwardly rigid, then real wages are downwardly rigid, so that losses in real output occur with no enhancement to trade flows. Unless real output increases in the union raise world output, and therefore consumption, or there is some other benefit to countries outside the union, welfare is unambiguously reduced.

The Dynamics of Monetary Integration

Regardless of the reasons for advocating monetary integration, once a decision has been made to adopt such a strategy, there are many possible paths to achieving a monetary union. Below, several alternative blueprints for a path to monetary union are explored:

1. 'Maastricht' approach (time-specified/gradualist);
2. Hayekian 'Hard-ECU' approach (competition/gradualist); and
3. 'Hawaiian' approach (shock-therapy).

The paths can vary according to both speed of transition and route taken to the final objective, however, the two are not mutually independent.

There are two basic approaches concerning the speed at which a monetary union is adopted, the gradualist approach (which is essentially an approach that has a specified timetable, or agreed-upon criteria before the next stage can begin) and the 'shock-therapy' or 'Hawaiian' approach to achieving monetary union. The 'Hard-ECU" approach (originally proposed by the UK) is based on contemporaneous currency circulation of the new currency (see Hayek, 1984), and therefore might be considered gradualist, but there is no certainty as to whether the process will actually yield monetary union, as it could conceivably reverse at any time.

The 'Maastricht' Approach

All 12 member states of the EU have now successfully ratified the Maastricht Treaty, which was signed in the small Dutch town from which it takes its name in December 1991. The treaty outlines the process of Economic and Monetary Union (EMU), where all 15 member states will potentially be part of a single market with a single money. The process of EMU began with Stage 2 of the Treaty provisions on 1 January, 1994, with the establishment of the European Monetary Institute (EMI) at Frankfurt-am-Main in Germany.

The Maastricht Treaty envisioned one particular route to MU, which consists of three stages, as follows:

- *Stage 1* (1 July 1990 to 31 December 1993) – in this stage, the EMS abolished all remaining capital controls, monetary cooperation between the EC central banks was strengthened and realignments of the ERM were possible;
- *Stage 2* (1 January 1994 to between January 1997 and January 1999) – in this stage, the EMI is established as a temporary institution to oversee transition to stage 3, all Member States will start the process leading to the independence of their central banks, the Commission and the EMI will establish whether the member states achieve or are moving towards achieving certain criteria as specified in the Treaty, and ERM realignments will be vigorously resisted; and
- *Stage 3* (from between January 1997 and January 1999 onwards) – in this stage, the exchange rates between the national currencies will be irrevocably fixed, the European Central Bank (ECB) will start operations, the ECU will become a currency in its own right and will circulate as the only currency in EU member states that have proceeded to the third stage.

The Maastricht approach was to set entry conditions, the convergence criteria, and to use the ERM as the stepping-stone from which to gradually reduce volatility until exchange rates could be fixed, after which a single currency could be substituted.

The economic convergence criteria are clearly laid out in the Maastricht Treaty, which is an approach unique to Europe. It is politically a recognition of a compromise approach to monetary union. The criteria are as follows (Article 109j):

i.   price stability – an annual average rate of inflation that does not exceed by more than 1.5 per cent that of, at most, the three best performing member states;

ii.   interest rates – observed over a period of one year, a Member State has had an average nominal long-term interest rate on government bonds that does not exceed by more than 2 per cent that of, at most, the three best performing member states in terms of price stability;

iii.   government deficits – the deficit should not exceed 3 per cent for the ratio of the planned or actual government deficit to gross domestic product at market prices;

iv.   Government Debt - the debt should not exceed 60% for the ratio of government debt to gross domestic product;

v.   ERM – respect for the 'normal' fluctuation margins provided for by the exchange rate mechanism of the EMS without severe tensions for at least the last 2 years before examination; a devaluation should not have occurred during this period.

Because of the extraordinary foreign exchange market events of 1992–93, criteria (v) has essentially been dropped by the EMI. (A kinder interpretation might be that it has been 'reinterpreted'.) Much has been written on these criterion, and in particular, the fiscal criteria (iii) and (iv) have been the focus of much attention (see Goodhart, 1991; Buiter, Corsetti and Roubini, 1993; Langfeldt, 1992; Papadia and Schioppa, 1993; Centre for Economic Policy Research, 1991; Corsetti and Roubini, 1993; among others).

The first two criteria are very well specified, and make economic sense in the context of the economic circumstances prevailing when the Maastricht Treaty was signed. If stable exchange rates are to be achieved, then inflation convergence in terms of tradable goods would be advantageous. In terms of criterion (ii) (long-term interest rates), high intra-EC capital mobility combined with criterion (v) (the ERM) would imply that long-term interest rate differentials would only occur with differential default risk. Eliminating such differential risk may be the motivation behind criteria (iii) (government deficits) and (iv) (government debt). As criteria (i) (inflation rates) and (ii) (long-term interest rates) are only entry conditions they appear to be sensible, not only because they are defined in relative terms, but also because they closely link the entry conditions so as to be dynamically consistent with the final objective.

Criteria (iii) and (iv) (government deficits and debt, respectively), in contrast, are absolute objectives that, *inter alia*, bear little relation to the eventual objective. Table 7.7 summarizes the Maastricht criteria.

Table 7.7   The Maastricht convergence criteria

Criteria		Nature	Entry condition?
i.	Inflation rate	Relative	Entry
ii.	Interest rate	Relative	Entry
iii.	Govt deficit	Static	Continuing
iv.	Govt debt	Static	Continuing
v.	ERM	Relative	Entry

It should be noted that the ERM conditions are really a 'relative' criterion because the ECU itself is a basket of all EMS currencies, and further, although the ERM may continue after stage 3 of EMU begins, as soon as all member states adopt the ECU, the ERM will cease to exist. Also, and most importantly here, the fiscal criteria would not be relaxed but act as a measure for ensuring that Article 104c(1) ('Member States shall avoid excessive deficits') of the Maastricht Treaty is not transgressed.

The Transition Process

Whatever approach is chosen to get to MU, there are various questions as to the component parts of the transition process. In this instance, five issues will be addressed:

a.   Should monetary union be accompanied by a further significant increase in economic convergence?
b.   Should MU be accompanied by national currency stability?
c.   Should the MU process incorporate a role for national central banks, and if so, what should it be?
d.   Should some form of fiscal federalism be developed in the transition to help Europe's periphery shoulder regional shocks?
e.   Should EU monetary institutions be developed before monetary union eventually occurs, and if so how?

Each of the generic approaches described in the section on the dynamics of monetary integration has different responses to these questions, and these are summarized in Table 7.8, where three specific examples of the three possible approaches to monetary union have been given. Maastricht's answer to the role of national central banks is as yet unclear, but central bank independence is seen as a priority and with the degree of fiscal federalism, there is a limit of 1.27 per cent of EU GDP (for 1999) in the stipulated projections for the EU

Table 7.8   The transition process to MU

		Maastricht	Hard ECU	Hawaiian
a.	Economic convergence?	Yes	No	No
b.	Currency stability?	Yes	No	No
c.	National bank role?	Independent	Yes	None
d.	Fiscal federalism?	Minimal	Yes	(Yes)
e.	EU monetary authorities?	EMI	Yes	Yes

budget. The 'Hawaiian' approach does not need any convergence, but requires complete cooperation on the part of the national central banks and also may require some resource transfer depending upon the rate at which the conversion is made. The 'Hard ECU' approach requires no economic convergence or currency stability but national central banks have to play a role in determining the speed at which the transition occurs, and indeed, whether it occurs at all. Some fiscal redistribution may be required for the 'Hard-ECU' approach, as regional shocks may endanger the efficacy of national fiscal policies because of the legal ability to substitute national currency for ECUs.

In terms of the reality of the current state of European monetary integration, the irony is that the economic convergence criteria specified in Maastricht will probably not be met by many of the member states by 1997 excepting Germany and Luxembourg (see De Grauwe and Gros, 1991; *Financial Times*, 1993, 1994b; and European Monetary Institute, 1994), and most member states are operating, if at all, under exceptionally wide fluctuation bands in the ERM (this is unlikely to change following evidence EMI President Lamfalussy gave to the European Parliament (see *Financial Times*, 1994a)). The role of national central banks is a moot point with many European governments (notably the UK) and the degree of fiscal federalism as envisaged under the Edinburgh plan has been attacked as inadequate (see Sala-i-Martin and Sachs, 1991). Only the development of EU monetary authorities appears to be on track, with the EMI firmly established as the precursor to the ECB.

REGIONAL POLITICAL INTEGRATION

For some, the whole notion of integration has become undesirable from a political perspective, with some arguing that the benefits of increased economic welfare will be outweighed by the threat to the nation state (see McMillan, 1994). In the European context, substantial divisions are apparent, particularly in Germany and the United Kingdom. In Germany (see *Financial Times*, 1995) the German finance ministry and the Bundesbank have been in disagreement for some time over the degree of political integration desirable. In the United Kingdom, recent outbursts by a group of British MPs in the spring and summer of 1995, together with the publication of a book by a member of the Commission's economic analysis division (Connolly, 1995), have sought to emphasize the differences between those who see EMU as a natural progression in order to protect and further entrench the gains of the single market from those who view Brussels as autocratic, inflexible and ambitious to harness as many political powers as possible. The latters' concerns are that the pursuit of economic gains from integration threatens to erode the power of national governments, sovereignty in policy and the social cohesiveness of the nation state. The preservation of national identity is clearly perceived to be an important issue, as it is elsewhere (it mirrors the debate currently unfolding in Canada concerning the future of Quebec). In the continental European context, though, cultural identity is firmly rooted in most member states, so these concerns have not been so strongly expressed. This issue will therefore not be addressed in any depth. A full description of the EU institutions and general issues concerning their development can be found in Sbragia (1992).

Background

The Werner Report (1971) (which was produced by the Werner Group, which was set up in 1969 after The Hague summit, to study plans for EMU), was the earliest attempt to specify a more concrete plan to achieve greater monetary and economic integration between member countries. It did not, however, specify any political integration among members of the community. During the Werner Group negotiations, it became clear (see Tsoulkalis, 1977 and De Grauwe, 1990) that two opposing groups had formed with views on strategies to attain MU. These groups were labelled the 'monetarists' and the 'economists', the former holding to the view that early progress in the monetary field would force an effective coordination of economic policies and the latter believing that harmonization of economic policies should take priority before any coordination of Community monetary policy. These two groups (in various guises) characterised much of the debate in the Maastricht discussions.

The issuance of the Delors Report in 1989 (Committee on the Study of Economic and Monetary Union, 1989) provided new impetus towards monetary and political unification in Europe and laid out the basis for the eventual treaty for unification, the Maastricht Treaty. The Delors Report was, in essence, a blueprint for a 'monetarist' approach (of a gradualist kind) to EMU.

There were two dissenting voices against the means of achieving monetary union, the UK government and the German government (with the Bundesbank). The UK government objected to the report on the basis that it ceded monetary sovereignty to a European monetary institution and that it implicitly sought the abolition of national currencies. The UK government issued two (HM Treasury) documents as alternatives to the Delors plan which embodied the Hayekian parallel-currency principle. The UK government, particularly under Margaret Thatcher's leadership, was deeply suspicious of plans for deepening political integration in the community. The Bundesbank's objections, on the other hand, were of an 'economist' nature. The Bundesbank wanted strict criteria to be incorporated into the plan before countries could proceed towards monetary union and the German government sought (most vocally) greater European political integration so that the European Central Bank (ECB) could be answerable to a European Parliament that possessed real powers. This stems from the Bundesbank's position within Germany as the protector of the currency, and directly answerable to Parliament rather than to the government of the day, but with a clear mandate to be an independent partner of the finance and economic ministries, when economic policies impinge on monetary affairs (see Henning, 1994 and Marsh, 1992).

It soon became clear that the 'Hard-ECU' proposal, while it obtained a polite reception, was unacceptable to most of the UK's European partners. At the Inter-Governmental Conference in Maastricht in December of 1991, agreement was reached on a compromise that satisfied the Germans. The UK, still uneasy about the loss of monetary sovereignty, along with Denmark at a later date, negotiated opt-out clauses.

It is interesting to note that the political stance of member states regarding increased political integration does not neatly divide along 'economist' and 'monetarist' lines. The Germans have long maintained that monetary integration, albeit with 'economist' preconditions, should be accompanied by political integration as it would provide a dialogue between what the French government called the '*pôle monétaire*', represented by the ECB and the '*pôle économique*' (represented by the European Parliament). Thus the independence of the ECB could only be achieved when an interdependence exists with a strong economic government.[2] 'Monetarist' France and Italy were initially favourable towards increased political integration, but lately, much to the delight of the British, the French government has adopted a 'softer' position, arguing that increased political integration is only acceptable if some degree of sovereignty is retained by member-state governments.

The Theory of Political Integration

The theoretical foundations for the theory of European integration were laid out more than a quarter century ago by Haas (1958), Lindberg (1963) and Nye (1968) among others. The theory of European integration developed by these political theorists was labelled 'neo-functionalist'. As Moravcsik (1993) notes, neo-functionalism predicts that the cumulative logic of economic integration will, if followed, lead to political integration via 'spillovers'. These 'spillovers' can be of a functional nature, whereby incomplete integration undermines the effectiveness of existing policies and thus pressures governments, or of a political nature, when a self-reinforcing institution-building process occurs at a supranational level, as officials become more autonomous and 'European' in their thinking. Tsoukalis describes this process as follows:

> Because economic tasks are functionally related to each other, it was expected that, once co-operation on some specific issues had been initiated, this would bring about a need both for a strengthening of such co-operation in the areas already covered by international agencies and for its extension to other related areas of economic policy. The process would continue until the moment that the nation-state would be virtually deprived of its autonomy. (1977, Chapter 2, p. 23)

Neo-functionalism is now regarded as unsatisfactory, not only because it predicted that integration would be a gradual and incremental process, where in fact it has proceeded in discrete jumps and through intergovernmental negotiations, but also because it predicted a large role for spillovers, whereas the empirical evidence tends to suggest that the functional spillovers are not of significant magnitude and that until recently, the supranational organizations have had very little perceived power (see Haas, 1975; Koehane and Nye, 1975; Taylor 1983).

More recently, Moravcsik (1993) has developed a liberal intergovernmentalist approach to the EU to replace the neo-functionalist theory. The approach consists of two parts: first the national governments define a set of interests (assuming rational governments) and then enter into a bargaining process to try to achieve those objectives (which are analysed using the theory of liberal intergovernmentalism and regime theory). This approach is seen as advantageous to many member states in that it can assist in domestic agenda-setting. Moravcsik further notes that in several instances regional integration was pursued as a means of employing the legitimacy that EU institutions enjoy so as to force domestic structural changes when significant inertia existed at home.

The one problem with applying such a liberal intergovernmentalist approach is that it assumes that the intergovernmental bargaining continues until consensus is reached. It appears, however, that the next Inter-Governmental Conference (IGC) will not see the emergence of a consensus, but a situation that has already been dubbed as a 'two-speed' EU, that is, two specific groups of member states, with those who are proceeding to the next and final stage of EMU, and those member states that do not find this last stage of the process desirable exercising their right to opt out. Even if one views this result as 'a consensus that agreement cannot be reached' other problems such as that of 'leviathan' governments with objectives that are different from those of the citizens that they represent (see Hayek, 1976) are not considered.

Other approaches to European integration exist, notably that of Taylor (1991), who proposes that a consociationalist model would best fit the emerging EU structure, given the current voting structure and entrenched national interests. Further, with the lack of cultural homogeneity in Europe, this model of political structure, which is usually associated with Switzerland, appears to be well-suited to divergent levels of economic development and cultural differences.

The Politics of 'Variable Geometry'

The current debate in the EU, prior to the conclusion of the 1996 Inter-Governmental Conference (IGC) centres around priorities: whether the EU should deepen integration between current Member States or should widen membership to include East European countries, at the expense of postponing or cancelling further substantive integration measures. Even if EMU proceeds as outlined in the Maastricht Treaty, that is by 1999, it is almost certain to involve a 'two-speed' process, with member states that satisfy the economic criteria introducing the ECU ahead of other member states, and with the possibility that Denmark and the United Kingdom may not even participate in EMU. This situation has been called 'variable geometry' in the political science literature.

There is agreement among member states on maintaining and strengthening the economic integration in terms of the single market concept, but there is fundamental disagreement on how this should be achieved. Some member states maintain that deepening economic integration is all that is necessary, while other member states claim that monetary integration is essential to protect the gains made in the single market in the light of the instability of the ERM of the EMS in 1992–93, while other member states claim that monetary integration is necessary, but will only be functional in a framework where supranational institutions are answerable to a European parliament that has real powers. Other issues such as a pan-EU social policy also divide member states, with the United Kingdom in particular, rejecting the concepts of a legislated minimum wage or a maximum number of hours of work for the EU as a whole (otherwise known as the social chapter).

The argument that monetary integration follows naturally from economic integration, is made on the assumption that full economic integration without exchange rate stability will produce incentives to competitively depreciate, which in turn will induce political pressure in member states for protectionist measures. As Eichengreen (1993) points out, the demise of the narrow-band ERM was probably due to speculative pressures in the foreign exchange market, which were inevitable once capital controls were removed (as part of the single market initiative). Thus there is a fear that deeper economic integration could lead to political tension between member states if measures are not taken to ensure exchange rate stability.

The argument for deeper political integration centres on two further issues:

1. What are the functional imperatives posed by the formation of the single market?
2. Given that the political nature of most monetary unions is federal in structure, and given that EMU will remove the monetary policy instrument from member-state governments, how should pan-EU fiscal policy be devised and implemented?

The functional imperatives which stem from the single market have been identified in such areas as harmonization of competition policy; reductions in state subsidies; coordination in the development of transport, energy and telecommunications networks; further liberalization in highly regulated sectors; and the coordination of member state social policies and the Commission's regional policy role. A detailed analysis of these imperatives is beyond the scope of this chapter.

Those who see further political reform as protecting and reinforcing the gains made by the single market also point to further development of central institutions along more democratic lines and majority voting in the European Council with regard to political issues. These items were not covered in the Maastricht Treaty, but they require resolution before and if further expansion of the EU takes place, so will likely figure large in the negotiations due to take place in the 1996 IGC (see *The Times* (1995) for some recent developments in this area).

As for the second of the issues, pan-EU fiscal policy is usually discussed under the general subject of fiscal federalism. Fiscal federalism is part of a branch of the public finance literature which deals with the assigning of different expenditure and tax/transfer competences to different levels of government (see Oates, 1972). Much of this literature assumes a static economy, so in a sense it is not applicable to the European situation, but it does have one important implication for EMU, which has been enshrined in Article 3b of the Maastricht Treaty: the principle of subsidiarity.

The concept of subsidiarity stems from the continental European tradition of Catholic social thought (see von der Groeben, 1987). Subsidiarity stipulates that a higher level of government should only assume responsibilities that cannot be taken care of effectively by a lower level of government. Implicit in this principle is a preference for national autonomy in regulation, so coordination, in terms of, for example, the formation of committees, is assumed preferable to harmonization or centralization (see Centre for Economic Policy Research, 1991). Harmonization is seen as a last resort, once attempts to coordinate policies between member states have failed.

Several questions arise here, notably, what are the reasons for attempting to implement the subsidiarity principle in practice? In answer to this question as to the use of subsidiarity as a competence assignment criterion, Courchene et al. (1993) provide three arguments as follows:

1. national differences in needs and tastes;
2. better democratic control of public services at a national level; and
3. decentralized supply of public goods and services encourages competition and innovation between national authorities.

The first of these arguments, in the EU context, is certainly not in dispute: it is the European reality. The second reason reflects the notion that decentralized decision-making brings government 'closer to the people' (see Tresch, 1981). The third argument is somewhat controversial, however, as it assumes that a sufficient degree of labour and capital (or corporate) mobility exists between member states. Certainly, since 1993, the free movement of labour and capital is possible, but cultural and linguistic differences inevitably inhibit labour mobility, and other factors such as natural resource availability constrain the movement of firms between member states.

Even if the third reason cited above (increased competition between national authorities) for the subsidiarity principle is set aside, the principle might be justified on the basis of the first two reasons. But in what circumstances should competences either be coordinated or passed to a supranational level of government, according to the principle of subsidiarity? In 1977, the MacDougall Report was published (Commission of the European Communities, 1977) which 'examined the criteria for assigning functions to the different levels of a multi-tier government' (Plender, 1991). The report identified three rationales for assigning competences, in addition to that of the principle of subsidiarity. These were: cross-border spill-over effects of national policies that give rise to externalities; economies of scale and/or indivisibilities in national policies; and the pursuit of homogeneity and/or fairness.

With spillover effects, the more integrated economies grow, the greater these spillover effects are likely to be. For economies of scale and/or indivisibilities, efficiency gains are cited as the benefit. The pursuit of homogeneity and/or fairness, however, is the most controversial. In terms of the homogeneity argument, this justification has already caused much debate within Europe following recent claims that the European Commission has not been meddling in areas where it has no competence.

REGIONAL INTEGRATION AND ECONOMIC CONVERGENCE

The political tension between those gaining and losing in a federalist structure is normally justified by the economic principles of fiscal federalism. The principle here is often called the 'resource flow' principle – that is, the resources should flow from richer to poorer member states. Hence regional disparities might be expected to diminish in a federalist structure. But the degree of political homogeneity is clearly a factor in the perceived desirability for the extent of 'resource flow', even if such economic benefits in terms of overall welfare improvement could be convincingly demonstrated. The experience of federations such as the USA, Australia and Canada is that language and cultural similarities and factor mobility engender a much greater level of acceptance for 'resource flow' in general and, more specifically, regional income redistribution. All mature federations have a substantial degree of expenditure and revenue centralization. Most of these countries are unilingual, bilingual, or trilingual at most, which suggests that linguistic and cultural differences might be a major impetus for the acceptability of resource flows.

As Courchene et al. (1993) point out, 'there is an inverse relationship between State public finance autonomy and interregional redistribution'. This claim directly follows from the fact that the capacity for interregional redistribution depends *ceteris paribus* on the size of the federal budget relative to the budgets of the member states. There are, therefore, in any federation, winners (the poorer member states) and losers (the richer ones) – which is usually referred to in political terms as 'fairness in the supranational budgetary process'. In most mature federations 'fairness' is an elusive concept in budgetary politics, as certain expenditures cannot generally be apportioned on a regional basis.

This naturally leads to a discussion of the nature of convergence within a more federal EU structure. Given no interregional income distribution, there are two views here on whether convergence will occur in an economic union – the most well known often being labelled the 'convergence hypothesis'. The convergence hypothesis states that spatial disparities will tend to disappear under an economic union due to international trade, capital flows and labour mobility. The opposing view stresses the existence of imperfect competition, economies of scale and externalities and so asserts that convergence in an economic union will be deflected due to 'cumulative causation' processes (see Prud'homme, 1993). Clearly, even if international trade has no additional effects in the EU, interregional income redistributions must be sufficiently large enough to offset any 'cumulative causation' processes for economic convergence to occur.

The whole notion of budgetary fairness is thus congruent to that of economic convergence. But economic convergence in reality under Maastricht is a moot issue, as the loss of two economic policy levers (monetary and exchange rate policies) leaves only two other levers (national fiscal policies and the EU budget itself). This could limit national governments when responding to asymmetric shocks and could potentially discourage convergence. The outcome logically depends upon the relative phasing of business cycles and the degree of asymmetric shocks between each member state and the ability of national governments and the European Commission through the EU budget, to respond through fiscal means.

Concerning the role of the EU budget, the medium-term evolution of the EU budget was decided by EU leaders at the Edinburgh summit in 1992. The budget will grow from just under 1.2 per cent of EU GDP to a limit of 1.7 per cent of EU GDP by 1999. Furthermore, it was decided that the Commission would be denied fiscal sovereignty (the ability to raise taxes independently of national governments) and would continue to raise most of its resources by a 'surcharge' on indirect taxes (VAT) collected by member states. This may seem to be at odds with other federations, but as Boadway and Keen (1994) have shown, regardless of whether EU has fiscal sovereignty, on efficiency grounds there is no reason to presume that intergovernmental transfer should go from higher levels of government to lower levels. There is also a legal prohibition from running a deficit at the EU level of government and EU expenditures are highly discretionary, with more than 80 per cent being directed to the Common Agricultural Policy or regional development. The inability to raise 'own resources', though, and to operate interpersonal income transfers, when compared with other more fiscally-sovereign federalist structures, makes the EU unique. This suggests that the reason that the EC budget is so minuscule in comparison with other more mature federations might be because of the political unacceptability of regional income redistribution and the associated addition of tax competencies to a centralized federal administration.

The fact that there will be little interregional income redistribution in the EC suggests that the ties binding most member states together will be far less substantial and resilient than in other mature federations. The reality of this fact spawns a whole series of corollaries, but most poignantly that the member states will need a great deal of fiscal latitude to deal with regional- or industry-specific disturbances and shocks, given that both monetary sovereignty and the exchange rate instrument will no longer be available to member states. As the EU budget cannot support compensatory redistributive initiatives to alleviate the effects of asymmetric shocks, this leaves, *in extremis*, national fiscal policies as the only policy lever available.

It should be noted that one other economic valve for responding to asymmetric shocks, *ex post*, is through labour migration. As has already been noted, cultural and linguistic differences (as well as interregional transfers themselves) tend to inhibit the rate of migration to high-growth regions.

CONCLUSIONS

Regional integration projects are now widespread. In Europe, integration has proceeded in the economic domain, with the formation of the single market, which was to be completed by 1993, and in the monetary domain, after the signing of the Maastricht Treaty in December 1991. Political integration is still in its infancy compared with other more mature federations.

But what can be learned from the European experience? The primary lesson to be learned is that the vision and objectives or goals that constitute that vision need to be fully specified in advance before the means to achieve them can be formulated. The use of the ERM of the EMS is a prime example of using an existing mechanism to achieve something for which it patently was not designed. If EMU is to be realized in the current political climate, the political of 'variable geometry' will undoubtedly dominate.

The natural adjoint to the economic issues surrounding the major obstacles to EMU, notably the fiscal criteria, is not primarily one of exchange rate instability, but rather that of the role of supranational institutions, particularly in relation to overall EU fiscal and monetary policy. With the abandonment of national currencies and therefore independent member-state monetary policy, the fiscal restraints imposed by the Maastricht Treaty protocol on excessive deficits, and the extremely limited size of the EU budget and the concomitant EU mandatory surplus, member states will be severely limited in their ability to respond to asymmetric shocks or unphased business cycles. The current Maastricht path and the criteria embodied in the approach to EMU will therefore not allow the ultimate objective of EMU to be attained for the regional bloc as a whole, and will lead to incomplete monetary integration. Such divisions within the EU will severely handicap any efforts to intensify political integration.

EMU is certainly not dead, but the process of keeping it alive has already compromised the objective of European exchange rate stability (the EMS) and will inevitably pose further economic problems and difficult policy choices. The opt-out clauses negotiated by Denmark and the UK illustrate that consensus in the EU no longer exists and it also demonstrates that to some, there are limits to what countries will sacrifice in order to deepen integration. Indeed, with the addition of three recent new members to the EU (Sweden, Finland and Austria), this begs the question as to the optimal number of signatures to regional integration arrangements and the question of broadening versus deepening such arrangements. Indeed, there is still wide disagreement among the member states of the EU on the appropriateness of pursuing a deepening of arrangements when it is likely that various Eastern European countries will be ready to join the EU in the not too distant future.

How is European integration unique? The major difference between the three regional poles is that in Europe, the strongest participant, Germany, is balanced by many other countries, which together provide a balance to counteract German dominance – in the other two regional blocs, a single country dominates the regional bloc. One corollary from this observation is that while this situation persists in the other regional blocs, it is highly unlikely that further integration will be viewed as politically acceptable or desirable. It appears, therefore, that widening the membership of these regional blocs will be a prerequisite for a deepening of integration arrangements.

NOTES

1. A similar analysis for North America finds that the correlations of disturbances suggest that there is some support for an east–west US split, with Western Canada joining the US North West, the US South West and Mexico. California fits more neatly with the eastern regions of the USA, while Eastern Canada apparently belongs on its own!
2. Communiqué du Conseil des Ministres, 5 December 1990.

REFERENCES

Allsopp, C., G. Davies and D. Vines (1995), 'Regional Macroeconomic Policy, Fiscal Federalism, and European Integration', *Oxford Review of Economic Policy*, **11** (2), pp. 126–44.
Artis, M. and M. Taylor (1994), 'The Stabilizing Effect of the ERM on Exchange Rates and Interest Rates', *IMF Staff Papers*, **41** (1), 123–48.
Artus, P., S. Avouyi-Dovi, E. Bleuze and F. Lecointe (1991), 'Transmission of U.S. monetary policy to Europe and asymmetry in the European monetary system', *European Economic Review*, **35**, 1369–84.
Bayoumi, T. (1994), 'A Formal Model of Optimum Currency Areas', *IMF Staff Papers*, **41** (4), 537–54.
Bayoumi, T. and B. Eichengreen (1993), 'Monetary and Exchange Rate Arrangements for NAFTA', *IMF Working Paper*, WP/93/20, March.

Begg, I., G. Gudgin and D. Morris (1995), 'The Assessment: Regional Policy in the European Union', *Oxford Review of Economic Policy*, **11** (2), 1–17.

Bini-Smaghi, L. and S. Vona (1989), 'The Effects of Economic Convergence and Competitiveness on Trade among the EMS Countries', in D. Hodgman and G. Wood, *Macroeconomic Policy and Economic Interdependence*, Basingstoke: Macmillan, pp. 272–326.

Boadway, R. and R. Keen (1994), 'Efficiency and the Fiscal Gap in Federal Systems', *Institute for Economic Research Discussion Paper*, No. 915, Queen's University.

Buiter, W., G. Corsetti and N. Roubini (1993), 'Excessive Deficits: Sense and Non-sense in the Treaty of Maastricht', *Economic Policy*, **16**, 58–90.

Cantwell, J. (1988), 'The Reorganisation of European Industries after Integration: Selected Evidence on the Role of Multinational Enterprise Activities' in J. Dunning and P. Robson (eds), *Multinationals and the European Community*, Oxford: Basil Blackwell, pp. 25–49.

Cavallo, D. (1992), 'Economic Reorganisation as a Prerequisite to Growth', in *Policies for Long-Run Economic Growth*, Kansas City: Federal Reserve Bank, pp. 149–56.

Centre for Economic Policy Research (1991), *Monitoring European Integration: The Making of Monetary Union*, Annual Report, London: Centre for Economic Policy Research.

Commission of the European Communities (1977), *Report of the Study Group on the Role of Public Finance in European Integration*, Brussels.

Commission of the European Communities (1990), *One Market, One Money*, European Economy 44, Directorate-General for Economic and Financial Affairs, Brussels.

Commission of the European Communities (1993), *The European Community as a World Trade Partner*, European Economy 52, Directorate-General for Economic and Financial Affairs, Brussels.

Commission of the European Communities (1994), *Competitiveness and Cohesion*, Fifth Periodic Report on the Social and Economic Situation and Development of the Regions in the Community, Luxembourg: Office for Official Publications of the European Communities.

Committee on the Study of Economic and Monetary Union (Delors Committee) (1989), *Report on Economic and Monetary Union in the European Community (Delors Report)* (with Collection of Papers), Luxembourg: Office for Official Publications of the European Communities.

Connolly, B. (1995), *The Rotten Heart of Europe: The Dirty War for Europe's Money*, London: Faber and Faber.

Corsetti, G. and N. Roubini (1993), 'Design of Optimal Fiscal Rules for Europe after 1992', in F. Giavazzi and F. Torres (eds), *Adjustment and Growth in the European Monetary Union*, Cambridge: Cambridge University Press.

Council of the European Communities, Commission of the European Communities (1992), *Treaty on European Union*, Luxembourg: Office for Official Publications of the European Communities.

Courchene, T., C. Goodhart, A. Majocchi, W. Moesen, R. Prud'homme, F. Schneider, S. Smith, B. Spahn and C. Walsh (1993), 'Stable Money – Sound Finances', *European Economy*, **53**.

Crowley, P. (1995), 'The Exchange Rate Mechanism of the European Monetary System: Volatility, Target Zones and Prospects', Unpublished Ph.D. thesis, McGill University, Montreal.

De Grauwe, P. (1990), 'The Liberalisation of Capital Movements and the EMS' in P. Ferri (ed.), *Prospects for the European Monetary System*, Basingstoke: Macmillan, pp. 159–77.

De Grauwe, P. and D. Gros (1991), 'Convergence and Divergence in the Community's Economy on the Eve of Economic and Monetary Union', in P. Ludlow (ed.), *Setting European Community Priorities 1991–92*, Brussels: Centre for Economic Policy Studies.

Dignan, T. (1995), 'Regional Disparities and Regional Policy in the European Union', *Oxford Review of Economic Policy*, **11** (2), pp. 64–95.

Dunning, J. and P. Robson (1988), 'Multinational and Regional Integration', in J. Dunning and P. Robson (eds), *Multinationals and the European Community*, Oxford: Basil Blackwell, pp. 1–24.

Eichengreen, B. (1993), 'European Monetary Unification', *Journal of Economic Literature*, **31**, 1321-57.

Emerson, M. (1991), 'The Transformation of Trade and Monetary Regimes in Europe', in *Policy Implications of Trade and Currency Zones*, Kansas City: Federal Reserve Bank, pp. 59–76.

European Monetary Institute (1994), *Annual Report 1994*, Frankfurt: European Monetary Institute.

Financial Times (1993), 'Europe keeps on tortuous path towards EMU', 17 February.

Financial Times (1994a), 'EMI drops call for narrow currency bands', 27 April.

Financial Times (1994b), 'Emu may not be dead, after all', 1 August.

Financial Times (1995), 'Bundesbank and Bonn split on Emu', 24 February.

Frankel, J. and S.-J. Wei (1993), 'Trade Blocs and Currency Blocs', *NBER Working Paper*, No. 4335, April.

Genberg, H. and F. Nadal De Simone (1993), 'Regional Integration Agreements and Macroeconomic Discipline', in K. Anderson and R. Blackhurst (eds), *Regional Integration and the Global Trading System*, New York: St. Martins Press, pp. 167–96.

Goodhart, C. (1991), 'National Fiscal Policy within EMU: The Fiscal Implications of Maastricht', *LSE Financial Markets Group, Special Paper*, No 45.

Greenaway, D. (1988), 'Intra-Industry Trade, Intra-Firm Trade and European Integration: Evidence, Gains and Policy Aspects', in P. Dunning and P. Robson (eds), *Multinationals and the European Community*, Oxford: Basil Blackwell Ltd, pp. 51–70.

Haas, E. (1958), *The Uniting of Europe: Political, Social and Economic Forces, 1950–1957*, Stanford, California: Stanford University Press.

Haas, E. (1975), *The Obsolescence of Regional Integration Theory*, Berkeley, California: Center for International Studies.

Hayek, F. von (1976), *Denationalization of Money*, Hobart Paper No. 70, The Institute of Economic Affairs, London.

Hayek, F. von (1984), 'The Future Unit of Value', in F. Salin (ed.), *Currency Competition and Monetary Union*, The Hague: Martinus Nijhoff, pp. 29–41.

Helpman, E. and P. Krugman (1985), *Market Structure and Foreign Trade*, Cambridge, MA: MIT Press.

Henning, R. (1994), *Currencies and Politics in the United States, Germany, and Japan*, Washington DC: Institute for International Economics.

Hoeller and Louppe (1994), 'The EC's Internal Market: Implementation, Economic Consequences, Unfinished Business', *OECD Economics Department Working Paper*, No. 147, OCDE/GD (94) 87, Paris.

Jacquemin, A. (1992), 'Corporate Strategy and Competition Policy in the Post-1992 Single Market', in W. Adams (ed.), *Singular Europe*, Michigan: University of Michigan Press.

Jacquemin, A. and A. Sapir (1991), 'Europe Post-1992: Internal and External Liberalisation', *American Economic Review*, **81**, 166–70.

Koehane, R. and J. Nye (1975), 'International Independence and Integration' in F. Greenstein and N. Polsby (eds), *Handbook of Political Science*, Andover, MA: Addison-Wesley Inc., pp. 363–414.

Krugman, P. (1991), 'The Move Towards Free Trade Zones', in *Policy Implications of Trade and Currency Zones*, Kansas City: Federal Reserve Bank.

Langfeldt, E. (1992), 'Economic Monetary Union: Design and Implementation', in R. Barrell (ed.), *Economic Convergence and Monetary Union in Europe*, London: National Institute of Economic and Social Research, pp. 58–69.

Lindberg, L. (1963), *The Political Dynamics of European Economic Integration*, Stanford, CA: Stanford University Press.

Marsh, D. (1992), *The Bundesbank: The Bank that Rules Europe*, London: Heinemann.

McCallum, J. (1993), 'National Borders Matter: Regional Trade Patterns in North America', *McGill University Working Papers in Economics*, No. 12.

McMillan, M. (1994), 'Continental Economic Integration: A Perspective on the Relative Threat to the Canadian Nation-State', *University of Alberta Economics Research Paper*, No. 23.

Moravcsik, A. (1993), 'Preferences and Power in the European Community: A Liberal Intergovernmentalist Approach', *Journal of Common Market Studies*, **31** (4), 473–524.

Morsink, R. and W. Molle (1991), 'Direct Investment and Monetary Integration', *European Economy*, Special Edition No. 1, 36–55.

Mundell, R. (1961), 'A Theory of Optimum Currency Areas', *American Economic Review*, **51**, pp. 657–65.

Mussa, M. (1979), 'Macroeconomic Interdependence and the Exchange Rate Regime' in R. Dornbusch and J. Frenkel (eds), *International Economic Policy*, Baltimore: Johns Hopkins University, pp. 160–203.

Nye, J. (1968), *International Regionalism*, Boston, MA: Little, Brown Publishers.

Oates, W. (1972), *Fiscal Federalism*, New York: Harcourt, Brace & Jovanovich.

Padoa-Schioppa, T. (1993), 'Tripolarism: Regional and Global Economic Cooperation, *Group of Thirty Occasional Paper*, No. 42, Washington, DC.

Papadia, F. and C. Schioppa, (1993), 'Economic Convergence and Monetary Union', in W. Gebauer (ed.), *Foundations of European Central Bank Policy*, Heidelberg: Physica-Verlag.

Plender, J. (1991), *European Community: The Building of a Union*, Oxford: Oxford University Press.

Prud'homme, R. (1993), 'The potential role of the EC budget in the reduction of spatial disparities in a European Economic and Monetary Union', *European Economy Reports and Studies*, No. 5.

Sala-i-Martin, X. and J. Sachs (1991), 'Fiscal Federalism and Optimum Currency Areas: Evidence for Europe from the US', *NBER Working Paper*, No. 3855, NBER, Washington, DC.

Sbragia, A. (ed.) (1992), *Euro-Politics: Institutions and Policymaking in the 'New' European Community*, Washington, DC: The Brookings Institution.

Taylor, P. (1983), *The Limits of European Integration*, London: Croom Helm Ltd.

Taylor, P. (1991), 'The European Community and the State: Assumptions, Theories and Propositions', *Review of International Studies*, **17**, 109–25.

The Times, (1995), 'France deserts Britain over majority EU voting', 15 September.

Tinbergen, J. (1965), *International Economic Integration*, Amsterdam: Elsevier Publishing Co.

Tresch, R. (1981), *Public Finance: A Normative Theory*, Texas: Business Publications.

Tsoukalis, L. (1977), *The Politics and Economics of European Monetary Integration*, London: George Allen & Unwin.

Ungerer, H. (1993), 'Political Aspects of European Monetary Integration', *EUI Working Papers*, European Policy Unit, EPU 93/2, Florence, Italy.

von der Groeben, H. (1987), *Legitimationsprobleme*, Baden-Baden: Nomos.

Vona, S. (1990), 'Real Exchange Rates and Trade Imbalances in the EMS' in P. Ferri, *Prospects for the European Monetary System*, Basingstoke: Macmillan, pp. 59–89.

Winters, A. (1993), 'The European Community: A Case of Successful Integration?', *CEPR Discussion Paper*, No. 755, January.

8. The economic effects of an East Asian trading bloc

Drusilla K. Brown, Alan V. Deardorff and Robert M. Stern

INTRODUCTION

In this chapter, we use a specially constructed version of the University of Michigan Brown–Deardorff–Stern (BDS) Computational General Equilibrium (CGE) Trade Model to estimate the potential economic effects of an East Asian Preferential Trading Bloc on the trade, output, and employment by sector as well as the real returns to capital and labour and the economic welfare of the members of an East Asian bloc, the United States, and the rest-of-world major trading countries/regions.

The chapter proceeds as follows. Previous research relating specifically to an East Asian bloc is reviewed in the next section. In the following section, we outline some of the essential features of the Michigan BDS CGE Trade Model. Next, the various scenarios investigated using the model are presented, together with the aggregate results of the model simulations. The sectoral results are then presented, and the final section contains our conclusions and implications for further research and policy.

A SURVEY OF THE RESEARCH ON AN EAST ASIAN TRADING BLOC

There has been considerable interest in the issue of whether East Asia in some sense already represents a natural trading bloc and whether it is in the interests of the countries in the region to pursue an explicit preferential trading arrangement or instead to opt to strengthen their ties multilaterally to the global trading system. It may be useful accordingly to review some of the highlights of the burgeoning literature on these issues before we turn in subsequent sections to our own research.

A Profile of the East Asian Economies

Exactly what countries constitute East Asia depends of course on where the boundaries are to be drawn. Thus, for example, the USITC (1993, p. 6) depicts the East Asia region to include Brunei, Cambodia, China, Hong Kong, Indonesia, Japan, North Korea, South Korea, Laos, Malaysia, Myanmar (Burma), New Guinea, the Philippines, Singapore, Taiwan and Thailand.[1] Also, as noted in USITC (1993, p. 47), a number of East Asian poles of economic growth can be identified, including Northeast Asia, Greater China, Greater ASEAN, Growth Triangle (Singapore–Johor–Riau) and Southern Indochina.

It is of course well known that East Asia has been experiencing truly remarkable rates of growth of output and foreign trade compared to other parts of the world. Further, as documented in Panagariya (1993, 1994), East Asia accounted for nearly one-fifth of world gross domestic product and one-third of the world population in 1990. Panagariya also finds that there has been a noticeable increase in the proportion of intra-East Asian trade between 1980 and 1990 from 29.9 per cent to 32.3 per cent and some fluctuation in the relative importance of East Asia's trade with North America: 26.0 per cent in 1980; 37.8 per cent in 1985; and 31.9 per cent in 1990. Panagariya further cites data on the direction of exports and imports for the separate East Asian economies that make evident the importance of trade with Japan, and the particular importance of subregional trade, involving China–Hong Kong–Taiwan and Singapore. Finally, Bannister and Braga (1994) present data on the sources of flows of foreign direct investment (FDI) in East Asia in the 1980s which document the shift away from North America in the first half of the decade towards East Asia – especially FDI from Japan, Hong Kong, Singapore and Taiwan – in the second half of the decade.[2]

Gravity-model and Other Analyses of an East Asian Trading Bloc (EATB)

Frankel (1991, 1994) and Frankel et al. (1993a,b) have carried out a number of studies pertinent to an EATB. They have relied for the most part on the use of a gravity-model framework in which intra-regional or bilateral trade is related to such variables as country proximity, economic size, per capita GNP, whether there is a common border, common language and other distinguishing characteristics. To the extent that these variables do not account for the observed bilateral trade, this is taken as evidence of a bias in favour of intraregional trade or against it. These authors have sought answers to three questions using the gravity-model approach: (1) whether the world is fragmenting into three separate and identifiable trading blocs (Americas, Europe and Pacific Asia) and, if so, what the associated welfare implications may be; (2) whether Japan is developing a de facto trade bloc, yen bloc, or FDI bloc in East Asia and the Pacific; and (3) what is the most natural trade bloc grouping for the Asia–Pacific region. Their findings pertinent to these questions are, respectively: (1) the model supports the existence of three broad regional blocs, and economic welfare might be increased or reduced depending on how inclusive the blocs are in terms of the degree of preferences that they afford; (2) there is no evidence that Japan is forming an explicit bloc in East Asia with respect to trade, use of the yen, or FDI; and (3) the most natural trade bloc grouping for the region is one that includes the United States and Canada together with the Asia–Pacific countries.[3] In addition, they find that, while there is a sizeable amount of intra-East Asian trade, this reflects in large measure the very rapid rates of economic growth in East Asia rather than an intraregional bias of trade flows. This last finding is also borne out in the gravity-model study by Dhar and Panagariya (1994) and in calculations of trade-intensity indexes for the East Asian countries by Bannister and Braga (1994).[4]

Some authors have used a more descriptive and analytical approach to the issues involving an EATB. These include studies by Yamazawa (1992), the USITC (1993), Panagariya (1993, 1994), Kirkpatrick (1994), and Anderson and Snape (1994). The USITC study is a useful compendium of information and discussion of the national economic strategies and performance of the individual East Asian countries, the ongoing subregional integration, trade and investment patterns, foreign aid, sectoral trade and investment activities in East Asia, and energy and environmental issues affecting trade, investment and integration in East Asia. Panagariya analyses whether East Asia should go regional by examining: (1) the likely economic effects of the 1992 plans for an ASEAN Free Trade Area (AFTA); (2) the economic desirability and feasibility of an EATB; and (3) the desirability of pursuit of nondiscriminatory, open regionalism along GATT lines in East Asia. His conclusions are negative with regard to the likely benefits of the AFTA and the formation of an EATB, whereas he grants that something possibly might be gained from a policy of open regionalism. This policy of open regionalism is also endorsed by Yamazawa, Kirkpatrick, and Anderson and Snape.[5]

Finally, there are two additional studies to be mentioned, both of which use a global computable general equilibrium (CGE) model to asses the consequences of Asian trade liberalization.[6] Martin, Petri and Yanagishima (1994) have a CGE model with seven goods and 19 regions. Their model assumes perfect competition with constant returns to scale, and national product differentiation according to the Armington assumption that goods can be distinguished by place of production.[7] Inter-industry (input–output) relations are not included explicitly in the model. They also make allowance, outside of the model. They allow for changes in FDI, increases in efficiency and increased competition, and growth in productivity. The country groups analysed include: (1) individual Pacific countries; (2) ASEAN (Indonesia, Malaysia, the Philippines, Singapore and Thailand); (3) East Asia (China, Japan, ASEAN, South Korea, Hong Kong and Taiwan); and (4) Pacific region (East Asia, Australasia, Canada and the United States). The extent of liberalization assumed is a reduction in post-Uruguay Round tariff protection by one-third of 1992 protection levels. The assumed reductions in barriers are applied on a most-favoured-nation (MFN) basis as well as preferentially for partners within the groups noted above. Their conclusions are as follows (pp. 28–9):

> The results show that the gains produced by Pacific liberalization initiatives can be indeed substantial. The gains are typically in excess of $100 billion and are concentrated among East Asian countries. These countries benefit not just because they are effective competitors for the newly-created markets for manufacturing exports, but also because they have significant initial distortions that can be eliminated by reducing protection. The largest gains are calculated for China and ASEAN, at around 5 per cent of GDP in the year 2000.
>
> Among the alternatives examined, scenarios involving broader Pacific liberalization – that is, scenarios which include North America and Australasia – tend to be superior to scenarios that are limited to East Asia, but not by much. Most-favored-nation scenarios tend to be substantially superior to discriminatory scenarios, especially when the 'actor' is East Asia rather than the Pacific as a whole. These broad conclusions are not affected by a range of alternative modeling specifications.

The second study is by Lewis, Robinson and Wang (1995), who use a global CGE model that consists of six countries/regions: the United States; Japan; the European Union (EU); the Asian NIEs (Korea, Taiwan and Singapore); China (including Hong Kong); and ASEAN4 (Indonesia, Thailand, the Philippines and Malaysia). This country/region coverage is assumed to represent much, but no means all, of the membership of APEC.[8] The Lewis et al. CGE model has ten sectors and four factors of production (two types of labour, land and physical capital) for each country/region and includes inter-industry (input–output) relations as well as a variety of domestic sectoral taxes. Their data base refers to 1992. They also assume perfect competition with constant returns to scale, and national product differentiation according to the Armington assumption. To complement the base solution of the model, allowance is made for three kinds of trade–productivity links: (1) sectoral productivity changes are related to sectoral imports of intermediate and capital goods, depending on the share of intermediate goods in total production; (2) externalities are associated with sectoral export performance, with higher growth yielding increased domestic productivity; and (3) there are further externalities associated with aggregate exports that are assumed to make the sectoral-embodied physical capital stock more productive. The sectoral data used in the modelling scenarios for agricultural and industrial products refer to post-Uruguay Round tariff rates and are supplemented by estimates of the tariff equivalents of non-tariff barriers especially in agriculture and textiles/ clothing.

A number of computational scenarios are run using the model: (1) creation of an Asian Free Trade Area (AFTA) covering all of the APEC countries/ regions noted above, without and with the three trade-productivity linkages noted; (2) an AFTA without China, an AFTA without the ASEAN4, and an AFTA without the United States; and (3) global trade liberalization that involves all of the countries/regions included in the model. The results of their various scenarios are as follows: (1) all of the countries/regions would benefit from an AFTA, except for the EU; (2) omitting China, the ASEAN4, or the United States from an AFTA makes the omitted country/region worse off and reduces the benefits for the other AFTA members; and (3) global trade liberalization dominates an AFTA in so far as it yields the largest gains of all and benefits each of the countries/regions included in the model.

While the Martin et al. and Lewis et al. CGE modelling simulations are not readily comparable because of differences in modelling structure and the design of their computational scenarios, they both suggest that there may be sizeable benefits from the creation of an Asian trading bloc arrangement. These studies are thus the closest to our own study, which also relies on a CGE modelling framework. However, as will be seen in the following section, the Michigan BDS CGE Trade Model has a number of different properties compared to these other models in so far as the Michigan model incorporates elements of imperfect competition, including economies of scale and product variety, and avoids strong terms-of-trade effects by allowing for product differentiation by monopolistically competitive firms rather than by country of production. A further important difference is that we will adopt a much narrower conception of Asia to include only Japan, South Korea, Singapore and Taiwan since these are the most advanced countries in the region and are therefore, in our view, more likely candidates for the formation of an EATB that could stand on its own and perhaps permit the United States to join as well. Leaving out China, Hong Kong and the other ASEAN nations, we can expect to get smaller effects than those calculated by Martin et al. and Lewis et al. Let us turn, then to consider some of the main features of the Michigan BDS CGE Trade Model.

THE MICHIGAN BDS CGE TRADE MODEL[9]

The CGE model used in this chapter is an extension of the model first constructed by Brown and Stern (1989) to analyse the economic effects of the Canada–US Trade Agreement (CUSTA), and later expanded by Brown et al. (1992a,b, 1994) to analyse the NAFTA and the extension of the NAFTA to some major trading countries in South America. In its further elaboration for present purposes, we model individually Japan, Singapore, South Korea and Taiwan as the potential members of an East Asian Trading Bloc (EATB) as well as the United States, Canada and Mexico which comprise the NAFTA.[10] A group of 27 other major industrialized and developing countries are combined to create an eighth 'country', and all remaining countries of the world are consigned to a residual rest-of-world to close the model. The sectoral coverage in each country/region includes 23 'tradable' (import–export) product categories covering agriculture and manufacturing and six 'non-tradable' categories covering services and government.[11]

The agricultural sector in each country is characterized as being perfectly competitive, and it is assumed that the products of this sector are differentiated according to the place of production. The manufacturing sectors in each country are characterized as being monopolistically competitive with free entry, and the products that are produced and traded are assumed to be differentiated by firm.[12] The reference year for the data base of the model is 1990. The input–output relations used in the model refer to different years, depending on the availability of national input–output tables.[13] More complete technical details, including a full statement and description of the equations and parameters of the model, are available from the authors on request. The data base and documentation for the model are also available from the authors.[14]

There are several important assumptions that either are built into the model or are implemented by the model for the present analysis. It is important that these be understood in interpreting the results to be reported below.

- *Full Employment* The analysis assumes throughout that the aggregate, or economy-wide, level of employment is held constant in each country. The East Asian Trading Bloc (EATB) to be analysed is therefore not permitted to change any country's overall rates of employment or unemployment. This assumption is made because overall employment is determined by macroeconomic forces and policies that are not contained in the model and are not themselves to be included in a negotiated agreement. The focus instead is on the composition of employment across sectors as determined by the microeconomic interactions of supply and demand with the sectoral trade policies that an EATB will alter.

- *Balanced Trade*   It is assumed that trade remains balanced for each country, or more accurately that any initial trade imbalance remains constant, as trade barriers are changed with an EATB. This assumption is intended to reflect the reality of mostly flexible exchange rates among the countries involved. It also, like the full employment assumption, is appropriate as a way of abstracting from the macroeconomic forces and policies that are the main determinants of trade balances.[15]

- *Fixed Relative Wages*   While the economy-wide wage in each country is permitted to adjust so as to maintain full employment, the wages across sectors are held fixed relative to one another. This permits the analysis to focus on the labour-market adjustments that an EATB might require, independently of any relative wage changes that may facilitate those adjustments.[16]

- *Fixed Labour Supply*   The total labour supply in each country is assumed to be held fixed in the analysis. This is not to say that changes in labour supply will not occur in the course of a phase-in of an EATB, but only that such changes are assumed not to be the result of such an agreement.[17]

The policy inputs into the model are the tariffs and non-tariff barriers (NTBs) that are currently (as of the early 1990s) applied to the bilateral trade of the individual East Asian and North American economies modelled explicitly with respect to each other and to the other two aggregated regions included in the model.[18] As will be noted below, in order to investigate the sectoral employment effects of an EATB, it will be assumed that the existing bilateral tariffs will be removed and NTBs will be relaxed all at one time rather than in stages.

When the policy changes are introduced into the model, the method of solution yields percentage changes in sectoral employment and other variables of interest for each country/region. Multiplying the percentage changes by the actual (1990) levels given in the data base yields the absolute changes, positive or negative, that might result if the bilateral tariffs/NTBs were removed all at one time. More realistically, of course, the removal of tariffs (and NTBs) in an EATB would almost certainly be phased in over a period of years. If information were available for the different phases, the model could in principle be solved sequentially taking into account the barrier reductions in each time period.

In addition to the sectoral effects which are the primary focus of our analysis, the model also yields results for changes in total exports, total imports, the terms of trade, the overall level of welfare in the economy measured by the equivalent variation, and the economy-wide changes in real wages and returns to capital. Because both labour and capital are assumed to be homogeneous and intersectorally mobile in these scenarios, we cannot distinguish effects on factor prices by sector. Nor, as noted above, can we distinguish effects on different skill groups or other categories of labour. In particular we are unable to address the important question of how a free trade area might affect the differential between the wages of skilled and unskilled workers.

While the bilateral removal of tariffs (and NTBs) constitutes the main change in trade policies that would occur with an EATB, there may be other changes as well. These relate especially to changes in FDI and to the cross-border movement of workers as the result of changes in the rate of return on capital and changes in real wages. While changes in FDI might very well occur, it seems much less likely in the East Asian context that cross-border movements of workers would take place due to changes in real wages. In any case, we shall not take cross-border movements of FDI and workers into account in the analysis that follows.[19] We also do not make any allowance for dynamic efficiency changes and economic growth.

COMPUTATIONAL RESULTS: AGGREGATE EFFECTS

The Scenarios

It is possible to use our CGE model to analyse various combinations of country membership in a free trade agreement. What we did initially was to assume that Japan and South Korea were the first of the East Asian countries to form a preferential bloc. We then assumed that Taiwan and thereafter Singapore become members. In each case, we eliminated the bilateral tariffs involved and solved the model for its effects on the individual East Asian countries as well as on the United States, Canada and Mexico and the remaining aggregate of the other major trading countries.

One question that immediately arises is what to assume about the reduction or elimination of the existing NTBs in the East Asian countries. Consonant with the spirit and conclusion of the Uruguay Round negotiations, the most desirable way to handle NTBs would be to represent them in terms of their tariff equivalents and then to assume that these NTBs would be eliminated. Unfortunately, we have been unable to obtain sufficient data to measure these NTB tariff equivalents. We decided accordingly to assume a scenario in which existing NTBs would be partially relaxed so as to permit a 50 per cent increase in the imports that had been constrained. This was implemented in the model by expanding a parameter representing quantitative restraint of imports for those sectors subject to NTBs. Handling NTBs in such a manner is by no means satisfactory, but our rationale is that it may be unlikely that the existing NTBs would be completely eliminated in the context of an EATB.

The remaining scenario was to assume that the United States opted to join the four-country EATB.[20] Altogether then, six scenarios were run, as follows:

A.   *Japan/South Korea Tariff Elimination*   Bilateral removal of all tariffs on trade between Japan and South Korea.

B.   *Japan/South Korea/Taiwan Tariff Elimination*   Same as Scenario A, plus removal of all bilateral tariffs between each of the three countries.

C.   *Japan/South Korea/Taiwan/Singapore Tariff Elimination*   Same as Scenario B, plus removal of all bilateral tariffs between each of the four countries. This constitutes the base case for the formation of an EATB, with bilateral tariff elimination only.

D.   *Japan/South Korea/Taiwan/Singapore Tariff Elimination plus Relaxation of Existing NTBs by 50 per cent*   Same as Scenario C, but allowing imports subject to NTBs to be increased by 50 per cent.[21]

E.   *East Asia Trading Bloc Tariff Elimination plus the United States*   Same as Scenario C, plus removal of all bilateral tariffs among the four EATB countries and the United States.

F.   *East Asia Trading Bloc Tariff Elimination plus Relaxation of Existing NTBs by 50 per cent, plus the United States*   Same as Scenario D, but allowing imports subject to NTBs to be increased by 50 per cent.

Table 8.1   *Average tariff rates among East Asian and NAFTA countries (percent)*

	Exporter						
Importer	Canada	Japan	S. Korea	Mexico	Singapore	Taiwan	United States
Canada	—	7.1	12.2	2.8	6.3	11.0	4.5
Japan	3.8	—	7.4	1.3	4.7	7.5	6.9
S. Korea	5.2	10.5	—	6.6	9.6	10.9	8.1
Mexico	7.5	13.9	13.1	—	14.6	15.3	11.4
Singapore	0.1	0.2	0.2	0.5	—	0.1	0.1
Taiwan	3.8	6.4	8.0	2.1	6.1	—	6.1
United States	1.1	3.5	6.2	1.2	3.9	6.5	—

Source: EATB data base. The bilateral tariffs are own-country, import-weighted averages of pre-Uruguay Round MFN tariff rates, using 1990 imports for weighting purposes. The original tariff rates for Canada, Japan and the United States came from the GATT tariff files for the Tokyo Round negotiations and the tariff rates for Mexico, South Korea, Singapore and Taiwan from national sources.

Table 8.2 Summary results of East Asian free trade: changes in country imports, exports, terms of trade, welfare and return to labour and capital

Country	Imports* (millions of dollars) (2)	Exports* (millions of dollars) (3)	Terms of trade percent change (4)	Equivalent variation Percent (5)	Equivalent variation millions of dollars (6)	Wage rate percent change (6)	Return to capital percent change (7)
A. JAPAN+SOUTH KOREA: Tariff elimination							
Canada	58.9	53.0	0	0	80.3	0	0
Japan	4,380.2	3,815.4	0.2	0.2	4,872.4	0.1	0.1
South Korea	3,547.6	4,297.7	-1.1	0.2	541.1	0.6	0.4
Mexico	21.0	12.2	0	0	30.5	0	0
Singapore	-17.9	-10.3	0	0	8.5	0	0
Taiwan	-30.8	-9.2	0	0	-46.7	0	0
United States	42.1	-54.1	0	0	211.6	0	0
Other	-48.3	1.3	0	0	-13.3	0	0
B. JAPAN+SOUTH KOREA+TAIWAN: Tariff elimination							
Canada	66.3	53.9	0	0	92.1	0	0
Japan	6,631.8	5,874.6	0.3	0.3	7,688.6	0.1	0.2
South Korea	3,840.1	4,646.4	-1.2	0.3	718.1	0.7	0.5
Mexico	26.2	12.5	0	0	34.8	0	0
Singapore	-16.7	15.6	-0.1	0.1	25.2	0	0
Taiwan	2,343.4	2,721.9	-0.5	1.1	1,718.7	1.1	0.9
United States	57.4	-133.4	0	0	232.9	0	0
Other	2.7	29.4	0	0	-160.3	0	0
C. JAPAN+SOUTH KOREA+TAIWAN+SINGAPORE: Tariff elimination							
Canada	67.2	51.3	0	0	117.1	0	0
Japan	6,863.8	6,280.1	0.2	0.3	8,529.5	0.1	0.2
South Korea	3,931.8	4,816.2	-1.3	0.3	797.5	0.7	0.5
Mexico	24.9	9.7	0	0	42.0	0	0

Singapore	557.3	350.8	0.4	1.1	379.2	0.9	0.7
Taiwan	2,530.5	2,992.5	−0.7	1.2	1872.0	1.2	1.0
United States	−4.7	−261.6	0	0	418.4	0	0
Other	−69.4	−52.2	0	0	227.5	0	0

D. JAPAN+SOUTH KOREA+TAIWAN+SINGAPORE: Tariff and NTB reduction

Canada	67.4	50.7	0	0	121.3	0	0
Japan	7018.0	6416.0	0.3	0.2	8,821.1	0.1	0.2
South Korea	3,987.1	4,883.9	0.4	−1.3	882.0	0.7	0.5
Mexico	25.2	10.1	0	0	43.3	0	0
Singapore	574.0	362.2	1.2	0.4	432.1	1.0	0.8
Taiwan	2,624.2	3,101.4	1.2	−0.7	1,977.3	1.3	1.0
United States	−22.6	−284.7	0	0	448.5	0	0
Other	−87.7	−70.0	0	0	338.2	0	0

E. JAPAN+SOUTH KOREA+TAIWAN+SINGAPORE+US: Tariff elimination

Canada	101.1	82.5	0	0	241.4	0	0
Japan	1,4013.2	13,963.1	0.7	0.1	19,783.2	0.3	0.4
South Korea	6155.0	7490.0	0.9	−2.0	2,018.9	1.1	0.9
Mexico	37.2	16.0	0	0	88.7	0	0
Singapore	1,207.5	833.9	1.9	0.7	648.8	1.6	1.4
Taiwan	5,247.1	5,318.8	2.5	−0.1	3,980.1	2.3	2.2
United States	11,977.7	11,336.4	0.2	0.1	10,039.9	0.1	0.1
Other	−20.0	60.2	0	0	539.2	0	0

F. JAPAN+SOUTH KOREA+TAIWAN+SINGAPORE+US: Tariff and NTB reduction

Canada	−292.6	−91.8	−0.1	−0.1	−637.4	−0.1	0
Japan	21,606.1	18,942.9	1.0	0.9	29,148.8	0.4	0.6
South Korea	8,858.2	9,571.6	1.7	−1.1	3,982.1	1.7	1.4
Mexico	134.1	78.4	0	0	−49.8	0	0
Singapore	1,651.6	1,109.7	2.3	1.0	813.9	2.2	1.8
Taiwan	5898.0	5,901.9	3.0	0	4,795.4	2.6	2.5
United States	18,244.6	20,462.2	0.3	−0.5	15,728.0	0.1	0.2
Other	−141.4	97.6	0	0	502.2	0	0

Note: *   Exports and imports valued in US dollar base period prices.

Average tariff levels currently applying to East Asian and North American trade are summarized in Table 8.1.[22] There we report the import-weighted average tariff applying to each pair of bilateral trade flows for the individual countries. Singapore's tariffs are virtually zero. South Korea has the relatively highest rates of the East Asian countries, varying from 5.2 per cent for imports from Canada to 10.5 per cent and 10.9 per cent for imports, respectively, for Japan and Taiwan. The tariffs for Taiwan are roughly equivalent to those of Japan. Mexico and Canada have relatively higher tariff rates as compared to the United States. The sectoral tariff rates are available from the authors on request.

As already mentioned, we do not have any systematic information on the tariff equivalents of NTBs for the East Asian and NAFTA countries. Rather, what we have are sectoral NTB trade coverage ratios. These are available on request. They indicate that the highest NTB trade coverage ratios are to be found in: agriculture and food products; textiles, clothing, leather products and footwear; wood products; and transport equipment. Also, the United States exhibits significantly larger and more comprehensive sectoral NTB trade coverage ratios than any of the East Asian or other NAFTA countries.

As already noted, we assumed initially in Scenario A that Japan and South Korea formed a free trade area (FTA) by eliminating their bilateral tariffs. We then added Taiwan (Scenario B) and Singapore (Scenario C) sequentially. Scenario C thus represents what we consider for our purposes to be the EATB. We could, of course, have altered the order and combinations of countries, but it did not seem worthwhile to do these additional runs of the model. Scenario D refers to the formation of an EATB with the elimination of bilateral tariffs together with an assumed reduction of NTBs that allows for a 50 per cent increase in the imports that had been constrained. Our final Scenarios (E and F) refer to an FTA that includes the EATB together with the United States with bilatral tariff removal alone and then with bilateral tariff removal plus a 50 per cent increase in the imports that had been constrained by NTBs. We turn now to our results.[23]

An overview of results on trade, terms of trade, welfare and factor payments from each of the scenarios is reported in Table 8.2. Perhaps the single most important number to consider in evaluating an EATB is the impact on economic welfare, that is, the 'equivalent variation' measure of the change in real gross domestic product (GDP).

Economic Welfare

In Scenario A, bilateral tariff removal between Japan and South Korea increases welfare in both countries by 0.2 per cent of GDP. There are relatively small increases in welfare for Canada, Mexico, Singapore and the United

States and small reductions in welfare for Taiwan and the other major trading countries. It is interesting that welfare tends to increase for the included partners as well as the acceding East Asian countries as the EATB is expanded. Furthermore, the formation of an EATB can be seen in Scenarios C and D to increase economic welfare for the three NAFTA countries as well as the other major trading countries. What appears to be happening is that the internal benefits to countries in an EATB are transmitted to non-member countries especially through the realization of scale economies and increased product variety. If the United States were to join with the four East Asian countries in the bilateral removal of tariffs, as in Scenario E, the positive effects on all member as well as non-member countries are even more enhanced. But this result does not hold up in Scenario F with bilateral tariff removal combined with NTB reduction, in so far as Canada and Mexico experience a reduction in welfare, although the welfare increases for the four East Asian countries and the United States become larger.

It should be noted that positive welfare gains are not inevitable when trade is liberalized on a preferential basis, though the presumption that each country will gain from joining an EATB is strong. Several different forces are at work determining the welfare effects of trade liberalization.

On the positive side, consumers are free to choose the least expensive source of goods from countries within the FTA. In addition, by expanding trading opportunities, each country has the option of specializing production in the range of goods in which it has a comparative advantage.

There are three other forces, however, that have an ambiguous effect on welfare. First, consumers are not able to choose freely among all foreign sources of goods because tariffs are removed only on included partners. Hence, consumption choices may be distorted by the preferential nature of the tariff liberalization. Second, a country's terms of trade could improve or deteriorate as a result of trade liberalization. If import prices rise and export prices fall, welfare gains stemming from specialization and exchange could be reversed. However, in most cases we expect that the terms-of-trade effects following liberalization by a small country will be too small to reverse other sources of gain. This is the case with an EATB, as can be seen from column (4) of Table 8.2. There tend to be negative terms-of-trade effects for South Korea and Taiwan, but they are relatively small and have not led to a net fall in welfare in columns (5) and (6). A third force determining the welfare effects of trade liberalization concerns the realization of economies of scale. Tariff liberalization is expected to have a pro-competitive effect on import-competing firms in each country. Without tariff protection, domestic firms feel competitive pressure from imports and may charge a lower price in order to compete.

In industries where there are significant economies of scale and, thus, declining average costs, the firm that charges a lower price may also have to increase output in order to break even. As the firm moves down its average total cost curve, the inputs required to produce a unit of output decline on average. If many of the firms in a country are forced by competitive pressure to economize on inputs in this way, then the country overall will be able to produce more than before the liberalization using the same inputs and technology. This gain from the realization of economies of scale enhances the more traditional gains from specialization and exchange.

However, scale gains, while likely, are not inevitable. Tariff liberalization is pro-competitive for import-competing firms. However, curiously, export firms experience an anti-competitive effect. As the trade partner lowers its tariffs, export firms now have easier access to foreign markets and, therefore, feel less competition. Such firms may respond by raising price and cutting back production, with adverse consequences for the economy overall.

Scale economies will be discussed in detail below. However, we find that for most countries firm output tends to rise, so that scale gains are generally positive.

Real Wages and Return to Capital

Having established that the welfare effects of an EATB that includes the four major East Asian countries plus the United States are positive for all participants, we next turn to the distributional consequences. In particular, we are interested in which factors of production are likely to gain and which to lose with formation of an EATB. The percentage changes in the real returns to labour and capital are reported in columns (6) and (7) of Table 8.2. What is striking in all the scenarios is that both factors of production gain and the distributional effects are minimal. For example in Scenario D, the increases in real wages range from 0.1 per cent in Japan to 1.3 per cent in Taiwan. The increases in the real return to capital range from 0.2 per cent in Japan to 1.0 per cent in Taiwan.

The fact that returns to both factors rise in most countries may seem inconsistent with the Stolper–Samuelson theorem. From this theorem, we expect that trade liberalization will raise the return to the abundant factor in each country while making the other factor worse off. However, in the context of a differentiated-products model with increasing returns to scale, like the one used for this study, other forces may be at work undermining Stolper–Samuelson-type mechanics.[24]

Scale effects work very much like the relative price effects articulated in the Stolper–Samuelson theorem to determine the implications of trade liberalization for factor prices. Scale effects, like price effects, tend to accrue to one factor only. For example, it can be shown that an increase in output per firm in an industry raises the real return to the factor used intensively in that industry and lowers the return to the other factor. Price and scale effects differ, however, in one important regard. If scale gains emerge across the board in nearly all industries, then both factors may gain. This is apparently the case in our model.[25]

We turn next to consider the sectoral results.

COMPUTATIONAL RESULTS – SECTORAL EFFECTS

Sectoral results for Japan, South Korea, Singapore, Taiwan and the United States are detailed in Tables 8.3–8.9 for Scenario D representing the effects of a four-country EATB and Scenario F that includes the four-country EATB plus the United States. For each country, the percentage changes in total exports and imports are reported in columns (2) and (3). Imports are decomposed by trade partner in columns (4) through (9). The percentage changes in industry output and number of firms are listed in columns (10) and (11). The percentage change in output per firm, which can be used to determine the extent to which economies of scale may be realized, are calculated by subtracting column (11) (change in number of firms) from column (10) (change in industry output). Finally, the percentage and absolute changes in employment are listed in columns (12) and (13). The results for Canada and Mexico and all seven countries from the other scenarios are available from the authors on request.

Scenario D

Considering first the sectoral results for Japan of the four-member-country EATB in Table 8.3, there are noteworthy percentage increases in total exports and imports (columns (2) and (3)) in virtually all sectors. Japan's bilateral imports (columns (4)–(9)) also show sizeable percentage increases from the other EATB member countries and relatively small increases from the three NAFTA countries. It is further evident in column (10) that Japan becomes more specialized in its relatively more capital-intensive industries, whereas output declines in its resource- and labour-intensive sectors (ISIC 1, 2 and 310–31). Japan also experiences positive scale-economy effects throughout all its manufacturing sectors (comparing columns (10) and (11)). The percentage increases in employment in column (12) are comparatively small as are thè declines, with the exception of the clothing sector (3.6 per cent). The largest absolute employment increases are in the machinery sectors (382, 383), whereas Japanese agriculture and labour-intensive manufacturing show absolute employment declines. Japan's non-tradable sectors can also be seen to expand.

Table 8.3 Scenario D: sectoral effects on Japan of East Asian bilateral tariff elimination and NTB reduction (percent change; 000 workers)

Sector	Exports	Imports	Bilateral imports						Output	No. firms	Change in employment	
			CND	SK	MEX	SNG	TAI	USA			Percent	1000s
	(2)	(3)	(4)	(5)	(6)	(7)	(8)	(9)	(10)	(11)	(12)	(13)
Tradables												
1 Agriculture	7.4	2.7	0.5	27.1	0.7	20.8	24.5	0.6	-0.5	0	-0.4	-19.1
310 Food	8.4	7.6	1.0	42.0	1.0	76.3	39.0	1.0	-0.3	-0.5	-0.4	-6.6
321 Textiles	2.9	7.1	0.5	34.6	0.5	23.8	27.9	0.7	-0.4	-0.6	-0.5	-4.7
322 Clothing	0.4	17.8	0.3	53.9	0.9	22.6	36.2	1.0	-3.4	-3.6	-3.6	-23.9
323 Leather products	7.7	4.6	0.3	46.8	0.5	27.5	47.3	0.3	-0.7	-0.9	-0.8	-0.5
324 Footwear	-1.8	30.7	0.4	57.7	0.2	44.1	60.1	0	-6.6	-7.1	-7.0	-3.2
331 Wood products	8.2	1.5	1.3	14.8	0.8	11.6	13.9	1.2	-0.1	-0.3	-0.2	-1.0
332 Furniture, fixtures	3.9	4.9	0.9	14.3	0.8	15.9	12.6	1.0	0.1	-0.1	-0.1	-0.2
341 Paper products	2.8	1.3	1.1	15.0	1.0	15.3	13.4	1.1	0.2	0	0	0.2
342 Printing, publishing	-0.2	1.3	1.2	4.1	1.2	-0.5	2.1	1.2	0.1	0	0	0.1
35A Chemicals	4.5	1.9	0.4	17.4	0.4	17.9	22.3	0.4	0.4	0.2	0.2	1.3

35B Petroleum products	12.6	0.5	0.7	1.3	0.6	0.2	2.9	0.6	0.4	0.1	0.2	0.1
355 Rubber products	0.6	2.6	0.8	12.7	0	11.9	12.2	0.9	0.2	0	0	0
36A Non-metal min. prod.	4.1	1.7	0.9	5.0	0.8	8.1	5.0	0.9	0.2	0	0.1	0.4
362 Glass products	5.2	3.4	0.7	15.2	0.6	24.3	14.4	0.7	0.4	0.2	0.2	0.2
371 Iron, steel	5.0	5.4	0.2	16.7	0.1	10.2	1.5	0.1	0.7	0.3	0.4	1.8
372 Non-ferrous metals	4.8	1.1	0.7	13.4	0.6	8.4	10.3	0.6	0.5	0.2	0.3	0.5
381 Metal products	3.1	3.9	0.8	16.1	0.7	12.8	6.6	0.7	0.2	-0.1	0	0.5
382 Non-elec. machinery	3.7	0.9	0.3	6.5	0.1	9.8	5.9	0.1	0.9	0.5	0.5	10.0
383 Electrical machinery	1.6	2.9	0.6	9.3	0.5	2.9	12.0	0.5	0.6	0.3	0.3	8.2
384 Transport equipment	0.7	0.9	0.4	15.4	0.6	6.9	9.9	0.3	0.3	0	0	0
38A Misc. mfrs.	0.9	3.1	0.5	22.5	0.7	10.8	14.4	0.7	0	-0.2	-0.2	-1.9
2 Mining, quarrying	0.7	0.8	1.3	1.8	1.2	-3.7	-3.0	1.2	-0.6	-0.7	-0.7	-0.4
Non-tradables												
4 Utilities									0.2	0	0.2	0.8
5 Construction									0.1	0	0.1	7.5
6 Wholesale trade									0	0	0.1	12.0
7 Transportation									0.1	0	0.1	3.9
8 Financial services									0	0	0.1	6.7
9 Personal services									0	0	0.1	7.2
Total	2.1	3.3	1.0	26.4	1.1	12.3	21.7	0.7	0.1	-0.3	0	0

Table 8.4 Scenario D: sectoral effects on South Korea of East Asian bilateral tariff elimination and NTB reduction (percent change; 000 workers)

Sector	Exports (2)	Imports (3)	Bilateral imports						Output (10)	No. firms (11)	Change in employment	
			CND (4)	JPN (5)	MEX (6)	SNG (7)	TAI (8)	USA (9)			Percent (12)	1000s (13)
Tradables												
1 Agriculture	24.6	0.9	-0.2	27.9	-0.7	22.1	39.3	-0.3	1.1	0	0.9	31.1
310 Food	25.0	-0.4	-2.5	38.7	-1.8	49.4	46.6	-2.0	0.8	0.5	0.3	1.2
321 Textiles	8.0	9.1	-3.9	24.7	-3.9	24.9	31.1	-3.6	7.4	6.0	6.2	38.1
322 Clothing	20.5	-13.8	-19.7	10.8	-19.0	15.3	19.6	-19.0	14.8	12.5	12.7	53.7
323 Leather products	6.9	4.4	-3.1	20.4	-3.0	25.8	29.0	-3.1	4.5	3.4	3.6	2.6
324 Footwear	9.2	-3.0	-9.5	12.9	-9.7	24.4	29.6	-10.1	6.7	5.2	5.3	2.7
331 Wood products	11.3	-0.7	0	24.9		25.0	24.9	0	0	-0.3	-0.2	-0.1
332 Furniture, fixtures	6.1	9.2	-2.5	26.2	-2.6	29.7	26.8	-2.5	-0.5	-1.0	-1.0	-0.7
341 Paper products	1.7	3.1	-1.1	25.1	-1.5	25.1	24.4	-1.0	0	-0.4	-0.5	-0.5
342 Printing, publishing	1.7	0.8	-1.2	4.1	-1.3	-2.9	8.8	-1.2	-0.3	-0.7	-0.7	-0.8
35A Chemicals	4.2	8.8	-2.1	24.8	-2.1	28.4	32.6	-2.0	0.1	-0.3	-0.4	-0.8

35B Petroleum products	1.3	7.8	-0.6	23.9	-0.7	21.8	16.7	-0.7	-1.2	-1.1	-1.3	-0.4
355 Rubber products	3.4	12.5	-3.6	25.1	-3.6	27.7	26.5	-3.5	1.0	-0.3	-0.3	-0.8
36A Non-metal min. prod.	3.4	8.7	-1.2	24.8	-1.3	26.0	23.8	-1.2	-1.1	-1.3	-1.4	-2.2
362 Glass products	5.2	13.3	-2.0	27.4	-2.0	36.7	27.6	-1.9	-1.7	-2.1	-2.2	-0.8
371 Iron, steel	7.6	8.9	-3.9	23.5	-3.9	19.3	9.5	-3.9	-0.5	-1.2	-1.1	-1.5
372 Non-ferrous metals	4.2	3.6	-1.2	24.4	-1.3	4.9	20.9	-1.3	-1.9	-2.0	-2.0	-1.0
381 Metal products	3.5	11.6	-2.3	26.7	-2.4	25.5	20.1	-2.4	-0.5	-1.1	-1.1	-3.1
382 Non-elec. machinery	0	10.8	-2.9	26.7	-3.1	25.4	23.2	-2.9	-4.6	-5.4	-5.4	-17.4
383 Electrical machinery	1.7	10.9	-4.9	24.0	-5.0	17.8	28.8	-5.0	-2.0	-2.9	-2.9	-21.0
384 Transport equipment	2.1	2.8	-2.7	25.3	-2.9	17.5	21.3	-2.6	0.1	-0.8	-0.7	-2.4
38A Misc. mfrs.	8.6	4.2	-6.6	22.4	-6.2	23.1	24.8	-6.0	3.3	2.1	2.1	8.7
2 Mining, quarrying	1.9	-1.2	-0.9	8.2	-0.9	4.0	4.3	-0.9	-0.4	-0.6	-0.6	-0.5
Non-tradables												
4 Utilities									0.2	0	0	0
5 Construction									-1.0	0	-1.1	-15.0
6 Wholesale trade									-0.4	0	-0.7	-27.6
7 Transportation									-0.7	0	-0.8	-7.8
8 Financial services									-0.3	0	-0.5	-5.0
9 Personal services									-1.1	0	-1.1	-28.8
Total	7.3	6.3	-2.0	24.7	-1.3	21.3	27.1	-2.7	0.4	2.8	0	0

Table 8.5 Scenario D: sectoral effects on Singapore of East Asian bilateral tariff elimination and NTB reduction (percent change; 000 workers)

Sector	Exports	Imports	Bilateral imports						Output	No. firms	Change in employment	
			CND	JPN	SK	MEX	TAI	USA			Percent	1000s
	(2)	(3)	(4)	(5)	(6)	(7)	(8)	(9)	(10)	(11)	(12)	(13)
Tradables												
1 Agriculture	3.2	4.3	4.1	9.7	6.0	4.4	4.6	4.3	3.5	0	3.4	0.1
310 Food	23.8	-2.0	-5.6	10.8	14.7	-8.4	23.5	-8.2	20.3	18.5	18.5	2.8
321 Textiles	2.6	1.7	-0.6	-1.5	10.7	-0.6	4.5	-0.3	2.0	0.7	0.7	0
322 Clothing	0.3	2.8	0.9	7.2	30.7	1.6	16.4	1.6	0.6	-0.9	-0.9	-0.3
323 Leather products	6.3	0.9	-0.8	-2.3	6.7	-0.6	6.3	-0.7	5.5	4.2	4.3	0
324 Footwear	6.9	1.1	-1.7	-9.0	8.2	-1.9	7.7	-2.3	5.6	4.2	4.2	0
331 Wood products	1.2	1.2	1.6	0.2	2.3	1.1	1.1	1.5	1.0	0	0	0
332 Furniture, fixtures	5.3	0.6	-0.5	3.8	6.5	-0.6	3.0	-0.4	4.3	3.2	3.3	0.2
341 Paper products	4.1	0.5	0.6	-0.5	1.8	0.5	-0.5	0.5	3.6	2.5	2.4	0.1
342 Printing, publishing	-1.5	2.7	2.9	1.7	3.8	2.8	1.9	2.9	0	-0.9	-0.8	-0.1
35A Chemicals	4.0	1.0	0.5	0.1	2.2	0.6	6.4	0.6	3.6	2.5	2.4	0.3

35B Petroleum products	0.3	1.4	1.8	4.0	3.4	1.8	0.9	1.8	0.1	-0.6	-0.6	0
355 Rubber products	3.8	0.7	0.5	-0.3	4.8	0.5	1.9	0.6	3.3	2.2	2.1	0
36A Non-metal min. prod.	1.3	1.5	1.9	1.1	1.7	1.8	-1.4	1.9	0.1	-0.7	-0.8	0
362 Glass products	10.3	3.5	2.6	1.9	2.2	2.5	1.4	2.6	10.6	9.3	9.4	0
371 Iron, steel	1.2	0.9	1.1	1.2	2.6	1.1	-11.1	1.1	0.7	0	-0.2	0
372 Non-ferrous metals	1.8	-1.0	-0.7	-1.2	-1.9	-0.9	-1.1	-0.8	0.5	-0.2	-0.3	0
381 Metal products	1.6	0.7	1.5	0.8	2.8	1.4	-6.0	1.5	0.1	-0.8	-0.9	-0.3
382 Non-elec. machinery	1.5	1.3	1.4	1.5	-1.0	1.2	-1.8	1.3	1.2	0.2	0.3	0.1
383 Electrical machinery	-3.0	0.7	1.1	0.7	1.5	1.0	4.3	1.0	-3.5	-4.2	-4.3	-6.7
384 Transport equipment	4.0	1.8	-0.4	7.4	4.6	-0.5	-0.3	-0.4	2.6	1.4	1.5	0.4
38A Misc. mfrs.	2.1	0.9	0.5	-0.2	7.3	0.7	3.3	0.8	1.8	0.6	0.6	0.2
2 Mining, quarrying	-3.7	1.1	3.3	1.3	3.6	3.3	-1.7	3.2	-3.8	-4.0	-4.1	0
Non-tradables												
4 Utilities									0.7	0	0.2	0
5 Construction									0.8	0	0.7	0.5
6 Wholesale trade									0.7	0	0.3	0.9
7 Transportation									0.2	0	0	0
8 Financial services									0.5	0	0.2	0.3
9 Personal services									0.5	0	0.5	1.3
Total	0.7	1.0	0.6	1.3	3.6	1.2	4.0	0.5	0.3	1.3	0	0

Table 8.6 Scenario D: sectoral effects on Taiwan of East Asian bilateral tariff elimination and NTB reduction (percent change; 000 workers)

Sector	Exports	Imports	Bilateral imports						Output	No. firms	Change in employment	
			CND	JPN	SK	MEX	SNG	USA			Percent	1000s
	(2)	(3)	(4)	(5)	(6)	(7)	(8)	(9)	(10)	(11)	(12)	(13)
Tradables												
1 Agriculture	14.9	5.1	2.7	32.5	69.6	2.8	26.3	2.6	2.6	0	2.6	27.2
310 Food	26.6	7.4	-1.2	39.4	61.1	-1.0	39.1	-0.7	3.0	2.1	2.0	3.1
310 Textiles	5.3	8.3	-4.8	15.8	27.8	-4.7	18.4	-4.5	3.6	1.2	1.4	3.6
322 Clothing	5.1	1.7	-3.1	14.2	44.8	-2.4	24.7	-2.4	2.7	0	0.3	0.3
323 Leather products	7.7	0.9	-1.0	2.8	12.9	-0.9	9.6	-1.0	6.9	5.0	5.2	3.0
324 Footwear	10.7	-2.6	5.6	-0.4	17.0	-5.8	11.4	-6.2	8.7	6.4	6.6	1.8
331 Wood products	3.9	2.6	0.6	22.2	42.3	0.1	4.5	0.5	1.3	0.2	0.3	0.2
332 Furniture, fixtures	1.1	5.2	0.4	19.8	21.8	0.3	24.5	0.4	0.7	-0.4	-0.3	0
341 Paper products	2.0	5.8	0.9	19.0	18.7	0.8	21.6	0.9	0.2	-1.0	-1.0	-0.9
342 Printing, publishing	-0.4	2.9	1.4	6.4	11.7	1.4	5.3	1.5	0.5	-0.6	-0.5	-0.2
35A Chemicals	6.5	0.7	-4.3	7.5	8.1	-4.2	10.8	-4.2	5.1	3.0	3.2	4.2

35B Petroleum products	4.2	3.6	2.2	8.1	4.4	2.2	3.0	2.2	-0.3	-0.8	-1.0	-0.2
355 Rubber products	2.0	14.4	-0.2	24.5	31.9	-0.2	27.8	-0.1	1.3	-0.6	-0.5	-0.3
36A Non-metal min. prod.	-1.6	13.4	2.0	24.8	23.0	2.0	19.8	2.0	-1.3	-2.1	-2.1	-2.2
362 Glass products	3.3	14.0	-0.5	22.6	22.9	-0.6	32.0	-0.5	-0.3	-1.7	-1.7	-0.3
371 Iron, steel	-1.6	15.9	2.2	25.3	27.2	2.1	23.2	2.2	-9.0	-9.1	-9.3	-6.8
372 Non-ferrous metals	5.6	3.3	0.8	12.0	9.2	0.7	2.2	0.7	1.1	0	0	0
381 Metal products	-5.3	14.9	2.7	24.8	30.9	2.6	27.5	2.7	-5.2	-5.8	-5.8	-15.3
382 Non-elec. machinery	-0.8	5.8	-2.2	14.0	11.7	-2.3	12.2	-2.2	-2.1	-3.5	-3.4	-4.6
383 Electrical machinery	4.0	3.1	-3.0	9.4	8.1	-3.1	4.4	-3.1	2.9	0.9	1.1	5.2
384 Transport equipment	0.4	11.2	-3.4	34.3	55.9	-7.0	21.3	-3.1	-3.0	-5.9	-5.6	-8.1
38A Misc. mfrs.	3.7	4.5	-0.8	11.1	16.3	-0.4	12.3	-0.4	2.0	0	0.2	0.7
2 Mining, quarrying	-1.9	1.9	2.5	2.1	6.5	2.6	-4.2	2.5	-2.3	-2.9	-2.7	-0.5
Non-tradables												
4 Utilities									0.1	0	-0.3	-0.1
5 Construction									-0.1	0	-0.2	-1.1
6 Wholesale trade									0	0	-0.2	-2.6
7 Transportation									0.1	0	0	-0.1
8 Financial services									-0.2	0	-0.4	-1.5
9 Personal services									-0.3	0	-0.3	-4.6
Total	4.4	5.4	-0.8	15.1	21.4	-4.2	10.8	-1.4	0.7	0.1	0	0

Table 8.7 *Scenario D: sectoral effects on the United States of East Asian bilateral tariff elimination and NTB reduction (percent change; 000 workers)*

Sector	Exports (2)	Imports (3)	Bilateral imports CND (4)	JPN (5)	SK (6)	MEX (7)	SNG (8)	TAI (9)	Output (10)	No. firms (11)	Change in employment Percent (12)	1000s (13)
Tradables												
1 Agriculture	0.2	-0.1	0	-1.2	1.1	0	-0.1	-1.5	0	0	0	1.6
310 Food	0	0.1	0	-1.3	1.8	0	18.6	1.3	0	0	0	0
321 Textiles	-0.1	0.3	-0.3	-0.4	3.7	-0.1	0.1	0.7	0	0	0	-0.2
322 Clothing	0.1	0.5	-0.7	-1.2	3.8	0	0	0.4	0	0	0	-0.1
323 Leather products	-0.5	0.5	-0.2	-1.6	7.3	0	4.2	6.9	-0.2	-0.2	-0.2	-0.1
324 Footwear	-0.8	1.3	0.1	-5.8	2.3	-0.1	2.9	4.7	-0.5	-0.5	-0.5	-0.4
331 Wood products	0.5	0	0.1	-1.3	0.9	-0.4	-0.8	-0.4	0	0	0	0.3
332 Furniture, fixtures	0.1	-0.2	0	-1.0	0.8	-0.1	2.2	-0.6	0	0	0	0.1
341 Paper products	0.1	0	0	-0.9	1.2	-0.1	1.7	-1.1	0	0	0	0
342 Printing, publishing	0.1	-0.2	0	-1.2	0.9	-0.1	-2.3	-0.9	0	0	0	0
35A Chemicals	-0.2	0	-0.1	-0.5	1.4	0	1.9	5.6	0	0	0	-0.3

35B Petroleum products	0.1	-0.2	0	-0.5	-0.7	0	-2.0	-2.5	0	0	0
355 Rubber products	0.1	0.1	-0.1	-0.8	4.0	-0.1	0.6	1.1	0	0	0
36A Non-metal min. prod.	0.1	-0.3	0	-0.6	-0.1	0	-2.1	-3.1	0	0	0.1
362 Glass products	0.1	-0.2	0	-0.7	-0.4	-0.1	8.7	-1.2	0	0	0
371 Iron, steel	-0.4	0	0	0	0.1	0	-0.1	-2.1	0	0	-0.1
372 Non-ferrous metals	0.2	0	0.1	-0.4	-0.9	0	-2.0	-0.3	0	0	0
381 Metal products	0.1	-1.2	0	-0.5	0.7	-0.1	-1.5	-6.4	0	0	0.4
382 Non-elec. machinery	-0.1	-0.1	0	0.1	-1.4	-0.1	-0.5	-2.8	0	0	-0.4
383 Electrical machinery	-0.2	-0.2	0.1	-0.2	0.3	0	-4.7	3.0	0	0	-0.6
384 Transport equipment	-0.1	0	0	-0.1	0.3	0	0.8	-0.6	0	0	-0.4
38A Misc. mfrs.	0	0.2	-0.3	-1.0	5.4	-0.1	0.1	2.1	0	0	-0.7
2 Mining, quarrying	0.2	-0.1	0	-1.9	0.4	0.1	-7.1	-4.7	0	0	0.2
Non-tradables											
4 Utilities									0	0	0
5 Construction									0	0	0
6 Wholesale trade									0	0	-0.1
7 Transportation									0	0	-0.1
8 Financial services									0	0	0.1
9 Personal services									0	0	0.5
Total	-0.1	0	0	-0.2	1.9	0	-3.1	1.1	0	0	0

215

Turning next to South Korea, it is evident in Table 8.4 that exports and imports increase in virtually all sectors, with the largest export increases in the resource- and labour-intensive sectors and the largest import increases in the capital-intensive sectors. This is a mirror image of what has just been noted for Japan, and it appears to be consistent with what we would expect the comparative advantage of the two countries to be. South Korea shows sizeable increases in its bilateral sectoral imports from the other three EATB countries and declines in its imports from the NAFTA countries. This latter result differs from what we noted for Japan. South Korea's increased speciali-zation is especially evident in the output results in column (10), and there is also broad indication of positive scale effects. It further appears that outputs decline in South Korea's non-tradable sectors, which is in contrast to the effects noted for Japan. These various output changes are reflected in the changes in employment in columns (12) and (13). The largest absolute em-ployment declines are in community, social, and personal services (–28,800), wholesale and retail trade (–27,600), and non-electric machinery (–17,400). The largest absolute employment increases are in clothing (53,900), textiles (38,100), agriculture (31,100), and miscellaneous manufactures (8,700).

The results for total exports and imports for Singapore in Table 8.5 are relatively smaller than those for South Korea, reflecting the fact that Singa-pore has virtually no tariffs and NTBs to begin with. The largest percentage export increases are in food products (23.8 per cent), leather products (6.3 per cent), footwear (6.8 per cent), furniture and fixtures (5.3 per cent), and glass products (10.3 per cent). The percentage changes in Singapore's bilat-eral imports are also small in comparison to South Korea. When we consider changes in output, however, because Singapore is small and has virtually no protection, it experiences increases in output in all sectors except electrical machinery and mining and quarrying. There is also evidence of positive scale effects across all of its manufacturing sectors. Finally, the absolute employ-ment effects in column (13) are all quite small, except for food products (2,800) and electrical machinery (–6,700).

The results for Taiwan in Table 8.6 show noteworthy percentage increases in total exports in most sectors and much larger percentage increases in total imports for all sectors except footwear. The pattern is similar to what was observed for South Korea, with the largest export increases in the resource- and labour-intensive sectors and the largest import increases in the capital-intensive sectors. Bilateral imports from the other EATB countries increase substantially and imports from the three NAFTA countries decline in several sectors. Taiwan's increased specialization in the labour-intensive sectors is evident in column (10), and scale economies appear across all of the manu-facturing sectors. The largest absolute employment increases are in agricul-ture (27,200), textiles (3,100) chemicals (4,200) and electrical machinery

(5,200). The largest employment declines are in iron and steel products (–6,800), metal products (–15,300), non-electric machinery (–8,100), and transport equipment (–8,100). Employment declines in all the non-tradable sectors.

Finally, let us consider the effects of an EATB on the United States. It can be seen in Table 8.7 that US exports are only slightly affected, both positively and negatively. There are somewhat larger percentage increases in imports, particularly of textiles (0.3 per cent, clothing (0.5 per cent), leather products (0.5 per cent) and footwear (1.3 per cent). US imports from Japan fall in practically all sectors. Imports particularly of consumer goods increase from South Korea, Singapore and Taiwan. The effects on US sectoral outputs are positive but very small, except in leather products (–0.2 per cent) and footwear (–0.5 per cent). Agriculture has the largest absolute employment increase (1,600). All other absolute changes in employment are negligible.

Scenario F

If an EATB were to be expanded to include the United States, it can be seen in Table 8.8 that Japan's total exports and especially its imports would increase by relatively large amounts across all sectors. The relative increases in Japan's bilateral imports from both the other EATB and NAFTA countries also become more pronounced. Further, we can see the same pattern of specialization as in Scenario D, with an expansion of output and employment in the capital-intensive and non-tradable sectors and a decline in the resource- and labour-intensive sectors. In manufacturing, the machinery and transport equipment sectors show absolute increases in employment in the 20,000 worker range. In agriculture, there is an absolute employment decline of 101,900 workers and in food products a decline of 29,100 workers. Textiles and clothing show declines of 6,700 and 32,500 workers, respectively.

Space limitations preclude our reporting the detailed sectoral results for South Korea, Singapore and Taiwan. But we may note that South Korea's bilateral imports from the other EATB countries remain sizeable, and there are more positive bilateral imports from both Canada and Mexico than we saw in the results for Scenario D for the EATB. With the United States included in an EATB, South Korea experiences a decline in output in its agricultural and food products sectors, while its output increases become larger in the labour-intensive sectors. There are employment declines in the machinery sectors, agriculture and food, and non-tradables and employment increases especially in textiles (73,600) and clothing (100,800). For Singapore, the major change in total exports is in clothing, 16.8 per cent compared to 0.3 per cent in Scenario D. The percentage increases in imports appear somewhat larger in Scenario F, and this is reflected as well in the bilateral

Table 8.8 Scenario F: sectoral effects on Japan of East Asian/US bilateral tariff removal and NTB reduction (percent change; 000 workers)

Sector	Exports (2)	Imports (3)	Bilateral imports CND (4)	SK (5)	MEX (6)	SNG (7)	TAI (8)	USA (9)	Output (10)	No. firms (11)	Change in employment Percent (12)	1000s (13)
Tradables												
1 Agriculture	7.0	14.4	2.2	23.9	2.8	19.8	19.5	33.7	-2.3	0	-2.2	-101.9
310 Food	10.1	29.2	4.7	39.2	4.3	74.2	36.4	67.7	-1.2	-2.0	-1.7	-29.1
321 Textiles	4.9	12.0	4.0	42.3	4.1	25.0	28.4	28.7	-0.3	-0.8	-0.8	-6.7
322 Clothing	4.9	25.4	4.0	69.2	4.8	35.0	40.6	34.6	-4.4	-4.9	-4.8	-32.5
323 Leather products	7.5	24.2	4.4	54.4	3.3	25.2	53.1	50.7	-1.9	-2.6	-2.6	-1.6
324 Footwear	-7.0	43.6	3.5	73.6	2.4	42.1	85.3	43.7	-8.6	-9.6	-9.5	-4.3
331 Wood products	9.2	6.0	6.5	10.2	2.2	7.2	14.0	9.4	-0.6	-1.3	-1.1	-4.8
332 Furniture, fixtures	6.6	10.3	5.3	13.3	4.1	13.1	23.0	16.7	0.3	-0.3	-0.2	-0.4
341 Paper products	2.2	9.2	7.8	13.4	4.7	13.7	9.6	12.7	-0.1	-0.5	-0.4	-1.4
342 Printing, publishing	-2.3	5.7	6.5	3.7	5.4	-2.9	0.2	7.3	0.2	-0.1	0	0.3
35A Chemicals	5.2	9.9	5.5	17.0	4.1	16.9	18.8	19.1	0.1	-0.5	-0.4	-2.1

35B Petroleum products	13.8	1.4	4.4	-0.7	4.6	-5.2	-0.1	8.8	0.7	-0.4	0	0
355 Rubber products	3.0	8.1	4.0	15.9	0.1	11.0	14.2	11.5	1.2	0.6	0.7	1.5
36A Non-metal min. prod.	10.6	4.0	5.1	3.4	4.4	5.6	1.8	15.0	0.7	0	0.2	0.8
362 Glass products	8.9	9.9	5.1	14.0	4.1	20.2	12.9	19.8	0.8	0.2	0.4	0.4
371 Iron, steel	10.1	6.5	3.0	15.3	2.9	7.6	-4.7	12.2	2.1	0.9	1.2	5.8
372 Non-ferrous metals	7.4	5.0	7.1	10.6	4.0	5.4	3.5	11.5	0.9	0	0.2	0.3
381 Metal products	7.1	9.1	4.6	15.6	4.1	12.0	6.7	19.1	0.7	-0.1	0.2	2.0
382 Non-elec. machinery	6.0	7.4	3.8	2.9	0.4	9.6	0.7	16.5	1.8	0.8	1.0	17.5
383 Electrical machinery	4.3	8.6	2.8	8.9	3.0	4.8	9.5	11.9	1.6	0.8	0.9	21.9
384 Transport equipment	10.3	8.1	-1.0	14.1	1.0	1.7	9.0	17.8	3.0	1.9	1.9	23.6
38A Misc. mfrs.	2.6	8.3	6.7	25.8	4.2	11.1	15.6	11.5	0.1	-0.5	-0.3	-4.1
2 Mining, quarrying	-2.8	3.0	7.1	-5.9	6.7	-15.5	-11.3	6.4	-3.7	-4.1	-3.8	-2.3
Non-tradables												
4 Utilities									0.5	0	0.6	1.9
5 Construction									0.3	0	0.4	21.8
6 Wholesale trade									0.2	0	0.3	39.0
7 Transportation									0.3	0	0.3	11.6
8 Financial services									0.2	0	0.4	19.3
9 Personal services									0.1	0	0.2	23.2
Total	6.3	10.1	5.7	29.6	6.2	10.1	21.2	23.0	0.5	-0.6	0	0

Table 8.9 Scenario F: sectoral effects on the United States of East Asian/US bilateral tariff removal and NTB reduction (percent change; 000 workers)

Sector	Exports	Imports	Bilateral imports						Output	No. firms	Change in employment	
			CND	JPN	SK	MEX	SNG	TAI			Percent	1000s
	(2)	(3)	(4)	(5)	(6)	(7)	(8)	(9)	(10)	(11)	(12)	(13)
Tradables												
1 Agriculture	9.7	0.1	1.1	1.6	-1.5	0.6	-1.4	3.7	2.2	0	2.2	73.6
310 Food	21.1	-0.8	-0.4	11.0	7.6	-0.9	22.0	11.1	1.0	0.8	0.9	16.4
321 Textiles	2.6	6.4	-0.8	25.9	33.2	-0.4	25.4	26.0	-0.5	-0.6	-0.6	-6.0
322 Clothing	3.9	7.2	-1.3	23.4	31.9	0	26.0	26.4	-1.4	-1.5	-1.5	-14.5
323 Leather products	14.2	-1.6	-2.0	2.3	21.0	-3.1	0.1	17.7	1.1	0.9	0.9	0.5
324 Footwear	0.4	15.0	-0.4	42.1	32.3	-1.6	34.2	47.9	-7.1	-7.4	-7.3	-6.0
331 Wood products	6.0	0.2	0.8	6.3	6.4	-3.2	0	3.3	0.5	0.4	0.4	2.5
332 Furniture, fixtures	1.8	5.8	0.2	9.3	11.6	-1.0	8.2	21.6	-0.4	-0.5	-0.4	-2.4
341 Paper products	3.7	1.5	2.1	2.2	5.6	-0.9	5.2	-2.6	0.3	0.1	0.2	1.2
342 Printing, publishing	1.0	-1.4	0.8	-4.3	-1.6	-0.3	-8.5	-4.0	0.1	0	0	0.3
35A Chemicals	4.8	1.0	0.7	11.1	16.7	-0.7	13.6	12.2	0.5	0.4	0.4	4.5

35B Petroleum products	4.8	-0.6	0.3	1.6	-6.2	0.5	7.2	-4.8	0.2	0.1	0.2	0.2
355 Rubber products	2.0	4.1	-0.7	8.8	15.8	-0.5	19.2	12.7	-0.3	-0.4	-0.3	-0.8
36A Non-metal min. prod.	3.8	3.5	0.5	22.4	20.7	-0.2	10.8	4.1	-0.1	-0.2	-0.2	-0.8
362 Glass products	4.0	2.5	0.3	17.1	16.5	-0.6	19.3	14.5	0.3	0.2	0.3	0.5
371 Iron, steel	2.9	6.7	-0.4	24.6	24.6	-0.4	23.8	19.5	-0.4	-0.6	-0.5	-2.7
372 Non-ferrous metals	5.5	0.5	2.3	7.4	5.7	-0.7	-6.8	0.8	0.4	0.3	0.3	0.9
381 Metal products	2.8	4.0	-0.1	13.8	17.2	-0.6	12.4	5.2	0	-0.2	-0.1	-1.9
382 Non-elec. machinery	3.6	1.7	-0.3	9.9	7.6	-3.9	14.9	-0.3	0.3	0.1	0.2	4.9
383 Electrical machinery	3.5	4.7	-2.4	9.2	13.3	-2.1	3.7	10.2	-0.1	-0.3	-0.3	-5.1
384 Transport equipment	3.0	6.6	-4.5	22.2	22.7	-1.8	6.2	11.3	-0.4	-0.7	-0.6	-14.5
38A Misc. mfrs.	2.6	3.7	1.7	8.7	24.9	-0.8	14.0	16.1	0	-0.2	-0.1	-1.5
2 Mining, Quarrying	2.3	-0.6	1.5	-9.0	8.2	1.6	-23.0	-13.0	0.4	0.3	0.4	3.0
Non-tradables												
4 Utilities									0	0	0.1	1.0
5 Construction									-0.1	0	0	-3.8
6 Wholesale trade									-0.1	0	0	-6.1
7 Transportation									0	0	0	0.8
8 Financial services									-0.1	0	0	-4.2
9 Personal services									-0.1	0	-0.1	-40.0
Total	4.9	3.6	-1.0	14.2	22.1	-0.4	7.0	15.8	0.1	-0.1	0	0

imports for all the countries noted. The output increases are most marked in food products and clothing, and these sectors show the largest absolute employment increases (2,400 and 3,100). The largest employment decline is in electrical machinery (–4,500). The results for Taiwan show significant percentage increases especially in labour-intensive exports as compared to Scenario D. There are also much larger percentage increases in total imports in all sectors except footwear. Bilateral imports are sizeable from all the countries shown in virtually all sectors. As in the case of South Korea, including the United States in an EATB enhances Taiwan's specialization in its labour-intensive sectors. The pattern of employment changes reflects the output changes, although in this scenario, there is a comparatively small increase in agricultural employment (1,900) compared to Scenario D (27,300).

Looking finally at the sectoral results for the United States in Table 8.9, expanding an EATB to include the United States has pronounced effects on both exports and imports. US exports increase in all sectors, most notably in agriculture (9.7 per cent), food products (21.1 per cent) and leather products (14.2 per cent). Imports increase in 18 of the 23 sectors, in particular textiles (6.4 per cent), clothing (7.2 per cent), footwear (15.0 per cent), furniture and fixtures (5.8 per cent), iron and steel products (0.2 per cent), electrical machinery (4.7 per cent) and transport equipment (6.6 per cent). There are sizeable increases in US imports from the four countries of the EATB. US imports from Canada decline in 11 of the 23 sectors. Output increases in agriculture (2.2 per cent), food products (1.0 per cent), leather products (1.1 per cent) and to a smaller extent in 11 other sectors. There is evidence of small but positive scale effects across manufacturing. The largest absolute employment increases are in agriculture (73,600), food products (16,400), chemicals (4,500) and non-electric machinery (4,900). The largest absolute declines in employment are in clothing (–14,500), electrical machinery (–5,100), transport equipment (–14,500), wholesale and retail trade (–6,100), financial services (–4,200) and community, personal and social services (–40,000).

CONCLUSIONS AND IMPLICATIONS FOR RESEARCH AND POLICY

Our purpose in this chapter has been to analyse the possible economic consequences of the formation of an East Asian Preferential Trading Bloc (EATB) comprising the four major trading countries in the region, namely Japan, South Korea, Taiwan and Singapore. To provide background for our analysis, we surveyed the burgeoning literature relating specifically to the formation of an East Asian bloc. Following this discussion, most of the chapter was devoted to using our Michigan BDS CGE Trade Model to analyse the effects of forming this bloc on the four East Asian countries themselves as well as on the United States, Canada, Mexico and the world's other major trading nations in the aggregate. We also analysed the effects of a bloc that consisted of the four East Asian countries together with the United States.

The version of the Michigan BDS CGE Trade Model used has eight countries/regions and 29 sectors. The sources of welfare improvement identifiable by the model include the traditional effects of changes in terms of trade and gains from specialization and exchange. They also include the effects of labour moving between sectors of different productivity, reflecting that wages in different sectors are in fact different. In addition, the presence of economies of scale, product differentiation, and imperfect competition among firms allows us to identify the contribution to economic well-being due to the procompetitive effects of trade liberalization, together with the effects of increased scale and variety.

Six liberalization scenarios were performed. The first scenario examined tariff removal between Japan and South Korea, and subsequent scenarios added Taiwan and then Singapore to the bloc grouping. A separate scenario combined bilateral tariff removal for the four countries together with an assumed 50 per cent expansion in imports that had been constrained by non-tariff barriers (NTBs). The final scenarios dealt with bilateral tariff removal alone and in combination with relaxation of NTBs for a bloc of the four East Asian countries plus the United States.

The results suggest that each of the four East Asian countries would gain from formation of an EATB. These gains range from 0.2 to 1.2 per cent of GDP for individual countries. Welfare tends to increase for the included partners as well as for acceding countries when the EATB is expanded. Further, the excluded countries/regions appear to benefit through the spillovers resulting from increases in the realization of scale economies and in product variety. The welfare results are even further enhanced when it is assumed that the United States also becomes a member of an EATB, although Canada and Mexico show negative welfare effects in the final scenario.

Within each country, the distributional consequences of the formation of an EATB appear to be relatively small. Indeed, it is interesting that both the real wage rate and return to capital rise in every country, with only one minor exception in the final scenario for Canada. The reason for this result is that there are large enough gains from the realization of economies of scale that accrue to both labour and capital so as to offset the negative effects that would otherwise be expected from the Stolper–Samuelson logic.

At a sectoral level, the results for Japan suggest sizeable relative increases in total exports and imports as well as in bilateral trade with the other East Asian countries if an EATB were to be formed. It is particularly noteworthy that Japan would become more specialized in its relatively more capital-intensive industries and in the non-tradable sectors, and that output and employment would decline in its agricultural and labour-intensive manufacturing sectors. The sectoral results for South Korea and Taiwan are mirror images of Japan in so far as these two nations would become more specialized in their resource- and labour-intensive industries and output and employment would decline in their more capital-intensive industries as well as in the non-tradable sectors.

The sectoral effects on US trade, output and employment are comparatively small as the result of formation of an EATB that excludes the United States. The negative effects are concentrated in textiles and clothing and leather products and footwear, and there is a positive effect in agriculture. The sectoral effects are considerably larger, however, when the United States itself is assumed to be part of an EATB. The largest employment increases occur in US agriculture and food products, chemicals and non-electric machinery. The largest employment declines occur in clothing, electrical machinery, transport equipment and in the non-traded sectors.

Our research is by no means the final word on the economic effects of the formation of an EATB. In particular, we have taken into account a bloc comprising only the four most advanced economies in the region and thus have excluded other countries such as China, Indonesia, Malaysia, Thailand and Australia/New Zealand, all of which are major participants in the broader Asia–Pacific setting. We have also abstracted from the changes that an EATB might have on foreign direct investment and have not made any allowance for dynamic changes in efficiency and economic growth. Further, if an EATB were to be formed, it would undoubtedly deal with a variety of other issues such as environmental and labour regulations and standards, intellectual property rights and liberalization of services sectors. Finally, we have not investigated whether a policy of open regionalism or a policy of global liberalization might be preferred to an EATB. Granting these limitations, our hope nonetheless is that our research provides some insights into the economic consequences of the removal of tariffs and relaxation of NTBs that would result from the formation of an EATB that included the Asian region's four most advanced economies in their own right as well as in conjunction with the United States. Taken in conjunction with the results of the aforementioned modelling studies by Martin et al. (1994) and Lewis et al. (1995), our study reinforces the conclusion that a broader economic grouping such as APEC would be welfare enhancing for the member countries. Yet it should also be kept in mind that multilateral trade liberalization would potentially yield even greater welfare gains globally as compared to .an Asia–Pacific regional trading arrangement.

NOTES

1. The East Asia region membership is to be distinguished from the membership of the Asia–Pacific Economic Corporation (APEC) grouping. Thus, Cambodia, North Korea, Laos and Myanmar are presently not members of APEC. APEC incudes all of the other countries noted as part of East Asia as well as Australia, Canada, Chile, Mexico, New Zealand and the United States.
2. It should be noted, however, according to Bannister and Braga (1994, p. 8), that the major outlet for Japanese FDI was in North America, which accounted for 45.1 per cent of total Japanese FDI in 1991 as compared to 15.1 per cent for East Asia.
3. For some related research on this issue, see Kreinin and Plummer (1994).
4. A trade-intensity index is measured by dividing the share of a country's exports going to a particular region by that region's share in world markets. For further details, see Bannister and Braga (1994, especially pp. 5–6 and Table 2).
5. Other studies that endorse open regionalism include Plummer (1994), World Bank (1994) and Wonnacott (1995). For additional perspectives on an EATB, see the papers by Petri, Saxonhouse, and Froot and Yoffie in Frankel and Kahler (1993).
6. For some partial equilibrium estimates of the effects of Asian regionalism on the United States, see Plummer (1994) and the references cited therein. These estimates are difficult to compare to those based on a CGE modelling framework which takes into account the effects between industries and countries.
7. The Armington assumption amounts essentially to providing monopoly power to each country in supplying its products, and, as a consequence, implies that there may be strong terms-of-trade effects when trade liberalization occurs.
8. The APEC members excluded from specific consideration are Australia, Brunei, Canada, Chile, Mexico and New Zealand. The Lewis et al. focus is thus narrower than what is contemplated in the Bogor Declaration of 15 November 1994, which commits APEC to implement an agreement on free and open trade and investment by the year 2020 for the developing economies and by the year 2010 for the developed economies. For additional details, see USITC (1995, pp. 14–16).
9. Readers who are not concerned with the technical details of the model being used may wish to proceed to the results of the analysis reported in the sections immediately following.
10. Hong Kong might be included as well in an EATB, although its imminent absorption by the People's Republic of China would make its membership in such a bloc unlikely. Singapore is presently a member of the Association of Southeast Asian Nations (ASEAN), but presumably could become a member of an EATB while retaining membership in ASEAN. Our decision to include Singapore as a member of an EATB reflects the fact that it is one of the most economically advanced and politically stable nations in Asia and thus could satisfy the preconditions for membership in an EATB. There are other countries in the larger Asia–Pacific region, such as Indonesia, Malaysia, Thailand, Australia and New Zealand, which might become members of an Asian trading bloc, but we shall exclude them for present purposes.
11. We have recently constructed a bilateral matrix of international trade in services for the 34 countries in the model's data base. Consequently, we are now able to treat all 29 sectors as tradable and to analyse the effects and interaction of liberalization of both merchandise trade and services. For some preliminary analysis along these lines, see Brown, Deardorff, Fox and Stern (1995).
12. It is thus being assumed that there are constant returns to scale in the agricultural sector and increasing returns to scale in the manufacturing sectors. The non-tradables sectors are treated as perfectly competitive, with constant returns. The assumption of national product differentiation for agriculture means that the so-called Armington assumption is being applied and that nations will have some degree of monopoly power in trade in this sector. For the manufacturing sectors, product differentiation by firm dispenses with the Armington assumption so that the potentially strong terms-of-trade effects associated with national monopoly power will be greatly diminished.

      Issues of the modelling of market structure are discussed in Brown and Stern (1989), where a variety of different imperfectly competitive market structures are used in analysing the economic effects of the CUSTA. For the current model, as noted, we use a structure of monopolistic competition, following Helpman and Krugman (1985), for all of the manufacturing industries. There is free entry of firms, each producing a different variety of a good, and producing it with a fixed cost and constant marginal cost in terms of primary and intermediate inputs. Varieties enter via a Dixit–Stiglitz (1977) aggregation function into both utility and production functions, with the implication that greater variety reduces cost and increases utility.

13.   It is always a problem to use completely up-to-date input–output tables because of ongoing changes in technology and productivity that would alter the input–output coefficients for particular sectors. However, our CGE model relies mainly on the intermediate input-value shares and the shares of primary factors as data. These shares tend to be more stable over time than physical input requirements. For amplification of this point, see Deardorff and Stern (1990, pp. 61–79).

14.   The main data used cover trade, production and employment, and these data come primarily from United Nations sources and to a lesser extent from national sources. The model parameters are constructed from the trade and input–output data for the countries included in the model and from published studies of trade and capital/labour substitution elasticities. For a comprehensive discussion of the data and parameters, see Deardorff and Stern (1990, pp. 37–45).

15.   The results reported below for changes in total exports and imports may appear to contradict this assumption of balanced trade. This is because what are reported are measures of the changes in *quantities* traded, which are relevant for output and employment changes. They are not the *values* of trade, which undergo additional change due to changing relative prices. It is the values of exports relative to imports that are held fixed by the balanced trade assumption.

16.   In effect then, we do not distinguish workers according to their skill characteristics and therefore how the wages and employment of different skill groups may be affected by an EATB. In Stern, Deardorff and Brown (1992), the US employment changes that might result from the NAFTA were decomposed by sector, occupation and geographic location.

17.   See Stern, Deardorff and Brown (1992) for analysis of the cross-border movement of labour between the United States and Mexico that may occur as a result of the NAFTA.

18.   The bilateral tariffs were constructed by weighting the pre-Uruguay Round, most-favoured-nation (MFN) line-item tariffs by bilateral imports so as to calculate the tariffs that each country applied bilaterally to its trading partners.

      The NTBs were calculated in terms of the percentage of trade subject to NTBs, based primarily on the NTB inventory data assembled by the United Nations Conference on Trade and Development (UNCTAD). These NTB measures are calculated by first making an inventory of existing NTBs classified by disaggregated import groupings, then determining the value of imports that are subject to any NTBs, and thereafter aggregating up to the sectoral level used in the model. Thus, a sector with a zero per cent NTB trade coverage is taken to be completely exempt from NTBs, while, say, an NTB coverage of 25 per cent is taken to mean that 25 per cent of the imports in that sector are subject to one or more NTBs. It is important to emphasize that these measures of NTB trade coverage are *not* the same as the tariff equivalents of the NTBs. For further discussion, see Deardorff and Stern (1990, pp. 23–5).

19.   For analyses of the relationships between FDI and trade, see the papers by Doner in Frankel and Kahler (1993) and Wells in Froot (1993).

20.   It is assumed for this purpose that the NAFTA is not in effect so that US bilateral tariffs and NTBs *vis-à-vis* Canada and Mexico are maintained at their pre-NAFTA levels.

21.   The model includes NTB coverage ratios that dampen the response of imports in a sector to changes in prices. This scenario has the constrained portion of imports increased by 50 per cent while the unconstrained portion responds normally to prices.

22.   See the note to Table 8.9 for information on how these tariff levels were calculated.

23. In the curse of our research we discovered that our initial model of the role of product variety, based on a Dixit–Stiglitz aggregation function for both utility and intermediate inputs, had a potential for implicitly unstable market adjustment. With costs being reduced (just as utility is increased) by variety, an increase in demand in an industry induces entry, greater variety, and therefore lower cost in downstream industries; the latter then raises demand still further. To prevent this mechanism from causing the near instability that we observed in initial runs with the East Asian data, we introduced a damping parameter into the Dixit–Stiglitz aggregator, reducing the benefits from variety by half.
24. For a further discussion of factor prices in a differentiated products model, see Brown, Deardorff and Stern (1993).
25. As already mentioned, we do not distinguish workers according to skill groups, so that we cannot determine if skilled and unskilled workers will be affected differently.

REFERENCES

Anderson, Kym and Richard H. Snape (1994), 'European and American Regionalism: Effects on and Options for Asia', *Journal of the Japanese and International Economies*, **8** (4), December, 454–77.
Bannister, Geoffrey and Carlos A. Primo Braga (1994), *East-Asian Investment and Trade: Prospects for Growing Regionalization in the 1990s*, The World Bank, unpublished paper.
Brown, Drusilla K., Alan V. Deardorff, Alan K. Fox and Robert M. Stern (1995), *Computational Analysis of Goods and Services Liberalization in the Uruguay Round*, in process.
Brown, Drusilla K., Alan V. Deardorff, David L. Hummels and Robert M. Stern (1994), *An Assessment of Extending NAFTA to Other Major Trading Countries in South America*, University of Michigan, unpublished paper.
Brown, Drusilla K., Alan V. Deardorff and Robert M. Stern (1992a), 'A North American Free Trade Agreement: Analytical Issues and a Computational Assessment', *The World Economy*, **15**, 15–29.
Brown, Drusilla K., Alan V. Deardorff and Robert M. Stern (1992b), 'North American Economic Integration', *Economic Journal*, **102**, 1507–18.
Brown, Drusilla K., Alan V. Deardorff and Robert M. Stern (1993), 'Protection and Real Wages: Old and New Trade Theories and Their Empirical Counterparts', Research Forum on International Economics, University of Michigan, Discussion Paper No. 331, May.
Brown, Drusilla K. and Robert M. Stern (1989), 'Computable General Equilibrium Estimates of the Gains from U.S.–Canadian Trade Liberalization', in David Greenaway, Thomas Hyclak and Robert J. Thornton (eds), *Economic Aspects of Regional Trading Arrangements*, London: Harvester Wheatsheaf, pp. 69–108.
Deardorff, Alan V. and Robert M. Stern (1990), *Computational Analysis of Global Trading Arrangements*, Ann Arbor: University of Michigan Press.
Dhar, Sumana and Arvind Panagariya (1994), *The Trading Blocs' Story and East Asia: Experiments with the Gravity Equation*, unpublished paper.
Dixit, Avinash K. and Joseph E. Stiglitz (1977), 'Monopolistic Competition and Optimum Product Diversity', *American Economic Review*, **67**, 297–308.
Frankel, Jeffrey A. (1991), 'Is a Yen Bloc Forming in Pacific Asia', in Richard O'Brien (ed.), *Finance and the International Economy*, 5, The AMEX Bank Review Prize Essays, Oxford: Oxford University Press, pp. 4–20.

Frankel, Jeffrey A. (1994), 'Is Japan Establishing a Trade Bloc in East Asia and the Pacific?', in Mitsuaki Okabe (ed.), *The Structure of the Japanese Economy*, London: Macmillan Press, pp. 387–415.

Frankel, Jeffrey A. and Miles Kahler (1993), *Regionalism and Rivalry: Japan and the United States in Pacific Asia*, Chicago: University of Chicago Press.

Frankel, Jeffrey A., Ernesto Stein and Shang-Jin Wei (1993a), 'Continental Trading Blocs: Are They Natural, or Super-Natural?, National Bureau of Economic Research, Working Paper No. 4588, Cambridge: NBER.

Frankel, Jeffrey A., Ernesto Stein and Shang-Jin Wei (1993b), *Trading Blocs: The Natural, the Unnatural, and the Super-Natural*, unpublished paper.

Frankel, Jeffrey A. and Shang-Jin Wei (1993), 'Trade Blocs and Currency Blocs', National Bureau of Economic Research, Working Paper No. 4335, Cambridge: NBER.

Froot, Kenneth (ed.) (1993), *Foreign Direct Investment*, Chicago: University of Chicago Press.

General Agreement on Tariffs and Trade (GATT) (1994), *Guide to GATT Law and Practice*, Analytical Index, V, Tables on Application of Article XXIV, 6th Edition. Geneva: GATT.

Helpman, Elhanan and Paul R. Krugman (1985), *Market Structure and Foreign Trade: Increasing Returns, Imperfect Competition, and the International Economy*, Cambridge, MA: MIT Press.

Kirkpatrick, Colin (1994), 'Regionalization, Regionalism and East Asian Economic Cooperation', *The World Economy*, **17**, 191–202.

Kreinin, Mordechai E. and Michael G. Plummer (1994), '"Natural" Economic Blocs: An Alternative Formulation', *The International Trade Journal*, **8**, 193–205.

Lewis, Jeffrey D., Sherman Robinson and Zhi Wang (1995), 'Beyond the Uruguay Round: The Implications of an Asian Free Trade Area', *China Economic Review*, forthcoming.

Martin, Will, Peter A. Petri and Koji Yanagishima (1994), 'Charting the Pacific: An Empirical Assessment of Integration Initiatives', *International Trade Journal*, **8** (4), 447–82.

Panagariya, Arvind (1993), 'Should East Asia Go Regional? No, No, and Maybe', The World Bank, Policy Research Working Papers, WPS 1209, Washington, DC: The World Bank.

Panagariya, Arvind (1994), 'East Asia and the New Regionalism in World Trade', *The World Economy*, **17**, 817–39.

Plummer, Michael G. (1994), 'Asian Regionalism and U.S. Interests', prepared for the Bureau of International Labor Affairs, US Department of Labor.

Stern, Robert M., Alan V. Deardorff and Drusilla K. Brown (1992), 'A U.S.–Mexico–Canada Free Trade Agreement: Sectoral Employment Effects and Regional/Occupational Employment Realignments in the United States', Appendix A in National Commission for Employment Policy, *The Employment Effects of the North American Free Trade Agreement: Recommendations and Background Studies*, Special Report No. 33 (October), Washington, DC: National Commission for Employment Policy.

US International Trade Commission (1993), 'East Asia: Regional Economic Integration and Implications for the United States', USITC Publication 2621, Washington, DC: USITC.

US International Trade Commission (1995), *International Economic Review*, January, Washington DC: USITC.

Wonnacott, Paul (1995), 'Merchandise Trade in the APEC Region: Is There Scope for Liberalization on an MFN Basis?', *The World Economy*, symposium on Global Trade Policy, 33–52.

World Bank (1994), 'East Asia's Trade and Investment: Regional and Global Gains from Liberalization', Development in Practice Series, Washington, DC: World Bank.

Yamazawa, Ippei (1992), 'On Pacific Economic Integration', *Economic Journal*, **102**, 1519–29.

9. Cross-border capital flows, corporate governance and developing financial systems in the Asia–Pacific region

J. Colin Dodds

The process of economic growth and development is not well understood (Patel, 1993), notwithstanding the voluminous literature. What we are aware of is a divergence of growth rates among industrialized and developing countries. The relatively high rates (World Bank 1993) in East Asia have attracted particular attention and are often contrasted with the low growth in Latin America. The East Asian countries are members of the Asia–Pacific Economic Cooperation Forum (APEC), which includes developing and industrial countries[1] committed to regional trade liberalization. The NAFTA states belong to this forum, which as a regional grouping functions to a degree in rivalry with the European Union.[2]

The high-growth processes in East Asia have had some common features. (Ito and Krueger, 1995). Trade policies have been liberalized, macroeconomic stability has been maintained, financial sectors have been deregulated, state firms have been privatized and there have been regional cooperative efforts (see de la Torre and Kelly, 1992; Kirkpatrick, 1994; Martin et al., 1994). The potential for increasing cross-border capital flows (both FDI and portfolio) is very great. The flows have developed momentum and this will continue, provided financial markets are open and investors have confidence in the disclosure and accountability of firms and in the functioning of securities markets. There is, however, increased systemic risk that has arisen from the greater financial integration.

High-volume Japanese and US capital flows dominate the Asia–Pacific pattern of economic activity and US portfolio investment has been attracted by high growth rates in Japan and the industrializing economies of East Asia. The flows of Japanese portfolio investment into the USA and Canada have been facilitated by the appreciation of the yen since the 1985 Plaza Accord. The internationalization and greater integration of financial systems is increasingly drawing Japan and East Asian financial institutions into global financial markets which are experiencing significant shifts in state and corporate governance structures. Countries in the region have interests in maintaining stable large-volume domestic funding for their industries – particularly the export sectors – and supplementing this with investment flows from lower-growth areas of the world economy. Greater financial openness brings with it the potential for greater market volatility and surges of portfolio flows, but the problems of indiscriminate deregulation and liberalization in Latin America (Bradford 1994 and Calvio et al., 1995), have not been present in East Asia.

While some of the other chapters in this book cover the increasing linkages of trade and FDI, this chapter extends the analysis to the implications of cross-border portfolio capital on financial markets and corporate governance structures. The focus is the Asia–Pacific region where intrazonal trade and capital flows (Kahn and Reinhart 1995) are developing rapidly while Japan (Helleiner 1992) and China are economic pivots. Other chapters in this book, which cover NAFTA and the EU, provide interesting parallels.

This chapter will illustrate that many countries in the region have been successful in tapping into cross-border capital flows, particularly FDI, and that this has led to stronger domestic competition, with easier access to foreign markets, but has changed the risk profiles of firms, as risk is borne by both domestic and foreign investors. However, the need to maintain domestic saving is critical: investment in these economies is still for the most part internally financed, increasingly from security markets. These markets are becoming integrated globally and this has the potential to change East Asian corporate governance structures.

GLOBAL FINANCIAL MARKETS

The new transnational and integrated financial marketplace that has emerged from deregulation and liberalization has led to financial innovation and the increased mobility of capital – FDI and portfolio. The development of unregulated Euro-markets in the 1960s became a catalyst for the liberalization and deregulation processes that began in the 1970s in the United States and the United Kingdom.[3] There is now an international competitive dynamic (Helleiner 1994a) as other countries, including developing ones, recognize the potential for regulatory drag on their economies and financial sectors. The dramatic opening of cross-border financial flows contrasts with piecemeal multilateral liberalization in the trade of goods and services (Edwards, 1995). The market-driven increased volatility of capital flows reinforces a change from the liberal Bretton Woods economic world (Helleiner, 1994b) in which countries could choose their own economic priorities, as policy instruments have been weakened in the more transnational marketized order (Sinclair, 1994).

Table 9.1 Global pattern of direct investment

	1976–80	1981–85	1986–90	1991	1992	1993	1994[1]
			(in billions of US dollars, annual averages)				
Total outflows	39.8	43.2	167.7	187.2	179.4	198.9	233.5
Industrial countries	39.1	41.4	158.6	177.7	161.4	168.4	197.8
of which: United States	16.9	7.6	25.3	31.3	41.0	57.9	58.4
Japan	2.3	5.1	32.1	30.7	17.2	13.7	17.9
United Kingdom	7.8	9.2	28.1	16.4	19.4	25.7	30.0
Other Europe	10.0	15.1	63.9	91.3	80.2	63.2	80.1
Developing countries[2]	0.8	1.8	9.1	9.5	18.0	30.5	35.7
of which: Asia	0.1	1.1	7.8	7.2	15.3	26.4	30.2
Latin America	0.2	0.2	0.6	1.3	0.8	2.2	2.9
Total inflows	31.7	55.3	152.4	152.0	153.2	177.4	239.7
Industrial countries[2]	25.3	36.2	126.8	108.7	94.8	96.8	135.1
of which: United States	9.0	18.6	53.4	26.1	9.9	21.4	60.1
Japan	0.1	0.3	0.3	1.4	2.7	0.1	0.9
United Kingdom	5.6	4.3	21.7	16.1	16.5	14.6	10.9
Other Europe	8.7	9.9	38.8	57.5	55.7	52.4	51.5
Developing countries[2]	6.4	19.1	25.6	43.3	58.4	80.6	104.6
of which: China	–	1.0[3]	3.1	4.4	11.2	25.8	33.8
Other Asia	2.1	4.6	12.1	20.5	26.2	25.5	33.3
Latin America	3.6	5.6	6.6	11.2	12.6	16.1	25.9

Notes:
1. Preliminary.
2. Including Eastern Europe.
3. 1982–85.

Source: BIS (1995), p. 66.

The data in Tables 9.1 and 9.2 illustrates the magnitude and volatility of capital flows. Table 9.1 shows the important roles of the USA and UK in the outflows and inflows of FDI. However, in outflows up to 1991, Japan equalled the USA. Japanese and US capital flows dominate the Asia–Pacific pattern of economic growth and we can identify the building of structural linkages first between Japan and the industrializing East Asian states, second between the USA and those states, and third, very asymmetrically, between Japan and the USA.

The Japanese flows are evidence of the strong influence of yen appreciation on firms manufacturing for East Asian and North American markets. There is a coherence in these flows which reflects relational bonds in the Japanese system of corporate governance, with informal entry barriers. The American flows enter industrializing East Asian states in competition against those from Japan, with less intercorporate cooperation, and penetrate Japan only on a very modest scale. Table 9.1 illustrates the absence of any significant inflows of FDI into Japan. In contrast to this, Japanese flows into the USA have until recently been at high volumes, and the direct Japanese investment position, on historical cost basis, is second only to that of the UK, but is perhaps strategically more significant.

Some other interesting trends to be noted are the increasing outflows from Asian developing countries as the region develops its intra-trade and investment patterns. In this regard the inflows into China have now reached significant levels. The data illustrate that Latin America has attracted increased FDI, (but still less than East Asia) – perhaps as a result of the policy reforms in the region and expectations of the expansion of NAFTA.

Turning to portfolio flows (Table 9.2), the data refer only to the two-way flows of the USA, Japan and Western Europe (particularly the UK, where the institutionalization of saving is a major factor). The table confirms a surge of investment, particularly in 1993 with a return in 1994 to the levels established in previous years. North American portfolio investment has been attracted by high growth in Japan and the industrializing East Asian states, while Japanese portfolio investment in the USA and Canada is facilitated by the appreciation of the yen. The portfolio movement each way across the Pacific reflects the financial interdependence between the USA and Japan, which is related in part to the US fiscal and trade deficits.

These data indicate contexts for investors and policy makers as they consider policy responses. The effects of deregulation and liberalization have been little understood (Underhill, 1995), but what is apparent is that national policy objectives and instruments are now conditioned by transnational markets, and a regulatory gap has emerged as accountability and supervisory controls have become diffused.

Table 9.2   Portfolio capital flows

	1976–80	1981–85	1986–90	1991	1992	1993	1994
	(in billions of US dollars, annual averages)						
Outflows[1]	21.3	63.5	182.6	267.3	244.1	424.7	232.6
United States	5.3	6.5	13.6	44.7	45.1	120.0	60.6
Japan	3.4	25.0	85.9	74.3	34.4	51.7	83.6
Western Europe[2]	12.6	32.0	83.1	148.3	164.6	253.0	88.4
Inflows[1]	26.4	68.4	172.3	354.1	305.8	520.3	175.5
United States	5.2	29.4	44.7	54.0	66.7	104.9	91.5
Japan	5.1	12.6	26.9	115.3	8.2	–11.1	34.7
Western Europe[2]	16.1	26.4	100.7	184.8	230.9	426.5	49.3

Notes:
1. Excluding official monetary movements.
2. Including intra-regional flows. Data for 1994 are partly estimated.

Source: BIS (1995).

Speculative surges of cross-border portfolio capital can weaken the links between a national financial system and a domestic real sector (Bradford, 1994 and Underhill, 1995). The dramatic fall in the Mexican stock market, the fall in the peso in early 1995, and financial crises in other Latin American countries had ripple effects extending to all emerging markets as MNEs and offshore investors critically re-evaluated their past and future decisions. The IMF was thus obliged to reassess the effectiveness of its surveillance of capital movements (IMF, 1995).

FINANCIAL AND CORPORATE GOVERNANCE

The structure of financial systems has varied quite markedly across countries, reflecting differences in history, culture and stages of economic development (Pauly, 1994). There is an increasing body of 'old' and 'new' literature which illustrates the critical role that the financial sector and financial markets can play in the growth process (Dodds, 1994). This raises interesting questions as to whether structural asymmetries can give competitive advantages (see, for example, Porter, 1994 and Kaufman, 1994). Concerns have been expressed that, in the USA at least, corporate governance, particularly with the growth of institutional ownership, may be fatally flawed (Porter, 1994), and a major impediment to US global competitiveness, and that lessons can be learned from structures found in other countries, including Germany and Japan (Prowse, 1995).

In Table 9.3 we recognize three types of financial systems within which there are different corporate governance structures. Shareholding is diffused in the outsider/market system and more concentrated in the insider systems. Taking these *seriatim*, in Type 1 (Table 9.3) there is a greater emphasis on financial contracting, transparency of transactions and codification procedures; ownership is generally dispersed and passive even though financial institutions often hold a significant percentage of the total stock. This is broadly reflective of the US and UK approaches and also those in Canada, Australia and New Zealand (Dodds, 1996). It is referred to as an *outsider* system because the shareholders are largely outside internal firm decision processes and focus more on risk-return factors; their portfolio selection and management decisions result in a greater propensity to trade their stock. As a result, turnover rates can be high and investors often have short investment horizons.

The flexibility and continuous auction nature of the capital market can lead company managers, given the agency relationship, to focus on policies which can raise short-term value rather than long-term strategic objectives (Edwards, 1994 and Porter, 1994). To do otherwise would invite forced corporate restructuring by the threat or onset of takeovers (Arshadi and Eyssell, 1995). The impact of takeovers is felt by many other stakeholders in the firm, including employees and lenders, and the motives may be asset-stripping or concentration of asset and/or market share rather than the enhancement of 'real value'. As a result, a number of US state legislatures have enacted laws to permit and in some instances to require Boards of Directors to consider and act on the interests of other corporate stakeholders. In the EU some of these stakeholders have constitutional powers. The potential for bankruptcy and dissolution of the firm can also condition financial managers and their financing policies, particularly in their assessments of leverage.

The openness of the ownership structure and cross-border portfolio flows in outsider systems is increasing the potential for cross-border mergers and acquisitions. The market for corporate control evident in mergers and acquisitions is not just one of correcting managerial failure (as measured by past corporate performance), but of 'a market in contending prospective strategies for firms' (Franks and Mayer, 1992, p. 8), particularly through hostile bids. The state generally plays a limited role in this system, focusing on prudential and supervisory issues, and the interplay of statute and regulatory controls places constraints on shareholder activism, whether individual or institutional. Legal rules in the USA, for example, have not encouraged shareholder oversight and have made it difficult and even dangerous for shareholder activism and intervention even when companies are in financial distress.

Although there is a logic to assuming that the interests of the individual shareholder and those of the professional managers of financial institutions

Table 9.3   *Financial structure and corporate control mechanisms, USA, Germany and Japan*

Control mechanisms	United States	Type of financial system Germany	Japan
	Type 1 – Outsider	Type 2 – Insider	Type 3 – Ultra-insider
Board independence/ power over management	Little	Greatest	Little formally. More influence informally through President's Club meetings. Substantial
Monitoring by financial institution stakeholders	Little	Substantial	Some
Monitoring by non-financial firm stakeholders	Little	Substantial	Some
Monitoring by individual stakeholders	Little	Important for those firms that are owner-managed	Little
Frequency of hostile takeovers	Frequent	Virtually non-existent	Virtually non-existent
Bank control over access to external finance	None	Possibly some	Substantial

Source: Adapted from Prowse (1995) Table 15, p. 39.

such as mutual and pension funds are identical, we cannot presume this. Indeed, professional fund managers may not share the same interests of improving corporate governance. They have a greater ability at diversification and the costs involved in direct monitoring can impact on their performance which for mutual funds in particular can be important as league tables are often utilized. They can informally pressure for information and may develop an investing relationship with the management of the firm. In a takeover battle they are often in a critical position by virtue of the concentration of their holdings to determine the outcome. Concerted action has legal implications in North America, although in the UK the formation of watchdog committees and legal challenges on the fiduciary responsibility of Boards are now quite common. However, recently in the USA. (e.g. IBM, Westinghouse and Kodak and the moves by the Securities and Exchange Commission (SEC) to relax proxy rules[4]) and the UK (Cadbury Committee, December 1992) the spotlight has now been placed on corporate governance (Prowse 1995). There is now a greater potential to reduce agency costs by collective action (Shleifer and Vishny, 1986 and Black, 1992).

In the *insider* systems, notably in Germany and Japan (ultra-insider) banks not only grant credit, but take equity positions (see Allen and Gale, 1995 and Andrews, 1994) and, in Japan, there is a high degree of reciprocity in equity ownership and commercial trade, with cross-shareholding by firms. As a result, there is a concentration of ownership and inside shareholders can assume major policy and monitoring roles in the firm. Transparency is low and the financial markets for corporate securities are generally less developed, as is the non-bank financial sector. In Japan, the Ministry of Finance intervenes at times to support stock prices, at the risk of raising concerns about market manipulation. While individuals do invest in the markets, the float of shares is generally low.

In this structure, corporate change and restructuring, with funding, is negotiated, with managerial expertise, particularly with banks, and usually at an early stage. While bankruptcies do occur, financial managers do not face the same external threats of hostile takeovers as they would in an outsider system. Management is given greater discretion, and performance is assessed by supervisory boards. These structures reduce the agency costs of other investors as well as the direct monitoring costs of banks. As hostile takeovers, including those from overseas, are rare, a strategic longer-term corporate investment capability is reinforced. In Japan, the structure is referred to as the *keiretsu system* (Kester, 1991). Its corporate governance gives a member firm independence of ownership and control, but with information sharing and selective interaction by stockholders to build and maintain long-term business relationships. The Main Bank takes on a direct monitoring role and acts as if it is a controlling shareholder (Nakatani, 1984).

The insider control systems have been efficient means of resolving the corporate agency issue. The market-driven financial innovation referred to earlier, however, and competitive pressures, together with the increased use of offshore security market financing, will bring about significant changes. There will be moves towards a more market-driven system and greater reliance on security markets. Combinations of 'old' and 'new' elements of financial contracting will evolve with prices established by world supply and demand.

DEVELOPING ASIA–PACIFIC FINANCIAL SYSTEMS

East Asian financial systems, led by Japan, have developed with policy-induced orientations towards the funding of outward-oriented industries, from domestic sources, with restraints on the movement of investment into world financial markets (Patrick and Park, 1994). In Table 9.4 the data illustrate not only high and increasing saving rates relative to all developing countries, but the importance of domestic saving, particularly from households (see Schmidt-Hebbel et al., 1992). Efficiency in the national financial markets has been lower, in certain respects, than in the more sophisticated North American and European markets. But the industrial funding has been generally larger and more stable. Notwithstanding this, the attraction of foreign saving can lead to significant spin-off effects in terms of technology transfer, marketing, and so on.

With changes in regulations, financial innovation, and greater sophistication on the part of participants, the household sector in East Asia is now more sensitive to yield, transaction costs and liquidity. There is now a wider array of financial instruments including cross-border ones, often with higher returns to savers, and this has had the effect of mobilizing new saving. As

Table 9.4   Developing countries – saving (in percent GDP)

	1971–93	1971–75	1976–81	1982–86	1987–90	1991–93
Asia						
Total saving	28.4	26.3	27.8	28.3	30.5	30.4
Domestic saving	27.5	25.3	27.0	27.0	30.0	29.5
Foreign saving	0.9	1.0	0.8	1.3	0.5	0.9
All developing countries						
Total saving	25.6	24.7	26.9	24.6	25.8	25.8
Domestic saving	24.3	23.9	25.4	22.6	24.9	24.5
Foreign saving	1.3	0.8	1.5	2.0	0.9	1.3

Source: Table 15, IMF (1993), p. 77.

security markets develop further in the region, the interest of investors can be developed and sustained. However, more savings may be invested indirectly via pension funds, mutual funds, and so on, and if there is a move to more institutionalized saving, it would likely lead to more active portfolio selection and management, increased international diversification, and further pressures for the integration of financial markets. It will probably also have an impact on corporate governance as institutional investors acquire greater shares of outstanding holdings. These investors, moreover, may be more active in asserting their fiduciary responsibilities to their clients (Black, 1992). In recent years such a trend has become apparent in North America and the UK. The trend, if it continues, will raise questions about how to exercise and control the responsibility that comes from institutional investor activism.

The new Asian patterns of private cross-border financial flows are radically different from those of the 1970s and early 1980s (Claessens, 1995). Table 9.5 illustrates that commercial bank loans, which dominated the earlier period, have been replaced by FDI and portfolio flows (equity and bonds). Cottarelli and Kourelis (1994) argue for policies to develop financial structures by encouraging markets for securities, including short-term ones, and by removing barriers to entry and encouraging capital mobility (Dodds, 1996). As Stiglitz (1993) has argued, well-developed capital markets are now seen as the 'hallmark of a developed economy' (p. 20). They bring about an efficient allocation of capital and provide avenues for saving. The latter requires security markets to ensure liquidity for investors. The emerging Asian markets have attracted cross-border portfolio investment, both direct and via mutual and pension funds, but the receiving countries need financial systems that can absorb the investment as well as give protection to investors. Indeed, investors' concerns about the economic and political fundamentals of

Table 9.5   Capital flows to developing countries in Asia (US$ billions)

	1971–76	1977–81	1982–88	1989–92	1991	1992
FDI	8.9	8.9	13.2	22.7	24.1	22.7
Portfolio equity	—	—	—	3.9	1.6	7.5
Bonds	0.7	1.4	5.2	3.9	4.2	6.5
Commercial bank loans	21.3	30.9	31.5	23.0	25.5	14.7
Suppliers and export credit	9.2	11.9	10.2	10.9	8.8	19.6
Official loans	42.2	36.0	32.7	29.8	29.8	24.5
Grants	17.7	10.8	7.2	5.7	6.0	4.6
Total in US$ (billions)	10.5	24.6	43.3	73.8	73.7	92.8
Total in constant US$ (billions)	19.8	25.7	40.8	59.8	59.0	73.4

Source: IMF (1993), Table 15, p. 77.

a country, its disclosure requirements, and the available liquidity are paramount issues.

In the Asia–Pacific region, although security markets are developing, many are still thin. Table 9.6 presents comparative data for 1994 Q.3 market capitalization and turnover in some of the East Asian markets. The data reveal that Malaysia has the highest market capitalization[5] and Taiwan has the highest turnover rate. Markets in the region have become attractive to off-shore investors because of the potential for higher average returns and for gains from diversification. Financiers in the region have incentives to invest offshore, to reduce risk by diversification.

Table 9.6   Emerging stock markets in the Asia–Pacific region (1994 Q.3)

	Market capitalization (US million)	Value of stock traded (US million)
Indonesia	43,976	2,809
Korea	183,295	61,140
Malaysia[1]	229,272	43,611
Philippines	52,570	4,382
Taiwan	222,988	223,878
Thailand	142,245	25,162

Notes: 1.   Data for Malaysian incorporated companies only.

Source: World Bank, Financial Flows and the Developing Countries, February 1995, Table A.7.

Harvey (1995) and Buckberg (1995) offer the most recent comprehensive analysis of these markets. Their findings are that there are very marked differences in the risk-return characteristics, and that returns are not as high as might be expected given the risks. Some of these results from the Buckberg Study (1995) are in Tables 9.7 and 9.8. However, the data also appear to confirm that segmentation still exists among markets, as well as market imperfections (Mullin, 1993) and, therefore, that full diversification may not be possible (Bekaert, 1995). Indeed, there are direct and indirect barriers to investment. The former include legal barriers such as ownership restrictions and taxation regimes, asymmetries of information, differences in accounting standards and investor protection. Nevertheless, many of these are now disappearing.[6]

The management of effective involvement in world financial markets has become a very demanding challenge for Japan and the high-growth industrializing East Asian states. They have interests in maintaining stable large-

Table 9.7   *Means and standard deviations of monthly total equity returns (including reinvested dividends), January 1985–December 1991*

	Mean	Standard deviation
Indonesia	−0.0215	0.1006
Korea	0.0194	0.0833
Malaysia	0.0079	0.0812
Philippines	0.0348	0.1101
Taiwan	0.0234	0.1591
Thailand	0.0261	0.0906
USA	0.0138	0.0513
Japan	0.0164	0.0786
Europe	0.0178	0.0574
World	0.0146	0.0488

Source: Buckberg (1995).

Table 9.8   *Total return correlations of international equity returns, January 1985–December 1991*

	Indonesia	Korea	Malaysia	Philippines	Taiwan	Thailand
Indonesia	1.00					
Korea	−0.11	1.00				
Malaysia	0.43	0.15	1.00			
Philippines	0.48	0.20	0.34	1.00		
Taiwan	0.18	0.05	0.30	0.12	1.00	
Thailand	0.48	−0.02	0.57	0.27	0.43	1.00
USA	0.20	0.26	0.57	0.30	0.20	0.42
Japan	−0.20	0.35	0.24	0.29	0.21	0.26
Europe	0.18	0.23	0.43	0.17	0.17	0.42
World	−0.01	0.36	0.51	0.26	0.26	0.46

Source: Buckberg (1995).

volume domestic funding for their industries, but also in supplementing this with investment drawn from lower-growth areas of the world economy which may have more sophisticated financial markets. They also have interests in maintaining a presence in world financial markets that will facilitate measures to control volatility. In both contexts, the interests of Japan and the industrializing East Asian states are basically complementary, but there is a divergence, related to asymmetries in structural interdependence.

THE EVOLVING PATTERN

Domestic and external pressures for financial liberalization and development have been operative in a larger context of increasing rivalries to raise levels of structural competitiveness. In these rivalries the principal objectives of financial policies are to increase productive use of domestic savings and incoming portfolio investment. Foreign direct investment policies in the industrializing East Asian states are intended to draw outside firms into outward-oriented manufacturing with expanding local linkages and technology transfers. However, in Japan the treatment of foreign direct investment is managed with much informal discrimination, from a position of strength rather than dependence. In this East Asian pattern, governmental capacities to regulate, deepen, and enlist the cooperation of their financial sectors differ significantly, with consequences for structural competitiveness and development. The differences in administrative capacity evidence contrasts in institutional development, in the rationality of elite preferences, in levels of technocratic and technological competence, and in degrees of functional responsiveness between economic ministries and corporate groups.

Japan ranks high on the dimensions affecting economic policy management, especially because of the bureaucracy's level of institutional advancement, rather high degrees of technocratic capability, supported by technological expertise, and strong synergies generated in its system of government–business relations. A distinctive feature of the political economy is its informal restraint on inward foreign direct investment, and a further distinctive feature is the external expansion of *keiretsu* ties as integrated groups of Japanese firms undertake foreign production. Dependence on incoming portfolio investment is moderate because of the large accumulated resources of many Japanese firms. In addition, the yields offered are moderate because common managerial strategies are to accept low profit margins in foreign markets, in order to consolidate and expand established positions while the yen remains appreciated.

Korea and Taiwan rank next because of somewhat weaker institutional development, lower levels of technocratic and technological competence and weaker synergies in government–business relations. These two states are more open to foreign direct investment, and, while they have sought to limit dependence on it, are substantially dependent on it for technology transfers, and have to implement more accommodating foreign direct investment policies because of weaker leverage in relations with major trading partners. Incoming portfolio investment is more in demand than in Japan, exerts more pressure for deepening of the local financial sectors, and tends to yield higher returns, in part because export performance is less hindered by currency appreciation.

The larger resource-rich ASEAN members, which are less industrialized, are institutionally less advanced, have relatively lower technological capabilities, and have less efficient systems of government–business cooperation. These states are more open to foreign direct investment, and more dependent on it for export expansion, but tend to attract outside firms into assembly-type manufacturing, with small technology transfers. Foreign portfolio investment is attracted, but in part by highly protected officially favoured firms that enjoy local monopolies yet lack international competitiveness. Local affiliates of foreign firms producing for export also attract international portfolio investment, and will tend to attract more of it as levels of protection for sheltered domestic enterprises are lowered, in the course of regional trade liberalization, since foreign shares of the domestic markets will increase. Considerable volumes of the inward foreign direct investment come from Korea and Taiwan, and there are also substantial flows of such investment between the larger ASEAN members, in which Chinese firms are very active.

In Pacific cross-investment, the prominent and rapidly growing Japanese manufacturing presence in the USA has been financed mainly by the accumulated export earnings of the participating firms, with support from major banks in the home economy, especially on the basis of *keiretsu* bonds. Efficiencies associated with this direct investment tend to be high because of synergies which reinforce risk-sharing commitments and which generate information flows that reduce investment uncertainties. Investment competition against US firms, to achieve advances in applied technology, is facilitated by strong relational intercorporate links, and these resist assimilation into the US system of corporate governance.

American direct investment in industrializing East Asia is less than Japan's, principally because of the long-standing attraction of Europe for US outward direct investment, but also because intense Japanese corporate interest in East Asia's resources and markets is a formidable challenge. The expanding Japanese direct investment position in the area in manufacturing and trading tends to facilitate increasing Japanese portfolio investment, and extensions of the Japanese financial system, on a scale that reduces the relative size of the US corporate presence.

Within the USA, its liberal foreign direct investment policy and open system of corporate governance allow wide scope for market forces, but with risks of greater vulnerability to stress and shocks in world financial markets. Administrative capacity to regulate the financial sector is affected by a fragmentation of authority between institutionally advanced structures and by conflicted policy processes in the US system of divided government. Government–business relations tend to be distant and somewhat adversarial, and have thus received very critical evaluations in policy debates on financial sector issues related to problems of structural competitiveness.

CONCLUSION

Cross-border capital flows are changing the landscape of national financial and corporate governance structures. Governments have relinquished many regulatory controls, and policies of privatization, in conjunction with financial innovations, are causing greater use of security markets. This raises important regulatory issues. For the USA the involvement of its financial sector in world financial markets has been a very demanding challenge because of downward pressures on its currency and stresses in its financial sector. There are also difficulties in the Japanese banking sector. These present very real systemic risks which need to be addressed through greater macro–economic and regulatory policy coordination.

Although financial systems and corporate governance structures differ, the continued growth of FDI, with increasing portfolio investment, will lead to a greater convergence towards a more market-driven global financial system. There are shifts in the market (outsider) financial structure of the United States and United Kingdom, with demands for greater transparency and accountability backed up by the increasing use of shareholder power. Likewise, in much of the EU and Japan, cross-border capital mobility will inevitably lead to shifts in corporate governance. With the diminishing role of banks as firms increasingly use capital markets securities, including those raised overseas, the insider systems will become market focused, with a greater potential for cross-border acquisitions. Nevertheless, major advantages will be gained wherever financial institutions are linked relationally with each other and with national manufacturing and trading enterprises.

As we have illustrated, the Asia–Pacific countries have attracted FDI and, increasingly, portfolio investment. These flows can be mutually reinforcing, for the continued mobilization and deployment of domestic saving, provided that the issues of accountability and disclosure are addressed. However, the greater shareholder activism now emerging in the USA and the UK, and the potential for cross-border acquisitions, will be felt in these markets. This will not only produce a shift in corporate governance, but will lead to further financial and corporate integration. With the recent free trade commitments within the APEC, this will strengthen intraregional integration.

NOTES

1. These include Australia, Canada, Chile, Japan, New Zealand and the United States.
2. As recognized, there are other smaller regional trading agreements in existence.
3. Helleiner (1994b) argues that both the UK and USA had 'hegemonic' interests in pursuing financial openness.
4. Including reforms on proxy rules and sponsorship of a round table in Corporate Govern-

ance and American Economic Competitiveness. In addition, the American Law Institute in 1991 in a Restatement of Trusts has attempted to move the interpretation of 'prudence' to one based on modern portfolio theory (MPT).
5. Excluding Hong Kong and Singapore.
6. The Asian Development Bank (ADB) has expressed concerns about shareholder protection in the region and this applies to both domestic and cross-border shareholders. They have called for greater transparency and a level playing field so as to avoid insider dealing, inaccurate corporate reporting and stock price manipulation. Given the greater global integration of markets, to be found in developing countries, including the Asia–Pacific region, significant shifts will occur in financial and corporate governance structures and the role of governments.

REFERENCES

Allen, F. and D. Gale (1995), 'A Welfare Comparison of Intermediaries and Financial Markets in Germany and the U.S.', *European Economic Review*, **39**, 179–200.

Andrews, D.M. (1994), 'Capital Mobility and Monetary Adjustment in Western Europe', *Policy Sciences*, **27** (4), 425–45.

Arshadi, N. and T.H. Eyssell (1995), 'On Corporate Governance; Public Corporations, Corporate Takeovers, Defensive Tactics and Insider Trading', *Financial Markets, Institutions and Instruments*, **4** (5), 74–103.

Bekaert, G. (1995), 'Market Integration and Investment Barriers in Emerging Equity Markets', *World Bank Economic Review*, **9** (1), 75–108.

BIS (1995), *Annual Report*, Basle: Bank for International Settlements.

Black, B.S. (1992), 'Institutional Investors and Corporate Governance: The Case for Institutional Voice, Continental Bank', *Journal of Applied Corporate Finance*, **5** (3) 19–32.

Bradford, C.I. (ed.) (1994), *The New Paradigm of Systemic Competitiveness: Toward More Integrated Policies in Latin America*, Paris: OECD, pp. 41–65.

Buckberg, E. (1995), 'Emerging Stock Markets and International Asset Pricing', *World Bank Economic Review*, **9** (1), 51–74.

Calvo, G., L. Leiderman and C. Reinhart (1995), 'Capital Inflows to Latin America: With a Reference to the Asia Experience', in S. Edwards (ed.) (1995), pp. 339–82.

Claessens, S. (1995), 'The Emergence of Equity Investment in Developing Countries: Overview', *World Bank Economic Review*, **9** (1), 1–17.

Cottarelli, C. and A. Kourelis (1994), 'Financial Structure, Bank Lending Rates and the Transmission Mechanism of Monetary Policy', *Staff Papers*, International Monetary Fund, **41** (4), 587–628.

de la Torre, A. and N.R. Kelly (1992), 'Regional Trade Arrangements', Occasional Paper No. 93, March, Washington: International Monetary Fund.

Dodds, J.C. (1994), 'The Funding of Pacific Industries', in G.K. Sletmo and G. Boyd, *Industrial Policies in the Pacific*, Boulder: Westview Press, Chapter 3.

Dodds, J.C. (1996), 'Pacific Financial Systems', in G. Boyd (ed.), *Structural Competitiveness in the Pacific*, Cheltenham: Edward Elgar Publishing (forthcoming), Chapter 3.

Edwards, F.R. (1994), 'Financial Markets and Managerial Myopia: Making America More Competitive', in Kaufman (ed.) (1994), Chapter 4.

Edwards, S. (1995), *Capital Controls, Exchange Rates and Monetary Policy in the World Economy*, Cambridge: Cambridge University Press.

Franks, J.R. and C. Mayer (1992), 'Corporate Control: A Synthesis of the International Evidence', Institute of Finance and Accounting, Working Paper No. 165–92, London Business School.

Grout, P. (1987), 'Wider Share Ownership and Economic Performance', *Oxford Review of Economic Policy*, **3** (4), 13–28.

Harvey, C.R. (1995), 'The Risk Exposure of Emerging Equity Markets', *World Bank Economic Review*, **9** (3), 19–50.

Helleiner, E. (1992), 'Japan and the Changing Global Financial Order', *International Journal*, **XLVII**, Spring, 420–44.

Helleiner, E. (1994a), 'Freeing Money: Why Have States Been More Willing to Liberalize Capital Controls than Trade Barriers?', *Policy Sciences*, **27** (4), 299–318.

Helleiner, E. (1994b), *States and the Re-emergence of Global Finance: From Bretton Woods to the 1990's*. Ithaca: Cornell University Press.

Herring, R.J. (1994), 'The Collapse of BCCI: Implications for the Supervision of International Banks', in Kaufman, (ed.) (1994), Chapter 8.

IMF (1995), 'Capital Account Convertibility: Review of Experience and Implications for IMF Policies', Occasional Paper No. 131, International Monetary Fund, Washington, DC.

Ito, T. and A.O. Krueger (1995), *Growth Theories in Light of the East Asian Experience*, Chicago: University of Chicago Press.

Jenkinson, T. and C. Mayer (1992), 'The Assessment: Corporate Governance and Corporate Control', *Oxford Review of Economic Policy*, **8** (3), 1–10.

Kahn, M.S. and C.M. Reinhart (1995), 'Capital Flows in the APEC Region', Occasional Paper No. 122, International Monetary Fund (March), Washington, DC.

Kaufman. G.G. (ed.) (1994), *Reforming Financial Institutions and Markets in the United States*, Boston: Kluwer Academic Publishers.

Kester, W.C. (1991), 'Japanese Corporate Governance and the Conservation of Value in Financial Distress', *Continental Bank Journal of Applied Corporate Finance*, **4** (2), 98–104.

Kirkpatrick, C. (1994), 'Regionalisation, Regionalism and East Asian Economic Cooperation', *World Economy*, **17**, 191–202.

Martin, W., P.A. Petri and K. Yanagishima (1994), 'Charting the Pacific: An Empirical Assessment of Integration Initiatives', *The International Trade Journal*, **VIII** (4), Winter, 447–82.

Mullin, J. (1993), 'Emerging Equity Markets in the Global Economy', *Federal Reserve Bank in New York Quarterly Review*, **18**, (2), Summer, 54–83.

Nakatani, I. (1984), 'The Economic Role of Financial Corporate Grouping', in M. Aoki (ed.), *The Economic Analysis of the Japanese Firm*, Amsterdam: Elsevier North-Holland Science Publisher B.V.

Patel, S.J. (1993), 'East Asia's Explosive Development: Its Relevance to Theories and Strategies', Working Paper No. 93.5, International Development Studies, Saint Mary's University, Halifax.

Patrick, Hugh T. and Yung Chul Park (1994), *The Financial Development of Japan, Korea and Taiwan*, Oxford: Oxford University Press.

Pauly, L.W. (1994), 'National Financial Structures, Capital Mobility and International Rules: The Normative Consequences of East Asian, European and American Distinctiveness', *Policy Sciences*, **27** (4), 343–63.

Porter, M.E. (ed.) (1994), *Capital Choices*, Boston: Harvard University Press.

Prowse, S. (1995), 'Corporate Governance in an International Perspective: A Survey of Corporate Control Mechanisms Among Large Firms in the U.S., U.K., Japan and Germany', *Financial Markets, Institutions and Instruments*, **4** (1), New York University, Salomon Center.

Schmidt-Hebbel, K., S.B. Webband and G. Corsetti (1992), 'Household Saving in Developing Countries: First Cross-Country Evidence', *World Bank Economic Review*, **6** (3), September, 529–47.

Shleifer, A. and R.W. Vishny (1986), 'Large Shareholders and Corporate Control', *Journal of Political Economy*, **94** (3), 461–88.

Sinclair, T.J. (1994), 'Between State and Market: Hegemony and Institutions of Collective Action Under Conditions of International Capital Mobility', *Policy Sciences*, **27** (4), 447–66.

Stiglitz, J.E. (1993), 'The Role of the State in Financial Markets', Proceedings of the World Bank Annual Conference on Development Economics, 1993, New York: World Bank.

Underhill, G.R.D. (1995), 'Keeping Governments Out of Politics: Transnational Securities Markets, Regulatory Co-operation and Political Legitimacy', *Review of International Studies*, **21** (3), 251–78.

World Bank (1993), *The East Asian Miracle: Economic Growth and Public Policy*, Washington DC: World Bank.

10. Designing institutions for global economic cooperation: investment and the WTO

Gilbert R. Winham and Heather A. Grant

The World Trade Organization (WTO) came into effect on 1 January, 1995, as a result of the success of the GATT Uruguay Round negotiation launched in 1986. The WTO represents a new departure in international trade, in that it includes new issues on the trade agenda, and it is a full-fledged international institution in place of what was mainly a contractual relationship under the GATT. The WTO places trade on the same institutional level as monetary relations and economic development, which are serviced by the International Monetary Fund (IMF) and the International Bank of Reconstruction and Development (IBRD), respectively.

Investment, or Trade-Related Investment Measures (TRIMs), was one of the new issues included in the Uruguay Round Final Act. Its inclusion in a trade agreement was controversial. As a separate issue, investment was addressed only on a minimal basis (as the name TRIMs implies) during the Uruguay Round negotiation. Consequently, the results of the TRIMs agreement are meagre, despite the fact that considerable progress was made on investment issues, in other Uruguay Round agreements, such as services and intellectual property. Following on this rudimentary beginning, many have called for new international negotiations on investment, either on a multilateral or plurilateral basis; or even for the creation of a new world investment organization.

At this writing in January 1996, negotiations on investment have been under way for six months in the OECD, with completion slated for the June 1997 meeting of OECD ministers.[1] However, there is considerable pressure to involve developing countries in these negotiations, which would involve establishing a consultation mechanism between the OECD and the WTO, or alternatively moving the negotiation to the WTO itself. For example, European Trade Commissioner Sir Leon Brittan has stated:

> I believe that developing countries have never been as receptive as they are today to the message that foreign direct investment is not a threat but a positive tool for

economic growth and for bringing in capital, technology, and management expertise. At a time when over half of new investment flows go to the developing world,
this is a global issue, that OECD countries cannot resolve alone.[2]

This sentiment has been recently supported by WTO Director General Renato
Ruggiero, who noted:

> The question that has been raised is whether, because of the substantive interlinkages
> between the subject matter of these [OECD] negotiations and WTO rules – for
> example, in the area of trade in services, intellectual property, and trade-related
> investment measures (TRIMs) – and because of the need to ensure a truly multi-
> lateral dimension that would enable the interests of all trading nations to be taken
> into account, it is desirable that the WTO decide at an early stage to initiate an
> examination of investment policy issues.[3]

This chapter will examine the subject of investment and its relationship to
the WTO. First, it will survey the nature and role of international investment
in the world economy, and its relationship to international trade. Second, it
will explore the case for new international rules for international investment.
Third, it will describe the accomplishments of the Uruguay Round, including
the establishment of the WTO and the new dispute settlement mechanism of
that body which would be important in a new investment regime.

Fourth, the chapter will examine in detail what was accomplished in the
Uruguay Round TRIMs agreement. It will also highlight two other agreements negotiated under the Uruguay Round with particular investment dimensions, namely the agreements on services and trade-related intellectual
property rights (TRIPs). Finally, it will propose a negotiating agenda for
multilateral talks, which is based on the more modern and forward-looking
rules included in the chapter on investment in the North American Free Trade
Area (NAFTA).

INVESTMENT IN THE INTERNATIONAL ECONOMY

The importance of foreign direct investment (FDI) to the global economy is
steadily increasing. In the decade of the 1980s the world economy became
globalized, which is apparent in the figures of FDI. Flows of FDI increased
by 30 per cent annually during the decade, about three times faster than the
growth of world exports and four times faster than world GNP. By 1990,
the global production of companies where ownership and financing lay
outside a host country was $5.5 trillion, while world exports of goods and
non-factor services were $4.0 trillion and gross world product was $22.6
trillion.[4] This relationship continued into the 1990s, when some 207,000
foreign affiliates sold $5.8 trillion in 1992, exceeding the value of global

Table 10.1[10]   *FDI inflows and outflows, 1982–1994 (billions of dollars and percentages)*

	1982–86	1987–91	1989	1990	1991	1992	1993	1994
	(annual average)							
Country	(Billions of dollars)							
Developed Countries								
Inflows	42	143	171	177	120	100	107	117
Outflows	53	184	215	228	184	174	181	192
Developed Countries								
Inflows	13	30	29	32	39	52	71	80
Outflows	1	7	11	10	7	10	12	12
Central and Eastern Europe								
Inflows	0.02	0.6	0.3	0.3	2	5	6	7
Outflows	0.008	0.02	0.02	0.04	0.01	0.04	0.04	0.06
All Countries								
Inflows	55	174	200	209	162	157	183	204
Outflows	55	192	226	239	191	184	193	204

Note: The levels of worldwide inward and outward FDI flows and stocks should balance; however, in practice, they do not. The causes of discrepancy include differences between countries in the definition and valuation of FDI; the treatment of unremitted branch profits in inward and outward FDI; treatment of unrealized capital gains and losses; the recording of transactions of 'offshore' enterprises; the recording of reinvested earnings in inward and outward FDI; the treatment of real estate and construction investment; and the share in equity threshold in inward and outward FDI.

exports of goods and services in that year which totalled $4.7 trillion.[5] It is clear that investment, besides trade, has become an essential route of access to foreign markets.

Foreign investment, and increasingly trade itself, is largely associated with transnational corporations (TNCs): indeed, 'only about one third of international transactions are not associated with TNC activity'.[6] The number of TNCs in the early 1990s has been estimated to be about 37,000 parent firms that control more than two million affiliates worldwide, not including numerous non-equity links.[7] Most TNCs originate in OECD countries: some two-thirds of parent firms, or 26,000, come from 14 major developed countries. The largest TNCs have enormous influence on output, employment, trade and so forth in the international economy: roughly one hundred of the top firms control about one-third of the world FDI stock. However, the largest firms no longer monopolize FDI. Whereas FDI was formerly characterized as being dominated by a few multinationals from countries such as the United States,

1982–86	1987–91	1992	1993	1994	1982–86	1987–91	1992	1993	1994
(annual average)					(annual average)				
(Share in total* percentage)					(growth rate** percentage)				
77	82	64	58	57	24	1	–16		9
98	96	95	94	94	25	9	–6	4	6
23	17	33	39	39	–0.4	13	32	36	13
2	4	5	6	6	11	28	47	21	3
0.03	0.4	3	3	3	3	278	91	22	23
0.01	0.01	0.02	0.02	0.03	53	7	336	–2	36
100	100	100	100	100	17	4	–3	17	11
100	100	100	100	100	25	9	–4	5	6

*   Based on preliminary estimates.
**   Calculated on the basis of FDI flows expressed in millions of dollars.

Source: UNCTAD, Division on Transnational Corporations and Investment estimates, based on International Monetary Fund, balance of payments tape, retrieved on 5 January 1995, and data from the Organization for Economic Cooperation and Development Secretariat.

Japan and Europe, now a greater number of small and medium-sized firms are participating as players in the field. It has been estimated that 'small and medium sized enterprises now account for one in ten of international investments made'.[8]

Foreign investment is traditionally associated with developed countries, both in terms of stocks and flows of FDI. Regarding global FDI stock through to 1993, developed countries have a dominant position and account for 97 per cent of total world outward FDI stock. On inward FDI stock, these countries accounted for 76 per cent of the total in 1993. Through to the 1990s, FDI flows also reflected the dominance of the developed countries. However, due in part to the collapse in Japanese investment, a sharp recession occurred in FDI activity in 1991 which was not reversed until 1994. Coming out of this recession, developing countries substantially increased their absorption of FDI inflows. Moreover, newly industrialized economies are increasingly participating as outward investors, both as investors within their own region and further afield.

The impact of the recession and change in developing country FDI patterns is reflected in Table 10.1. Total FDI inflows peaked in 1990, declined by about one-quarter, and then nearly reached the 1990 peak by 1994. The share of FDI inflows received by developing countries doubled between the years 1987 and 1992, rising from 17 to 33 per cent. The trend continued after the FDI recession of the early 1990s, and in 1993 developing countries accounted for 39 per cent of the FDI received, which is almost twice the average that the developing countries received throughout the 1980s. If this development is maintained over time, it will change the nature of worldwide TNC activity.

FDI inflows to developing countries are not evenly disbursed, and 80 per cent of the investment went to only ten countries. Major recipients come from Latin America and Asia, and especially China, which accounted for about 80 per cent of the increase in FDI inflows to all developing countries in 1993. By contrast, FDI flows to Central and Eastern European countries have grown little in the early 1990s, and the share of FDI flows of African countries to all developing countries declined to 5 per cent in 1993 compared to an average of 11 per cent during 1986–90.

The increases of FDI flows to developing countries are a result of increased growth rates, but they are also connected to policy changes in those countries. Many developing countries have recently liberalized their trade regimes (including TRIPs and services), which was demonstrated by the support developing countries gave to the Uruguay Round. Liberalization of the FDI regulatory framework also followed trade liberalization in some countries, and increased the opportunities for the formation of mergers and acquisitions, which are a less costly and hence preferred form of FDI. Additionally, some developing countries undertook privatization programmes, and by necessity opened participation in these programmes to foreign investors. Privatization is often viewed as producing a one-time influence on FDI flows, but in fact additional post-privatization investments often follow an initial investment.[9]

To sum up, it appears that to this point in the development of the world economy, economic factors have favoured growth in transborder flows of investment between mainly developed countries. This may now be changing, with the result that private FDI flows between developed and developing countries, and between developing countries themselves, may be much more characteristic of global investment patterns of the future. This fact puts great emphasis on the development of a multilateral rules-based investment regime.

THE CASE FOR MULTILATERAL INVESTMENT RULES

Several governments and individual leaders have recently called for negotiations towards a multilateral agreement on investment. One such call – from Sir Leon Brittan – noted that the basis for a more general agreement had been laid in the more than 600 bilateral investment treaties (BITs) that OECD countries have signed, mostly with non-OECD countries.[11] However, the multiplicity of treaties has produced a complex and uneven basis of regulation for international investors. What is needed is a more uniform set of rules with broader application, and particularly rules that will limit the frequent exclusions taken in investment treaties for 'domestic laws, regulations and policies'.

The call for a general investment agreement has been challenged from two sides. On the one hand, if investment flows are increasing in the world economy, is an agreement necessary or will competition for investment itself (that is, the market) produce all the liberalization in national investment regimes that is needed? The answer is that FDI flows to relatively few countries in part because of the unevenness of investment regimes, especially in developing countries. Furthermore, the investment that is available is often of a highly speculative and short-term nature. It appears that improving the investment regime could improve the quality of investment as well.

On the other hand, there is the argument that investment *rules* are no longer as critical in the investment decisions by firms as is the general *climate* for investment. This latter concern goes to the overall functioning of the market, and is a matter especially of competition policy and R&D, relations with financial institutions, the role of state ownership versus publicly traded companies, corporate concentrations, access to professional resources, and the like. The answer is that the importance of the investment climate does not negate the benefits of clear and workable rules. It is often only in negotiating general rules that national governments become aware of the climate issues that also impact on business decisions in their jurisdictions.

As FDI increases worldwide, the obstacles faced by investors and potential investors in foreign markets become more apparent and underscore the need for worldwide liberalization in the regulation of investment. Such issues constitute the basis for any future negotiation on investment. For purposes of this analysis, these issues can be divided into five broad categories: (1) market access; (2) discrimination; (3) transparency; (4) security of investment; and (5) effective market access.

In the first category pertaining to market access, the obstacles relate to lack of opportunity for investors to establish themselves (that is, the right to establish) within a particular country, due particularly to a myriad of restrictions that can be placed against foreign investment. For example, a host country may limit access to foreign investors in particular sectors of the economy, such as those in which the government may have a vested interest, for example, state monopolies or areas given protection from competition by foreign investors under the country's constitution. In developed countries, restrictions limiting the right to establish tend to be found in the natural resources and services sectors, but in developing countries the restrictions are more numerous, and can include outright prohibitions on foreign investment; performance requirements on foreign investors in exchange for admission to the market; ownership restrictions; local control over foreign affiliate decision-making; and various types of operational restrictions, such as the hiring of nationals.

The second category of obstacles faced by investors pertains to discriminatory treatment by foreign government both in relation to other foreign investors, and to domestic investors. In trade parlance these forms of discrimination demonstrate an absence of most-favoured-nation (MFN) treatment, and national treatment. For example, a host country may discriminate between the nationality of foreign investors and allow access to some and not to others based strictly on considerations of nationality. Or, discrimination may take the form of less-favourable rules and regulations governing the conduct of foreign investors within the domestic market and in competition with national investors. Today, many nations are moving towards regimes that provide some measure of MFN and national treatment for foreign investment, but the rules are rarely iron-clad, and as noted by Nymark and Verdun: 'In practice ... the elimination of discrimination is tempered by exceptions'.[12] For example, in the agreements on services in the WTO and NAFTA, the procedure employed to reduce discrimination was to enunciate broad liberalizing concepts in the main text of the agreement, followed by additional language qualifying or adhering to the principles in specific sectors. Similarly, one can expect the elimination or containment of exceptions to be the main subject of negotiations on international investment.

The third category of obstacles concerns transparency and predictability in the regulatory schemes governing foreign investment in the host country. Governments often are reluctant to commit themselves to clear public guidelines on foreign investment; consequently, foreign investors are faced with a notable lack of clarity in the rules or conditions that govern access to foreign markets. Such lack of clarity may serve to promote indecision or delays in investing because of uncertainty about one's rights and obligations, or about the procedures that are followed in applications for investment. Evidence on these matters is anecdotal, but nevertheless persuasive. For example, Leon Brittan notes that: '[w]ould-be European investors in China told me only recently that they knew to whom to apply for an investment licence, and had done so. But they had no means of knowing whether their application was being processed, what considerations were being applied by those examining it or when they might expect a reply'.[13] This example suggests how transparency of rules and procedures is a minimum condition that should be met in any multilateral investment agreement.

The fourth category pertains to the security of investment and covers a wide range of specific concerns about the treatment of investments by a host country. One concern is unfair and/or uncompensated expropriation, which is a longstanding concern in international law in the relations between investors and host states. Another concern is the freedom to repatriate profits, which is essential in promoting flexibility in the management of globalized production. Yet another concern is access to a fair and effective dispute settlement mechanism in lieu of being forced to take cases to domestic courts which may not provide the expertise or procedural guarantees needed to settle international claims. All three of these matters are traditional concerns of overseas investors, but they are no less important than the more modern problems confronting international investment, and indeed they often constitute the *sine qua non* of any successful regime.

The fifth category of obstacles is effective market access, which is an emerging concept and not yet clearly defined. Effective access concerns whether different jurisdictions provide something like 'equivalent competitive opportunity' to investors and/or traders operating from outside that jurisdiction.[14] Defining effective market access is difficult, because the conditions that assure or deny effective access are often sector specific. For example, Canadian financial service providers receive national treatment in the US market, but effective access is nevertheless limited by the US banking regulations. Similarly, effective access to the Japanese auto market is limited by the *keiretsu* pattern of vertical and horizontal integration of that industry.

In tackling the concept of effective access, it is useful to distinguish between government and private barriers.[15] Especially in high-tech sectors, government can affect access to markets through policies on standards, subsidies or government procurement. Already there are codes of conduct in these areas dating as far back as the GATT Tokyo Round of 1979, but modern practices are sufficiently subtle so as not to be inconsistent with international codes, yet still effective in competitive high-tech industries so as to deter access to foreign producers. These barriers are further compounded by private barriers that are nominally beyond the reach of government regulation. The most important of these barriers are the Japanese *keiretsu*, which have been the subject of extended bilateral debate between Japan and the United States in the Structural Impediments Initiative (SII) negotiations. It is likely that similar negotiations over issues of effective access will continue on a bilateral and plurilateral basis between the Triad (United States, European Union and Japan) or OECD countries into the future. These issues represent the cutting edge in the debate over the liberalization of international investment policy and practices, and they raise problems that are confronted especially in the relations between advanced industrialized countries.

Turning to the more general problems of international investment, there was a lively debate over whether negotiations on a multilateral investment agreement should be conducted in the WTO, or in a less universal and perhaps more facilitating setting like the OECD. This matter was the subject of discussion at the private level, with US business groups favouring action in the OECD while Japanese groups wanted the issue to be handled in the WTO.[16] The debate was joined by EU Commissioner Leon Brittan, who, after earlier calling for action in the WTO, agreed to support talks in the OECD contingent on action also being taken in the WTO [17]

As earlier noted, work on a multilateral investment agreement was launched at the May ministerial meeting of the OECD. The OECD provides two advantages in that analytical work can be supported by the research capacities of the OECD, and that initial discussions will be held among developed countries that have the most in-depth experience with international investment. However, if the goal is to establish a universal investment regime, which is desirable given the increasing diversification of FDI flows today, then it will be necessary to conduct negotiations in the WTO where especially developing countries would be included. It could be a serious error, as noted by Michael Hart, to negotiate new investment rules among OECD countries and then invite developing countries to join in.[18] Furthermore, the WTO offers a desirable negotiating forum because of the contractual nature of its regime, which would offer greater promise that the rules negotiated would be carried out in practice. A negotiation of investment issues in the WTO would build upon a solid rules-based system of international economic policy established in the Uruguay Round negotiation, that itself would be more complete and effective with the addition of a multilateral investment agreement.

ACCOMPLISHMENTS OF THE URUGUAY ROUND

There are three main accomplishments of the Uruguay Round negotiations that have implications for a multilateral investment agreement and that merit discussion in this chapter: (1) the establishment of the WTO; (2) a new and improved state-to-state dispute settlement mechanism; and (3) the negotiation of the TRIMs, services and TRIPS agreements. The first two points will be addressed in this section, while the third point merits discussion in a separate section following this one.

The World Trade Organization

The establishment of the World Trade Organization on 1 January 1995, brings to a close a chapter of GATT history which began more than 50 years ago with the idea of creating an international trade organization in conjunction with the implementation of the GATT.[19] That idea failed to materialize until now, and the GATT was forced to take on an institutional role that it was ill-designed to perform. By the time the Uruguay Round was launched in 1986, it was determined that more than 200 legal instruments comprised the GATT system.[20] Moreover, the obligations set out in these instruments did not apply to all contracting parties as the acceptance of the agreements or codes negotiated during the Tokyo Round was optional, thereby creating a hotchpotch of rights and obligations flowing between parties.

Primarily as a result of the fragmentation of the system, it was decided in the Uruguay Round that the results of the negotiation would have to be accepted as a single undertaking by signatories or else not at all. Furthermore, it was determined that a strong institutional base in the form of an international trading organization was required in order to implement the results of the negotiations and lead the international trading system confidently and effectively into the future.

To this end, the WTO was born. The Agreement by which it was established, namely the WTO Agreement, forms the centrepiece of all the agreements negotiated during the Round. Four Annexes to the WTO Agreement form an integral part of it, and contain the individual agreements reached in specific sectors such as services, textiles, intellectual property, investment, dispute settlement and subsidies and countervailing measures, to name but a few. Except for the agreements in procurement, dairy, aircraft and bovine meat, all the results of the Round are binding on all signatories. This includes the dispute settlement procedures set out in Annex 2.

The functions of the WTO are described as follows: (1) to facilitate the implementation and administration of the WTO Agreement; (2) to serve as a forum for negotiations; (3) to administer the Dispute Settlement Understanding (DSU); (4) to administer the Trade Policy Review Mechanism (TPRM);[21] and (5) to cooperate with the IMF and the IBRD 'with a view to achieving greater coherence in global economic policy-making' (Article III).

In view of the fifth identified function, an international trade organization finally takes its proper place alongside the IMF and the IBRD in order to participate in global economic policy-making. Clearly, the WTO is well placed to make a considerable contribution in this area, given its broad reach into diverse sectors of the economy.

It should be noted that another important feature of the WTO Agreement are the rules governing decision-making. The WTO Agreement sets out explicit rules governing the adoption of decisions, including those involving the interpretation of provisions or the amendment of an agreement, and waiver of a Member's obligation. Generally, decisions are adopted by consensus as was previously the practice under the GATT. However, whereas formerly consensus was reached if all Members explicitly agreed to the adoption of a decision, now it is defined as having been reached where no Member explicitly objects to its adoption. If no consensus is reached, a vote must take place. The level of support required for a vote to pass will vary depending upon the nature of the decision to be made; for example, is it intended to amend a substantive feature of the WTO Agreement, or else to establish a consistent interpretation of a provision?

The rules are a significant improvement over past practice. In particular, they will ensure that a disputing party will no longer be able to block the adoption of a panel report. The importance of this point will be discussed further below. Another important result is that Members will no longer be required to wait for the initiation of a Round of negotiation in order to amend an agreement. This will significantly improve the ability of the WTO to respond to current issues in a timely manner. Furthermore, in the context of this chapter, it means that any amendments to, say, the TRIMs Agreement could be dealt with relatively quickly without necessarily waiting for the completion of negotiations in other areas.

Very briefly, the structure of the WTO is as follows: at the top of the hierarchy is the Ministerial Conference which is composed of representatives of all Members. The Conference is responsible for carrying out all the functions of the organization, and in its absence, is replaced by the General Council, similarly composed of representatives of all Members. Since the Ministerial Conference is generally composed of Members' senior trade ministers, and is only required to meet once every two years, the replacement of the Conference by the General Council ensures the continued functioning of the Organization all year round. The General Council is also responsible for discharging the responsibilities of the Dispute Settlement Body[22] and the Trade Policy Review Body.[23] In addition, a variety of councils and committees are responsible for overseeing the functioning of the various agreements as well as reporting to the General Council on specific topics such as trade and development and restrictions on trade. Finally, the day-to-day operation of the Organization is conducted by the WTO Secretariat, headed by a Director-General.

Dispute Settlement

The new rules on dispute settlement in the WTO go a long way in addressing the frustrations previously experienced by GATT contracting parties which had led parties in the past to take unilateral action against other parties, instead of seeking recourse under the GATT.[24] A discussion of the WTO's Dispute Settlement Understanding is important to this chapter because it applies to all agreements, including those in respect of TRIMs, services and TRIPS. One of the most important contributions the WTO could make to a global investment agreement is its dispute settlement mechanism.

The DSU maintains the essential nature of the dispute settlement mechanism previously developed under the GATT in that it encourages parties to reach a mutually satisfactory solution to a dispute between them before resorting to formal dispute settlement or arbitration. Nevertheless, if consultations fail, the DSU provides recourse to a dispute settlement panel generally in order to examine whether a measure maintained by another Member is inconsistent with that Member's obligations under an agreement. However, even where a panel has been established, the parties to the dispute may resort at any time to good offices, conciliation or mediation in an attempt to resolve the matter.

Unlike the GATT provisions, however, the establishment of a panel is automatic unless the Dispute Settlement Body (DSB)[25] decides by consensus against it. Where such a request is made, a panel of three persons is formed. The panel is required to conduct its examination either based on standard terms of reference set out in the DSU, or in accordance with discrete terms crafted by the chairman of the panel in consultation with the parties. Once the panel is established, it is expected to issue a report on the matter within six months, or within three where the matter is considered to be urgent, such as where perishable goods are involved. In no case, however, is the process to go beyond nine months.

The panel process is adjudicatory in nature. Parties are provided with an opportunity to make submissions to the panel in both written and oral form, and to comment on the other party's submissions. Each stage in the process is governed by very strict timeframes in order to ensure that the panel completes its examination and issues its report within the specified period of time.

Once the panel has considered all the submissions, including oral argument, it is required to issue the descriptive sections of its report to the parties for comment, after which it issues an interim report to the parties, including its findings and conclusions. Once finalized, the report is distributed to Members, who may comment on it before it is considered for adoption by the DSB. Even though the DSB is given time to consider the report, adoption of the report is automatic unless the DSB decides by consensus to reject it, or a party notifies the DSB of its intention to appeal the report to the Appellate Body.

The creation of a standing Appellate Body is one of the innovations of the DSU and provides a second review of the matter on questions of law or legal interpretation. Similar to the panel process, the appeal process is expected to be concluded expeditiously. The timeframe for completion of the appeal procedure is not to exceed 60 days or at the outside limit, 90 days. Similar to the panel report, the Appellate Body's report is released to Members, but is expected to be adopted unconditionally by the DSB within a month of its release unless the DSB unanimously rejects it.

In the event that a panel or the Appellate Body concludes that the measure in issue is inconsistent with a party's obligations under an agreement, it is expected to recommend that the party bring the measure into conformity, and possibly suggest ways in which this could be done. If a non-conforming party does not comply with the recommendations, it must either provide compensation or else face retaliatory action by the prevailing party.

First in a succession of provisions governing enforcement is the obligation on the non-conforming party to notify the DSB within a month of the adoption of the report of the party's intentions with regard to the recommendations. Where it fails to implement the recommendations within a reasonable period of time, the prevailing party may seek mutually satisfactory compensation from the other party, failing which, it may, with the authorization of the DSB, suspend the application of concessions or obligations to the other party. The scope of concessions that may be suspended is hierarchical. First, an effort must be made to suspend concessions within the same sector in which the non-conforming measure exists. However, if suspension in that sector is not practical or effective, concessions or obligations in other sectors, under the same agreement, may be suspended. Where neither of these options is practical or effective, the DSU permits cross-retaliation into other agreements. In other words, the prevailing party may suspend concessions or obligations under a different WTO agreement than the one in which the offending measure exists, thereby giving a party a broad scope of potential remedies. In any event, the level of suspension may only be equal to the level of nullification or impairment induced by the non-conforming measure and not greater. Where the level of suspension is disputed, the matter may be referred to arbitration .

There were many improvements made to the dispute settlement provisions of the GATT under the DSU. In general, it can be said that it provides much more effective and expeditious dispute settlement than previously. The procedures are detailed and transparent. The time limits by which certain steps must be completed are moreover explicit, thereby ensuring that disputes will be resolved within a relatively short period of time from the moment the panel is established to the adoption of the panel or Appellate Body's report, right through to the suspension of concessions or obligations. A standing Appellate Body will, furthermore, ensure greater consistency in legal interpretations of the provisions of the agreements, and provide an additional element of security by providing a second opportunity for review, particularly in view of the more or less automatic adoption of panel reports.

As already noted, both the establishment of a panel and the adoption of the panel report are more or less automatic under DSU provisions. These are significant improvements given that formerly, non-conforming parties would often delay the establishment of a panel by drawing out consultations at the outset of proceedings, or else block the adoption of a panel report. As already mentioned, previously GATT parties had to agree unanimously to the adoption of a report in contrast to the current requirement that Members must unanimously agree not to adopt it in order for it to be rejected.[26]

The enforcement provisions are similarly more effective than before. The DSU sets out a rigorous surveillance mechanism to review the implementation of adopted reports and, moreover, expeditious arbitration where a dispute arises about what constitutes 'a reasonable period of time' for implementing recommendations in a particular case, or about the appropriate level of suspension of concessions or obligations. Furthermore, a non-conforming party is expected to bring the offending measure into conformity with its obligations or else face retaliatory action. As a result, a prevailing party will always obtain some form of relief if the panel finds in its favour if the party chooses to exercise its rights under the DSU. Of particular benefit to the investment sector is the notion of cross-retaliation. This provision expands the scope of remedies available for investment matters into the trade area, thereby underscoring the close relationship between trade and investment.

A final point that needs to be made is that the DSU forecloses the opportunity for Members to take unilateral action instead of resorting to the dispute settlement procedures established pursuant to the DSU. Article 23, entitled 'Strengthening of the Multilateral System' imposes on Members the obligation to seek recourse to the DSU rules and procedures for resolving disputes arising out of the nullification or impairment of benefits, or an impediment to a Member achieving an objective under the WTO agreements. This provision codifies the Members' commitment to the proper functioning of the DSU, which is backed up by what would appear to be 'a genuine system of enforceable rules and remedies',[27] that should serve to instil confidence in the WTO system.

INVESTMENT PROVISIONS IN THE WTO

As already mentioned, investment was one of the three new issues addressed during the Uruguay Round, along with services and TRIPs, and the results of the investment negotiations *per se* are set out in the TRIMs Agreement. Having said this, it is to be noted that both the agreements reached in services and TRIPs also contain provisions having a direct impact on investment and, therefore, merit some discussion in this chapter in order to obtain a more rounded appreciation of the scope of investment coverage in the WTO agreements.[28]

The Agreement on Trade-related Investment Measures

The scope of the TRIMs Agreement is limited to trade in goods and does not extend to services. Generally, the TRIMs Agreement prohibits Members from applying any trade-related investment measure that is inconsistent with the principles of national treatment (Article III, GATT 1994) and the general elimination of quantitative restrictions (Article XI, GATT 1994). For greater transparency, the Agreement sets out an illustrative, but not exhaustive, list of inconsistent TRIMs. Specific TRIMs targeted by the list include those imposing requirements in respect of domestic sourcing, import–export trade balancing, import substitution, access to foreign exchange and export restrictions.

The TRIMs Agreement does provide some flexibility with respect to compliance, by providing Members with a transition period for the ultimate elimination of trade-distorting TRIMs. Generally, non-conforming measures were to have been eliminated by 1 January 1996, but developing and least-developed countries are given an additional four and six years, respectively, within which they are obliged to comply. A Member's individual circumstances may, however, be taken into account in extending the time limit.

During the transition period, a Member may not modify the measure so as to increase its degree of inconsistency, but it may extend it to a new investment under limited circumstances in order to avoid disrupting competition between that investment and other enterprises, specifically where the new investment is producing like products to those of the already affected enterprises.

Another obligation imposed on Members includes becoming more transparent in the administration of its TRIMs. Specifically, the Agreement obliges Members to notify the WTO Secretariat as to the publications in which TRIMs are set out. Furthermore, it requires Members to afford 'sympathetic consideration to requests for information, and afford adequate opportunity for consultation', on matters raised by another Member arising from the Agreement (Article 6, para. 1).

In sum, the TRIMs Agreement prohibits the application of new TRIMs which are inconsistent with the principles of national treatment and the general elimination of quantitative restrictions, and provides for the general elimination of already-existing measures within specific timeframes. Furthermore, it provides for greater transparency and notification of already-existing measures. The limitations of the Agreement are primarily its scope, both in that it applies solely to measures affecting trade in goods and in that the Illustrative List of non-conforming TRIMs is relatively narrow as compared to the broad list of performance requirements banned under the NAFTA investment chapter. It should be noted, however, that the Agreement provides for the mandatory review of its operation within five years of its entry into force which review could result in the expansion of the scope of the non-conforming TRIMs identified in the Illustrative List. Such a review would also consider whether the Agreement should be complemented with provisions on investment and competition policy.

The General Agreement on Services (GATS)

As its name implies, the GATS is limited to measures affecting trade in services and does not extend to trade in goods. The GATS applies specifically to all services other than those supplied in the exercise of governmental authority.[29] Given the comprehensiveness and complexity of the GATS, this chapter will merely highlight some of the main aspects of the Agreement as they apply to investment matters .

Investment in the services field is given coverage under the GATS by virtue of the definition of trade in services, which includes the supply of a service 'by a service supplier of one Member, through commercial presence in the territory of any other Member' (Article 1, para. 2(c)). Commercial presence is defined as 'any type of business or professional establishment, including through (i) the constitution, acquisition or maintenance of a juridical person, or (ii) the creation or maintenance of a branch or a representative office, within the territory of a Member for the purpose of supplying a service' (Article XXVIII). A related, and significant, additional definition of trade in services includes the supply of a service 'by a service supplier of one Member, through presence of natural persons of a Member in the territory of any other Member' (Article 1 para. 2(d)). This definition recognizes the essential link between suppliers and commercial presence.

The GATS consists of three elements, namely: a framework of general obligations and disciplines; a series of national schedules that set out each Member's sector-specific commitments primarily in regard to market access and national treatment; and finally, a series of annexes which set out discrete conditions pertaining to individual sectors.

The basic investment-liberalizing provisions of the GATS pertain to Members' obligations in respect of extending (1) MFN treatment; (2) market access; and (3) national treatment to services and suppliers of services. A Member's obligation to apply these principles to all sectors is, however, not absolute.

Although Members are generally obligated to extend MFN treatment to all services and suppliers, a Member may have exempted certain inconsistent measures in a particular sector or subsector from this obligation prior to the entry into force of the Agreement and on such terms as it dictated. In principle, such exemptions should not exceed ten years and are reviewable within five years in order to assess whether the underlying basis for the exemption continues to exist. An exemption should terminate on the date provided for in the stated exemption.

Moreover, the extent to which a Member is obliged to provide market access and national treatment is self-determined, although subject to negotiation. Unlike in the TRIMs and TRIPS Agreements, there is no general obligation on Members to either prohibit the application of new measures inconsistent with these principles, or to eliminate already-established measures within a specific period of time. Each Member is required to set out in its national schedule the sectors in which it commits itself to extending these principles and on what terms and conditions. Accordingly, a Member may exempt itself from applying these principles in a specific sector by not committing itself through its national schedules to do so. Of course, the consequence of such an approach is to encourage one's trading partners to do the same.

The degree to which an investor will ultimately benefit from MFN treatment is largely tied to the scope of commitments made by a host country in respect of market access and national treatment.[30] It is noteworthy that a significant number of developed countries granted unrestricted access and national treatment in respect of all types of commercial presence, with some developing countries provided comparable bindings. Moreover, 'virtually all' developed countries and many developing countries also committed themselves to open access to intracorporate transferees,[31] thereby significantly improving the global investment climate.

It should be noted, however, that the long-term benefits of such commitments are lessened to some degree by the fact that any commitment may be modified or withdrawn after three years from the date the commitment entered into force (or one year as a form of safeguard measure in emergency situations). The three-year period does, however, provide at least some stability during the initial years of the Agreement. Where a Member intends to modify or withdraw a commitment, it is required to give notice of its intentions and be prepared to provide compensation on an MFN basis for any resulting benefits lost to other Members .

The GATS also imposes certain transparency requirements on Members. These requirements include publishing notice of all measures of general application affecting the operation of the Agreement, as well as giving notice of domestic laws and regulations affecting trade covered by its commitments as set out in its national schedule. With respect to the level of transparency resulting from the scheduling of commitments, Pierre Sauvé notes that while it provides for a fair degree of transparency in the sectors and subsectors subject to the commitments, such an approach results in no information being provided in respect of sectors not subject to any commitments.[32]

Other noteworthy provisions of the GATS include those: (1) allowing Members to extend preferential treatment to certain foreign suppliers engaged in 'substantive business operations' in the territory of a party to an economic integration agreement, such as the NAFTA; (2) obliging Members to provide a supplier with a domestic review mechanism and remedy, if appropriate, for administrative decisions affecting trade in services; (3) requiring Members to ensure that monopolies and exclusive suppliers do not abuse their position in competing in the supply of a service outside the scope of their monopoly rights, in the context of committed sectors and subsectors; and finally (4) obliging Members to refrain from applying restrictions on international transfers and payments except in the case of balance-of-payments or external financial difficulties.

Similar to the TRIMs Agreement, the GATS provides for future negotiations to be held within five years of the Agreement's entry into force, in the case of GATS, 'with a view to achieving a progressively higher level of liberalization' (Article XIX).

The Agreement on Trade-related Intellectual Property Rights

It is important in considering the issue of investment in the WTO that in developing rules aimed at the protection of trade-related intellectual property rights, the Agreement on TRIPs goes a long way towards fostering a sense of security among potential investors that their foreign investments will have a minimum standard of protection in a host country once the provisions of the Agreement have been phased in.[33]

Certain aspects of the Agreement on TRIPs which are noteworthy for investment are the applicability of the principles of MFN and national treatment to this area, the obligation on Members to provide effective and appropriate means for the enforcement of rights accrued by both national and foreign rights holders under the Agreement, as well as the overriding application of the WTO Dispute Settlement Understanding.

THE NAFTA INVESTMENT CHAPTER

While the WTO may be the preferred forum in which to develop global investment rules, one might equally argue that the NAFTA is to be preferred as a model for developing the substance of those rules. Chapter 11 of NAFTA

provides a complete code governing the regulation of both inward and outward investment between Canada, the United States and Mexico, which
apply to investments in both goods and services. In so doing, it addresses
many of the obstacles and concerns faced by investors and potential investors
in a foreign market. These obstacles were discussed in the second section of
this chapter in the following categories (1) market access; (2) discrimination;
(3) transparency; (4) security of investment; and (5) effective market access.

NAFTA's investment chapter is divided into two separate sections, the first
section (A) sets out rules pertaining to the first deals addresses investment
matters, while the second section (B) provides rules for dispute settlement.
Section A goes far beyond the minimalist approach of the WTO TRIMs
Agreement which only covered trade-distorting investment measures, specifically in respect of trade in goods. NAFTA applies to investment in both goods
and services. At the outset, the chapter established a broad definition of
investment by including not only FDI (that is, an investment made by and
under the control of a foreign head office), but also equity and debt securities,
loans and interest, real estate and capital commitments: in other words virtually all types of investments that are made across national boundaries. Such a
broad definition means that more investment activities are protected by the
NAFTA rules than many other investment agreements. Coverage is also extended to investors incorporated in a NAFTA country regardless of the investor's country of origin.

Market Access

It will be recalled that market access concerns the right to establish, which
can be restricted in many ways. NAFTA limits the parties' capacities to apply
such restrictions in two areas. First, NAFTA substantially limits the use of
performance requirements, and goes much further than the WTO TRIMs
Agreement.

NAFTA provides that specific performance requirements are explicitly
prohibited, including (1) export performance, (2) local content, (3) domestic
sourcing, (4) trade balancing, (5) technology transfer and (6) restrictions on
who the investor may supply its goods and services to. Other prohibited
performance requirements include (1) local content, (2) domestic sourcing,
(3) trade balancing, and (4) domestic sales and export balancing, which are
imposed on investors in exchange for a subsidy or other benefit. However, a
party may condition the receipt of a subsidy or other benefit on the performance of requirements in respect of (1) locating production, (2) providing a
service, (3) training or employing workers, (4) constructing or expanding
production facilities or (5) carrying out research and development in the
party's territory.

Second, NAFTA prohibited measures that require senior management positions to be filled by individuals of a certain nationality, or that require a majority of the board of directors to be of a certain nationality or be resident in that party's territory .

A final point is that in Annex III (Activities Reserved to the State), Mexico excluded in principle investment in certain economic sectors, such as petroleum. The fact that these exclusions were itemized in Mexico's case, and were not taken at all by Canada or the United States, indicates that the principle of market access is promoted in other areas of economic activity.

Discrimination

The NAFTA imposes on the parties the obligation to provide both MFN (Article 1103) and national treatment (Article 1102) to investors of the other parties and their investments, specifically in respect of the (1) establishment, (2) acquisition, (3) management, (4) conduct, (5) operation, (6) sales and (7) other disposition of investments, subject to specific exceptions or reservations negotiated by each party. Prohibited measures include requiring that a minimum level of equity be held by nations of the host country other than nominal qualifying shares, and that an investor sell or otherwise dispose of an investment on the basis of the investor's nationality. NAFTA also provides for national treatment in other areas of the overall agreement, notably in services and financial services. With regard to national treatment, Gestrin and Rugman have observed: '[t]he cornerstone of the NAFTA investment provisions are, the national treatment requirements which are written into the investment, services and financial services Chapters (Articles 1102, 1202, 1405)'.[34]

Transparency

It should be noted that Chapter 11 does provide for substantial exceptions and reservations to the obligations set out above. While the exceptions and reservations may be criticized for their scope as they diminish the value of the code in addressing the concerns of investors or potential investors in all sectors of the economy, a more positive focus for the purpose of this discussion is the level of transparency in the listing of parties' exceptions and reservations. Each party's derogations from the investment rules are set out in Schedules contained in a series of Annexes to the NAFTA. Four of the seven Annexes contain both exceptions and reservations to the investment rules of Chapter 11. Annex I lists reservations for existing measures and liberalization commitments; Annex II sets out reservations for specific sectors, subsectors or activities for future measures; Annex III specifies activities reserved by Mexico for the state; while Annex IV lists exceptions from the obligation to provide MFN treatment.

The derogations are set out in a very detailed form. The type of information that is generally set out in the Schedules gives investors considerable knowledge about the non-conforming measures so that they may govern their investment activities accordingly. For example, for each non-conforming measure the following information is generally set out: the sectors, subsectors and industry classification to which an exception or reservation applies; the type of reservation (that is, from MFN or national treatment, or specific performance requirements); the level of government making the reservation; the specific measure in issue and a description of it; and finally, any commitments by that party to phasing out the measure in the future.[35]

While reservations and exceptions at the federal level were set out in the Agreement by the time it came into force on 1 January 1994, provincial and state governments were given until 1 January 1995 to indicate the non-conforming measures which they intend to maintain. An obligation is imposed on both levels of government not to make their non-conforming measures more restrictive, except for measures which specifically pertain to certain sectors explicitly excluded from the application of this provision.

Security of Investment

Specific obstacles addressed by the NAFTA include the inability of investors to repatriate profits, expropriation without compensation or recourse, and ineffective dispute settlement. With respect to the *repatriation of profits*, Chapter 11 circumscribes a party's authority to restrict the free movement of currency derived from, or relating to, an investment, or to oblige or penalize an investor that fails to transfer amounts derived from investments in the territory of another party. The rules further provide that transfers are to be permitted in a freely usable currency at the market rate of exchange. These provisions, however, do not restrict a party from preventing a transfer through the equitable and non-discriminatory application of laws governing bankruptcy, securities trading and criminal matters.

The NAFTA also provides investors with protection from unfair and uncompensated *expropriation*. Under the Agreement, a party may not expropriate, or take some other measure tantamount to an expropriation of, an investment except for a public purpose. Furthermore, the expropriation must be done on a non-discriminatory basis, in accordance with due process and most importantly, on payment of compensation. Compensation is required to be equivalent to fair market value immediately before the expropriation took place and must not reflect any changes in the value resulting from general knowledge of the party's intention to expropriate. Furthermore, compensation must be paid without delay and be fully realizable, generally including interest from the date of expropriation until the date of payment.

As already indicated above, Section B of Chapter 11 provides for *dispute settlement* for investment matters. Unlike the general dispute settlement provisions contained in Chapter 20 of NAFTA, or the dispute settlement mechanism developed in the WTO, the mechanism in Chapter 11 provides for investor–state arbitration. Such a mechanism is very progressive in view of the needs of investors vis-à-vis their host governments. State-to-state does not always fulfil the needs of investors. The party of an investor may have different priorities than an investor and be influenced by the prospect that making a claim against another party may have a negative impact on diplomatic relations with that party. Moreover, there is little incentive for a party to find a fast and speedy resolution to a dispute where it involves but a single investor or investment.[36]

The dispute settlement provisions provide that an investor may submit to arbitration, a claim that a party has breached one of its obligations under Section A and the investor, or an investment on whose behalf the investor is making the claim, has incurred loss or damage as a result of the breach. Such a claim must be submitted within three years of when the investor first knew or should have known of the alleged breach and the loss or damage arising out of it.

Before proceeding to formal arbitration, disputing parties are encouraged to attempt to settle the claim through consultation or negotiation. Where, however, formal arbitration is pursued, an investor is given a choice of rules under which it may bring its claim, the choice of which will vary depending on whether the party of the investor and the disputing party are signatories to a particular international instrument. Depending upon the circumstances, the arbitration may be conducted under the rules contained in the International Centre for the Settlement of Investment Disputes (ICSID) Convention, the Additional Facility Rules of ICSID or the United Nations International Commission on Trade Law (UNCITRAL) Arbitration Rules, subject to the extent to which they are modified by the specific provisions contained in Section B of Chapter 11.

Effective Market Access

The NAFTA was only partially successful in this area. On the one hand, NAFTA did pursue an 'integrative approach' to rule-making on investment,[37] which attempts to reflect in international rules the relationships that exist in corporate decision-making, between trade, investment, services, intellectual property and competition policy. Furthermore, NAFTA incorporated a far-reaching TRIPs code, which was largely similar to the WTO agreement in that area. However, NAFTA made little progress with rule-making on competition policy (Chapter 15) and it excluded issues of competition policy from the generally-effective NAFTA dispute settlement mechanism. Nor did NAFTA tackle informal or non-governmental barriers to investment. These new issues will have to await a further stage in the development of international rules on investment.

CONCLUSION

It is probable that rules for international investment will be negotiated in the world community in the coming years. This chapter has argued that such negotiations should be conducted in concert with the WTO, especially because the universal aspects of that organization would involve the developing countries in any new investment regime. Further, the chapter has suggested the NAFTA chapter on investment as a useful model to structure a multilateral investment agreement. The NAFTA addresses many of the areas identified as obstacles to foreign investment, and it was negotiated between two developed countries (one a long-standing capital importer) and a (then) developing country. From this perspective, NAFTA should be a useful precursor for negotiations between developed and developing countries in the WTO.

The NAFTA experience suggests that the biggest difficulty with a multilateral investment agreement is likely to be the derogations from general rules that individual countries will insist upon, but it provides a mechanism for making exceptions that provides transparency and, therefore, greater likelihood that such exceptions will be removed with further negotiation. More importantly, the NAFTA broadens the concept of investment and thereby makes it more consistent with the environment in which firms are operating in the international economy.

NOTES

1. 'OECD Group Begins Negotiations on Multilateral Investment Pact', *International Trade Reporter* (Washington, DC: Bureau of National Affairs), 4 October 1995, 1655.
2. 'Quad Partners Agree to Consider Investment Rules in WTO Earlier', *International Trade Reporter* (Washington: Bureau of National Affairs), 25 October 1995, 1758.
3. 'Ruggiero Report Assesses Trade Body's First Year', *International Trade Reporter*, (Washington, DC: Bureau of National Affairs), December 13, 1995, 2052.
4. See DeAnne Julius, 'International Direct Investment: Strengthening the Policy Regime', in Peter B. Kenen, *Managing the World Economy Fifty Years After Bretton Woods* (Washington, DC: Institute for International Economics, 1994), pp. 278–9.
5. UNCTAD Secretariat, 'Recent Developments in International Investment and Transnational Corporations: Trends in Foreign Direct Investment' (Geneva: UNCTAD Secretariat, 21 February 1995), p. 5 (hereinafter referred to as the UNCTAD Report). All the statistics cited in this section are from the UNCTAD Report unless otherwise indicated.
6. Ibid., p. 19.

7. 'World Investment Report: Transnational Corporations, Employment and the Workplace' (New York: United Nations, 1994) p. xxi.
8. 'Smoothing the Path for Investment Worldwide', Address by the Rt. Hon. Sir Leon Brittan, QC, to the European–American Chamber of Commerce, Washington, DC, 31 January 1995, p. 4.
9. UNCTAD Report, *supra*, note 5 p. 11.
10. Reproduced from the UNCTAD Report, *supra*, note 5, p. 8.
11. Brittan, *supra*, note 8, p. 10.
12. Alan Nymark and Emmy Verdun, 'Canadian Investment and NAFTA' in Alan M. Rugman (ed.), *Foreign Investment and NAFTA* (Columbia, South Carolina: University of South Carolina Press, 1994), p. 144.
13. Brittan, *supra*, note 8, p. 8.
14. Nymark and Verdun, *supra*, note 12, p. 146.
15. See Sylvia Ostry, 'New Dimensions of Market Access: Challenges for the Trading System', Presented at the OECD Round Table on New Dimensions of Market Access in a Globalizing World Economy, Paris, 1 July 1994.
16. 'Japan Business Groups Disagree on Forum for Investment Rules', *Inside U.S. Trade*, 17 March 1995.
17. 'Brittan Backs OECD Investment Talks, But Also Wants WTO Action'. *Inside U.S. Trade*, 31 March 1995.
18. Michael Hart, 'What's Next: Negotiating Rules for a Global Economy', in *New Dimensions of Market Access in a Globalising World Economy* (Paris: OECD, 1995), p. 9.
19. For an in-depth discussion of the history of the GATT leading towards the establishment of the WTO, see Gardner Patterson and Eliza Patterson, 'The Road from GATT to WTO', *Minnesota Journal of Global Trade*, **3** (1), Spring 1994, pp. 35–59.
20. Debra P. Steger, 'The Significance of the World Trade Organization for the Future of the Trading System', (Washington, DC: The American Society of International Law Annual Meeting, 6 April 1994), p. 3.
21. This mechanism provides for the periodic review of each Member's trade policies and practices, including in respect of TRIMs, services and TRIPS. The purpose of the TPRM is to provide greater transparency and disclosure of Members' policies and practices, as well as encourage Members to adhere to their commitments under the WTO Agreements. Whereas the TPRM was operated on a provisional basis under the GATT (since 1989), it became a permanent feature of the WTO as a result of the Uruguay Round negotiations. For an historical and analytical discussion of the TPRM, see Victoria Curzon Price, 'New Institutional Developments in GATT', *Minnesota Journal of Global Trade*, **1** (1), Fall 1992, 96–105.
22. See note 25, *infra*.
23. The Trade Policy Review Body monitors WTO Members' trade policies and practices pursuant to the TPRM.
24. For a more in-depth discussion of the frustrations experienced by contracting parties in respect of the GATT dispute settlement mechanism and the evolution of the WTO Dispute Settlement Understanding, see Judith H. Bello and Alan P. Holmer, 'U.S. Trade Law and Policy Series no. 24: Dispute Resolution in the New World Trade Organization: Concerns and Net Benefits', *The International Lawyer*, **28** (4), Winter 1994, 1095–104; Andreas F. Lowenfeld, 'Remedies Along with Rights: Institutional Reform in the New GATT', *American Journal of International Law*, **88** (3), July 1994, 477–88; and Michael K. Young, 'Dispute Resolution in the Uruguay Round: Lawyers Triumph Over Diplomats', *The International Lawyer*, **29** (2), Summer 1995, 389–409.
25. The DSB is established by the General Council and is composed of representatives of all WTO Members. Its function is to administer all dispute settlement procedures.
26. Lowenfeld, *supra*, footnote 24, p. 479.
27. Ibid., p. 481.
28. For a more in-depth discussion of the investment provisions in the WTO Agreements, see Pierre Sauvé, 'A First Look at Investment in the Final Act of the Uruguay Round', *Journal of World Trade*, **28** (5), 1994, 5.

29. For a comprehensive discussion of the GATS, see Mary E. Footer, 'The International Regulation of Trade in Services Following Completion of the Uruguay Round', *The International Lawyer*, **29** (2), Summer 1995, 453–81.
30. Ibid., p. 465.
31. Canadian Statement on Implementation: Agreement Establishing the World Trade Organization, *Canada Gazette*, Part I, 31 December 1994, 4921.
32. Sauvé *supra*, footnote 28, p. 11.
33. For an in-depth discussion of the Agreement on TRIPS, see J.H. Reichman, 'Universal Minimum Standards of Intellectual Property Protection under the TRIPS Component of the WTO Agreement', *The International Lawyer*, **29** (2), Summer 1995, 345–87.
34. Michael Gestrin and Alan M. Rugman, 'The NAFTA Investment Provisions: Prototypes for Multilateral Investment Rules?' (Paris: OECD, 14 February 1995), p. 6.
35. Gestrin and Rugman have referred to NAFTA derogations as a 'negative list', that is, where signatories are obliged to identify each existing measure that is inconsistent with the basic liberalizing provisions (for example, Articles 1102, 1103) of the agreement. This can be contrasted to the blanket 'grandfathering' mechanism used in the Canada–US Free Trade Agreement. Gestrin and Rugman, *supra*, note 34 pp. 8–9.
36. Julius, *supra*, note 4, p. 275.
37. Gestrin and Rugman, *supra*, footnote 34, p. 3.

11. Political entrepreneurship for collective management

Gavin Boyd

In the Triad pattern of economic relations between the industrialized democracies questions of collective management arise because of market changes and structural transformations associated with high-volume trade and higher-volume transnational production. As markets are increasingly linked, their efficiencies and failures assume international dimensions, shaped more and more by international firms, and governments acting alone have very limited capacities to guide or control these effects. National economic structures are altered more and more as transnational enterprises implement production and marketing strategies while intensifying rivalries in the course of which weaker firms are driven into declines. The spread of gains between countries is uneven, as the more integrated national political economies, notably Japan and Germany, promote greater efficiencies in their systems and tend to retain the loyalties of their international firms. The less integrated and less advantaged states can cooperate for improved macromanagement and for bargaining with the more integrated states, but their potentials tend to be affected by problems of coalition building.

The corporate competition for market shares causes policy competition, as most governments strive to promote higher levels of structural competitiveness that will result in increased growth and employment. There are cumulative effects, while the advantages of the more integrated states increase, and these states tend to have greater scope for discretion on questions of international economic cooperation. Such questions have much significance for the less integrated states, because of their lower levels of structural competitiveness, and because their efforts to raise those levels tend to be hindered by problems of governance. Through cooperation with each other, these states can bargain with the advantaged governments: the incentive can be strong, but what can be achieved will of course depend on concerted efforts, which internal divisions make difficult.

The Triad pattern has evolved with expanding commerce and cross-investment, linking less integrated and more integrated national political economies, with imbalances that have reflected the greater structural competitiveness of the latter, but also the effects of differences in bargaining leverage on questions of market openness. Within the pattern a system of collective management has evolved only in the European Union, and this is highly significant as the outcome of a common political will to promote regional economic integration under a structure of cooperative governance. In this system, deepening integration has been increased through the formation of the single market, aid is given for the development of backward areas, and industrial policy initiatives have indicated a potential for reducing disparities in intrazonal structural competitiveness.[1]

The evolution of the European Union has contributed to a reactive regional emphasis in US foreign economic policy, partly because of imperatives to overcome persistent trade deficits, and partly because European bargaining strength in Atlantic trade relations has been strengthened. The main result of the US policy shift has been the formation of the North American Free Trade Area, in which deepening integration is facilitated by advances towards the formation of a single market, without commitments to establish a system of collective management.[2] A secondary result of the change in US policy has been interest in Asia–Pacific economic liberalization, but the superior bargaining strength which was used with considerable effect in negotiating the North American Free Trade Area agreement has less scope for leverage in dealing with Japan and the industrializing East Asian states.

In the Asia–Pacific context extensive, rapid, but imbalanced deepening integration has developed because of strong Japanese trade and investment penetration of the USA and industrializing East Asian states. An integrated Japanese international production system for North America has been linked with one in East Asia. The US interest in Asia–Pacific economic liberalization has been primarily an expression of hopes for securing wider access to the Japanese and other East Asian markets.

In a comparative perspective the European system of regional collective management has become especially significant as an endeavour from which instructive lessons can be drawn for the building of other regional systems of economic cooperation and of structures for governance of the world economy. Problems of advanced political development in the member states, and at the Union level, affect the evolution of the European system, but it has demonstrated how substantially representative institutionalized cooperative decision-making can engage with tasks of managing a common market. Advances towards the formation of a regional monetary system are enabling Union-level authorities to become a source of fiscal discipline, for improved macromanagement in member states that have been lacking structural competitiveness.

The development of the European Union has been an achievement of constructive political entrepreneurship, beginning with its founders in the 1950s, and continuing, after lapses, with the vigorous direction of the European Commission under Jacques Delors in the 1980s and early 1990s, which resulted in the formation of the single market.[3] Franco-German leadership for the regional integration endeavour supported the Commission's work for the establishment of the single market.

While the European Union has been becoming a more advanced system of collective management, constructive political entrepreneurship has been lacking elsewhere in the Triad pattern. Imbalances in structural interdependencies and the transformations of markets and economic structures, however, have made the development of comprehensive systems of economic cooperation more and more necessary. For the building of such structures political entrepreneurship is imperative, especially because strains associated with the structural imbalances are tending to increase. The effects of these strains on policy processes limit interest in economic cooperation.

COMPETITIVE MACROMANAGEMENT

Intensifying corporate rivalries for world market shares drives policy competition between governments, to increase gains from the global trading and production systems.[4] Policy orientations tend to focus on this competition, to raise levels of structural competitiveness while gaining more favourable access to foreign markets. The degrees to which structural competitiveness can be enhanced depend on levels of integration in each national political economy and the extent to which policy-making can be consensual and holistic, with long-term objectives, but of course also depend on the openness of trading partners. Policy choices of course are made in the contexts of differing patterns of political and security ties or antagonisms which affect the openness of those partners. The policy competition tends to limit recognition of benefits attainable through cooperation with other governments, while causing opportunities for such cooperation to be viewed instrumentally, rather than with integrative intentions.

Large states, with high levels of structural competitiveness based on substantial integration in their national political economies, and with bargaining strength resulting from the size of their economies, are advantaged. Japan and Germany are in this category, but are situated differently because of political and security factors. Japan, in relative political isolation but benefiting from substantial access to the US market that was originally facilitated by security links, has bargaining leverage in that relationship because of considerable US dependence on the confidence of Japanese investors who have aided the financing of large US fiscal deficits.[5] Germany, enjoying political bonds with other members of the European Union, benefits from their acceptance of its role as the dominant state in the region, and its use of bargaining leverage is limited by the obligations and restraints of collective decision-making in the Union.[6]

Large but less integrated national political economies have lower levels of structural competitiveness, and thus tend to use their bargaining strength for compensating advantages in trade and investment interactions. Their capacities for using leverage effectively and for increasing their structural competitiveness however, are typically hindered by problems of governance; these can generate pressures to impose burdens of adjustment on other states, and can encourage exploitations of nationalist feelings directed against such states. Hence there can be emphasis on managing foreign economic relations very independently. The USA and Britain, as examples of states in this general category, are situated differently in the Triad pattern, the USA having extensive scope for assertive management of its foreign economic relations while Britain operates within the European collective decision-making system.

Small and medium-sized national political economies are disadvantaged not only by weaker bargaining power on trade and investment issues but also by limitations on their potentials for structural competitiveness, as their economies are not large enough to support major diversified centres of innovation, and their international firms have to operate without extensive domestic market bases. Their governments, exposed to the bargaining leverage of larger states, have incentives to seek preferential accommodation with the trade and investment interests of those states but also to join regional economic cooperation arrangements in which coalitions can be formed for collaborative bargaining, and in which collective decision rules may restrain leverage by larger member states. Small and medium-sized European states benefit, in terms of shared economic sovereignty, from membership of the European Union. Canada and Mexico, however, are not similarly advantaged, and have to relate individually to the USA as the dominant member of the North American Free Trade Area.[7]

In interactions with transnational enterprises seeking to exploit trade and investment opportunities, large integrated national political economies have more bargaining strength than less integrated ones of similar size, and considerably more than small and medium-sized ones, especially those that are less integrated. The related differences in structural competitiveness, in contexts with differing degrees of market openness, and differing degrees of penetration through foreign direct investment, mainly determine relative gains from involvement in global commerce, and their cumulative effects.

Complex imbalances result in the Triad pattern of structural interdependencies, and these are sources of stress for the disadvantaged states, while contributing to the consolidation of strong positions gained in the world economy by the larger, more integrated, and structurally more competitive states, which experience smaller losses of economic sovereignty. The largest and potentially most disruptive imbalances are in the USA–Japan relationship, in which the import-drawing effects of heavy US fiscal deficits are facilitating Japanese penetration of the US market. Other major but less threatening imbalances are in Atlantic relations, due principally to high-volume production in Europe by US firms for the single market. Significant imbalances are also developing in Japan's relations with industrializing East Asian states, primarily because of Japanese investment in assembly-type manufacturing for export to the USA and Europe, but only on a modest scale to the home economy.

In the USA–Japan relationship competitive macromanagement is difficult for the USA because of problems of governance associated with a lower level of integration in its political economy. Intense individualism and much distrust in its society perpetuate weaknesses in its aggregating structures and fragmentation in its intercorporate system. Its system of divided and limited government has to operate with much conflict between aggressively expressed interests, in line with a tradition of aloofness from industry and commerce, which is sustained indirectly by low corporate esteem for the administration. There is little scope for industrial and other policy measures to promote structural competitiveness, and the dynamics of intensely pluralistic decision-making thus cause emphasis on trade policy leverage against other states, for improved market access. The policy process, however, in effect allows trade imbalances to increase, not only because extensive compromises necessitate heavy deficit spending but also because firms are given incentives to produce abroad rather than in the home economy, partly because of the deficit spending.[8]

In the Japanese political economy, strong horizontal and vertical cohesion sustains more functional policy-making which causes superior structural competitiveness. Bargaining strength is weaker than that of the USA, but tends to increase because of Japanese purchases of US government debt and large-scale manufacturing in the USA. American leverage to open the informally protected Japanese market is resisted, and this is possible partly because the USA enlists only moderate European support. The large imbalances in structural interdependence call for constructive responses, and these would be feasible because of Japan's rather high degree of internal unity, but leadership is lacking, and while the relationship remains conflicted strong currents of economic nationalism tend to motivate exploitation of the USA's weaker structural competitiveness.[9]

In Atlantic economic relations increased gains are in prospect for US firms, because of their operations in Europe, and, while exports to Europe grow slowly, the US economy benefits from substantial European direct investment, and moderate increases in imports from Europe. European decision-makers are challenged because the positions of their firms in the Union market are directly affected by the large and more competitive US corporate presence.[10] Greatly increased European corporate expansion within the single market is imperative, and this could be assisted by reductions of the flow of European direct investment into the USA. That flow indicates some lack of confidence in Europe's prospects, as well as optimism about the scope for operations in the USA, and while it continues there is a danger that Union firms will lose shares of the single market and thus have weaker domestic bases to support operations in the USA.[11]

Improved macromanagement is necessary in most European Union states, especially to lower the heavy costs of government, and this is difficult because of generally weak political support for fiscal discipline, except in Germany. It is also difficult because many European firms are attracted to collaboration with US enterprises in the Union, and become less responsive to the policy concerns of their home governments. The need for improved European macromanagement is indeed urgent – to overcome regional growth problems and to cope with external issues. There are also imperatives to work for active Atlantic collaboration, to ensure more balanced interdependent growth. Ethnic, cultural and political affinities can facilitate such political entrepreneurship, and the European potential is considerable because of the aggregating and advocacy as well as planning functions of the European Commission.

In East Asia the emerging hierarchical pattern of structural interdependencies centred on Japan allows that state wide scope for independent initiatives. Industrializing East-Asian states attract Japanese direct investment into outward-oriented assembly operations which increase exports from those states but entail rises in imports from Japan and provide only restricted technology transfers. The technological capabilities of those states, especially the larger ones in the Association of South-East Asian Nations, are tending to fall further behind those of Japan, because of smaller resources, lower levels of technocratic competence, and insufficient political will to promote advances in innovative capacity. The expanding Japanese regional production system tends to draw local firms into subordinate affiliations with its operations directed at the US and European markets, while restricting access to the Japanese domestic market.[12] The industrializing East Asian states lack solidarity that would enable them to collaborate on issues of interdependent growth, and Japan is not significantly challenged by their dissatisfactions with bilateral trade deficits; their generally favourable trade balances with the USA offset those deficits.

Japanese policy could shift towards the development of more symmetrical economic links with the industrializing East Asian states, but strong economic nationalism causes a high degree of continuity in administrative measures and corporate strategies that are building a zone of relatively dependent states. This regional involvement encounters US rivalry, but the US corporate presence is smaller and is growing at a slower pace. The Japanese presence is becoming more influential because of the efficiencies and bargaining strength of the extended national intercorporate system, the support of a large official aid programme, and the projection of a growth model that has considerable appeal for governments in the industrializing East Asian states.[13]

IMPERATIVES FOR COOPERATION

Issues of equity and efficiency in the Triad pattern demand attention. Equities and inequities are mixed in the imbalanced spreads of gains from Euro-Pacific commerce and associated with these are international market efficiencies and failures. Diverse government functions and failures, with cross-border dimensions, are in the pattern, and associated with these are achievements and problems responsible for differing levels of political development. The government failures entail 'democratic deficits' as the interests of communities and states are affected by policies adopted without sufficient accountability, and by corporate actions facilitated by such policies.

In Europe and North America the issues of equity and efficiency are posed in contexts in which policy orientations over the past two decades have been influenced by shifts in elite preferences towards greater reliance on market forces and reduced government economic involvement. These shifts have evidenced concerns about public sector inefficiencies, high costs of government, welfare state burdens and problems of inflation control. In the USA, the policy reorientations have been associated with pervasive business distrust of government, attributable in part to the disjointed effects of pluralistic pressures on the administration's regulatory, promotional and taxation measures. In Europe the policy shifts have reflected much anxiety about slack growth and high unemployment, and the formation of the single market has been seen primarily as an advance allowing wider scope for independent corporate activities.

With the emphasis on market forces there have been varying degrees of fiscal tightening. Allocative discipline has been strong in Germany, to cope with the high costs of national unification, but has been considerably weaker in the USA, where heavy fiscal deficits have been persisting since the early 1980s. The Japanese administration maintained fiscal discipline through the 1980s but since 1991 has provided substantial stimulus to overcome a recession caused by the collapse of a property boom and by falls in export revenue due to currency appreciation. Monetary tightening in Germany to reduce inflation has lowered growth throughout the Union in recent years, but in Japan there has been considerable monetary loosening, to assist economic recovery and moderate upward pressures on the currency.

The growth potential of international market forces has been given much prominence in US foreign economic policy. Imperatives for economic cooperation have been affirmed with emphasis on the anticipated benefits of general market openness, which would allow increased specializations and large economies of scale and scope. European attitudes have been less enthusiastic, reflecting awareness that markets and economic structures would be changed, more and more, by the operations of transnational enterprises.[14] European perspectives have been more open to recognition that trade and investment liberalization sets requirements for the coordination of competition and industrial policies, so that the spread of gains can be to some extent controlled.

Increasing efficiencies in internationalizing markets result from the operations of transnational enterprises maximizing the use of globally dispersed locations, while internalizing functionally related market activities and playing larger roles in world trade. The activities of these enterprises, together with those of national firms engaged mainly in exporting, result in increases in international oligopoly power, especially in high-technology sectors. There are externalities, moreover, which affect numerous communities and industries in many national political economies. Public goods issues are evident, and these are linked across borders: greater order and stability are necessary. With the expansion of linkages between national markets, the disruptions resulting from changes in corporate structures and strategies pose adjustment problems that are difficult for governments and firms to engage with because of uncertainties and coordination failures.[15]

All these issues are encountered in a setting dominated by volatile capital markets decoupled from the real economy. Financial markets, internationalized more than product markets, fail in service to the real economy by drawing large funds away from productive investment into high-volume speculative transactions. This rent seeking causes much volatility, which is constantly manipulated on an extensive scale. There is inadequate monitoring of financial institutions, despite general recognition of the serious effects of insolvencies. Virtually preferential financing of large firms demonstrating short-term profits contributes to oligopolistic trends in product markets. Insolvencies tend to limit access to financing by firms under sound management, especially because risky firms can offer high returns, but also because lending agencies lack information. Because of uncertainties due to informational failures, moreover, insolvencies can have contagious effects as investors seek greater security. Insolvencies often follow speculation in real estate, which can offer much higher returns than investment in manufacturing, although the social returns are typically lower. The most risky and highest-volume speculation, however, is in currency markets, and this can have severe effects on national economies coping with debt loads and trade deficits.[16]

All the efficiencies and failures in product markets and financial markets indicate imperatives for comprehensive management of the Euro-Pacific structural interdependencies which are affected. Such management is necessary for the promotion of orderly growth in the economies which are being linked, and for their equitable sharing in the gains from international trade and production. While intensifying rivalries for world market shares are causing governments to work for greater structural competitiveness in their economies, the systemic logic guiding their efforts can be seen to have wider applications in the evolution of linkages between those economies.

To be comprehensive, the necessary collective management will have to be integrative, excluding manipulative behaviour that could lead to bargaining outcomes determined by capacities for leverage. Sensitivities to questions of equity will have to be active, with acceptance of obligations deriving from extended accountability – that is to foreign communities affected by the externalities of national policies. Considerable changes in national policy orientations and styles will thus be required. Leadership functions and domestic patterns of interest representation will have to be aligned with the integrative imperative, so as to express goodwill towards partner states and commitments to the building of international trust.

Liberal political traditions express hopes of high-principled behaviour by citizens enjoying freedom under limited governments, and by members of those governments, responding to the aspirations of their citizens.[17] The extensive imbalanced linkages which have evolved between national political economies now obligate adaptations of liberal thought. These have to recognize losses of economic sovereignty to international firms, the complex forms of policy interdependence, the losses of home-country loyalties by enterprises expanding transnational operations and the problems of governance caused by political leaders striving to maximize electoral support with the collaboration of major interest groups.

Considerable streams of economic advice to governments express a philosophy of unprincipled pursuit of personal gain. This encourages emphasis on vote-maximizing criteria in policy choices, and on the use of incentives to secure public cooperation with those choices. The ethos of a national political economy can thus evolve in ways opposed to the expectations of liberal traditions: with the pursuit of instrumental values moral standards can decline, weakening the social organization of trust and limiting growth potentials by hindering collaborative entrepreneurial ventures.[18] Adaptations of liberal thought in line with imperatives for collective management can thus become difficult.

Where issues of international cooperation are viewed instrumentally, with reliance on relative bargaining strengths, interactions between governments tend to be only moderately productive, in terms of common interests. Distrust and manipulative intent are sources of caution, and oblige concentration on short-term objectives, because of doubt about the commitments of partners. The prospective gains from instrumental cooperation, it must be stressed, depend on bargained arrangements, mainly about market openness, and on degrees of structural competitiveness that can exploit those arrangements; hence shifts in the spread of gains have to be anticipated, together with changes in the utility of agreed commitments.[19]

In more integrated national political economies liberal government is undermined less by economic advice appealing solely to self-interest: on a basis of relational political contracting there is active cooperation between authority structures, with limited power, and economic groups. This collaboration is a source of advantages in managing cooperation with less integrated national political economies, as there can be more successful competition, within cooperative arrangements, and substantial benefits can be offered to the less integrated national political economies. These considerations can help understanding of the need for liberal political thought to become open to systemic logic, through recognition of functional requirements for administrative–corporate complementarity, in conditions of interdependence under competitive pressures; the role of the liberal state can be redefined, in terms of requirements for balanced domestically-based growth, and further redefined to meet needs for balanced interdependent growth.[20] With these adaptations liberalism can become more explicitly high principled.

LEADERSHIP CAPABILITIES

The capabilities required for comprehensive collective management relate to transnational consensus building and the design of cooperative arrangements that can become increasingly productive while being guided by that consensus building. The development of leadership capacities for transnational consensus building is difficult because of the diversity of elite perspectives within and between mostly countries, and because the political fortunes of contenders for office mostly depend on skills for identifying with particularistic attachments and loyalties in the contexts of those perspectives. Where there is broad internal consensus on macromanagement tasks, however, this can have an external demonstration effect, as has been illustrated by Germany's significance as an example of fiscal discipline within the European Union.

Where contests for office are sharpened by disputes over ways of overcoming slow growth, high unemployment, and suboptimal sharing in gains from international commerce, appeals to key interests and particularistic ties tend to become politically very rewarding. The political psychologies of elites can thus be shaped more and more by absorption in community and sector-specific vote-maximizing strategies. Such inwardness has been evident in varying degrees within the numerous less integrated European Union members.[21] More effective collective management in the Union, which could be activated by member governments, could increase the regionalization of national political processes, with productive effects, but the necessary will and capacities are lacking, and general confidence in the growth potential of more advanced political integration is low. The benefits of the single market have been below expectations for all members because of the recession caused by the high costs of German unification, and popular support for further progress towards the establishment of a federal system has been weak.[22]

Of the larger European states Germany has regional leadership potential, based on size, a high degree of integration in its political economy, its macromanagement achievements, and its contributions to Union monetary stability. Germany has the largest share of the single market, that is after the extensive intrusive involvement of American firms. Strong functional solidarity in its intercorporate system, with much responsiveness in consultative links between that system and the administration, sustains orderly growth. The administration operates with a tradition of consensus for rational rather than vote-maximizing policy, and accordingly of cooperation between the major political parties – the Christian Democrats and the Socialists, with support from the principal interest groups. Efficient management of the economy, with fiscal discipline, has ensured stability for long-term corporate planning, with the security of relational financing by banks deeply involved in the ownership and guidance of manufacturing firms.[23]

Solidarity in the German system is maintained through intensive multilevel socialization. This solidarity can sustain a policy of regional engagement for building political union in Europe, but elite attitudes are influenced by awareness that the strengths and achievements of the German political economy could be weakened if a more advanced system of regional collective management were dominated by the voting power of numerous inefficiently administered states. Those states could be expected to burden Germany with the costs of their failures, while becoming more resentful at the imbalances in regional growth. German elite opinion could thus become divided about the issue of regional political union, and majority sentiment could focus on the benefits of maintaining a strong integrated political economy in a weak structure of collective management.[24]

The building of a national social market economy, which has been a Christian Democratic objective, has not been extended into a regional endeavour: there is no commitment to transform the Union in line with that ideal. Other Christian Democratic groups in the Union are weak, and affinities with conservative parties in France and Britain relate mainly to their emphasis on free market forces, in opposition to socialist parties which have been further to the left than the German Social Democrats. Ties with those socialist parties have been given little prominence by the German Social Democrats, and in several Union members socialist organizations have been politically disadvantaged by popular awareness of the difficulties of managing welfare states.[25]

Germany's most active trade and investment links are with France, and these are responsible for the most significant processes of social integration in the Union. The scope for German advocacy of a European Union design in France, however, is very limited, because of the persistence of cultural and political divisions, and French sensitivities to economic asymmetries in the relationship with Germany. There is a recent history of French association with Germany in the leadership of the European Union, but this has evidenced ambivalence regarding prospects for the representation of French interests in a transition to some form of European federalism.[26]

France has higher moral status, as memories of wartime German barbarism survive throughout the Union. There is a potential for regional leadership based on identification with the concerns of Union members sharing less in the benefits of the single market. Strong nationalism, however, tends to be expressed in France's relations with those members, and intense individualism which is also part of the national culture tends to have divisive effects in the political economy. The intercorporate system is fragmented, institutional development is hindered, and the development of a broad policy consensus is made difficult. Elite socialization processes are less patterned than in Germany, and, on this account, as well as because of a concentration of power at the presidential level, contests for high office tend to be influenced very strongly by personality factors. Intense high-level absorption in the manipulation of popular responses to those factors limits capacities for communicating with other Union audiences.[27]

The French administration has to cope with very difficult macromanagement problem which understandably dominate its perspectives on relations with partners in the single market but which complicate the tasks of involvement in the Union. In 1994 a recession which had begun in 1992 had pushed unemployment to about 12 per cent of the workforce, and the fiscal deficit, which had been 2 per cent of GDP in 1991, had risen to 4.1 per cent, that is above the 3 per cent limit allowed for entry into the European Monetary Union. While the recession was due in a large measure to slack growth and high interest rates in Germany – related to the costs of reunification – it was also attributable to the accumulated effects of high welfare costs, high taxation and low levels of business investment, compared with Germany's. Government efforts to reduce spending, especially on welfare, were causing domestic strains during 1995.[28]

Britain's scope for making positive contributions to the development of the Union system of collective management has been restricted by status as a reluctant partner in the European integration endeavour, and as a country experiencing industrial decline. Macromanagement has been hindered by a lack of cohesion in the intercorporate system, class-based tensions in industrial relations, a cleavage between manufacturing and financial interests, and large differences between the policy orientations of the two major political parties. A policy consensus for adjustment and growth has not been achieved.[29] Unemployment was about 8.4 per cent of the work force in 1995, while the fiscal deficit in 1994 was about 7 per cent of GDP; total government debt in 1994 had been 48 per cent of GDP, that is about 13 per cent higher than in France.

The British Conservative Party has some affinities with Germany's Christian Democrats, in terms of economic policy preferences, and fewer affinities with France's conservative parties. The British Labour Party can relate to the major German and French socialist groups, but under the constraints of popular concerns about losses of national identity in an integrated Europe, and of imperatives to compete against Conservative appeals to middle-class voters in Britain. Initiatives by British Conservative or Labour leaders to assert a strong role in European collective management would probably bring few domestic political benefits, and could be expected to succeed only if exceptionally positive German and French responses were forthcoming.[30]

At the Union level the transnational political organizations represented in the European Parliament are weak and generally unstable coalitions, subject to change with shifts in the affiliations of the national parties on which they are based; they are not involved in the selection of candidates for European parliamentary elections, as this function is monopolized by national parties. Multiparty systems in several member states are represented in a fragmented assortment of European parliamentary groups, and only in the German case is there a significant concentration of representation in two of those groups – the Party of European Socialists and the (Christian Democrat) European People's Party. French representation has been split several ways and has involved several changes in affiliations. Because of their weak structures and lack of institutional links with local organizations the transnational political organizations have little capacity for advocacy on issues of regional collective management.[31]

A significant advocacy role at the Union level, however, has been possible for the European Commission, on the basis of its mandate to aggregate the interests of member countries and make proposals to the Council of Ministers for further advances in economic and political integration. The Commission undertakes and sponsors studies offering authoritative economic advice to member governments as a group. Such studies contributed to the generation of a common political will to complete the formation of the single market by 1992, and have prepared the way for monetary union, to facilitate the operation of that market.[32] Increased majority voting in Union decision-making, for improved collective management, has also become possible partly because of Commission initiatives.

A very constructive Commission role was asserted under the energetic presidency of Jacques Delors, but the appointment of another strong figure to succeed him was made difficult by the negative attitude of the British Conservative government in 1994. The scope for Franco-German cooperation in leadership of the Union thus became more significant, despite the weaknesses of the Union's transnational political parties. Such cooperation could give impetus to the development of Commission advocacy for more comprehensive and more dynamic European collective management, especially to strengthen the positions of Union firms in the single market. As a more active source of economic advice to member governments the Commission could devote special efforts to the development of a more innovative and wider-ranging Union technology policy, to overcome lags in this area which assist US and Japanese penetration of the single market.[33]

American leadership capabilities for the promotion of collective management outside the Union context are in several respects less significant. The USA experiences very difficult problems of governance because of the low level of integration in its political economy. Pressures to externalize the costs of macromanagement failures are strong, because of the dynamics of interactions that generate domestic compromises necessary for legislative and executive action. Policy-making, conflicted because of aggressive assertions of unaggregated interests, is reactive, with short-term horizons. Cooperation with other states, viewed very much with cost-externalizing concerns, tends to be evaluated mainly with reference to potentials for effective leverage, to extract trade and investment concessions from states with weaker bargaining strength.

Aggregating capabilities in the American system are weak because of the fragmentation of business associations and the organizational weaknesses of the major political parties.[34] Numerous policy research institutes compete for elite attention, but the flow of advice to members of the administration and legislators contributes to information overload. Decisions tend to be reached by the administration incrementally, disjointedly and experimentally – more so than in states where governments enjoy stable legislative support and respond to organizationally stronger business groups and political parties.[35] The operation of the US system depends very much on presidential leadership capabilities, which tend to be overextended because of emphasis on maximizing the projection of the chief executive's qualities. These leadership capabilities are typically shaped in very unpatterned processes of elite socialization: the institutional weaknesses of the political parties are reflected in a multiplicity of idiosyncratic factors which express the strong individualism of the national culture.

Questions of collective management were not introduced into the negotiation of the North American Free Trade Area, in which the USA could in effect relate separately to Canada and Mexico, with superior bargaining power. Opportunities to expand NAFTA, through the inclusion of more Latin American states, have been seen as occasions for bilateral interactions with the prospective partners. The option of negotiating regional trading arrangements has been given wider expression through participation in discussions of trade and investment liberalization in the Asia–Pacific Economic Cooperation forum, but these have offered less scope for bilateral leverage, because of Japan's involvement and the potential for coalition bargaining in the Association of South-East Asian Nations.

In relations with the European Union the USA encounters a powerful challenge to its bargaining strength, which has been exerted to reduce Union agricultural protection and subsidies for European industries. US interest has been shown in proposals for Atlantic free trade, but there is no significant capacity for advocacy that would reach into policy processes in the Union members. There is a capacity for interaction with the European Commission, but to be persuasive this would have to overcome Union concerns about the vulnerabilities of European firms in the single market, due to their generally modest sizes and technological lags.[36] To initiate a drive for Atlantic trade liberalization and assert leadership of the process would require a sustained effort, over several years, by a well-structured US organization.

At the global level the USA has sought to assert a very active leadership role for liberalization of the international trading system and the development of the World Trade Organization. The promotion of consensus for general market opening however was subordinated to the use of leverage for trade concessions from the European Union and Japan during the Uruguay Round and subsequent interactions. In exchanges related to the formation of decision-making structures within the World Trade Organization the US administration has sought to maximize its influence mainly through collaboration with major European Union members, in continuity with its strategy under the former General Agreement on Tariffs and Trade. European interest in assisting the development of a strong role by the World Trade Organization, however, has been less active than that of the USA, and there is a recent history of Atlantic rivalry for an effective voice on global trade issues. As the World Trade Organization has more than 120 members, and its charter is vague about the staffing of its constituent units, the Atlantic rivalry is continuing, but neither EU nor US objectives will be served without much cooperation.[37] Scope for US leadership has been limited because of dependence on European collaboration related to shared interests in North–South and East Asian contexts, and this dependence will tend to increase as the European Union expands.

The international trading system will be more open, under the World Trade Organization, if most of the participating states observe its principles, but this is very uncertain. The scope and complexity of the agreement establishing the Organization must be expected to make its proceedings highly politicized. The utility of its dispute settlement procedures will depend on the quality of its panels and the willingness of larger states to respect their decisions. The organization has to build credibility through fairness, which will require substantial high-level political commitments. Trade experts reviewing the Uruguay Round agreement have expressed concern about the continued use of section 301 measures by the USA against 'unfair' trade practices, and about the probability that Voluntary Export Restraints will not be eliminated but may go 'underground', or be replaced, in effect, by anti-dumping measures.[38]

CONSTRUCTIVE STATECRAFT

All the deficiencies in Triad leadership capabilities obligate urgent consideration of systemic development imperatives posed by largely unguided deepening integration, which is continuing with further losses of economic sovereignty, international market failures, imbalances in the benefits of trade and transnational production, and problems of governance in numerous disadvantaged countries. Initiatives to promote comprehensive collective management of the evolving structural interdependencies will have to be highly constructive.

The systemic development imperatives will have to be met mainly by interactive responsiveness between collective management institutions, national administrations and corporate managements. Regulatory functions, relating to competition policy and market openness, will be less important than the coordination of corporate investment production and trading decisions through consultative exchanges activating responsiveness between managements and officials at the two levels of authority. The exchanges will be productive if technocratic assessments of sectoral potentials and concerns with the public interest can be blended with the narrower perspectives of managerial planning.[39] Patterns of regional alliance capitalism could then be formed, thus establishing social market economies above the national level.

New constructive statecraft could start with projects for regional government–corporate consultations, focusing on possibilities for coordinating direct investment decisions, on a long-term basis, in line with shared techno-cratic concerns to promote complementarities. Meanwhile endeavours could be made to promote stability in international financial markets. The projects for government–corporate cooperation could thus become transregional, ini-tiated both by intercorporate groups and national administrations. Networks evolving out of these projects could link with financial policy institutions and associations for more effective regulation of the global financial system, to reduce its volatility and the draining of funds away from productive functions into its high-volume speculative activities.

More integrated national political economies would have advantages in projects for regional government–corporate consultations. Relational ties be-tween firms in the more integrated states would tend to facilitate the develop-ment of networks with foreign firms lacking such affiliations, and would help concerted interactions with governments participating in the consultations. In the European Union the German intercorporate system, because of its cohe-sion, is a source of advantages for its firms as they seek collaborative links with enterprises in other Union members. If the European Commission were sponsoring consultations on cooperative direct investment planning, however, the general impetus given to regional corporate networking would tend to balance the collective advantages of German firms. In the Pacific, because of the absence of a strong common institution like the European Commission, there would be less basis for optimism: the advantages derived by Japanese firms from their integrated intercorporate system would probably not be significantly diminished.

In consultations between the European Commission and Union industrial associations very large firms have assumed the most active roles, on the basis of superior research and advocacy capabilities.[40] More broadly inclusive representation would be desirable in Commission-sponsored projects for co-operative regional direct investment planning. If these were to begin the rationale would have to be set out in Commission-sponsored studies of deliberative councils facilitating information exchanges with high analytic content between technocratic and managerial levels, and referring especially to Japanese experience.[41] The Commission's Directorates, which would have to serve as sponsors, could of course become highly politicized, with inten-sive representations by member governments, and the prospect of this could discourage positive responses. The rationale, moreover, could well become controversial, because of opposition based on faith in free market forces. Since the numerous less advantaged Union members would have the most to gain, however, majority opinion could well support an active Commission role. Leadership within the Commission could enhance prospects for such a role, and the development of such leadership would probably depend very much on French policy.

France has substantial technocratic capacities, shaped by a tradition of planning that sought to overcome problems of informational market failure and promote concerted entrepreneurship. Functional responsiveness conducive to corporate innovation has tended to be limited by authoritarian tendencies in that tradition, but adaptation in the light of the Japanese and other East Asian experiences could facilitate highly productive technocratic–corporate interactions.[42] France has a vital interest in promoting more balanced complementarity with Germany and higher interdependent growth in the rest of the Union. In Germany the well-established pattern of government–business relations has evolved with financial sector guidance of manufacturing firms, and this has in effect limited requirements for an industrial policy. Germany has thus been able to emphasize the efficiencies of free market forces in endeavours to shape a common Union policy orientation.

European government–corporate consultations could be paralleled by similar Atlantic consultations. The scope for collaborative direct investment planning, however, could be restricted by a lack of US administrative support, and by American corporate reluctance to participate. The necessary transregional cooperation, therefore, would probably require more energetic leadership than the European endeavour. This leadership, moreover, would have to be largely European, with vigour inspired by awareness that much of the growth potential of the single market is at stake. It would also have to be more actively European because the promotion of complementarity through government–corporate consultations would be more controversial in the USA than in Europe, encountering no doubt considerable corporate opposition and criticism from US economists.[43] Controversies over the utility of the discussions could cause US administrative cooperation to diminish.

European leadership in the sponsorship of Atlantic direct investment planning conferences would be more effective if a substantially innovative common industrial policy were being implemented in the Union. This would be difficult but if it could be initiated it would arouse the interest of numerous US manufacturing and service enterprises and associations, and would enable European participation to be well coordinated, with significant capacities for inducing the strategies of US firms to converge with the preferences of European industry groups. Opportunities for constructive new statecraft in the European Union can thus be seen to have a double significance. Deepening integration in the Union could be brought under responsive collective technocratic guidance for higher growth, and there could be concerted engagement with problems of imbalanced Atlantic structural interdependence.

The European Union's Atlantic and global status could be strengthened, meanwhile, by the assertion of a strong stabilizing role in world financial markets. Further advances towards monetary union in Europe would make such a role feasible, and more desirable, especially to cope with volatility associated with strains in the US financial system.[44] Monetary union has became essential for growth in the single market, in which transaction costs are more burdensome for most Union firms than for larger US and Japanese enterprises, and in which the weaker currencies are exposed to speculative attack, notably by US operators. The European Monetary Union, moreover, as a source of pressure for fiscal discipline, would aid regional growth by reducing costs of government.

Greater stability in international financial markets is necessary because their volatility obligates general caution in longer-term investment decisions, occasions high profits for investments drawn away from productive use, and contributes to strains in the USA, as the top currency state under stress because of weaknesses in its financial sector and its unsustainable fiscal deficits.[45] American political will to achieve fiscal discipline, institute strong financial regulation, and curb speculation in global financial markets is weak. Hence there is scope for forceful European intervention, based on the strengths of a monetary union, to bring more order into the financial markets, and extend the monetary union's pressures for fiscal discipline into Atlantic relations.

Pacific economic relations offer fewer opportunities for constructive European involvement than the Atlantic context, but there are incentives to seek understandings with Japan about transregional and global issues. There are shared concerns about stability in world financial markets and stresses in the US economy, and Japanese penetration of the single market is a growing challenge.[46] European diplomacy, moreover, can assist the development of a more active Japanese political role in the Pacific and at the global level, helping to overcome the degree of isolation Japan has experienced because of strains with trade deficit states, including especially the USA.

European status in the Pacific has been weakening because of a diminishing corporate presence in East Asia, relative to those of Japan and the USA, and neglect of opportunities to build rapport with members of the Asia–Pacific Economic Cooperation forum on questions of transregional collaboration.[47] Because of the stresses in USA–Japan relations, however, and the difficulties of evolving a constructive new regional statecraft in the USA, as well as in Japan, the European potential to promote consensus for collective management is significant.

Europe's integration experience can be made especially relevant for industrializing East Asian states confronting imbalances in gains from regional commerce and the prospect of increasing technological lags. The relevance of the European experience will of course become greater if an innovative Union industrial policy is implemented. European economic advice, however, would be challenged by the demonstration effect of the Japanese model of alliance capitalism. European diplomacy of course cannot argue more persuasively for methods of government–business cooperation to improve structural competitiveness, but the Union's evolving system of collective management is an example of cooperation for less industrialized states. Despite its deficiencies, this institutionalized collaboration has collective advantages which indicate how industrializing East Asian states could benefit from representative governance of a Pacific system of economic cooperation, with some capacity for evolving a common industrial policy.[48]

In conjunction with a diplomacy drawing Japan into more active Pacific and global roles, the European integration experience can also be made relevant for Japanese participation in building an Asia–Pacific system of collective management, to function in partnership with the European Union. Interaction with Japan for this purpose would be a very complex endeavour, because of the social distances and the established orientation of Japanese policy towards consolidating a central position in East Asian economic relations. Japanese advantages in bilateral dealings with industrializing East Asian states have been very useful for that policy, and there could be fears that reductions of these advantages in a regional system of economic cooperation would not be sufficiently offset by the benefits of involvement in such a system. A major concern would be the possibility of having to cope with a coalition of industrializing East Asian states willing to align with the USA in order to extract concessions on trade and investment issues from Japan.[49]

An opportunity for constructive European diplomacy would be to initiate active dialogues with Japan and the Association of South-East Asian states on Euro-East Asian economic cooperation. These would provide occasions for the development of understandings between the East Asian participants about basic principles of such cooperation, and of cooperation with each other. With such understandings Japan could anticipate a more equal balance of bargaining power in the Pacific, which would relieve concerns about the USA's strength as the dominant state in the North American Free Trade Area. The basic understandings about principles of cooperation meanwhile would have the more important effect of committing Japan to integrative rather than instrumental dealings with the industrializing East Asian states.

PROSPECTS

Choices about the building of systems for collective management are being posed in contexts of internationalized market efficiencies and failures and government efficiencies and failures, with shifts in the imbalanced spreads of gains from world production and trade, and continuing volatility in financial markets largely decoupled from the real economy. Problems of advanced political development in the Triad pattern are related to government failures, and affect capacities for constructive statecraft in line with imperatives for orderly systemic development. These become stronger as structural inter-dependencies rise.

Progress towards the establishment of an advanced system of collective management by the European Union may enable it to take initiatives for the development of increased Atlantic economic cooperation and for the building of an associated pattern of trade and investment collaboration in East Asia. The further integration that is necessary in Europe will depend very much on leadership by France and Germany, and will have very positive growth poten-tial if their perspectives converge in support of a common Union industrial policy, with an emphasis on overcoming European technological lags. If the more integrated Union functions with increased consensus and achieves higher growth more attention will tend to be given to its external economic relations, and interest in expanding commercial ties with the high-growth East Asian states will become more active.

For the development of more extensive and more constructive external engagement a vital preparatory function would be the sponsorship of policy papers by the European Commission. This could be given impetus by the interests of European corporate groups in East Asia's opportunities, but that might not be sufficient to initiate studies examining fundamental options for the Union in that area. Because of the complexity of those options and the probability that they would require long-term endeavours, advocacy and pro-motional activities by the Commission could well be cautious and sensitive to indifference or opposition among Union members. German commercial in-volvement in East Asia is on a larger scale than France's, and most of the other Union states have only minor roles in East Asian trade.[50]

European corporate interest broader than that focusing on East Asia could support Commission proposals for expanded Atlantic economic cooperation. Such interest could develop more readily, because of the strength of estab-lished commercial links, and the prospects for less complex and less risky engagement, despite the advantages of US firms with a strong presence in the single market. Intensive US bargaining for freer Atlantic trade would be in prospect, with probably little US interest in exploring possibilities for estab-lishing a system of Atlantic collective management. The opportunities to press for freer trade would tend to receive more US attention than European proposals for direct investment planning conferences. On the European side, interest in freer Atlantic trade would no doubt be less active, and cautious because of the probability of unequal gains, with deepening US penetration of the less-industrialized European economies.

US policy is likely to remain short term, reactive and conflicted, with emphasis on market-opening leverage against trading partners, to counter the import-drawing effects of large fiscal deficits. Regional applications of that leverage will probably lead to extensions of NAFTA through essentially bilateral arrangements. Protracted resistance to such leverage in East Asia, however, will have to be expected, with some losses of US bargaining strength because of increasing vulnerabilities in the complex policy interdependence with Japan. The formation of an elite consensus for economic cooperation in regional integration arrangements above the free trade level will be unlikely, because of the persistence of macromanagement difficulties caused by intense pluralism.

The export increases from US market-opening diplomacy in Latin America will probably be modest, partly because US firms will tend to serve the regional markets more and more through production in the area. The export gains which do result moreover are not likely to compensate for slow trade expansion in East Asia, where Japanese competition is very intense. Domestic pressures for trade policy activism will thus no doubt remain strong, narrowing foreign economic policy perspectives that might otherwise be open to wider cooperation with the European Union. The US relationship with Japan, it must be stressed, is therefore likely to remain strained, and accordingly the European potential for constructive engagement with Japan may well become very significant. The major opportunity in that relationship would be to build consensus on a doctrine of cooperation based on European policy learning, through collective management, and on Japanese policy learning in the evolution of alliance capitalism. *A concept of regional integration and transregional cooperation based on Euro-Pacific alliance capitalism could thus emerge.*

Stability in financial markets could be achieved through policies based on such a concept. A structure for collective management could regulate and guide financial sectors, to ensure that the funding of industry would be their primary task. If a strong monetary union is established in Europe this will be a significant advance towards the stabilization of financial markets, and could prepare the way for authoritative change that would discipline Union financial sectors in the service of the real economy. The German system of alliance capitalism, in addition to functioning as the basic structure in the regional monetary union, could become linked with the less unified French system, in support of the European financial regulatory authority. Affinitive change in the mixed European pattern of corporate governance could follow, with manufacturing and trading firms acquiring stable bonds with financial institutions and reducing their vulnerabilities to stock market changes.[51] A European system of regional alliance capitalism could be formed, with potentials for higher growth, and with a reduced drain of investment into the speculative activities in world financial markets.

Rent-seeking attractions in world financial markets draw some funds away from the German system of alliance capitalism, through inducements given to German banks, while those markets offer alternative arm's-length financing to German manufacturers. French and other Union business communities are influenced both by the rent-seeking attractions and the prospects for international financing. Competition between Union governments to facilitate the development of national centres for international capital hinders initiatives for concerted policies that would build a stable and dynamic system of regional alliance capitalism. The investment drain, which is tending to grow larger, makes policy learning in the common interest an urgent requirement, and thus challenges the planning and advocacy capacities of the European Commission.

Commission endeavours could anticipate French support, as President Chirac has been a strong advocate of international cooperation to curb speculation in world financial markets. Widening regional recognition of requirements for stronger financial regulatory and supervisory functions could also be anticipated. The European Central Bank, under the 1992 statute of the Council of European Communities, is to be responsible for Union monetary policy, but banking supervision is to remain with member governments, although the management of monetary policy can be made difficult by bank failures, and by the problems of financial institutions outside the banking system.[52] There is a strong case for establishing a Union financial regulatory system, for greater stability and more efficient funding of industry. The formation of such a system, moreover, would facilitate concerted management of financial policy interactions with the USA. US policy demands national treatment for US financial firms in Europe, even though European financial firms have less than equal scope to operate in the USA's more functionally regulated system.[53]

An emerging system of European alliance capitalism could become a significant force not only for order in world financial markets but also for the development of transregional complementarity, with North America and with East Asia. The necessary European policy learning would have to be wide ranging, to draw fully on lessons in the Union's integration experience, in the political evolution of member countries, and in the development of the Japanese integrated political economy. The interconnections between national problems of political development and difficulties in building a European system of collective management would have to be studied in depth, in order to formulate and promote consensus on a doctrine of harmonious and functional regional integration. Vital elements in this doctrine would have to be principles of corporate governance and national governance generalized from the Japanese experience and related to issues of functional convergence in the European Union's enterprises, industry groups, business associations, political organizations, and authority structures.

Efforts to promote more balanced complementarity with North America could be undertaken in conjunction with the policy learning, which hopefully would have positive knowledge intensive effects. If the complementarity is sought with emphasis on assisting the development of consultative links that can aid coordinated direct investment planning for major projects impetus may be given to cooperation between North American firms, as well as between European enterprises. Widening Atlantic cooperation could then be in prospect. Meanwhile European engagement with opportunities for collaboration in East Asia could contribute to more symmetrical growth in the Pacific, with reduced tension in the USA–Japan relationship as it was being drawn into closer association with the Atlantic pattern of complementarity. All this would help to reduce and simplify the global economic agenda, while preparing the way for management of the world trading, production and financial systems through collaboration between regional authorities.

NOTES

1. For a comprehensive review of the EU see Emile Noel, 'Future Prospects for Europe', *Government and Opposition*, **30** (4), Autumn 1995, 452–68.
2. See Murray Smith, 'The North American Free Trade Agreement: Global Impacts', in Kym Anderson and Richard Blackhurst (eds), *Regional Integration and the Global Trading System* (New York: St Martin's Press, 1993), and references to NAFTA in *Journal of the Japanese and International Economies*, **8** (4), December 1994, *Special Conference Issue on Regionalism*.
3. See George Ross, 'Inside the Delors Cabinet', *Journal of Common Market Studies*, **32** (4), December 1994, 499–523 and Helen Drake, 'Political Leadership and European Integration: The Case of Jacques Delors', *West European Politics*, **18** (1), January 1995, 140–60.
4. See John H. Dunning, 'The Competitive Advantage of Countries and the Activities of Transnational Corporations', *Transnational Corporations*, **1** (1), February 1992, 135–68.
5. See reference to large Japanese official purchases of US dollar securities in Martin Feldstein, 'American Economic Policy in the 1980s: A Personal View', in Martin Feldstein (ed.), *American Economic Policy in the 1980s* (Chicago: University of Chicago Press, 1994), p. 73.
6. See Klaus H. Goetz, 'National Governance and European Integration: Intergovernmental Relations in Germany'', *Journal of Common Market Studies*, **33** (1), March 1995, 91–116.
7. See Smith, cited.
8. Tax incentives are significant factors in US foreign direct investment decisions. See references to US taxation in Alberto Giovannini, R. Glenn Hubbard and Joel Slemrod (eds), *Studies in International Taxation* (Chicago: University of Chicago Press, 1993).
9. See comments on the dangers of conflictual behaviour in the relationship in C. Fred Bergsten and Marcus Noland, *Reconcilable Differences? United States–Japan Economic Conflict* (Washington DC: Institute for International Economics, 1993) and Laura D'Andrea Tyson, *Trade Conflict in High Technology Industries* (Washington DC: Institute for International Economics, 1992).
10. See figures on the US direct investment position in Europe on a historical cost basis, *Survey of Current Business*, **74** (6), June 1994, 42–62. The real value of US majority-owned affiliates in Europe is very much higher.
11. On the prospects for Union firms in the single market see Stephen Young and Neil Hood, 'Inward Investment Policy in the European Community in the 1990s', *Transnational Corporations*, **2** (2), August 1993, 35–62.
12. See Richard F. Doner, 'Japanese Foreign Investment and the Creation of a Pacific Asian

Region' in Jeffrey A. Frankel and Miles Kahler (eds), *Regionalism and Rivalry: Japan and the United States in Pacific Asia* (Chicago: University of Chicago Press, 1993), pp. 159–214, and John Ravenhill, 'The Japan Problem in Pacific Trade', in R. Higgott, R. Leaver, and J. Ravenhill (eds), *Pacific Economic Relations in the 1990s* (Boulder: Lynne Rienner Publishers, 1993), pp. 106–32.

13. See Gavin Boyd, 'Japan's Structural Competitiveness', in Gavin Boyd (ed.), *Structural Competitiveness in the Pacific* (Cheltenham, UK: Edward Elgar, 1996).

14. On the activities of firms in an integrated market see John Cantwell, 'The Reorganization of European Industries after Integration: Selected Evidence on the Role of Multinational Enterprise Activities', in John H. Dunning and Peter Robson (eds), *Multinationals and the European Community* (Oxford: Blackwell, 1988), pp. 25–50.

15. Extensive restructuring is anticipated in the European Union. See Young and Hood, cited.

16. See symposium on capital markets, *Policy Sciences*, **27** (4), 1994, and Joseph E. Stiglitz 'The Role of the State in Financial Markets', *Proceedings of the World Bank Annual Conference on Development Economics*, 1993, 19–62.

17. See Jenny Stewart, 'Rational Choice Theory, Public Policy, and the Liberal State', *Policy Sciences*, **26** (4), 1993, 317–30.

18. See discussion of the importance of trust in Mark Casson, *Entrepreneurship and Business Culture* (Aldershot: Edward Elgar, 1995).

19. Instrumental perspectives tend to be reflected in legalistic manipulation of texts specifying obligations. See indications of such manipulation in US trade policy in Anne O. Krueger, 'US Trade Policy and the GATT Review', *The World Economy*, issue on Global Trade Policy, 1995, 65–78.

20. See comments on the efficiency effects of public–private sector interactions in deliberative councils mentioned by Colin I. Bradford, 'The New Paradigm of Systemic Competitiveness: Why it Matters, What it Means, and the Implications for Policy', in Colin I. Bradford (ed.), *The New Paradigm of Systemic Competitiveness: Toward More Integrated Policies in Latin America* (Paris: OECD, 1994), pp. 41–68.

21. See Robert Harmel, Uk Heo, Alexander Tan and Kenneth Janda, 'Performance, Leadership, Factions and Party Change: An Empirical Analysis', *West European Politics*, **18** (1), January 1995, 1–33; Andrew Appleton, 'Parties under Pressure: Challenges to "Established French Parties"', *West European Politics*, **18** (1), January 1995, 52–77; Jeremy Richardson, 'The Market for Political Activism: Interest Groups as a Challenge to Political Parties', *West European Politics*, **18** (1), January 1995, 116–39; and Andrew Gamble, 'Economic Recession and Disenchantment with Europe', *West European Politics*, **18** (3), July 1995, 158–74.

22. See *West European Politics*, **18** (3), July 1995, Special Issue on The Crisis of Representation in Europe.

23. See Stephen Prowse, *Financial Markets, Institutions and Instruments* (New York: Stern School of Business, New York University, 1995). For an assessment of the German system's stability see Ann L. Phillips, 'An Island of Stability? The German Political Party System and the Elections of 1994', *West European Politics*, **18** (3), July 1995, 219–29.

24. The Europeanization of German policy-making increases general awareness of the policy interdependencies within the Union. See Goetz, cited.

25. On party links within the Union see Rudy Andeweg, 'The Reshaping of National Party Systems', *West European Politics*, **18** (3), July 1995, 58–78.

26. See Robert Ladrech, 'Europeanization of Domestic Politics and Institutions: The Case of France', *Journal of Common Market Studies*, **32** (1), March 1994, 69–88.

27. See Andrew Appleton, 'Parties under Pressure: Challenges to "Established" French Parties', *West European Politics*, **18** (1), January 1995, 52–77.

28. See Paul R. Masson (ed.), *France: Financial and Real Sector Issues* (Washington, DC: International Monetary Fund, 1995), and *France: OECD Economic Survey, 1994* (Paris: OECD, 1994).

29. See *Oxford Economic Review*, **9** (3), Autumn 1993, symposium on UK Economic Policy.

30. See discussion of British attitudes in Andrew Scott, John Peterson and David Millar,

'Subsidiarity: A "Europe of the Regions" v. the British Constitution?', *Journal of Common Market Studies*, **32** (1), March 1994, 47–68.

31. See Andeweg, cited.

32. See Ross, cited, and review of Commission activities in *Journal of Common Market Studies Supplement*, 1994, 40, and previous issues.

33. See Ruud Smits, Jos Leyten and Pim Den Hertog, 'Technology Assessment and Technology Policy in Europe: New Concepts, New Goals, New Infrastructures', *Policy Sciences*, **28** (3), August 1995, 271–99.

34. See William D. Coleman, 'State Traditions and Comprehensive Business Associations', *Political Studies*, **XXXVIII** (2), June 1990, 231–52, and Steven Kelman, 'Adversary and Cooperationist Institutions for Conflict Resolution in Public Policymaking', *Journal of Policy Analysis and Management*, **11** (2), 1992, 178–206.

35. See M. Stephen Weatherford, 'The Puzzle of Presidential Leadership: Persuasion, Bargaining, and Policy Consistency', *Governance*, **7** (2), April 1994, 135–64, and Ronald C. Moe, 'Traditional Organizational Principles and the Managerial Presidency: From Phoenix to Ashes', *Public Administration*, **50** (2), March/April 1990, 129–40.

36. See Smits, Leyton and Hertog, cited, and Kirsty S. Hughes, 'Trade Performance of the Main EC Economies Relative to the USA and Japan in 1992 – Sensitive Sectors', *Journal of Common Market Studies*, **XXX** (4), December 1992, 437–54.

37. See John H. Jackson, 'The World Trade Organization: Watershed Innovation or Cautious Small Step Forward?', *The World Economy*, symposium on Global Trade Policy, 1995, 11–32, and *OECD Documents: The New World Trading System: Readings* (Paris: OECD, 1994).

38. See *OECD Documents: The New World Trading System: Readings* (Paris: OECD, 1994).

39. This observation refers to the Japanese model of technocratic–managerial interaction, assessed in Michael L. Gerlach, *Alliance Capitalism* (Berkeley: University of California Press, 1992) and Martin Fransman, *The Market and Beyond* (Cambridge: Cambridge University Press, 1990).

40. See Michael Calingaert, 'Government–Business Relations in the European Community', *California Management Review*, **35** (2), Winter 1993, 118–33.

41. This observation is based on the reference to deliberative councils in Bradford, cited.

42. For a review of the recent history of French industrial policy see Jeffrey A. Hart, *Rival Capitalists* (Ithaca: Cornell University Press, 1992), Chapter 3.

43. See Roger G. Noll, 'Structural Policies in the United States', in Samuel Kernell (ed.), *Parallel Politics: Economic Policymaking in Japan and the United States* (Washington DC: Brookings Institution, 1991), pp. 230–80.

44. See *American Economic Policy in the 1980s*, cited, Chapter 8, and Frederic S. Mishkin, 'Preventing Financial Crises: An International Perspective', *Supplement to Manchester School Papers in Money, Macroeconomics, and Finance*, **LXII**, 1993, 1–40.

45 See Symposium on Capital Mobility, cited, and Mishkin, cited.

46 See Mark Mason, 'Elements of Consensus: Europe's Response to the Japanese Automotive Challenge', *Journal of Common Market Studies*, **32** (4), December 1994, 433–54, and 'Europe and the Japanese Banking Challenge', *Journal of Public Policy*, **13** (3), July–September 1993, 255–78.

47. *Implementing the APEC Vision*, the comprehensive Third Report of the Eminent Persons' Group, August 1995 (Singapore: APEC Secretariat, 1995) reflects little interest in transregional cooperation that would encourage European initiatives. The European Union was denied observer status at the 1993 APEC Summit in Seattle.

48. Industrializing East Asian states would have difficulties adjusting to regional trade liberalization. See references to the ASEAN countries in *Pacific Economic Relations in the 1990s*, cited.

49. Ibid., and see Gavin Boyd, cited.

50. See *Structural Competitiveness in the Pacific*, cited.

51. See references to the European systems in Prowse, cited.

52. See Charles Goodhart and Dirk Schoenmaker, 'Should the Functions of Monetary Policy

and Banking Supervision be Separated?', *Oxford Economic Papers*, **47** (4), October 1995, 539–60.
53. See references to the EC's Second Banking Directive in Thomas O. Bayard and Kimberly Ann Elliott, *Reciprocity and Retaliation in US Trade Policy* (Washington, DC: Institute for International Economics, 1994).

Index